Origins of
the New South
FIFTY YEARS LATER

*Origins of
the New South*
FIFTY YEARS LATER
The Continuing Influence of a Historical Classic

edited by
JOHN B. BOLES and
BETHANY L. JOHNSON

Louisiana State University Press Baton Rouge

Copyright © 2003 by Louisiana State University Press
All rights reserved
Manufactured in the United States of America
First printing
Cloth
12   11   10   09   08   07   06   05   04   03
5   4   3   2   1
Paper
12   11   10   09   08   07   06   05   04   03
5   4   3   2   1

Designer: Amanda McDonald Scallan
Typeface: Sabon and Optima
Typesetter: Coghill Composition, Inc.
Printer and binder: Thomson-Shore, Inc.

Library of Congress Cataloging-in-Publication Data:

   Origins of the new South fifty years later : the continuing influence of a historical classic /
      edited by John B. Boles and Bethany L. Johnson.
         p.   cm.
      Includes bibliographical references (p.) and index.
      ISBN 0-8071-2905-4 (alk. paper)—ISBN 0-8071-2920-8 (pbk. : alk. paper)
      1. Woodward, C. Vann (Comer Vann), 1908–   Origins of the new South, 1877–1913.   2.
   Southern States—History—1865–1951.   3. Southern States—Social conditions.   4.
   Woodward, C. Vann (Comer Vann), 1908–   5. Woodward, C. Vann (Comer Vann),
   1908—Political and social views.   6. Historians—Southern States—Biography.   7. Southern
   States—Historiography.   I. Boles, John B.   II. Johnson, Bethany L., 1974–

   F215.W85 2003
   975'.041—dc21

                                                                                    2003047645

The paper in this book meets the guidelines for permanence and durability of the Committee
on Production Guidelines for Book Longevity of the Council on Library Resources. ⊗

Contents

Preface

For the more than one thousand members of the Southern Historical Association who attended the reception following the opening session of the annual meeting in Birmingham on November 11, 1998, it truly was a special occasion. The affair, at the Birmingham Museum of Art, featured plentiful food and drink, impressive art, lively music, and an infectious, energetic buzz of conversation. But all knew what gave the event a pizzazz uncommon even for the convivial SHA: this reception was really a ninetieth birthday party for C. Vann Woodward. Everyone strained to see the great man, and finally, there he was, looking exactly as he had looked—it seemed—for decades: tall, apparently rather shy, but distinguished in an old-fashioned courtly way, wearing his softly muted checkered sport coat and greeting friends and admirers with a subdued smile.

Yet this mild man had first vigorously challenged the accepted interpretations of southern history sixty-five years ago with a stirring biography of Tom Watson, and he then followed that with a bold analysis of the entire four decades following Reconstruction that still shapes the contours of our interpretation of that era. His later book on the origins of segregation in the turn-of-the-century South educated and inspired a generation of southerners. In the three decades following the publication of that book, he perfected the art of the historical essay, with book review after book review that sometimes seemed to say more than the original book did. And in his eighth decade he produced magisterial editions of Mary Chesnut's diaries. Somehow, in the midst of all this scholarship, he had mentored several dozen outstanding students, many of whom had earned great distinction in their own right. C. Vann Woodward was and had long been a star in the academic firmament, and the respect that he was universally given was palpable that evening in Birmingham.

Shortly after Woodward's birthday party, plans were set into motion to commission articles assessing the lasting significance of his *Origins of the New South, 1877–1913,* a volume in the History of the South series, for the November 2001 issue of the *Journal of Southern History,* reprinted here. As these plans were progressing, Vann Woodward, age ninety-one, died at his home in Hamden, Connecticut. He never knew of the theme issue underway, much less the symposium at Rice University into which the plans soon evolved. Few academic books have a shelf life of more than a few decades, and rare indeed is it for one to continue to dominate a field after fifty years the way *Origins* does. Not everyone may accept all its interpretations, but it is still the starting point, the benchmark, for every book written on the post-Reconstruction era.

Scholars are divided as to what exactly has given *Origins* such staying power: certainly its research basis gives it authority; its writing style sparkles, soars, and moves the reader; its bold, revisionist interpretations envelop and shape much of what we all think. Students are sometimes surprised to discover in it the origins of what they had simply come to take for granted about the post-Reconstruction South. Like the man who discovered he had been speaking prose all his life, graduate students learn that *Origins* had shaped their understanding of the era and region through its pervasive influence on their teachers and textbooks. And yet while Woodward had quite self-consciously reacted against how and what he was taught in the 1930s, in ways he may not have anticipated the book found surprisingly widespread acceptance from the very beginning in part because the field in 1951 had already begun to change.

Although one more or less typical review reported that Woodward "has cut his way through a tangle of facts that would stagger the average historian . . . [his] book has blazed a new trail," that was, strictly speaking, not exactly accurate. Beginning in the 1930s and continuing into the 1940s several other scholars—W. E. B. Du Bois, Francis B. Simkins, Robert H. Woody, Vernon L. Wharton, Arthur S. Link—had published works that critiqued the moribund field that Woodward had originally reacted to, and they pointed the general direction that new interpreters would take. Of course World War II also intervened between Woodward's graduate career and the publication of *Origins,* and the war in many ways transformed southern attitudes. And Woodward's *Tom Watson* itself—the best single-volume biography in the literature of southern history—had advanced many of the interpretations laid out more broadly in *Origins.* So for specialists *Origins* represented less a radically new perspective in 1951 than a brilliant synthesis (with an elaboration and filling in of many details) of an already emerging interpretation. In a sense, Woodward turned the blazed trail into a wide highway. In part at least because the scope of *Origins* was broader than any of the individual studies yet published, it had an enormous interpretative impact on the historical academy. To an unusual degree, scholars have been following the way Woodward paved ever since, and even those later scholars who suggest a new direction begin their journey with his book. This collection of articles analyzes the scholarly reputation of that 1951 volume and its author: it reveals praise and criticism but always respect. From an early book review published in 1952 to the articles first presented at the 2001 symposium and the three previously unpublished commentaries on those papers, this is a history of the reception and influence of a historical classic.

Neither this book nor the symposium that inspired it would have been possible without the skilled and energetic cooperation of Evelyn Thomas Nolen, Patricia Bellis Bixel, Patricia Dunn Burgess, Scott P. Marler, and my coeditor Bethany L. Johnson of the *Journal of Southern History,* and all of us were assisted by our present group of southern history graduate students. Evelyn supervised the original copyediting of the articles by Sheldon Hackney, James Tice Moore, and Carl V. Harris, and the five articles that resulted from the 2001 symposium were copyedited with equal care and dedication by Bethany with the assistance of Scott. The symposium was funded by a grant from the Southern Historical Association and by grants from three different divisions of Rice University, which for more than four decades has generously supported the editorial offices of the *Journal of Southern History* and, more generally, the study of southern history at Rice.

*Origins of
the New South*
FIFTY YEARS LATER

Introduction

C. Vann Woodward and the Reconstruction of the New South

Origins of the New South was indeed a singular achievement. As the essays in this volume demonstrate, there are few works of southern history that had as profound an effect on the master narrative of events in the American South, both through the long-standing acceptance of its interpretive framework and, ironically, through its ability to provoke criticism, inspire further research, and promote revision. However, its prominence and longevity, not to mention its author's proclivity to cast himself as the rebel outsider who accidentally found himself in the historical profession, have somewhat obscured the book's own origins. With a better understanding of the context of *Origins*, it begins to make sense how this book, which its author famously called "a sort of historiographical black mass in the eyes of true believers," instantly became a pillar of southern historiography, almost universally acclaimed upon its publication. It also helps us understand how

C. Vann Woodward, who considered himself somewhat of "a free agent" in the historical profession and hence relatively unencumbered by the usual political niceties that dictated careers, was elected to the leadership of the Southern Historical Association (SHA)—the supposed refuge for those same "true believers"—the very year *Origins of the New South* was published.[1] These apparent paradoxes can best be explained by locating the book and its author within the context of the changing historical profession in the South. The years between 1934, when the Southern Historical Association was established, and 1951, when *Origins* was published, were a watershed period in southern historiography.

The establishment of the History of the South series itself (of which *Origins* is the ninth volume) was an important symbol of those changes. As James C. Cobb explains in his contribution to this collection, the idea to publish a multivolume, cooperative series on the history of the South arose simultaneously yet independently in the minds of University of Texas professor Charles W. Ramsdell and Louisiana State University professor Wendell Holmes Stephenson in the fall of 1937. Ramsdell proposed a five-volume series as a way to fulfill the terms of a bequest left to the University of Texas by George W. Littlefield—a wealthy cattleman and Confederate veteran who, after being angered by the interpretation of southern history contained in textbooks used at the university, was encouraged to make a major donation to fund a collection of historical documents and "to see a history written of the United States with the plain facts concerning the South . . . fairly stated." Stephenson, the editor of the *Journal of Southern History,* conceived of a ten-volume series, provided that financing for such a venture could be obtained. The two editors soon learned of each other's projects through their contacts with many of the same historians about contributing a volume. "It is a peculiar coincidence that two such plans should be started simultaneously," Ramsdell conceded, "but probably it is a good indication that something of the sort is needed."[2] A few weeks later, at the 1937 meet-

---

1. C. Vann Woodward, *Thinking Back: The Perils of Writing History* (Baton Rouge, 1986), 22, 61–66 (first quotation on p. 63; 147–48 in this volume); Woodward to H. C. Nixon, February 4, 1949, quoted in Sarah Newman Shouse, *Hillbilly Realist: Herman Clarence Nixon of Possum Trot* (University, Ala., 1986), 165 (second quotation); Woodward to J. Carlyle Sitterson, November 17, 1950, Series A1, Folder 78, Southern Historical Association Records #4030 (Southern Historical Collection, Wilson Library, University of North Carolina at Chapel Hill; hereinafter cited as SHC).

2. James P. Hendrix Jr., "From Romance to Scholarship: Southern History at the Take-Off Point," *Mississippi Quarterly,* 30 (Spring 1977), 196–99 (first quotation on p. 198); Fred

ing of the Southern Historical Association, Ramsdell and Stephenson conferred about the feasibility of combining the two projects, and by December they agreed to a jointly sponsored, ten-volume series, financed by the Littlefield Fund and published by Louisiana State University Press. The series was formally announced in the May 1938 issue of the *Journal of Southern History*.[3]

Assigning the volumes, however, was no simple task. Stephenson and Ramsdell agreed that "each contributor must be either a mature and recognized scholar in his field or a young man who shows marked promise."[4] However, potential authors who had "no training or experience in the South" were not considered: both Ramsdell and Stephenson believed that "a man who has lived in the South or who has received a part of his training in the South has a much better understanding of Southern people and problems than one who has not had that advantage."[5] In its founding intentions,

---

Arthur Bailey, "Free Speech and 'the Lost Cause' in Texas: A Study of Social Control in the New South," *Southwestern Historical Quarterly*, 97 (January 1994), 464–67; Charles W. Ramsdell to Thomas P. Abernethy, November 4, 1937, Box 3N290, Ramsdell Papers (Center for American History, University of Texas at Austin); Wendell H. Stephenson to E. Merton Coulter, November 4, 1937, Box 55, Stephenson Papers (Rare Book, Manuscript, and Special Collections Library, Duke University, Durham, N.C.); Abernethy to Stephenson, November 11, 1937, Box 50, Stephenson Papers; Ramsdell to Abernethy, November 11, 1937, Box 3N290, Ramsdell Papers (second quotation).

3. Charles W. Ramsdell to Thomas P. Abernethy, December 12, 1937, Box 3N290, Ramsdell Papers; "Memorandum of Agreement between the Trustees of the Littlefield Fund for Southern History (Located at Austin, Texas) and the University of Louisiana at Baton Rouge, Louisiana," March 14, 1938, Box 3N292, Ramsdell Papers; *Journal of Southern History*, 4 (May 1938), 263–64. A press release on the series was sent to the regular press the following year, once all the authors had been lined up. Donald Coney to Wendell H. Stephenson, January 19, 1939, and reply, January 21, 1939, Box 53, Stephenson Papers; *Journal of Southern History*, 5 (May 1939), 278.

4. "A History of the South, 1607–1940 (in ten volumes): General Plan," n.d. [ca. 1938], History of the South Folder, Box 61, Stephenson Papers. That the contributors be professionally trained historians was an implied requirement: the editors had to turn away several earnest amateurs seeking to peddle their manuscripts to the series. "We received a number of letters of this kind," Stephenson informed the president of LSU, who had forwarded one such entreaty to Stephenson's office, "which we answer as tactfully as possible." Stephenson to Paul M. Hebert, September 25, 1939, Box 61, Stephenson Papers; see also D. L. Lewis to Stephenson, May 4, 1939, and reply, May 29, 1939, Box 63, Stephenson Papers; and Blanche W. Salter to Stephenson, May 9, 1939, and reply, May 15, 1939, Box 69, Stephenson Papers.

5. Wendell H. Stephenson to Charles W. Ramsdell, May 20, 1938 (quotation), and reply, May 25, 1938, Box 3N292, Ramsdell Papers. Ramsdell, a native Texan, received his Ph.D. from Columbia University, where he had been one of William A. Dunning's students. Stephen-

then, the series epitomized a particular moment in the development of professional southern historiography—a moment when it was no contradiction to declare that "objectivity is a prime requisite for the Series," while asking that it "be tempered with a sympathetic understanding of the fundamental factors and problems which made the South Southern and the Southerner think and react as he did." Observers felt confident that the series would "be a landmark in Southern historiography for many years to come."[6]

As Cobb explains in his essay herein, assigning the ninth volume was one of the most controversial and complicated decisions that Ramsdell and Stephenson made. It was well recognized by historians eagerly anticipating the series that a history of the post-Reconstruction decades in the South was desperately needed. "There are so many dark spots in the history of the South which this work should clear away," historian Thomas D. Clark wrote in support of the series. "I am embarrassed at times in my course on the New South for materials on certain aspects of the section." The editors' first choice as an author for Volume IX, Benjamin B. Kendrick, ultimately turned down the opportunity, citing his fear that "there simply doesn't exist enough monographic material in the field to make possible the writing of anything like a definitive volume on southern history for the thirty years embraced."[7] C. Vann Woodward, fresh from the success of his first book, *Tom Watson, Agrarian Rebel,* happily accepted the assignment when it finally came from the series editors. The chance to "lay down the main lines

son, the son of Indiana Quakers, came to Louisiana State University in 1927 after doctoral training at the University of Michigan, where he had been a student of U. B. Phillips. Despite his midwestern roots, Stephenson considered himself a southerner; his attendance at an American Historical Association meeting in Providence, Rhode Island, a decade after his arrival in Baton Rouge, led him to remark, "Being a Southernor [*sic*], I did not feel much at home among so many Yankees." Obituary for Charles W. Ramsdell, *Journal of Southern History,* 8 (August 1942), 446–47; Wendell H. Stephenson, "Charles W. Ramsdell: Historian of the Confederacy," in Stephenson, *Southern History in the Making: Pioneer Historians of the South* (Baton Rouge, 1964), 184–204; Thomas D. Clark, "Wendell Holmes Stephenson, 1889–1970: Master Editor and Teacher," *Journal of Southern History,* 36 (August 1970), 335–49; Stephenson to E. Merton Coulter, January 8, 1937, Box 55, Stephenson Papers (quotation); Stephenson to Fletcher M. Green, October 7, 1956, Folder 246, Green Papers #4265 (SHC).

6. "A History of the South, 1607–1940: Editorial Suggestions and Directions," n.d. [ca. September 1942], and Robert H. Woody to Wendell H. Stephenson, May 3, 1943, both in History of the South Folder, Box 61, Stephenson Papers.

7. James C. Cobb, " 'On the Pinnacle in Yankeeland': C. Vann as a [Southern] Renaissance Man," *Journal of Southern History,* 67 (November 2001), 728–31 (175–78 in this volume); Thomas D. Clark to Wendell H. Stephenson, June 28, 1938, Box 53, Stephenson Papers; Benjamin B. Kendrick to Charles W. Ramsdell, January 16, 1939, Box 3N303, Ramsdell Papers.

of interpretation and to do something fairly definitive," as Cobb and Robert C. McMath Jr. tell us in this collection, excited Woodward and sustained the young historian through the twelve years it took to complete the book.[8]

The tenets of that interpretation and their revisionist ramifications are discussed with great detail and insight in the essays that follow. What concerns us here is their reception in 1951. As Woodward recalled in his reflection on the origin of *Origins,* reprinted here, he expected his effort at "revisionary subversion" to draw mostly "indignation and protest" from southern historians, but he was stunned that the book received a range of responses "from tolerance to respect to unqualified applause."[9] *Origins,* then, did turn so-called historical orthodoxy on its ear, but the historical profession in the South, after three decades of growth, research, and development, was largely ready and willing to see tables turned. Far from being a lone wolf, Woodward was part of an emerging coterie of white revisionist historians, well placed in southern colleges and universities and, for the most part, respectfully regarded by the Southern Historical Association—historians who had been given space and hearing at both the SHA annual meetings and in the pages of the *Journal of Southern History.* They joined an even longer tradition of African American historians who had not yet gained access to the white institutions of the profession. "Readers of his *Tom Watson* know what to expect of Professor Woodward," Roger W. Shugg, himself a challenger of southern historical orthodoxy, admitted in his review of *Origins.*[10] Indeed, perhaps *Origins of the New South* met with

---

8. Charles W. Ramsdell to C. Vann Woodward, March 6, 1939, and reply, March 11, 1939, Box 3N303, Ramsdell Papers; Woodward to Glenn W. Rainey, March 26, 1939, Folder 1, Box 22, Glenn W. Rainey Papers (Special Collections Department, Robert W. Woodruff Library, Emory University), quoted in Cobb, " 'On the Pinnacle in Yankeeland,' " 731 (178 in this volume), and in Robert C. McMath Jr., "C. Vann Woodward and the Burden of Southern Populism," *Journal of Southern History,* 67 (November 2001), 741 (190 in this volume).

9. Woodward, *Thinking Back,* 65 (first quotation), 66 (second and third quotations) (149–50 in this volume).

10. Roger W. Shugg, review of *Origins of the New South,* by C. Vann Woodward, *Mississippi Valley Historical Review,* 39 (June 1952), 141. Shugg's book, *The Origins of Class Struggle in Louisiana: A Social History of White Farmers and Laborers during Slavery and After, 1840–1875* (Baton Rouge, 1939), earned him the enmity of Frank L. Owsley and his students for applying a perceived Marxist edge to the story of the white yeoman farmer. As Owsley privately wrote, from the title alone it was clear that Shugg "has misused the material." Owsley to Cleanth Brooks, November 5, 1939, Correspondence, *Southern Review* Collection (Beinecke Rare Book and Manuscript Library, Yale University, New Haven, Conn.). See also Owsley's review of Shugg's book in *Journal of Southern History,* 6 (February 1940), 116–17; and Herbert Weaver to Owsley, June 5, 1944, Folder 5, Box 6, Owsley Papers (Special Collec-

such a radiant reception because its readers in some ways had been expecting it. In this respect, it may be useful to think of *Origins* as the culmination, rather than the seminal point, of an intellectual trajectory in southern historiography. This requires us to look beyond *Origins* as a single work of history to consider briefly the changing shape of the historical profession in the South after the founding of the Southern Historical Association in 1934.

To many mid-twentieth-century observers, the establishment of the Southern Historical Association portended a new, organized defensiveness in southern historical scholarship. In a fifteen-year retrospective of the annual presidential addresses of the association, H. C. Nixon found that the speeches, "pretty well spiked with the hard liquor of polemics," had baldly refused to admit that there was "anything inherently wrong with the South, or anything to criticize." The Southern Historical Association, Nixon argued in another article, enshrined a historiographical "conservative revolt" by giving form to the "interlinked doctrines of regional patriotism and conservation." Robert F. Durden observed that the SHA seemed at its founding "the vanguard of a defensive, almost neo-Confederate sectionalism." Christopher Lasch asserted that the presidential addresses, presumably representative of the scholarship of SHA members, "collectively constitute a manifesto against change in the interpretation of history (as well as against change in history itself)."[11]

---

tions and University Archives, Jean and Alexander Heard Library, Vanderbilt University, Nashville, Tenn.). Lawrence D. Reddick, in the *Journal of Negro History*, 25 (January 1940), 116, disagreed. Southern history has suffered from stereotypes of the planter, the slave, and the poor white, he argued: "Needless to say there were other types and even the planters, slaves and poorer whites were other than so described by sentimentalists and *I'll-take-my-stand*ers. A generation of more realistic scholars is rising up to describe the whole Southern society and to show the intense conflict which continually shook its foundation."

11. H. C. Nixon, "Paths to the Past: The Presidential Addresses of the Southern Historical Association," *Journal of Southern History*, 16 (February 1950), 35 (first quotation), 37 (second quotation); Nixon, "Southern Regionalism Limited," *Virginia Quarterly Review*, 26 (Spring 1950), 164–65 (third quotation); Robert F. Durden, "The Southern Historian Engagé," *South Atlantic Quarterly*, 64 (Autumn 1965), 509; Christopher Lasch, review of *The Pursuit of Southern History: The Presidential Addresses of the Southern Historical Association, 1935–1963*, ed. George Brown Tindall, and *Southern History in the Making*, by Wendell H. Stephenson, *Civil War History*, 11 (November 1965), 284. There is no denying that many SHA leaders were sectionally truculent. A. B. Moore, president in 1942, prided himself on the antinorthern "doctrine" of his address on economic abuses of the South and privately considered himself a "propagandist" historian. Benjamin B. Kendrick's presidential address was so critical of the North that he felt obliged to add a disclaimer to the published version. "Since the outbreak of war between Japan and the United States and with similar hostilities with Germany and Italy apparently inevitable," Kendrick wrote the *Journal of Southern History* editor

Such monolithic conceptions of conservative white southern historians banded together against all argument and debate, however, distort our understanding of the professionalization of history in the South by preventing us from examining the fissures, created by both internal and external forces, that eventually cracked open the South to allow a broader narrative of regional history and identity to emerge. These countertrends actually existed within the Southern Historical Association from the very beginning. As early as 1937, more conservative leaders were afraid that the association had been "taken out of the hands of the men who organized it" and had become "dominated by Yankeeized Southerners." They also doubted that their traditional defenses of the white South met with "much agreement" from the general membership.[12] Their perception of the shrinking historiographical space for traditional interpretations of the Civil War, Reconstruction, and their aftermath was no paranoid delusion. More generally, some SHA leaders felt that "there is too much patching of old quilts in our Association, and that someone is going to be compelled to call for something new [one] of these days."[13]

The "solid" historiographical South initially fractured most seriously over interpretations of Reconstruction and its consequences. The consensus that Dunning school historians and most southern whites had attained regarding this period had begun to crumble in the 1930s. Revisionist Reconstruction historiography best challenged what white southern historians thought they knew about their past. To be sure, African American historians had long disputed the prevailing white view of Reconstruction as a period

---

just after the bombing of Pearl Harbor, "I think it would be in order for me to add . . . the following sentence. 'The author wishes it understood that while he recognizes the necessity for complete national unity now that the country is at war, he sees no reason to modify any part of the interpretation he has placed upon events preceding the outbreak of war.'" A. B. Moore to Frank L. Owsley, March 26, 1943, Folder 8, Box 4, Owsley Papers; Moore, "One Hundred Years of Reconstruction in the South," *Journal of Southern History*, 9 (May 1943), 153–80; Benjamin B. Kendrick to Fred C. Cole, December 9, 1941, Box 63, Stephenson Papers; Kendrick, "The Colonial Status of the South," *Journal of Southern History*, 8 (February 1942), 3 n. 1.

12. Thomas Perkins Abernethy to Frank L. Owsley, February 5, 1937, Folder 8, Box 1, Owsley Papers (first quotation); Allen Tate to Owsley, April 14, 1940, Folder 11, Box 5, Owsley Papers (second quotation); Albert Simpson to Owsley, January 13, 1941, Folder 22, Box 4, Owsley Papers. "The 'Yankeeization' of southern history and of those who teach and write about it is one of the most persistent, if unacknowledged, characteristics of the historical craft's professionalization process," one unhappy practitioner has more recently argued. Grady McWhiney, "Historians as Southerners," *Continuity*, 9 (Fall 1984), 11.

13. James W. Patton to Fletcher M. Green, January 13, 1941, Folder 73, Green Papers.

of regional oppression, "Negro domination," graft, greed, ignorance, scalawags and carpetbaggers, terror and tumult, and corruption, occasionally conceding that they may still have been "too close to the history of reconstruction to expect better treatment" but always insisting that the histories coming from white pens did not yet represent the "truth."[14] Moreover, there was still a rigid opposition to change of any sort among an older generation of white southern historians—so much so that Woodward later described his introduction to historical writing as a "craft devoted primarily . . . to summing up, confirming, illustrating, and consolidating the received wisdom, the regional consensus that prevailed uniquely in the South of the 1930s." But a growing number of white SHA historians in the 1930s and 1940s did not ignore these challenges, and the reinterpretation of Reconstruction spurred debates not only on the role of African Americans in the South but more generally on the place and function of revisionism in professional history. African American historian Charles H. Wesley presciently charged that such reinterpretation demanded the entire "reconstruction of history."[15]

Although Claude G. Bowers was most responsible for the widespread popularization of the Dunning school interpretation of Reconstruction through his best seller *The Tragic Era*, Walter Lynwood Fleming best epitomized that consensus to the founding generation of the Southern Historical Association. Fleming was honored as an intellectual parent by the "Twelve

14. Review of *Reconstruction in Georgia*, by C. Mildred Thompson, *Journal of Negro History*, 1 (July 1916), 344 (quotation); review of *The Tragic Era*, by Claude G. Bowers, *Journal of Negro History*, 15 (January 1930), 117–19; Rayford W. Logan, "An Evaluation of the First Twenty Volumes of the *Journal of Negro History*," *Journal of Negro History*, 20 (October 1935), 405; Alrutheus A. Taylor, "Historians of the Reconstruction," *Journal of Negro History*, 23 (January 1938), 16–34. For revisionist arguments by African American historians see W. E. Burghardt Du Bois, "Reconstruction and Its Benefits," *American Historical Review*, 5 (July 1910), 781–99; John R. Lynch, "Some Historical Errors of James Ford Rhodes," *Journal of Negro History*, 2 (October 1917), 345–68; Luther P. Jackson, "The Education Efforts of the Freedmen's Bureau and Freedmen's Aid Societies in South Carolina, 1862–1872," *Journal of Negro History*, 8 (January 1923), 1–40; Alrutheus A. Taylor, "The Negro in South Carolina during the Reconstruction," *Journal of Negro History*, 9 (July 1924), 241–364; Taylor, "The Negro in the Reconstruction of Virginia," *Journal of Negro History*, 11 (April 1926), 243–415; and Taylor, "Historians of the Reconstruction," 16–34. See also Stephen Gilroy Hall, " 'Research as Opportunity': Alrutheus Ambush Taylor, Black Intellectualism, and the Remaking of Reconstruction Historiography, 1893–1954," *UCLA Historical Journal*, 16 (1996), 39–60.

15. Woodward, *Thinking Back*, 23; Charles H. Wesley, "The Reconstruction of History," *Journal of Negro History*, 20 (October 1935), 411–27.

Southerners" who wrote *I'll Take My Stand* in 1930 and by the history faculty of Louisiana State University, who named their new lecture series in southern history after him.[16] He was also the subject of two historiographical articles in the *Journal of Southern History*. The first, written by University of North Carolina professor Fletcher M. Green, praised Fleming for instigating the trend in Reconstruction historiography to study the social and economic, rather than the strictly political, aspects of the period. (The article was criticized by *Journal* referees, however, for its "eulogistic tone.") The second, written by Vanderbilt University professor William C. Binkley and printed in the *Journal* less than three years after Green's essay, was less certain of how Fleming's interpretations had stood the test of time but admired the historian for his commitment to the South. Fleming "was one of the few who came back [to the South after graduate school], not of necessity but of deliberate choice; and he came back with a vision." He therefore stood as both a precedent and an example for many of the founding members of the SHA.[17]

Fleming's critics were vocal, however, and gradually made themselves heard among white southern historians. By extolling Fleming, *Journal of Negro History* editor Carter G. Woodson argued, Fletcher Green had allied

16. Peter J. Sehlinger and Holman Hamilton, *Spokesman for Democracy: Claude G. Bowers, 1878–1958* (Indianapolis, 2000), 122–23; Walter L. Fleming, *Civil War and Reconstruction in Alabama* (New York, 1905). The dedication page in Twelve Southerners, *I'll Take My Stand: The South and the Agrarian Tradition* (New York, 1930), reads: "This book is dedicated in love and admiration to Walter L. Fleming: Historian; Professor of History and Dean of the Graduate School of Vanderbilt University; to whom some of the contributors owe doctrine and example, and all would offer this expression of perfect esteem." The first program of the Fleming Lectures similarly praised Fleming as an "impartial yet sympathetic" southern historian. "The Walter Lynwood Fleming Lectures in Southern History," n.d. [1937], Box 57, Stephenson Papers. See also Burl Noggle, *The Fleming Lectures, 1937–1990: A Historiographical Essay* (Baton Rouge, 1992), 1–8.

17. Fletcher M. Green, "Walter Lynwood Fleming: Historian of Reconstruction," *Journal of Southern History*, 2 (November 1936), 498; Wendell H. Stephenson to Green, May 9, 1936, Folder 35, Green Papers (first quotation); Green to Stephenson, May 19, 1936, Series A1, Folder 2, SHA Records; William C. Binkley, "The Contribution of Walter Lynwood Fleming to Southern Scholarship," *Journal of Southern History*, 5 (May 1939), 154 (second quotation); Binkley to Herbert A. Kellar, July 17, 1938, Folder 30, Box 2, Binkley Papers (Special Collections and University Archives, Jean and Alexander Heard Library, Vanderbilt University). Of Reconstruction, Fleming once wrote, "I firmly believe that no one but a Southern man can write that history." Walter L. Fleming to R. Heath Dabney, February 13, 1930, Box 1, Richard Heath Dabney Papers (Special Collections Department, University of Virginia Library, Charlottesville).

himself with a "propagandist who made himself the defender of the anti-Negro Ku Klux Klan regime." W. E. B. Du Bois similarly connected Fleming to a group of historians who "believe[d] the Negro to be subhuman and congenitally unfit for citizenship and the suffrage." Other critics, like Fisk University professor Horace Mann Bond, were more willing to allow Fleming the prejudices of his time and class but concluded that despite what "Reconstruction meant to Fleming, we may now agree that it involved social, economic, and political redefinition of the *status* of varied economic and racial groupings." White SHA historians would not yet adopt wholesale the reinterpretation of these supposedly "caustic" Fleming critics, but most conceded the role revisionism must play in new times and contexts. The result was the most fundamental historiographical debate members of the Southern Historical Association faced in the organization's first decades.[18]

It might be helpful to focus the discussion on the reception of a single revisionist history of Reconstruction before turning to the ways some members of the SHA finally opened themselves up to a reinterpretation of their most cherished historiographical tradition. No other work of history would serve this purpose as well as W. E. B. Du Bois's *Black Reconstruction,* published in 1935. Du Bois's study, which is only the most famous of a long line of African American additions to and revisions of Reconstruction history, departed from the assumption that Reconstruction was a real effort to recreate the class and racial order of the United States that had lasting if incomplete beneficial effects. Du Bois's interpretation was hardly recognizable to those readers who saw only the "horrors of the deconstruction called reconstruction," and it ended with a cutting criticism of the antiblack stance of most white historians.[19] Historians today generally assume that such a

---

18. [Carter G. Woodson], "Notes: In American Magazines," *Journal of Negro History,* 22 (January 1937), 122–23 (first quotation); W. E. Burghardt Du Bois, *Black Reconstruction: An Essay toward a History of the Part Which Black Folk Played in the Attempt to Reconstruct Democracy in America, 1860–1880* (New York, 1935), 731 (second quotation); Horace Mann Bond, "Social and Economic Forces in Alabama Reconstruction," *Journal of Negro History,* 23 (July 1938), 291 (third quotation); William M. Brewer, review of *Negro Education in Alabama,* by Horace Mann Bond, *Journal of Negro History,* 24 (April 1939), 227; Fletcher M. Green to Wendell H. Stephenson, May 19, 1936, Series A1, Folder 2, SHA Records (fourth quotation); Curtis W. Garrison, review of *Negro Education in Alabama,* by Horace Mann Bond, *Journal of Southern History,* 5 (August 1939), 404–5.

19. Du Bois, *Black Reconstruction,* 711–29; J. D. Eggleston to Charles W. Ramsdell, March 20, 1937, Box 3N302, Ramsdell Papers (quotation); Green, "Walter Lynwood Fleming," 506–7.

sweeping indictment of the white southern historical tradition was largely ignored by the historical profession.[20]

In fact, the argument was most certainly not ignored by white historians in the South. Du Bois's study—and the revisionism it exemplified—inspired responses ranging from casual conversation to scholarly panels, short reviews to review essays. At least one Dunning-trained historian even added *Black Reconstruction* to his course reading list.[21] To say that white southern historians responded does not mean that they were convinced by Du Bois's accusations that white historians wrote racist propaganda more than history. Nor does it mean that his argument that African Americans "restored the South to the Union[,] established a new democracy, both for white and black, and instituted the public schools" single-handedly transformed the majority's understanding of Reconstruction. As Du Bois himself recognized, he would not be able to persuade the reader who "regards the Negro as a distinctly inferior creation," incapable of a creative role in human history, of the truth of his interpretation. As predicted, some readers rejected Du Bois out of hand for his strict criticism of white historians.[22] Many others

---

20. Eric Foner, *Reconstruction, 1863–1877: America's Unfinished Revolution* (New York, 1988), xxi; Bruce Clayton, "No Ordinary History: W. J. Cash's *Mind of the South,*" in Charles W. Eagles, ed., *The Mind of the South: Fifty Years Later* (Jackson, Miss., 1992), 16; LaWanda Cox, "From Emancipation to Segregation: National Policy and Southern Blacks," 205 n. 15, and Harold D. Woodman, "Economic Reconstruction and the Rise of the New South, 1865–1900," 254, both in John B. Boles and Evelyn Thomas Nolen, eds., *Interpreting Southern History: Historiographical Essays in Honor of Sanford W. Higginbotham* (Baton Rouge, 1987); Peter Novick, *That Noble Dream: The "Objectivity Question" and the American Historical Profession* (Cambridge, Eng., 1988), 231–32; August Meier and Elliott Rudwick, *Black History and the Historical Profession, 1915–1980* (Urbana, 1986), 279 (on Du Bois's reaching only "those already convinced"). *Black Reconstruction* was not reviewed by the *American Historical Review:* John Hope Franklin, "Mirror for Americans: A Century of Reconstruction Historiography," in Franklin, *Race and History: Selected Essays, 1938–1988* (Baton Rouge, 1989), 389. David Levering Lewis provides an exception to this assumption in *W. E. B. Du Bois: The Fight for Equality and the American Century, 1919–1963* (New York, 2000), 365, by expressing surprise at how widely reviewed *Black Reconstruction* was.

21. J. G. de Roulhac Hamilton to Christian Dick, May 8, 1939, Folder 136, Box 5, Hamilton Papers #1743 (SHC).

22. Du Bois, *Black Reconstruction,* 713 (first quotation), iii (second quotation), 731–37. Many white readers despised Du Bois's annotated bibliography, which separated his sources into categories like "Standard—Anti-Negro," "Propaganda," indifferent and fair historians, and "Negro historians." See Wirt Armistead Cate to Frank L. Owsley, October 10, 1935, Folder 1, Box 2, Owsley Papers; Revilo Pendleton Oliver to Owsley, October 14, 1935, Folder

failed to give Du Bois full historical hearing because of his Marxist interpretation of class and race relations in the Reconstruction South. *Journal of Southern History* editor Wendell H. Stephenson, for example, admitted that he did not possess the intellectual tools to distinguish between history underpinned by Marxist theory and communist "propaganda." A sympathetic Francis Butler Simkins, Du Bois's reviewer in the *Journal of Southern History,* agreed that *Black Reconstruction*'s emphasis on "Marxian philosophy . . . does not leave sufficient room for consideration of the constructive achievements of the Negroes during Reconstruction."[23] Still other historians, including Woodward, gained something constructive from their reading of *Black Reconstruction.* Woodward sent Du Bois a copy of his 1938 *Journal of Southern History* article, "Tom Watson and the Negro in Agrarian Politics," with a note acknowledging Du Bois's influence on the work. Similarly, Woodward's dissertation advisor at the University of North Carolina, Howard K. Beale, insisted that "every future historian must reckon with" *Black Reconstruction.*[24] With white historians in the South reading

14, Box 4, Owsley Papers; and Benjamin B. Kendrick to Charles W. Pipkin, November 27, 1935, *Southern Review* Collection.

23. Wendell H. Stephenson to Robert H. Woody, October 26, 1937, and reply, November 1, 1937, Box 74, Stephenson Papers; Francis B. Simkins, review of *Black Reconstruction,* by W. E. B. Du Bois, *Journal of Southern History,* 1 (November 1935), 531. See also Ralph J. Bunche, "Reconstruction Reinterpreted," *Journal of Negro Education,* 4 (October 1935), 568; Avery O. Craven, review of *Black Reconstruction, American Journal of Sociology,* 41 (January 1936), 535–36; E. Merton Coulter, review of *Black Reconstruction, Georgia Historical Quarterly,* 20 (March 1936), 95; Arthur C. Cole, review of *Black Reconstruction, Mississippi Valley Historical Review,* 23 (September 1936), 278–80; Benjamin B. Kendrick, "History as a Curative," *Southern Review,* 1 (Winter 1936), 540–50; Kendrick, review of *Dusk of Dawn,* by W. E. B. Du Bois, *Journal of Southern History,* 7 (February 1941), 119–21; and T. Harry Williams, "An Analysis of Some Reconstruction Attitudes," *Journal of Southern History,* 12 (November 1946), 472. Many African American reviewers, by contrast, hardly mentioned the Marxist framework to concentrate praise on the constructive role African Americans played in Du Bois's interpretation. See Meier and Rudwick, *Black History and the Historical Profession,* 101–2; and Mary McLeod Bethune, "Clarifying Our Vision with the Facts," *Journal of Negro History,* 23 (January 1938), 13. For a general overview of the book's reception see Jessie P. Guzman, "W. E. B. Du Bois—The Historian," *Journal of Negro Education,* 30 (Autumn 1961), 381–83.

24. C. Vann Woodward to W. E. B. Du Bois, April 3, 1938, Papers of W. E. B. Du Bois (microfilm ed.; Ann Arbor, Mich., 1981), reel 49, frame 851; C. Vann Woodward, "Tom Watson and the Negro in Agrarian Politics," *Journal of Southern History,* 4 (February 1938), 14–33; Howard K. Beale, "On Rewriting Reconstruction History," *American Historical Review,* 45 (July 1940), 809. See also [Rayford W. Logan], review of *Reunion and Reaction,* by C. Vann Woodward, *Journal of Negro History,* 36 (October 1951), 446.

the work of Du Bois and other black historians, the process of debate opened the door, though tentatively and incompletely, to a reconsideration of the white Reconstruction consensus.[25]

A central part of this revisionism was locating the Reconstruction moment in a much longer view of southern history; it is this manifestation that connects *Origins,* which was designated to begin after Reconstruction, to the prior revisionist works. "[T]he tendency to cut Reconstruction off from the Civil War that preceded it and the Bourbon and Populist eras that followed has led to misinterpretation," Howard K. Beale argued in 1940. "We need to restudy as a whole the period from 1850 to the turn of the century in order to understand the segment of it that has usually been bounded by the years 1865 and 1877."[26] Woodward wrestled with his volume's assigned dates—they seemed unnatural to him; he wanted to de-emphasize them, perhaps by not even putting them in the title or on the book's spine; and he anticipated overlap between his and the preceding volume. He even successfully convinced the series editors to push the dates of his volume back to 1877 from the 1880 they had planned: "I am unable to find a logical and organic beginning point later than 1877," he admitted in a progress report. Woodward's struggle with his story's starting point was perhaps one reason that he broke away from work on *Origins* to write *Reunion and Reaction,* another book that garnered largely positive reviews. (The *Journal of Southern History* reviewer welcomed the revisionist contribution but also hoped that "future revisionists will not ignore the interpretations of the Dunning-Fleming school"—a fair indication of midcentury white southern historians' attempt to embrace change while clinging to the old.)[27]

---

25. William B. Hesseltine, "A Quarter-Century of the Association for the Study of Negro Life and History," *Journal of Negro History,* 25 (October 1940), 440–49; Williams, "Analysis of Some Reconstruction Attitudes," 469–86. For a more extensive discussion of black historians and the Southern Historical Association see Bethany L. Johnson, "Regionalism, Race, and the Meaning of the Southern Past: Professional History in the American South, 1896–1961" (Ph.D. dissertation, Rice University, 2001), esp. chap. 6.

26. Beale, "On Rewriting Reconstruction History," 813 (quotation), 815.

27. *Journal of Southern History,* 4 (May 1938), 264; C. Vann Woodward to Wendell H. Stephenson, May 9, 1941, Box 74, Stephenson Papers; Woodward to Stephenson, October 13, 1942, History of the South Folder, Box 61, Stephenson Papers (first quotation); Woodward to E. Merton Coulter, May 4, 1943, History of the South Folder, Box 61, Stephenson Papers. On Woodward, *Reunion and Reaction: The Compromise of 1877 and the End of Reconstruction* (Boston, 1951), see its reviews by Jeter A. Isely in *American Historical Review,* 57 (October 1951), 178–79; by Rayford W. Logan, in *Journal of Negro History,* 36 (October 1951), 445–50; by Daniel M. Robison, in *Journal of Southern History,* 18 (February 1952), 93–95

Beale's assessment of the status of Reconstruction studies went on to call for "a younger generation of Southern historians to cease lauding those who 'restored white supremacy' and instead to begin analyzing the restorationists' interests to see just what they stood *for* in opposing the Radicals." He appealed to Francis B. Simkins, Woodward, Horace Mann Bond, Paul Lewinson, Vernon L. Wharton, Roger W. Shugg, James S. Allen, and W. E. B. Du Bois to continue their important work along these lines. He set out a list of topics that needed investigation, many of which formed the core of *Origins of the New South*: a reanalysis of the connections between the Radicals, the Independents of the 1870s and 1880s, and the Populists as groups that "tried political co-operation of Negroes and whites"; an examination of the origins of industrialism, farm problems, business control over state government, and labor issues; and an appraisal of the accomplishments and effects of the Reconstruction governments. With such a call to arms, it is not surprising that *Journal of Negro History* writer William Brewer exclaimed in his review of *Origins*, "Within a decade Beale's dream of 1940 is partially realized."[28]

Woodward, then, may have conceived of himself and his History of the South series contribution as a "mole to subvert the establishment," but he was clearly in good company. Moreover, as it happens, these revisionists were in many ways actually welcomed in the seats of authority and power in the white southern historical profession. (The access of black historians of the South to these same institutions was much more difficult to arrange

---

(second quotation on p. 94); and by Arthur K. Kooker, in *Mississippi Valley Historical Review*, 38 (March 1952), 717–19; and Woodward, *Thinking Back*, 45–57.

28. Beale, "On Rewriting Reconstruction History," 808 (first quotation), 809–10, 823 (second quotation); Brewer, review of *Origins of the New South*, 206. For Woodward's company of revisionists see Francis Butler Simkins and Robert Hilliard Woody, *South Carolina during Reconstruction* (Chapel Hill, 1932); Francis B. Simkins, "New Viewpoints of Southern Reconstruction," *Journal of Southern History*, 5 (February 1939), 44–61; Woodward, *Tom Watson, Agrarian Rebel* (New York, 1938); Horace Mann Bond, *Negro Education in Alabama: A Study in Cotton and Steel* (Washington, D.C., 1939); Bond, "Social and Economic Forces in Alabama Reconstruction," 290–348; Vernon L. Wharton, "The Negro in Mississippi, 1865–1890" (Ph.D. dissertation, University of North Carolina at Chapel Hill, 1940), published as *The Negro in Mississippi, 1865–1890* (Chapel Hill, 1947); Paul Lewinson, *Race, Class, and Party: A History of Negro Suffrage and White Politics in the South* (New York, 1932); Shugg, *Origins of Class Struggle in Louisiana*; and James S. Allen, *Reconstruction: The Battle for Democracy, 1865–1876* (New York, 1937). Precursors also include Alex M. Arnett, *The Populist Movement in Georgia: A View of the "Agrarian Crusade" in the Light of Solid-South Politics* (New York, 1922). See also Novick, *That Noble Dream*, 232–34.

yet, even so, had started in earnest by the time *Origins* was published.)[29] Beale's paper described above, for example, was an invited presentation to the 1939 annual meeting of the Southern Historical Association, held in Lexington, Kentucky, as part of a panel designed to showcase the most recent approaches to southern historiography. The session reportedly attracted a large audience of members and nonmembers alike. Afterward, the editor of the *Journal of Southern History* begged for Beale to submit the paper for publication to the SHA organ, but Beale claimed he had already promised it to the *American Historical Review,* where it duly appeared.[30]

This successful SHA session was followed up the next year by a panel that contrasted older interpretations with the emerging revisionist perspectives. The program chair envisioned a roundtable, where older Dunning school historians like J. G. de Roulhac Hamilton, C. Mildred Thompson, and Charles W. Ramsdell would discuss changes they would make to their classic Reconstruction studies in light of new findings. Hamilton, for one, was not interested in participating. "As a matter of fact," he told the program chair, "if the revised point of view is that of Beale's paper [at the 1939 meeting], I haven't any interest in taking the matter seriously." Hamilton felt Beale's class-oriented approach was "so apparently detached from the facts of the case" and "so lacking in historicity" that it did not merit further discussion. Stephenson thought that Beale and Francis B. Simkins should not be put on the program again so soon, partially for diversity purposes and partially because "the Association was treated to their revisionists attitudes during the last program."[31] The association was nonetheless treated

29. Woodward, *Thinking Back,* 44; Johnson, "Regionalism, Race, and the Meaning of the Southern Past," chap. 6.

30. James W. Patton, "Fifth Annual Meeting of the Southern Historical Association," *Journal of Southern History,* 6 (February 1940), 81–83; Wendell H. Stephenson to Howard K. Beale, November 6, 1939, and December 7, 1939, and reply, January 13, 1940, all in Box 52, Stephenson Papers; Beale, "On Rewriting Reconstruction History," 807–27. Beale's fellow panel member, J. G. Randall, also hoped that Beale's paper would be published in the *Journal,* as it was "more suggestive of new angles and new points of view than my own." Randall to Stephenson, November 10, 1939, Box 69, Stephenson Papers. Randall's article, "The Civil War Restudied," appeared in the *Journal of Southern History,* 6 (November 1940), 439–57.

31. A. B. Moore to J. G. de Roulhac Hamilton, May 13, 1940, and reply, June 5, 1940, Folder 143, Hamilton Papers; Wendell H. Stephenson to John P. Dyer, April 9, 1940, Box 57, Stephenson Papers. For the classic studies in question see Hamilton, *Reconstruction in North Carolina* (New York, 1914); C. Mildred Thompson, *Reconstruction in Georgia: Economic, Social, Political, 1865–1872* (New York, 1917); and Charles W. Ramsdell, *Reconstruction in Texas* (New York, 1910).

to another discussion of revisionist Reconstruction historiography in Charleston in 1940. Simkins and Robert H. Woody restated their contention that revisionists (including Du Bois) had made positive changes to the understanding of Reconstruction and assorted issues by focusing squarely on the problems of race and class as well as on its constructive achievements. Most interesting, however, was C. Mildred Thompson's concession that if she had it to do over again, she would include in her state study of Georgia more analysis of social and economic aspects of Reconstruction, she would extend the study through 1890, and " 'most of all' she 'would want to know more about the part of the Negroes themselves in securing and maintaining their freedom.' "[32]

Although the value of the older state studies was defended from the floor at the Charleston meeting by another Dunning student, something approaching an alternative consensus was vaguely visible on the horizon—an approach that promised humanity and agency to the freedpeople, attention to the constructive benefits the South had attained as the result of Reconstruction, and the shortcomings and unfinished nature of the nation's democratic promise. For a growing contingent of the southern historical profession, to traditionalists' dismay, "Beale's article was considered the law and the gospel." Moreover, the Southern Historical Association and the *Journal of Southern History* were giving this revisionism succor. (A revisionist article on Reconstruction by T. Harry Williams that appeared in the *Journal,* for example, had first been rejected by the *American Historical Review* as too "controversial.") The New South could not suffer the same old representation with this kind of new starting point.[33]

The History of the South series editors envisioned a "continuous, integrated narrative" in ten volumes. To this end, "[e]ach contributor to the series must evince a spirit of co-operation . . . with other contributors, especially with those contributing the volumes just preceding and following his

---

32. Albert B. Moore, "Sixth Annual Meeting of the Southern Historical Association," *Journal of Southern History,* 7 (February 1941), 67.

33. Moore, "Sixth Annual Meeting of the Southern Historical Association," 66–68; E. Merton Coulter to Wendell H. Stephenson, November 16, 1942, History of the South Folder, Box 61, Stephenson Papers (first quotation); T. Harry Williams to William C. Binkley, May 14, 1946, Series B2, Folder 100, SHA Records (second quotation); Williams, "Analysis of Some Reconstruction Attitudes," 469–86. See also Bernard A. Weisberger, "The Dark and Bloody Ground of Reconstruction Historiography," *Journal of Southern History,* 25 (November 1959), 427–47; Avery O. Craven, review of *Reconstruction: After the Civil War,* by John Hope Franklin, *Journal of Southern History,* 28 (May 1962), 255–56; and Franklin, "Mirror for Americans," 384–98.

own."[34] The editors' dream of a seamless narrative, however, broke down between E. Merton Coulter's *The South during Reconstruction,* published in 1947, and Woodward's *Origins of the New South,* and no amount of cooperation could have remedied the situation.[35] Woodward's arguments in *Origins* were based on the budding revisionist consensus on Reconstruction and its aftermath, yet the Reconstruction volume of the History of the South series provided anything but a revisionist perspective. Series coeditor Wendell H. Stephenson had tried to get Coulter to tone down his attitude—to be fairer to the freedpeople and less hostile to the Reconstruction governments—to no avail. "I am a little nonplussed as to what other attitude anyone would have me assume," Coulter indignantly responded. "My attitude is based on common sense and practical facts, on two years of research among the sources, and not on some 'revisionist' point of view assumed more through predilections than through a consideration of the cold facts." Stephenson had apparently implied that Coulter would "lose [his] 'reputation'" due to his perspective on the period. While Stephenson tried to backpedal his comments, privately he still worried about how Coulter's book—the first in the series to be published—would be received. "If you have misgivings in regard to . . . publications that have passed under your editorship," Stephenson told Roger W. Shugg, "you can understand how I feel about Coulter's *The South During Reconstruction.* . . . I am glad that I am not called upon to review the manuscripts which I edit."[36]

Sure enough, Coulter's contribution to the series, though respectfully received by those of an earlier generation called upon to review it for scholarly historical journals, was increasingly panned by the rising generation, both privately and publicly. "It's a crying shame the way the profession has reviewed Coulter's godawful book on Reconstruction," T. Harry Williams confided to a friend. "Isn't someone going to have the courage to say it's based on race prejudice and distortion of the sources?" H. C. Nixon argued

---

34. "A History of the South, 1607–1940: Editorial Suggestions and Directions" (first quotation); "A History of the South, 1607–1940 (in ten volumes): General Plan" (second quotation).

35. Woodward recognized the potential problem of overlap, and he requested a copy of Coulter's final chapter so as to minimize repetition. He did not explicitly worry about interpretive differences, however. See Woodward to Wendell H. Stephenson, October 13, 1942, Box 61, History of the South Folder, Stephenson Papers.

36. E. Merton Coulter to Wendell H. Stephenson, November 16, 1942, and reply, November 26, 1942, History of the South Folder, Box 61, Stephenson Papers; Stephenson to Fletcher M. Green, December 8, 1947, Folder 146, Green Papers; Stephenson to Roger W. Shugg, December 11, 1947, Box 29, Stephenson Papers.

that Coulter did "an excellent job" given the limitations of his perspective and framework, "committing no sin to disturb the ashes or memory of the benefactor, Major George W. Littlefield, C. S. A." John Hope Franklin wrote an extended review essay criticizing Coulter's Reconstruction study for the *Journal of Negro Education,* which he then distributed to five hundred historians across the country. Manning J. Dauer called *The South during Reconstruction* nothing but a "historical romance."[37] Such criticism stuck in Coulter's craw for years afterward; he never seemed to grasp that his so-called objective point of view had been obliterated in accusations of racial bias. As one historian has noted, "The real significance of Coulter's volume is not so much what he said but that it was the last major work on Reconstruction to set forth that particular point of view."[38]

The extent to which Coulter's views were severely out of step with an emergent, more liberal consensus in the southern historical profession became even clearer from the near-unanimous approval that greeted the publication of *Origins* in 1951. Contrary to Woodward's expectations, the scholarly reviewers in historical journals tended toward unabashed praise. In his review for the *Journal of Southern History,* reprinted in this collec-

---

37. For positive reviews of E. Merton Coulter, *The South during Reconstruction* (Baton Rouge, 1947), see J. G. de Roulhac Hamilton, in *Journal of Southern History,* 14 (February 1948), 134–36; Wirt Armistead Cate, in *American Historical Review,* 53 (April 1948), 565–67; Frank L. Owsley, in *Annals of the American Academy of Political and Social Science,* 258 (July 1948), 153–54; and Henry H. Simms, in *Mississippi Valley Historical Review,* 35 (June 1948), 133–34. For critical reviews see T. Harry Williams to William B. Hesseltine, n.d. [ca. 1948], quoted in Novick, *That Noble Dream,* 349 n. 45; H. C. Nixon, in *Journal of Politics,* 10 (August 1948), 568–69; David H. Donald, "Southern Memory," *New Leader,* July 31, 1948, p. 11; John Hope Franklin, "Whither Reconstruction Historiography?" *Journal of Negro Education,* 17 (Autumn 1948), 446–61; Franklin to Wendell H. Stephenson, October 9, 1948, Box 12, Stephenson Papers; Manning J. Dauer, "Recent Southern Political Thought," *Journal of Politics,* 10 (May 1948), 346; Dewey W. Grantham Jr., "Southern Historiography and *A History of the South,*" *American Quarterly,* 5 (Autumn 1953), 255–57; and Weisberger, "Dark and Bloody Ground of Reconstruction Historiography," 434.

38. Michael Vaughan Woodward, "Ellis Merton Coulter and the Southern Historiographic Tradition" (Ph.D. dissertation, University of Georgia, 1982), 189; Coulter to J. G. de Roulhac Hamilton, April 3, 1954, Folder 191, Hamilton Papers; Coulter, "Communications," *Pacific Historical Review,* 23 (November 1954), 425–29; Joe Gray Taylor, "The White South from Secession to Redemption," in Boles and Nolen, eds., *Interpreting Southern History,* 182 (quotation); Franklin, "Mirror for Americans," 384–98. For another reassessment of the pros and cons of Coulter's work see John David Smith, "E. Merton Coulter, the 'Dunning School,' and the Civil War and Readjustment in Kentucky," *Register of the Kentucky Historical Society,* 86 (Winter 1988), 52–69.

tion, Allen W. Moger called Woodward "one of the most capable and realistic historians in the whole field." University of Wisconsin professor William B. Hesseltine wrote in the *American Historical Review*, "Beyond all question this is the most valuable book that has been written about the South in these years. Because of its freshness of view and its critical scholarship in a period long neglected, it is the most useful volume of 'A History of the South' that has appeared." In the *Mississippi Valley Historical Review* Roger W. Shugg praised *Origins* as "one of the masterpieces of our historical literature" that "every student of our recent past will grow wiser by reading." John Hope Franklin informed readers of the *Journal of Negro Education* that Woodward had told "the entire story of the beginnings of the New South," and Franklin called *Origins* "a masterful treatment of this difficult subject" that would be "a landmark in American historiography." William M. Brewer, the *Journal of Negro History* reviewer, found *Origins* "indispensable" and concluded, "Very probably no previous American historian has interpreted the New South with as complete freedom from bias and guile as Woodward has done." David H. Donald and Dewey W. Grantham added their kudos, both arguing that *Origins* was perhaps the best book to date in the series.[39] Francis Butler Simkins even took a shot at Coulter in his review of *Origins* for the *Saturday Review*, praising Woodward for "refus[ing] to adopt the amoral practice of many historians of justifying deeds in terms of the age."[40]

Though *Origins*, too, eventually became the target of thoughtful critics, as the essays in this volume illustrate, its longevity is partially attributable to its encapsulation of the new trend of historiography of the American

---

39. Allen W. Moger in *Journal of Southern History*, 18 (November 1952), 519 (21 in this volume); William B. Hesseltine in *American Historical Review*, 57 (July 1952), 994; Roger W. Shugg in *Mississippi Valley Historical Review*, 39 (June 1952), 142; John Hope Franklin in *Journal of Negro Education*, 21 (Spring 1952), 175; W. M. Brewer in *Journal of Negro History*, 37 (April 1952), 206; David H. Donald, "After Reconstruction," *The Nation*, May 17, 1952, p. 484; Grantham, "Southern Historiography and *A History of the South*," 268. Reviewers in southern state historical journals also lauded Woodward's work; see the reviews by Wood Gray, in *Maryland Historical Magazine*, 47 (September 1952), 254–55; by Lawrence Burnette Jr., in *Virginia Magazine of History and Biography*, 60 (April 1952), 342–44; by Jefferson Davis Bragg, in *North Carolina Historical Review*, 29 (July 1952), 446–47; and by S. Walter Martin, in *Georgia Historical Quarterly*, 36 (June 1952), 192–93.

40. Francis B. Simkins, "After Reconstruction," *Saturday Review*, 35 (February 23, 1952), 12. In *The South during Reconstruction*, Coulter had pointedly chosen "to write this volume in the atmosphere and spirit of the times here portrayed rather than to measure the South of Reconstruction by present-day standards" (p. xi).

South—an approach that guided southern historians, black and white, through the civil rights movement and beyond. This trend promised to explain the problems of the modern South of the first half of the twentieth century. It located the South's troubles not in Confederate defeat, as an earlier generation of white southern romanticists had, nor in the oppression and corruption of Reconstruction, as the Dunning school historians had, but in the origins of the New South itself—in the denial of democracy to freedpeople and white yeoman farmers; in the imposing strictures of Jim Crow laws and customs; in the debilitation of falling prices, debt, and agricultural failure; in the exploitation of land and labor. In retrospect *Origins* seems to be a book whose time had come.

ALLEN W. MOGER

Allen Wesley Moger, a native Virginian, received his Ph.D. from Columbia University in 1940, and his dissertation, quickly published, was entitled The Rebuilding of the Old Dominion: A Study in Economic, Social, and Political Transition from 1880 to 1902 *(Ann Arbor, 1940). Woodward cited it in* Origins's *"Critical Essays on Sources" as one of three "highly valuable studies of Virginia history." Moger spent his long and distinguished teaching career at Washington and Lee University, capping his scholarly career in 1968 with the publication of* Virginia: Bourbonism to Byrd, 1870–1925 *(Charlottesville, 1968). Moger's 1952 review of Woodward's book praised its honesty, its realism, its depth of research, and its writing style—characterizations of the book that have stood the test of time. Moger forthrightly warned those who wanted a defensive, romantic history of the South that they should avoid* Origins *because Woodward frankly revealed the selfishness, the expediency, the exploitation, the corruption, and the racism of the era. Moger described that time as the "background to the present South" and "essential to an understanding of the section today," suggestive of how at least some post–World War II southerners recognized the problems of the region that needed addressing. In a subtle way, Woodward was preparing a new generation to break free of old attitudes and practices that had held the region back and oppressed many of its people. He hoped his work would contribute to the origins of a truly new South.*

Review of *Origins of the New South, 1877–1913*

In this volume Mr. Woodward further substantiates his position as one of the most capable and realistic historians in the whole field of southern history. To the usual qualities of a trained scholar he brings unusual powers of perception and co-ordination. It is not the kind of book that will please those who like to emphasize the good and the beautiful and to minimize the unfavorable and the true. The story is as honest as is humanly possible, and the conclusions reached are well substantiated by the evidence given. Anyone who tries to write honestly in the history of this period will inevitably find material and reach conclusions which will be displeasing to those who are prone to laud the policies and actions of our fathers. The period covered was one of despair and hope for the South. The characters who made the history were human beings faced with immediate and insuperable problems,

Reprinted from *Journal of Southern History,* 18 (November 1952), 519–23.

and the selfishness, expediency, exploitation, and benevolence which characterized the period are revealed in this book. The background of the present South, so essential to an understanding of the section today, is explained more effectively and realistically in this volume than in any that this writer has read.

The term "New South" did not represent a place or a period but was primarily a slogan, a rallying cry, to popularize a South which was to win prosperity by copying the business and materialistic philosophy of the North. The "ambition of the South is to out-Yankee the Yankee," said Henry Watterson in 1877, the year of the Compromise which is treated more fully by Woodward in *Reunion and Reaction.* The word "Bourbon," so often used to designate those who were supposed to control the New South, is properly discarded because of the confusion and inconsistency with which it was used during the period. The use of "Solid South" is considered misleading because, while the racial issue usually made the section solid in national elections, the cleavage on local social, economic, and political issues was enormous.

The term "Redeemers" is appropriately used to designate those who rescued the South from the carpetbaggers and who remained in control for some years afterwards. They sought to realize enormous profits from railroading and industry under benevolent and subservient governments. While the new group possessed enough of the old planter class to give it respectability and win public confidence, the vast majority of the industrial leaders of the period came of nonslaveholding parents. They were often the same ones who sought to glorify the "Lost Cause," and this policy served to strengthen their position as leaders of the new industry. While admitting that the South's extreme poverty and need for capital made their program appear benevolent, Mr. Woodward, in viewing their work in the South as a whole, is inclined to disparage the motive of benevolence in carrying out their program. The Redeemers—and their spiritual successors—had more permanent influence on the South than the Republican Radicals or the leaders of the Confederacy because they "laid the foundations in matters of race, politics, economics, and law for the modern South." A long list of defalcations and financial looseness on the part of the Redeemers in various states causes the author to feel that their reputation for scrupulous honesty in the handling of public funds is hardly deserved. They, in most cases with honest intentions, promised "pure government first, free government afterwards," but failed to give either.

The farmer and the common man were "unredeemed." "If Reconstruction ever set the bottom rail on top . . . Redemption seemed to leave little doubt that the bottom rail was still on the bottom." In making this observation the author does not ignore other causes for the poverty of the lower classes. He demolishes the persistent idea that the end of slavery brought landholding and freedom to the poor whites. "The evils of land monopoly, absentee ownership, soil mining, and the one crop system, once associated with and blamed upon slavery, did not disappear with that institution but were instead, aggravated, intensified, and multiplied." The lien system and sharecropping were "not a plot but a makeshift" that "grew out of the ruins of the old regime." This new system, "together with the heritage of military defeat and pillage, would have been enough to keep generations of Southern farmers in a slough of depression." The convict lease system, the desertion of the Negro by his old Republican friends and even the northern churches, the widespread use of women and children in the new factories, and the frequent alliance between employers and state governments to defeat the efforts of labor to organize are other topics treated under "Mudsills and Bottom Rails."

The idea of "caste as a method of social control" evolved as the common whites came more and more into conflict with the Negroes for wages and opportunities and as the whites of the upcountry rose and demanded the vote to protect themselves, especially during and after the time of the Farmers' Alliance and Populism. This intensified hostility to the Negro reached its height in the decade at the turn of the century. The "Mississippi Plan" to eliminate the Negro as a voter was followed by all the states, and segregation laws and customs became more general and rigid. The "Atlanta Compromise," advanced by Booker T. Washington, had much influence in its purpose to "resolve the antagonisms, suspicions, and aspirations" of the Negro and the two groups of whites, North and South. Washington believed that if his fellow Negroes would quietly pursue education, personal worth, and material advance rather than political and social equality they would win the respect and co-operation of southern whites. To win the respect of northern investors and philanthropists and southern employers, he urged Negroes to rely upon paternalism rather than labor unions, and thrift and virtue rather than agitation, to improve their position. Washington's compromise was a *modus vivendi* in time and place. Practical, he simply did not emphasize ultimate aims. His philosophy was severely challenged by W. E. B. Du Bois, but Washington's influence with his race was impregnable until after his death in 1915.

The readability of a history book depends on the subject matter as well as on the writer. Telling a story based on the happenings in thirteen states leaves little time for lively personal portrayals or thrilling detail, but all of the writing in this book is good, and some of it approaches brilliance. The story at times is intricate because of the number of states involved and because the ways of politicians are bewildering, the machinations of businessmen difficult to decipher, and local and class cleavages confusing; but each chapter is constructed with perception and skill which leaves the reader with a clear understanding of the subject. The chapter on "The Divided Mind of the South"—divided between the new ideals of businessmen and developers and the "Lost Cause" of "warriors and orators"—is one of the best. If anyone doubts the colonial status of the New South, he should read the chapter on "The Colonial Economy." In 1898 the Southern Development Association was formed with headquarters in New York "to promote the colonization and improvement of the South," according to one of the organizers from Georgia. After reviewing much convincing evidence, the author concludes: "Like republics below the Rio Grande the South was limited largely to the role of a producer of raw materials, a tributary of industrial powers, an economy dominated by absentee owners . . . with the attendant penalties of low wages, lack of opportunity, and poverty."

A significant southern progressive movement—for whites only—is realistically reviewed, and the efforts of northern philanthropists and certain liberal southern leaders to improve education, to restrict child labor, to improve farm methods, and to eradicate hookworm are given proper attention. An excellent chapter discusses literature, the conditions of higher education, and the great power of churches in the section. The volume ends with an account of the part played by the South in the electing of Woodrow Wilson in 1912 and the new position occupied by southern political leaders in national politics as a result of that election.

There is little that deserves adverse criticism. A statement on page 104 is misleading. The phrase "This Way Freemen" was the much emphasized slogan of the Virginia Conservative-Democratic Convention of 1883 as an appeal to all Virginians to unite and overthrow what they considered the tyranny of William Mahone. It was not primarily an appeal for Negro votes. The Democratic party in Virginia used the popular primary to choose statewide candidates beginning in 1905, and because of the expense to the party and the candidates the primary was operated by the state after 1913 (p. 372). The convict lease system was abolished by Virginia in 1893 rather than later (p. 424). As a whole, this is one of the ablest and best volumes in an excellent series. It has an invaluable bibliography.

Sheldon Hackney, one of C. Vann Woodward's many distinguished students, wrote the first sustained retrospective of Origins of the New South, 1877–1913, *on the twentieth anniversary of its publication, and at the time* Origins *seemed to be enjoying an unusually long honeymoon. There were glimmers of criticism and some suggestive new work that called into question particular aspects, but the overwhelming impression Hackney had of the book's reputation in 1971 (when he first presented the paper that became this article) was the essential "durability" of its overall thesis. Subsequent work, he wrote, had "been for the most part complementary and supplementary rather than contradictory." Hackney suggested that in addition to its substantial research base, its graceful writing, and the plausibility if not simply correctness of its overall interpretation, the book's unusual staying power had been enhanced by its emphasis on economic matters—the perennial struggle between the haves and have nots—and a tragic vision of the South shared with novelist William Faulkner. Woodward's recognition of "the likelihood of failure and the necessity of struggle" struck a familiar chord in 1950s America, an attitude toward life probed deeply by theologian Reinhold Niebuhr. (Even the contemporaneous reappraisal of the New England Puritans in the hands of such scholars as Perry Miller and Edmund S. Morgan implicitly praised the Puritans for such an ethos.) In its competing themes of irony and tragedy,* Origins *seemed to fit the times. The fact that two other books with much narrower focus but similar interpretations appeared in the same year— Albert D. Kirwan's* Revolt of the Rednecks: Mississippi Politics, 1876–1925 *(Lexington, Ky., 1951) and Allen J. Going's* Bourbon Democracy in Alabama, 1874–1890 *(University, Ala., 1951)—and were both favorably reviewed in the* Journal of Southern History *a year before* Origins *was indicates another reason for* Origins's *reception.* Origins *built on an emerging revisionism of the pre–1930 scholarship, absorbed the new viewpoints, extended the arguments, and moved far beyond them to construct a broad-based interpretation of the entire era. To recall those earlier writings that helped point the direction Woodward took so boldly in no way lessens his achievement in* Origins. *Rather, it helps us understand why his great book was so quickly and almost universally praised when it appeared. It soon became the foundation on which practically the entire edifice of subsequent scholarship was built.*

Origins of the New South in Retrospect

One of the facts of intellectual life that makes publishers happy and students sad is that every generation writes its own history. The elapse of more than the traditional span of two decades since the publication of *Origins of the New South* by C. Vann Woodward[1] makes it an appropriate time to wonder whether a new generation has begun to alter Woodward's masterful portrait

---

Reprinted from *Journal of Southern History*, 38 (May 1972), 191–216.
1. Woodward, *Origins of the New South, 1877–1913* (Baton Rouge, 1951).

of the South between 1877 and 1913. Of the three general sources of revisionist impulses—new information, new questions, new world views—all have had ample time and sufficient cause to wash away Woodward's version of the origins of the New South. Yet, given the amazing frequency with which the generational waves are now rolling over our cultural breakwaters, the remarkable thing is that there has been so little fundamental challenge to the outlines of the story established by Woodward twenty years ago.

Of one thing we may be certain at the outset. The durability of *Origins of the New South* is not a result of its ennobling and uplifting message. It is the story of the decay and decline of the aristocracy, the suffering and betrayal of the poor whites, and the rise and transformation of a middle class. It is not a happy story. The Redeemers are revealed to be as venal as the carpetbaggers. The declining aristocracy are ineffectual and money hungry, and in the last analysis they subordinated the values of their political and social heritage in order to maintain control over the black population. The poor whites suffered from strange malignancies of racism and conspiracy-mindedness, and the rising middle class was timid and self-interested even in its reform movement. The most sympathetic characters in the whole sordid affair are simply those who are too powerless to be blamed for their actions.

Such a somber view differs sharply from the confident optimism exuded by the New South school of historians such as Philip Alexander Bruce, Broadus Mitchell, Paul H. Buck, and Holland Thompson.[2] Embellished by various degrees of hyperbole, their principal theme was that of sectional reconciliation and the casting off of the dead hand of the past. "Most of the real Southern colonels are dead," Holland Thompson wrote in 1919, "and the others are too busy running plantations or cotton mills to spend much time discussing genealogy, making pretty speeches, or talking about their honor. Not so many colonels are made as formerly, and one may travel far before he meets an individual who fits the popular idea of the type. He is likely to meet more men who are cold, hard, and astute, for the New South has developed some perfect specimens of the type whose natural habitat had been supposed to be Ulster or the British Midlands—religious, narrow, stubborn, and very shrewd."[3] "New South" for Thompson meant not only this

---

2. For an intelligent brief discussion of the New South school, see Paul M. Gaston, "The 'New South,'" in Arthur S. Link and Rembert W. Patrick, eds., *Writing Southern History: Essays in Historiography in Honor of Fletcher M. Green* (Baton Rouge, 1965), 321–26.

3. Thompson, *The New South: A Chronicle of Social and Industrial Evolution* (New Haven, 1919), 203–4.

new spirit of enterprise but a desire to accept the results of the Civil War as the best thing that could have happened, to face the future without rejecting the past, and the determination to play a part in national life. "Economically," Thompson maintained, "the South has prospered in proportion as the new spirit has ruled."[4]

Thompson himself was very cautious about his claims as regards the real economic changes in the South, but he was typical of the New South historians in many other things. In accord with the interpretation of Reconstruction then dominant, that associated with the name and work of William Archibald Dunning, Thompson viewed Reconstruction as a fiasco of disorder and dishonesty. Consequently, the men who returned the South to (conservative white) home rule, the Redeemers, appeared in a favorable light. Even though Thompson indulged in no cult of the Redeemers, he presented them as honest men justifiably concerned about white supremacy. Their only fault, according to Thompson, was perhaps an unhealthy fixation upon maintaining low taxes to the detriment of progressive services such as good schools and good roads. Toward the irrational and ill-informed rebellion of the Populists against their natural and traditional leaders, Thompson was condescendingly tolerant. Similarly, he pictured cotton-mill operatives as content with their lot except when stirred up by malcontents and agitators, and the political conflict of the Progressive movement is largely swallowed up in Thompson's account by the general swell of a developing social consciousness which resulted in humanitarian reforms and more schools, roads, and hospitals. The South looked to the future with a sense of well-being and optimism.

Though the Black Reconstruction myth already had been subjected to effective criticism by the time Woodward wrote, the buoyant picture of the succeeding era created by the New South historians still stood. It had been deflated neither by the attacks from the right by the Agrarians nor from the left by regionalists such as Howard W. Odum and Rupert B. Vance. Thus the themes that wound their way through *Origins of the New South,* camouflaged though they were by a gently seductive prose style and by subtle qualifications, were nonetheless a radical departure, one that not only veered to the left in response to Depression-era outlooks but that recast the story of the late nineteenth-century South. No longer could historians write as if the central conflict of the period pitted disembodied forces representing the agrarian past and the industrial future against each other. Henceforth the contending parties would be considerably more corporeal.

---

4. *Ibid.,* 192.

Phrased baldly, the thesis of *Origins of the New South* builds from the perception that though the Civil War deflected the course of southern history and altered the nature of southern society, there was considerable continuity between the policies of the Radical Republican governments of Reconstruction and the Conservative Democratic regimes established by the Redeemers. Regardless of who was in power, railroads and other special interests continued to enjoy privileges granted by government. The final act of Redemption itself took place as part of the electoral crisis of 1876–1877 when a Whiggish alliance between southern Democrats and national Republicans arranged to swap the presidency for home rule, political patronage, and internal improvements, an arrangement made possible through the good offices of that selfless public servant, Thomas A. Scott of the Pennsylvania Railroad. Railroads were the only national force strong enough to bring the warring sections and parties together.

So, Redemption was not a restoration. The old planter aristocracy was not returned to power with the Democratic party because the party had received a large admixture of Hamiltonian-Whig-industrial elements, dynamic components that quickly rose to the top of the party. Conservative in most matters, the *mésalliance* that was the Democratic party was liberal in its use of fraud and violence to achieve Redemption, in its creation of a corrupt political system to maintain itself in power, and in the frequency with which its officeholders absconded with public funds. Frightening the poor whites into line with the specter of black domination and holding planter opposition within bounds by playing upon their fear of poor-white insurgency, the Redeemers captured the slogans of white supremacy and home rule and used these banners to cloak the pursuit of their own political and economic purposes. The history of the New South period, according to this view, is largely the story of how the Redeemers ruled in a manner that was against the interests of the mass of common people.

Debunking the Redeemers was one of the most important contributions of *Origins of the New South*. In their previous incarnation, they had been seen often as heroic statesmen and at worst as a trifle shortsighted because of their policies of minimum government and maximum financial stringency. Now it is clear that Redemption was no moral demarcation.

Nor was it an economic demarcation dividing a glorious agrarian past and a glorious industrial future, as the New South ideologues would have it. Despite their glowing rhetoric, the South had to run hard just to keep from losing ground. Over the period from 1877 to 1913 the South's percentage of the nation's manufacturing establishments and its share of capital engaged in manufacturing remained constant. Never, in fact, had the South been more distinct from the North in every measure of wealth and social well-being and never more similar in the values espoused by the leaders of the two sections. Contrary to what some previous historians had believed, according to the *Origins of the New South,* high profits as well as moral fervor account for the growth of cotton mills in the South, a growth that began long before the 1880 date emphasized by New South historians. Contrary also to the romantic notions of Wilbur J. Cash and Broadus Mitchell, members of the new middle class were not the sons of the old planter aristocracy. More often than not they derived from the families of urban merchants or men of the professions. Wherever they came from, economic history does not explain why the captains of industry were in control, because the industrial revolution simply did not happen.

The reasons for the slow rate of industrial development are not far to seek. The South's was a colonial economy. It remained overwhelmingly a region of staple-crop agriculture and extractive industries. This meant that southerners bought almost all their manufactured goods, and not a little of their food, from outside the region. Not only that, but southern railroads and other establishments in the modern sector were increasingly controlled by outside capital. Profits that might have been reinvested in southern enterprise or helped to stimulate the local economy were drained off to the North. More important, decisions affecting the economic health of the region were made by men in northern boardrooms who had a vested interest in maintaining it in its colonial status. Industrialization under the New South formula hurt the South, for the Redeemers were not simply advocating industrialization, they were arguing for laissez-faire capitalism and a changed way of life. This cultural treason could not be hidden by the nostalgic view of the Old South created in the 1880s to dissolve the Great Recantation in the syrup of romanticism.

Political conflict during the New South period consisted of sporadic insurgencies by the "wool-hat boys," frequently supported by the obsolescing planter aristocracy, against the Redeemer coalition and its alliance with the capitalist East. After twenty years of falling farm prices the agrarian uprising finally coalesced in the Populist movement and burst the bonds of the Democratic party in 1892 only to be decisively defeated in 1896 after a fatal decision to attempt fusion with the Democrats under the pennant of free silver held aloft by William Jennings Bryan. *Origins of the New South* presents the Populist movement in the tradition of *The Populist Revolt* of John

D. Hicks as a rational, economic-interest political movement.[5] Contrary to Hicks, who slighted the southern branch of populism and the issue of race relations within populism, Woodward argued that populism was stronger and more radical in the South than in the West and that southern Populists made a sincere, though doomed, effort to effect a political alliance with blacks on the basis of economic self-interest. The ingrained racist feelings of the white Populist constituency contributed to the downfall of populism.

As if determined not to be handicapped by the same problem, the progressives, who inherited the mantle of reform from the Populists, aided or acquiesced in disfranchisement and fashioned a brand of progressivism for whites only. Like progressivism outside the South, southern progressivism was urban and middle class. Though indigenous, with tinges of picturesque leadership and sectional rhetoric, it contained all the varieties of reform thought and action that were present on the national scene, and its leaders attacked business and finance as vigorously as did those anywhere. The problem with progressivism was that it did not go far enough, "it no more fulfilled the political aspirations and deeper needs of the mass of people than did the first New Deal administration."[6] The progressives carried over a strain of humanitarianism adapted from the tradition of patrician paternalism of the old ruling class. Nevertheless, the South that returned to national political power with Woodrow Wilson in 1913 after an absence of two generations was a very different region from the South that had attempted to establish its independence in the 1860s. A new middle-class leadership had guided it back into the mainstream of American life.

If one may apply labels without implying value judgments, *Origins of the New South* is a Beardian analysis. It is concerned throughout with the cynic's question: Who is in control and what are they after? It seems to accept at times the dualistic world view of the Populists and progressives themselves, a view in which the world is an arena of conflict between two contending forces: the classes versus the masses or business versus the people.[7]

---

5. Hicks, *The Populist Revolt: A History of the Farmers' Alliance and the People's Party* (Minneapolis, 1931).

6. Woodward, *Origins of the New South*, 395.

7. That Charles Beard's interpretation of the motivations of the makers of the Constitution was actually pluralistic is one of the points of Lee Benson's excellent analysis in his book, *Turner and Beard: American Historical Writing Reconsidered* (Glencoe, Ill., 1960), but there are senses in which Marx was not a Marxist either. There is a rich literature on the historiography of Beardianism: Cushing Strout, *The Pragmatic Revolt in American History: Carl Becker and Charles Beard* (New Haven, 1958); Robert A. Skotheim, *American Intellectual Histories*

Similar views of the nature of conflict in the era of the Constitution, the early Republic, Jacksonian America, the secession crisis, Reconstruction, progressivism, and the New Deal have been destroyed or superseded during the last twenty years of historiography. To the extent that *Origins of the New South* is a Beardian analysis, and its deviations from the Beardian model will concern us later, one must wonder how much of it has survived the chippings and scrapings of scholars in the 1950s and 1960s.

There has been a gratifyingly large volume of monographic literature in the field since 1951, making this appear to be a case of the general preceding the particular. This is not unusual. As David H. Fischer reminds us, "The monographs do not commonly come first and the general interpretations second. Instead some master architect—not master builder—draws a rough sketch of a pyramid in the sand, and many laborers begin to hew their stones to fit. Before many are made ready, the fashion suddenly changes— pyramids are out; obelisks are in."[8] The real surprise in this case is that the pyramid still stands. There has been no major challenge to *Origins of the New South,* except for the demurrers registered against its interpretation of trends in race relations, which are outside the concern of this essay, and certainly there has been no new master architect to offer a different design. The excellent essays by T. Harry Williams and Dewey W. Grantham Jr., the only two essays attempting a broad overview of southern politics between 1877 and 1913 to appear since the publication of *Origins of the New South,* follow the main furrows plowed by Woodward,[9] as do the most recent texts, *The South Since 1865* by John S. Ezell, *The South Since Appomattox* by Albert D. Kirwan and Thomas D. Clark, and *The American South* by Monroe Billington.[10] This is not to argue that the contributions to the field in the last twenty years have not been significant, for they have been. It is merely

---

and Historians (Princeton, 1966); David W. Noble, *Historians Against History: The Frontier Thesis and the National Covenant in American Historical Writing Since 1830* (Minneapolis, 1965); Richard Hofstadter, *The Progressive Historians: Turner, Beard, Parrington* (New York, 1968); Charles Crowe, "The Emergence of Progressive History," *Journal of the History of Ideas,* 27 (January–March 1966), 109–24.

   8. Fischer, *Historians' Fallacies: Toward a Logic of Historical Thought* (New York, Evanston, and London, 1970), 5.

   9. Grantham, *The Democratic South* (Athens, Ga., 1963), and Williams, *Romance and Realism in Southern Politics* (Athens, Ga., 1961).

   10. Ezell, *The South Since 1865* (New York and London, 1963); Clark and Kirwan, *The South Since Appomattox: A Century of Regional Change* (New York, 1967); Billington, *The American South* (New York, 1971).

to say that they have been for the most part complementary and supplementary rather than contradictory.

The contradictions within *Origins of the New South* are nevertheless heightening in several important places. One of the most striking and original contributions of Professor Woodward in this book has been his revision of the story of the Compromise of 1877, the deal by which Rutherford B. Hayes was awarded the contested presidential election of 1876 by southern forbearance in exchange for his promise to withdraw the last of the federal troops from South Carolina, Louisiana, and Florida and to appoint David M. Key to the postmaster generalship, thus bringing Reconstruction to a formal close. In a brilliant piece of detective work reported first in *Reunion and Reaction*[11] and then more briefly in *Origins of the New South,* Woodward uncovered an economic aspect of the deal and argued that the famous Wormley House bargain was a charade masking political and economic arrangements made in more discreet ways by representatives of Hayes and Whiggish southern politicians. Among the most active of the "honest brokers" was Tom Scott, who stood to gain a federal subsidy for his faltering Texas and Pacific Railroad, a project in which southern congressmen were interested for a variety of reasons.

One of the problems with this marvelous conspiracy, which captures in microcosm the Woodward view of the economically motivated Whiggish alliance of southern Redeemers and the capitalist East behind a movie-set façade of loyalty to the Old South, white supremacy, and home rule, is that though one can be sure the conspiracy existed and that Hayes gave his assurances through intermediaries that he would honor his end of the bargain, including "internal improvements of a national character," we do not know how committed Hayes was to specific economic aspects of the deal. Similarly, the link between the performance of the southern congressmen during the electoral crisis and the efforts of the Texas and Pacific lobby are inferential and circumstantial. After compiling a mass of evidence lending weight to the theme of persistent Whiggery, Thomas B. Alexander has expressed surprise that so few items in the Hayes papers refer to economic matters, and he suggests that given their backgrounds perhaps the southern congressmen would have behaved as they did in 1877 even without a conspiratorial bargain.[12] A recent biography of David M. Key by David M. Abshire, using

---

11. Woodward, *Reunion and Reaction: The Compromise of 1877 and the End of Reconstruction* (Boston, 1951).

12. Alexander, "Persistent Whiggery in the Confederate South, 1860–1877," *Journal of Southern History,* 27 (August 1961), 305–29.

Key papers not available to Woodward, reinforces Woodward's reconstruction of events, though Abshire understandably places more importance than Woodward on the necessity of Key's role.[13] Despite the new evidence, however, there are still gaps filled only by inference and doubt. The problem is cast into an even murkier state by the fact that Key had not been a Whig, though his political associates had, and by Professor Alexander's researches into the identity of antebellum Whigs which lead to the conclusion that there was little to differentiate Whig from Democratic voters except ideology.[14]

Whatever the social status of Whigs before the war, there have been some doubts expressed about Woodward's view of their role after the war. Lillian A. Pereyra's biography of James Lusk Alcorn describes a Whig who persisted by joining the Republican party, a path taken by some other Whigs in Mississippi, particularly in the early days of Reconstruction.[15] Allen W. Moger, in his thorough reexamination of Virginia political history from the Bourbons to Byrd, denies the validity of the persistent Whiggery theme in Virginia and argues that attitudes rather than old party affiliations motivated the men in control of the Virginia Democracy. This highlights the ambiguity in Woodward's account between Whiggery as an institutional loyalty and Whiggery as an aristocratic ideology, but Professor Moger's impression is sharply contradicted in the more detailed account of Virginia politics during the Reconstruction era by Jack P. Maddex Jr.[16] According to Maddex, former Whigs accounted for approximately half of the Conservative party's leadership and, more important, the Conservative party adapted itself to postwar realities by adopting the values which had characterized the Union Whigs before the war. Even though Maddex portrays the Conser-

13. Abshire, *The South Rejects a Prophet: The Life of Senator D. M. Key, 1824–1900* (New York, Washington, and London, 1967).

14. Alexander et al., "The Basis of Alabama's Ante-Bellum Two-Party System," *Alabama Review,* 19 (October 1966), 243–76; Alexander et al., "Who Were the Alabama Whigs?" *ibid.,* 16 (January 1963), 5–19; Grady McWhiney, "Were the Whigs a Class Party in Alabama?" *Journal of Southern History,* 23 (November 1957), 510–22.

15. Pereyra, *James Lusk Alcorn, Persistent Whig* (Baton Rouge, 1966); David Donald, "The Scalawag in Mississippi Reconstruction," *Journal of Southern History,* 10 (November 1944), 447–60; Allen W. Trelease, "Who Were the Scalawags?" *ibid.,* 29 (November 1963), 445–68; William C. Harris, "A Reconsideration of the Mississippi Scalawag," *Journal of Mississippi History,* 32 (February 1970), 3–42.

16. Moger, *Virginia: Bourbonism to Byrd, 1870–1925* (Charlottesville, 1968); Maddex, *The Virginia Conservatives, 1867–1879: A Study in Reconstruction Politics* (Chapel Hill, 1970).

vatives as forward-looking modernizers rather than agents of the colonial power as in the Woodward account and though he departs from Woodward in other small ways, he provides impressive confirmation of the major lines of interpretation in *Origins of the New South*.

A more substantial contradiction comes in the case of South Carolina where the Woodward thesis does not fit. According to William J. Cooper Jr., the South Carolina Bourbons were not former Whigs nor were they the agents of northern capital. Far from being new men, they were the offspring of planters. Political conflict in the Bourbon period, writes Cooper, did not take the form of class antagonism but was the outgrowth of other alignments, chiefly intrastate sectionalism.[17]

The import of Cooper's findings for the thesis of *Origins of the New South* is less clear because South Carolina may be a special case. As Cooper himself points out, the major reason for Whiggery not to persist in postwar South Carolina politics is that there was no significant Whig party before the war. In addition, Cooper's portrait of Tillmanism as something other than a class movement supports Woodward's view of Tillman as a charlatan in his role as a radical agrarian leader.

This leaves the question of whether South Carolina Bourbonism was in fact a restoration of the antebellum planter aristocracy or whether even in South Carolina the Civil War marked a significant interruption and redirection of the political structure. One statistical fact that historians should become aware of and attempt to explain is the dramatic shift in the occupational base of the political elite in the South between the 1850s and the 1880s. Ralph A. Wooster's painstaking quantitative studies of the power structure in the 1850s reveal that South Carolina was the most elitist of the southern states in terms of the economic status of its state officeholders.[18] Almost two-thirds of the South Carolina legislators in 1850 and in 1860 were planters or farmers, yet two-thirds of Cooper's sample of forty-three members of the postbellum elite was composed of lawyers, though the fathers of most of them had been planters. This implies a shift in the social basis of politics that is consistent with the views expressed in *Origins of the New South*. Future analyses should disclose whether or not Cooper is justified in taking the South Carolina Bourbons so much at their own evaluation in attributing their actions to a system of values deriving from a firm loyalty

17. Cooper, *The Conservative Regime: South Carolina, 1877–1890* (Baltimore, 1968).

18. Wooster, *The People in Power: Courthouse and Statehouse in the Lower South, 1850–1860* (Knoxville, 1969).

to the Old South, in attributing their defeat to rhetorical obsolescence rather than to clashes of class and economic interests, and in cleansing them of the charge of industrial Quislinghood by imputing innocence to the observation that "The Conservatives welcomed industry to South Carolina and worked to create a favorable atmosphere for its growth."[19]

The crucial question of continuity or discontinuity across the Civil War involves more than simply the antebellum political identity of the dominant element of the postbellum Democratic party. Wilbur J. Cash, the South's foremost mythmaker, incorporated into his spellbinding evocation of the Piedmont mentality the New South propaganda's image of the planter's son becoming first a captain of cavalry and then after the war a captain of industry as the civilization of the Old South blended into the New South with scarcely a ripple in the social structure.[20] Woodward has dissented from this picture by implication in *Origins of the New South* and more explicitly in a recent publication.[21] William B. Hesseltine's study entitled *Confederate Leaders in the New South* takes some beginning steps toward a rigorous analysis of this problem by tracing the postwar careers of 656 Confederate officers.[22] His finding that they overwhelmingly held influential positions in society in the late nineteenth century is a welcome piece of evidence for the continuity school, but it is not a definitive answer for several reasons. We do not know much about the antebellum backgrounds of the Confederate officer corps as a group or about the degree of political dominance of Hesseltine's sample in the postbellum years or the extent to which the postbellum careers of Hesseltine's leaders are a fair sample of the postbellum careers of the surviving members of the antebellum elite. One of the next steps toward an answer to the continuity question should be a prosopographical study of the southern political elite in the 1880s. A comparison of the social origins and affiliations of the elites of the 1880s and the 1850s should tell us something about the transformation of the South in the era of the Civil War and lead us on to fruitful refinements of the question of continuity.

Woodward's mosaic of discontinuity includes an explication of the divided mind of the New South in which the dual loyalties of the Redeemer appear to be a more or less conscious exercise in Catoism. Recent histories,

---

19. Cooper, *Conservative Regime,* 120.

20. Cash, *The Mind of the South* (New York, 1941), 205.

21. Woodward, "W. J. Cash Reconsidered," *New York Review of Books,* 13 (December 4, 1969), 28–34.

22. Hesseltine, *Confederate Leaders in the New South* (Baton Rouge, 1950).

such as those by Cooper and Moger, tend to take the Redeemer's professions of loyalty to the values of the Old South civilization more seriously than Woodward. This is also true of Paul M. Gaston's beautiful and authoritative intellectual analysis entitled *The New South Creed*.[23] Economic regeneration, national reconciliation, and racial adjustment were the major motifs of New South propaganda, in and around which played the idea of sectional self-determination and even dominance. Emulating the conquerors, the New South theorists thought, was the best way of getting rid of them. Though it is a major contribution to our understanding of the proponents of southern industrialization, Gaston's study is not primarily revisionist. He agrees with the judgment that the New South theorists served the region poorly by rationalizing industrialization on the disadvantageous terms set by northern capitalists, and he reinforces the perception of discontinuity by demonstrating how a revolutionary regime mobilizes the symbols of tradition in the service of change.

Those who resist change generally attract much less attention from historians than those who advocate it, particularly when the advocates win, and the South in the late nineteenth century is no exception to this rule. Clement Eaton takes a small step toward rectifying this oversight in his Lamar lectures, published as *The Waning of the Old South Civilization, 1860–1880's,* in which he places great emphasis upon "the tenacity of old forces and ideas rooted in the soil of the ante-bellum South."[24] A biography of Charles Colcock Jones which is now in progress should also add to our appreciation of the backward-looking elements in the New South.[25] That the plantation as a system of agriculture was not destroyed by the Civil War and emancipation is a well-known fact documented by Roger W. Shugg's study of Louisiana, reiterated by J. Carlyle Sitterson's study of the cane sugar industry, and incorporated by Woodward in *Origins of the New South*.[26] We are still in need of detailed studies of landownership, rural mobility patterns, and local

---

23. Gaston, *The New South Creed: A Study in Southern Mythmaking* (New York, 1970).

24. Eaton, *The Waning of the Old South Civilization, 1860–1880's* (Athens, Ga., 1968).

25. J. William Berry of Princeton University is studying Jones for his Ph.D. dissertation under the direction of Arthur S. Link. See also Hugh C. Davis, "An Analysis of the Rationale of Representative Conservative Alabamians, 1874–1914" (Ph.D. dissertation, Vanderbilt University, 1964).

26. Shugg, "Survival of the Plantation System in Louisiana," *Journal of Southern History,* 3 (August 1937), 311–25; Sitterson, *Sugar Country: The Cane Sugar Industry in the South, 1753–1950* (Lexington, Ky., 1953).

economies and politics before we can be certain as to the effects of the Civil War upon southern social structures.

Robert L. Brandfon, in his study of the development of a rich plantation agriculture in the Yazoo-Mississippi Delta after the Civil War, contends that the postbellum planter, of whose origins we are still uncertain, differed from the antebellum planter in being conscious of the need for efficiency: "Underneath the romantic 'moonlight and magnolia' was the businesslike quest for profits."[27] Whether profit orientation was less a part of the planter's consciousness before the Civil War than after is an important topic for future scholarship,[28] but for the present Brandfon reminds us that the modernizers of the New South had an agricultural as well as an industrial policy. Brandfon thinks that both policies rested upon an unjustified and ultimately detrimental faith in the beneficence of outside capital, thus reinforcing the interpretive scheme of *Origins of the New South*.

In this regard Brandfon is in good company. Most of the state monographs done since 1951 reinforce much more than they revise about *Origins of the New South*. This is true of Albert D. Kirwan's narrative of Mississippi politics from 1876 to 1925 and of Allen J. Going's treatment of Alabama public life in the Bourbon period, both of which appeared soon after the publication of *Origins of the New South*.[29] Other than the deviations already discussed, Moger's account of Virginia throughout the late nineteenth century conforms to Woodward's patterns, as do those of Raymond H. Pulley on Virginia, Joseph F. Steelman on North Carolina, James S. Ferguson on Mississippi, William W. Rogers on Alabama, and William I. Hair on Louisiana.[30] Aside from Sheldon Hackney, who tends to see the Populists in

---

27. Brandfon, *Cotton Kingdom of the New South: A History of the Yazoo Mississippi Delta from Reconstruction to the Twentieth Century* (Cambridge, Mass., 1967), viii.

28. See Robert E. Gallman, "Self-Sufficiency in the Cotton Economy of the Antebellum South," *Agricultural History*, 44 (January 1970), 5–23. This entire issue, edited by William N. Parker, is devoted to papers on "The Structure of the Cotton Economy of the Antebellum South" and is available in book form from the Agricultural History Society.

29. Kirwan, *Revolt of the Rednecks: Mississippi Politics, 1876–1925* (Lexington, Ky., 1951); Going, *Bourbon Democracy in Alabama, 1874–1890* (University, Ala., 1951).

30. Pulley, *Old Virginia Restored: An Interpretation of the Progressive Impulse, 1870–1930* (Charlottesville, 1968); Steelman, "The Progressive Era in North Carolina, 1884–1917" (Ph.D. dissertation, University of North Carolina, 1955); Steelman, "Vicissitudes of Republican Party Politics: The Campaign of 1892 in North Carolina," *North Carolina Historical Review*, 43 (October 1966), 430–41; Steelman, "Republican Party Strategists and the Issue of Fusion with Populists in North Carolina, 1893–1894," *ibid.*, 47 (July 1970), 244–69; Rogers,

Alabama as much more opportunistic than does Woodward,[31] the only direct attempt to revise a part of the story of the southern uprising has been that mounted by Robert F. Durden in *The Climax of Populism,* in which he argues from a close examination of the evidence that the Populists at the national convention in 1896 were not duped by a conspiratorial leadership into fusion with the Democrats.[32] Agreeing with Norman Pollack on at least this point, Durden suggests that fusion was not a desertion of principles but was logically seen by many Populists as the best next step toward general political reform. Despite the divergent results of their textual analyses, Durden and Woodward share a basic sympathy with populism understood as an economic interest group composed of rational but oppressed farmers. That this interpretation has probably survived the brilliant revisionist rendering of populism fashioned by Richard Hofstadter in *The Age of Reform* can be seen in the work of Theodore Saloutos.[33]

The neglect-of-the-losers rule has also applied to the other minority party, the Republicans. Allen W. Trelease's quantitative assessment of the identity of the scalawags lends credence to the assumption of continuity among poor whites in the upland South from Unionist sentiments in 1860 to scalawag Republicanism during Reconstruction to Independentism during the Gilded Age to populism during the 1890s.[34] This progression may be traced in the various monographs covering state politics in the late nineteenth century, and particularly in Moger and Rogers of the post-1951 books. Vincent P. De Santis and Stanley P. Hirshson overlap considerably in charting the ebb and flow of national Republican policy on the Southern Question.[35] Olive Hall Shadgett's study of Republicanism in Georgia under-

---

The One-Gallused Rebellion: Agrarianism in Alabama, 1865–1896 (Baton Rouge, 1970); Hair, *Bourbonism and Agrarian Protest: Louisiana Politics, 1877–1900* (Baton Rouge, 1969).

31. Hackney, *Populism to Progressivism in Alabama* (Princeton, 1969). Helen G. Edmonds, in *The Negro and Fusion Politics in North Carolina, 1894–1901* (Chapel Hill, 1951), also exposes the opportunism of the Populist racial policies, but otherwise the fusion forces appear progressive in her pages.

32. Durden, *The Climax of Populism: The Election of 1896* (Lexington, Ky., 1965).

33. Hofstadter, *The Age of Reform: From Bryan to F.D.R.* (New York, 1955); Saloutos, "The Professors and the Populists," *Agricultural History,* 40 (October 1966), 235–54; and Saloutos, *Farmer Movements in the South, 1865–1933* (Berkeley, 1960). For an extensive bibliography on populism, with an introduction discussing the state of the field, see Sheldon Hackney, ed., *Populism: The Critical Issues* (Boston, 1971).

34. Trelease, "Who Were the Scalawags?"

35. De Santis, *Republicans Face the Southern Question: The New Departure Years, 1877–1897* (Baltimore, 1959); Hirshson, *Farewell to the Bloody Shirt: Northern Republicans and the Southern Negro, 1877–1893* (Bloomington, 1962).

lines the fact that national Republicans did not drop their efforts to build a southern base in 1877.[36] Successive attempts to court white allies from various sectors of society to link with captive black Republican votes were all wrecked on the rocks of white supremacy. Mistreated, defrauded, manipulated, and abandoned though they were, black Republicans managed to play a significant role in southern politics well into the 1890s before disfranchisement and cynical apathy ushered in the era of "post office Republicanism." We need somehow to gain access to the political life within the black community during the last third of the century.

With blacks relegated to unthreatening political roles, the whites were free to divide, or so the theory went. One of the unsolved, even unposed, riddles of twentieth-century southern politics is why a two-party system did not develop after disfranchisement. The absence of an opposition party, of course, did not mean the absence of conflict, because fierce conflict did occur between personal followings or through intrastate sectionalism. The question really is why was there not enough strength or persistence in the factional alignments for one or more opposition parties to emerge. State parties have usually been organized from above in response to the needs of national politics, and the Republican party certainly tried to create client organizations in the southern states in the late nineteenth century. The frequent shifts in tactics and the taboo attaching to the party of Lincoln and Grant certainly encouraged Democratic loyalty among whites, and then Solid South allegiances were frozen into place by habit and by the fact that white Republicans soon quit trying to build a strong party when they discovered the benefits of rotten-borough politics. That much of the answer is already in the literature. But when one considers that all these barriers, including an increasingly powerful black electorate, were overcome after World War II when the southern Republican party began to grow in response to the development of a heterogeneous urban culture, then one begins to suspect that there was something more than racism and habit underlying the one-party system. It may be that a homogeneity of economic interests and culture among whites was the real perpetuator of the Solid South. The argument that Democratic hegemony was supported by the voters because of the disproportionate power in national affairs accruing to long tenure rests, in fact, on the assumption that the electorate is not in conflict over the interests which such power is to serve, an assumption that has been less and less valid since the New Deal.

---

36. Shadgett, *The Republican Party in Georgia from Reconstruction Through 1900* (Athens, Ga., 1964).

Woodward's intuition that the Populist period resembled the era of the New Deal was not a distorted view. Both were dominated by economic depressions and experienced a reorientation of politics in which class had an increased influence on voter decisions. Since the publication of *Origins of the New South,* however, we have been made increasingly aware of the cultural component of Populist voting. Populists derived not only from inferior economic strata but from a rural segment of society that was being left behind by advancing technology and an increasingly urban society. They were defending a rural way of life, a culture, as well as a way of earning a living. Recent scholarship on politics in nineteenth-century America emphasizes the extent to which cultural divisions, and particularly ethnic identity, rather than class, served as the basis of political divisions.[37] The implications of this are at least two: that the success of populism was inhibited to the extent that it was a departure from the more normal cultural bases of political divisions at the time, and secondly, that with the defeat of populism and the success of disfranchisement there were few bases of political division left in the predominantly agricultural South except personal popularity, family loyalties, intrastate sectionalism, moral questions such as prohibition, and similar ephemeral alignments.

The result was that progressivism in the South took place within the Democratic party. Since the publication of *Origins of the New South,* and since the path-marking essay by Arthur S. Link in 1946,[38] historians have been elaborating the idea that there was such an animal as southern progressivism.[39] State studies, such as those by Hackney, Pulley, Kirwan, and Moger, have added much, and there is an extensive journal literature,[40] but biographies have played the central role in developing our knowledge of southern progressivism. The list is long, including Hoke Smith by Dewey Grantham, James Stephen Hogg by Robert C. Cotner, George Washington

---

37. Paul Kleppner, *The Cross of Culture: A Social Analysis of Midwestern Politics, 1850–1900* (New York, 1970); Lee Benson, *The Concept of Jacksonian Democracy: New York as a Test Case* (Princeton, 1961).

38. Link, "The Progressive Movement in the South, 1870–1914," *North Carolina Historical Review,* 23 (April 1946), 172–95.

39. For instance, see Anne Firor Scott, "A Progressive Wind from the South, 1906–1913," *Journal of Southern History,* 29 (February 1963), 53–70; Herbert J. Doherty Jr., "Voices of Protest from the New South, 1875–1910," *Mississippi Valley Historical Review,* 42 (June 1955), 45–66; William D. Miller, *Memphis During the Progressive Era, 1900–1917* (Memphis, 1957); and Pulley, *Old Virginia Restored.*

40. See the bibliographical essay by Dewey W. Grantham Jr., in Link and Patrick, eds., *Writing Southern History,* 410–44.

Cable by Arlin Turner, Napoleon B. Broward by Samuel Proctor, Charles Brantley Aycock by Oliver H. Orr, Andrew Jackson Montague by William E. Larsen, Edward H. Crump of Memphis by William D. Miller, Josephus Daniels by Joseph L. Morrison, Josiah William Bailey by John R. Moore, James K. Vardaman by William F. Holmes, and Edgar Gardner Murphy by Hugh C. Bailey.[41] Together with some perceptive comments about southern progressivism in Robert H. Wiebe's stimulating interpretation, *The Search for Order*,[42] these works confirm the fact that the South experienced the full variety of reform ranging from the businessman's drive for efficiency to proper middle-class concern for good government to hostility toward special economic interests, particularly toward those that were large and Yankee, to humanitarian concern for the wards of society and its weaker members. Through all of this, no one has solved the paradox of how a region so different from the rest of the nation in its history, its economic condition, and its social structure could produce a Progressive movement differing in no special sense from the national movement.

Other than a tendency to produce colorful and extravagant leaders, one of the few distinguishing traits of southern progressivism was its sponsorship of modernization with a proviso for economic home rule. The progressive politician's charge that there was a Yankee conspiracy to keep the South in colonial bondage, which peeks shyly from between the lines of *Origins of the New South*, has been downgraded but not banished during the past two decades.[43] John F. Stover's book, *The Railroads of the South, 1865–1900*, traces the unrelenting extension of control of northern financial interests

---

41. Grantham, *Hoke Smith and the Politics of the New South* (Baton Rouge, 1958); Cotner, *James Stephen Hogg: A Biography* (Austin, 1959); Turner, *George W. Cable: A Biography* (Durham, 1956); Proctor, *Napoleon Bonaparte Broward: Florida's Fighting Democrat* (Gainesville, 1950); Orr, *Charles Brantley Aycock* (Chapel Hill, 1961); Larsen, *Montague of Virginia: The Making of a Southern Progressive* (Baton Rouge, 1965); Miller, *Mr. Crump of Memphis* (Baton Rouge, 1964); Morrison, *Josephus Daniels Says . . . : An Editor's Political Odyssey from Bryan to Wilson and F.D.R., 1894–1913* (Chapel Hill, 1962); *Josephus Daniels: The Small-d Democrat* (Chapel Hill, 1966); Moore, *Senator Josiah William Bailey of North Carolina: A Political Biography* (Durham, 1968); Holmes, *The White Chief: James Kimble Vardaman* (Baton Rouge, 1970); Bailey, *Edgar Gardner Murphy: Gentle Progressive* (Coral Gables, 1968). Also see Bailey, *Liberalism in the New South: Southern Social Reformers and the Progressive Movement* (Coral Gables, 1969).

42. Wiebe, *The Search for Order, 1877–1920* (New York, 1967).

43. Clarence H. Danhof, "Four Decades of Thought on the South's Economic Problems," in Melvin L. Greenhut and W. Tate Whitman, eds., *Essays in Southern Economic Development* (Chapel Hill, 1964), 7–68.

over the southern railroad system,[44] and George W. Stocking explains the inability of Birmingham to benefit from her natural advantages in making steel by reference to the discriminatory basing-point system used by United States Steel.[45]

On the other hand, David M. Potter, in an overlooked investigation, argues that railroad rate differentials between sections existed from the earliest time but that competition among railroads prevented appreciable territorial discrimination until after 1920 when connecting lines began to lose their independence and the Interstate Commerce Commission formalized the regional freight-rate structure of the private associations.[46] The study by Calvin B. Hoover and Benjamin U. Ratchford, *Economic Resources and Policies of the South,* flatly states that high freight rates were never a major barrier to the economic development of the South.[47] Much controversy surrounds the role of railroads in economic growth in the nineteenth century,[48] and as the most powerful economic and political institutions of the period they will continue to interest historians. Recent studies, however, have tended to focus on issues other than colonialism or to emphasize the contributions made by railroads to the development of the South.[49]

The matter on which there is the widest agreement at the present is that,

44. Stover, *The Railroads of the South, 1865–1900* (Chapel Hill, 1955). The best monograph documenting the impact of railroads on politics is James F. Doster, *Railroads in Alabama Politics, 1875–1914* (University, Ala., 1957).

45. Stocking, *Basing Point Pricing and Regional Development: A Case Study of the Iron and Steel Industry* (Chapel Hill, 1954). See also Justin Fuller, "History of the Tennessee Coal, Iron, and Railroad Company, 1852–1907" (Ph.D. dissertation, University of North Carolina, 1966).

46. Potter, "The Historical Development of Eastern-Southern Freight Rate Relationships," *Law and Contemporary Problems,* 12 (Summer 1947), 416–48.

47. Hoover and Ratchford, *Economic Resources and Policies of the South* (New York, 1951), 78.

48. See Robert W. Fogel, *Railroads and American Economic Growth: Essays in Econometric History* (Baltimore, 1964); Albert Fishlow, *American Railroads and the Transformation of the Ante-Bellum Economy* (Cambridge, Mass., 1965); and Peter D. McClelland, "Railroads, American Growth, and the New Economic History: A Critique," *Journal of Economic History,* 28 (March 1968), 102–23.

49. Leonard P. Curry, *Rail Routes South: Louisville's Fight for the Southern Market, 1865–1872* (Lexington, Ky., 1969); Maury Klein, *The Great Richmond Terminal: A Study in Businessmen and Business Strategy* (Charlottesville, 1970); and Klein, "The L & N Railroad and the South, 1865–1893: A Case Study in Regional Development," paper presented at the annual meeting of the Southern Historical Association, Louisville, Kentucky, November 11–14, 1970.

contrary to the utopian visions of the New South spokesmen, no great leap or qualitative change occurred in the economy of the South until after 1940.[50] The South remained an economy of low incomes, labor-intensive enterprises, and primary industry. The question has been, why so little change in that pattern?

In addition to the possibility of a colonialist conspiracy, several answers are available. William H. Nicholls has pinned the blame on the attitudes and values of southerners themselves in his book, *Southern Traditions and Regional Progress*, a position disputed by William E. Laird and James R. Rinehart, who argue that capital stringency was the chief culprit in tying farmers to inefficient forms of agriculture and thus inhibiting industrialization.[51] Nicholls's colleague Anthony M. Tang, in an empirical investigation of development in twenty contiguous counties in the Georgia–South Carolina Piedmont, avoids that particular chicken-and-egg argument by raising another one. Applying an industrial-urban matrix approach to farm income differentials, Tang argues persuasively that the productivity of southern farmers did not keep pace with the national average because of the lack of nearby industrial developments offering markets and part-time employment. Without the flexibility such opportunities provide, farm families are eventually unable to adapt successfully to changes in the agricultural market.[52]

The implication of this argument is that one-crop agriculture, the crop-lien system, and other malevolent institutions of the South would have collapsed as urban-industrial demands increased. Another implication is that insufficient out-migration hurt farm areas, and it may be as a hindrance to out-migration that the "passive" factor of values enters the picture, rather than as in the Nicholls formulation as a negative factor in entrepreneurial

---

50. Thomas D. Clark, in *The Emerging South* (New York, 1961), suggests that the crucial changes began with the failure of the cotton crop in 1921 but agrees, in *Three Paths to the Modern South: Education, Agriculture, and Conservation* (Athens, Ga., 1965), that no economic revolution had yet occurred in 1940. This question can be most authoritatively followed in George B. Tindall, *The Emergence of the New South, 1913–1945* (Baton Rouge, 1967). Gerald D. Nash provides an informed guide to existing literature and future possibilities in "Research Opportunities in the Economic History of the South After 1880," *Journal of Southern History,* 32 (August 1966), 308–24.

51. Nicholls, *Southern Tradition and Regional Progress* (Chapel Hill, 1960); Laird and Rinehart, "Deflation, Agriculture, and Southern Development," *Agricultural History,* 42 (April 1968), 115–24.

52. Tang, *Economic Development in the Southern Piedmont, 1860–1950: Its Impact on Agriculture* (Chapel Hill, 1958).

decisions. For instance, lacking local markets or employment opportunities in the late nineteenth century, southern farmers had the option to stay with the increasingly inadequate subsistence level of farming or to migrate to the city. It is difficult to explain their unwillingness to go to cities, as European immigrants by the millions were doing, unless the standard of living on the farm was actually better or farmers preferred a lower standard of living in the country to opportunity in a strange and alien city. As to the reasons for the scarcity of urban-industrial matrices in the South, one may trace the causes back to slavery, the plantation system, the topography of the South with its excellent interior river systems, or the commercial orientations of the original settlers. That is still an open question.[53] Meanwhile, we must find out more about the history of those urban centers that did exist.

Much more work is also needed on the problem of economic development, or the lack of it, and the process of economic growth in the period from the Civil War to World War II. Given all the barriers to growth— capital destruction in the Civil War, investment opportunities elsewhere, the absence of urban centers and of a large urban middle class, low levels of education and public services, the scarcity of skilled labor, and all of the special problems faced by latecomers to the process of industrialization—it may be that historians have been asking the wrong question about growth. Nothing in the theory of regional economics would predict equilibrating capital flows, so perhaps we should not be seeking explanations for the slow rate of growth in the economy of the post–Civil War South but rather for the fact that it kept pace at all.[54] There has been, in fact, a general convergence of per capita incomes between the South and the nation, even though it has converged by fits and starts with a major reversal in the 1920s.[55] Furthermore, this has been accomplished despite the slow and late capital inflows from the North and despite the high rate of population growth. Any explanation must accommodate all these facts, and that is a great challenge.

Another great challenge stems from wondering about the causes for the instability of the Redeemer regimes which were defied by independent

---

53. A suggestive essay on antebellum urbanization in the South is provided by Julius Rubin, "Urban Growth and Regional Development," in David T. Gilchrist, ed., *The Growth of Seaport Cities, 1790–1825* (Charlottesville, 1967), 3–21.

54. See, for instance, Harry W. Richardson, *Regional Economics: Location Theory, Urban Structure and Regional Change* (London, 1969), 330.

55. Richard A. Easterlin, "Interregional Differences in Per Capita Income, Population, and Total Income, 1840–1950," in National Bureau of Economic Research, *Trends in the American Economy in the Nineteenth Century: Studies in Income and Wealth* (Princeton, 1960), 73–140.

movements and torn by factional feuds even before they suffered the Populist revolt. Barrington Moore's analysis of sporadic rural political activity in England is very suggestive, whether or not it is correct, in tracing the source of unrest to the destruction of communal values by the enclosure movement. For Moore, in general, the evolution from noncommercial to commercial agriculture is the underlying cause of agrarian revolution.[56] Even though this concept is not at all foreign to American historians, it points to an unexplored source of tensions in the relationship between yeoman farmers and planters, a relationship about which we do not yet know enough either before or after the Civil War, nor do we know how it was changed by the war and its associated disruptions.

The outcome of any analysis of change across the Civil War very much depends upon one's conception of antebellum society. *Origins of the New South* employs a class and sectional analysis of the postbellum period that could comfortably interlock with the model of the Old South being developed by Eugene D. Genovese. Using concepts derived from Gramsci and Marx, Genovese posits a noncapitalistic, cohesive, and self-conscious planter aristocracy whose values infuse the entire society.[57] In the sequel, Woodward might have argued that the Redeemer regimes were unstable precisely because they were not based upon a popularly accepted system of values. The notables had made a much more rapid transition to capitalistic values, represented by the eastern alliance, than could the commoners, whose allegiance to old values is expressed in the desire to unite with the West. Without the controls provided by shared values, the Redeemers depended on fraud, emotional appeals to racial solidarity, and a low profile that would not excite voter opposition. But the economic crisis of the late 1880s shook loose the planter support from the Redeemer regimes and set the agrarian revolt on its course. As it gained momentum and drew more of the wool-hat set into its vortex, it spun leftward leaving disaffected planters in its wake.

Other starting points would lead to different outcomes. Morton Rothstein has suggested the utility of considering the Old South as a dual economy typical of developing nations.[58] Capitalistic planters, pursuing

---

56. Barrington Moore Jr., *Social Origins of Dictatorship and Democracy: Lord and Peasant in the Making of the Modern World* (Boston, 1966).

57. Genovese, *The Political Economy of Slavery: Studies in the Economy and Society of the Slave South* (New York, 1965); Genovese, *The World the Slaveholders Made: Two Essays in Interpretation* (New York, 1969).

58. Rothstein, "The Antebellum South as a Dual Economy: A Tentative Hypothesis," *Agricultural History*, 41 (October 1967), 373–82.

commercial profits through their links to distant markets, compose the modern sector; slaves and nonslaveholding whites who were only marginally concerned with production for the market make up the traditional sector. The linkage between the plantation, as both store and market, and the yeoman farmer completes a picture of a communal agriculture being practiced under the umbrella of an extensive commercial plantation system.[59] If this view is tenable, and there is much to recommend it, then one of the most far-reaching effects of the Civil War was to force both white and black farmers from the traditional sector into commercial agriculture where they were unable to survive. At the same time planters were shedding paternalistic roles to concentrate on their commercial functions. Whether one takes the cool, long view that this amounted to modernization and therefore was ultimately good, or whether one sees it as a devastating human ordeal, one result is the same: agrarian protest. Populism may have been the cry of the rural masses for the re-creation of a noncommercial community.

If historians are to place significance on the transition of poor whites from communal to commercial agriculture, we need to know a great deal more about southern agricultural communities before and after the Civil War, and we particularly need social histories of black and white tenant farmers. In the sophisticated local studies that will produce the needed knowledge there must be a careful distinction made between "refuge farmers" and "venturing farmers," and this distinction should rest not upon the technology employed but upon the motive for farming.[60]

But until research produces new insights, the reality is that the pyramid still stands. *Origins of the New South* has survived relatively untarnished through twenty years of productive scholarship, including the eras of consensus and of the new radicalism, and remains the last of the Beardian syn-

---

59. There is an extensive and illuminating literature on this unresolved set of issues. The best beginning point now is William N. Parker, ed., "The Structure of the Cotton Economy of the Antebellum South," *Agricultural History*, 44 (January 1970), 1–165. See also Lewis E. Atherton, *The Southern Country Store, 1800–1860* (Baton Rouge, 1949); Frank L. Owsley, *Plain Folk of the Old South* (Baton Rouge, 1949); and Fabian Linden, "Economic Democracy in the Slave South: An Appraisal of Some Recent Views," *Journal of Negro History*, 31 (April 1946), 140–89.

60. Wayne C. Rohrer and Louis H. Douglas, *The Agrarian Transition in America: Dualism and Change* (Indianapolis, 1967); Douglas C. North, "Location Theory and Regional Economic Growth," *Journal of Political Economy*, 63 (June 1955), 243–58; John Friedman and William Alonso, eds., *Regional Development and Planning: A Reader* (Cambridge, Mass., 1964). A step forward in the increasing sophistication of local studies is made by George C. Rogers Jr., *The History of Georgetown County, South Carolina* (Columbia, S.C., 1970).

theses. How can we explain this phenomenon? One possible answer is that Woodward is right about his period. Such an explanation has a certain elegance, and in this case even a bit of plausibility despite the notorious elusiveness of historical truth. The impeccable research that is evident in the volume has earned the respect of historians who have covered the same ground later, proving again that there is no substitute for knowing the primary sources. Nevertheless, correctness may be summarily dismissed as sufficient cause of longevity on the ground that revisionists have never been noticeably deterred by the absence of serious flaws in the body of knowledge they wished to revise.

There is also the matter of literary grace, present in full measure in *Origins of the New South*. Frederick Jackson Turner's famous essay is a pertinent example of the lasting power of an appealing prose style. Furthermore, Woodward is adept at synthesis and generalization and an absolute genius with the carefully qualified observation, a quality that has caused some difficulty when readers have not been as careful as the writer. Having granted all this, one still feels by instinct that some additional factor is at work and that it must be linked to Woodward's essential gift, which is a gift for irony.

The most arresting irony detected by Woodward is that America's most peculiar section, set apart from the rest of the nation by the very un-American experiences of guilt, defeat, and poverty, is not at all peculiar in the context of world history. For historians who characteristically ask how a people's experience helps to explain its behavior, there is an even more profound irony to be found in the high concentration of spread-eagle patriotism in the former Rebel states. It is another testimonial that suffering is not always ennobling and another demonstration of the fierceness with which outsiders adopt the myths and pretensions of the group to which they wish to belong. The touching intensity with which Johnny Cash simultaneously celebrates Indians, convicts, God, and the American flag is but a dramatic instance of the real irony of southern history, the dual identity which is the result of a double history.

The national and the southern identities are acquiring more and more common ground. Sensitive Americans today are learning what southerners learned a hundred years ago: that defeat is possible, that suffering is real, that failure to honor moral commitments brings retribution, that the past exacts its tribute from the present, that society is a complex and not very tractable set of human relationships and needs. The world of *Origins of the New South* is therefore at the same time familiar and instructive. It is a world of grandiose and pious pronouncements and tawdry performances in which big men fail and little men suffer. The message that emerges from *Origins of the New South* and from the whole body of Woodward's work is that history is a burden that weighs upon the present, structuring and restricting it. This is also a major theme of William Faulkner's work, particularly of *Absalom, Absalom; The Unvanquished;* and *The Sound and the Fury.* Though not as happy a message as the faith of the progressive historians nor as certain as that of the new radicals, it nevertheless harmonizes with some pervasive contemporary moods.

This is an age in which people attempt to find meaning in the meaninglessness of things. Historians, of course, are barred by the nature of their craft from dealing in the Absurd, or at least in the literary brand of it. Practitioners of the Absurd are engaged in dismantling appearance, eliding the boundary between illusion and reality, demonstrating the essential lack of pattern and predictability beneath our commonsense understanding of the world. Historians, on the other hand, begin with the assumption that the past is a patternless jumble of phenomena on which the historian must impose his own order or one that he may find lying about. The models currently available for borrowing are not very reassuring. When one turns to our literature he finds McMurphy, Yossarian, Herzog, Portnoy, the graduate, Norwood, and a long stream of nonheroes. As Charles A. Reich contends in *The Greening of America,* the modern American feels so powerless that he is unable to conceive of a hero who can alter fate by taking action. Thus, Humphrey Bogart in *Casablanca* may be the last American hero.[61]

As the whimsical popularity of cartoon heroes implies, we have turned Carlyle upside down. When Charles Portis wrote a story of real gumption and guts, he called it *True Grit,* set it in the nineteenth century, and made it a parody of a true-life reminiscence. David Douglas Duncan's portfolio of photographs of frontline soldiers in Vietnam, for another example, is entitled *War Without Heroes.*[62] The young, the mobile, and the metropolitan, having lost their sense of original sin and their belief in transcendent values, evidently find it difficult to imagine a hero. How ironic in such a time that we should still find compatibility in literature that documents original sin and assumes transcendent values. This springs in part from the South's old

---

61. Reich, *The Greening of America* (New York, 1970), 146. Reich himself is a prophetic hero of the universal variety described by Joseph Campbell in *The Hero with a Thousand Faces* (New York, Evanston, and London, 1949), who suffers separation, travels in the land of death overcoming obstacles, and returns to give to mankind a redemptive message providing new sources of power. But that is a different kind of hero.

62. Duncan, *War Without Heroes* (New York, 1970).

role as foil and counterpoint for national moods, but it comes in part also from the link between the nonheroic sensibility of the present and the theme in Woodward and Faulkner of the individual being bullied about by fate, crushed by outside forces over which he has no control, or victimized by conspiracies of the strong. Populists and modern nonheroes have in common the fact that they are victims, yet they frequently enlist our sympathies and enlarge our vision of humanity by their willingness to struggle.

There are few heroes in *Origins of the New South,* and the few who do appear are of the tragic variety. Tom Watson is such a faulted hero, if one has compassion and empathy enough to understand him and those for whom he spoke. A hero while losing, he was transformed by defeat into a successful villain, only to be consumed by his own hatred. It is a theme worthy of William Faulkner's tragic vision of the South, a vision shared by Woodward to an extent stopping somewhat short of fatalism. *Origins of the New South* would provide a familiar context for Faulkner's characters: the decaying Sartoris family suffering for the sin of slavery, the opportunistic Compsons doomed for their materialistic rejection of the land, patrician Coldfields with enlightened racial views, poor whites like Hope Hampton who behave with honor despite racial prejudice, blacks who achieve dignity and respect like Lucas Beauchamp and Dilsey, and, of course, the Snopes tribe, filtering into the growing towns from the backcountry, taking control and losing out, transforming the South for better and worse, but always struggling.

Woodward's sensibility is both Beardian and Faulknerian, and the combination of the two is the source of the continuing appeal of *Origins of the New South.* Richard Hofstadter observed that, "As practiced by mature minds, history forces us to be aware not only of complexity but of defeat and failure: it tends to deny that high sense of expectation, that hope of ultimate and glorious triumph, that sustains good combatants. There may be comfort in it still. In an age when so much of our literature is infused with nihilism, and other social disciplines are driven toward narrow positivistic inquiry, history may remain the most humanizing among the arts."[63] Woodward is certainly a humanizing historian, one who recognizes both the likelihood of failure and the necessity of struggle. It is this profound ambiguity which makes his work so interesting. Like the myth of Sisyphus, *Origins of the New South* still speaks to our condition. And who knows? Perhaps one day we will get that rock to the top of the hill. But, having learned my skepticism at the master's knee, I doubt it.

---

63. Hofstadter, *Progressive Historians,* 466.

"Origins of the New South in Retrospect"
Thirty Years Later

The Jubilee year for C. Vann Woodward's *Origins of the New South* was 2001. We learn from Leviticus 25:1–23 that God, speaking to the children of Israel through Moses, prescribed that every seventh year should be a Sabbath year, during which the fields would lie fallow; after a week of Sabbath years there should be a Jubilee year in which debts are to be forgiven, ancestral lands restored, slaves released from bondage, and freedom proclaimed throughout the land.

I exercised my privilege as a liberated bondman during Jubilee to return home to my ancestral topic, only to discover how much the topic has changed since my last visit. Thirty-two years ago, in 1971, I was invited to deliver a paper at the spring meeting of the Organization of American Historians evaluating *Origins* as it celebrated its twentieth birthday and as

a second edition was being published.[1] Being young and foolish, and wanting a trip to New Orleans, I accepted. I was on leave that academic year
doing research on the civil rights movement. My notes on civil rights continue to gather mold, of course, and I am still trying to figure out how such
a revolutionary book as *Origins* could have gone a full generation without
attracting major revisionists. It was not that historians had ignored the era,
as confirmed by Charles B. Dew's 110-page critical essay on authorities that
was included in the second edition.[2] Woodward himself was a little surprised that no fundamental challenge had arisen, but in his disarming intellectual memoir, *Thinking Back: The Perils of Writing History,* he agreed
with me that in 1971 the "pyramid still stands."[3] Most significantly, he
made no revisions for the second edition of *Origins;* he simply added a brief
foreword.

What accounts for the staying power of *Origins?* Thirty years ago I
somewhat facetiously suggested that the longevity of *Origins* might be
traced to the correctness of Woodward's interpretation, but I dismissed that
possibility as unlikely because soundness of argument had never deterred
critics before. Instead, I suggested that the tragic story that Woodward told
resonated in an era of disillusionment, when the shock troops of multiple
social justice movements had produced a society at war with itself at home,
just as it found itself fighting an unpopular and unwinnable war abroad—a
war without heroes, just as *Origins* is a history without heroes. Without
naming it, Woodward's *Origins* attacked the meta-narrative of American
exceptionalism, the national myth that all problems have solutions, that the
solutions are to be found in the application of human reason and technology, and that the United States, as the world's exemplar of freedom through
democracy, is so blessed that progress and success are inevitable.

The resilience of this national self-image is amazing. It has not only been
revived in recent years, but it colors the way we see even the Gilded Age.
Yes, there was the genocide of the Native Americans, the disastrous desertion of recently freed slaves in the South by the federal government and the
northern public, the corruption of affairs by politicians of Lilliputian stature

---

1. The essay, reprinted above, first appeared as "*Origins of the New South* in Retrospect,"
Journal of Southern History, 38 (May 1972), 191–216.

2. C. Vann Woodward, *Origins of the New South, 1877–1913* (2d ed., Baton Rouge,
1971).

3. C. Vann Woodward, *Thinking Back: The Perils of Writing History* (Baton Rouge,
1986), 67 (150 in this volume).

and business tycoons with morals to match, the brutality of the Robber Barons, the exploitation of immigrants and blue-collar laborers, the wretched lives lived by the "other half," the subjugation of colonial populations, and the exclusion from immigration of non-European peoples. Nevertheless, if you squint properly, the Gilded Age can be seen as a continuation of the inevitable march of progress: there was the romance of rapid urbanization and industrialization, the taming of the West, the creation of great American fortunes, a dramatically rising standard of living, the emergence of the United States as a world power, and the rise of Progressivism, a reform movement aimed at checking all of the abuses mentioned above. If you keep your eyes fixed on the nation, and ignore real people, it is a heroic success story.

For the South, however, the story was different; there was unrelieved poverty, agricultural depression, social dislocation, and racial friction. Promising a new Eden in which southerners would live with modern comforts without having to give up their traditional values, the New South crusade produced a lot of running hard just to stay in place—a place at the bottom of the income, wealth, and power distribution. Nevertheless, the conventional view of the period 1877–1913 that Woodward replaced was pretty much the version that would have been written by Henry W. Grady or the most self-serving conservative Redeemer, full of hope, progress, and the justification of white supremacy. In contrast, Woodward's story in *Origins* was of a time and place in which defeat, poverty, and gloomy prospects were everyday realities for a lot of Americans. His sense of historical contingency and the likelihood of failure spoke to the crisis of confidence that began in America in the mid-1960s and lasted until the mid-1990s.

From our current vantage point in the Jubilee year, it is possible to see patterns that were not so evident in 1951 or even in 1971. We can see, for instance, that Woodward, the genteel controversialist, was constantly probing the past for lessons that would speak to the most fundamental issues of the current day: the politics of scarcity, racial justice, and the dangers of national self-righteousness. It is a mistake, Woodward was saying in *Origins,* to assume that our national story flowed continuously forward without conflict or serious disruption, encapsulated in the myths of innocence, success, and affluence. Woodward was engaged in the old game of using the history of the South to instruct the nation.

Though he did not specifically object to my "malaise" theory to explain the bulletproof nature of *Origins* through its first twenty years, his own explanation was that there was a different sense in which the times favored his theme of discontinuity across the Civil War. Because the 1950s and 1960s witnessed huge discontinuities in southern life, he reasoned, the profession was willing to entertain the idea that the Civil War had occasioned a similar fundamental break with the past.

To use a Woodwardian technique against the master, I need only point out that as change in the South has accelerated over the succeeding thirty years, occasioning greater and greater distance between its present reality and its mythic past, the ranks of the naysayers to the Woodward discontinuity theme have also swelled, contrary to what should have happened if his explanation were correct. My own current guess about the delayed-action doubters is that Woodward had done such a prodigious amount of archival research for *Origins* that it took a long time for even a brash challenger to master the primary sources in some comfortable niche sufficiently to mount a credible challenge.

However charmed the youth of *Origins*, its adulthood since 1971 has been productively normal. Historians have been swinging their sledgehammers from various angles with mounting ferocity. Consequently, *Origins* is dented, discolored, tattered, and torn, but it is still there, still the mandatory starting point for any serious study of the South between 1877 and 1913. On the other hand, there are now alternative opinions on every major question. Rather than having an uncontested narrative, we have rubble heaps of fascinating arguments dotting the countryside. Woodward relished it. Let me point out the major ruins and historical sites.

Origins opens with a synopsis of *Reunion and Reaction,* Woodward's economic conspiracy theory of the Compromise of 1877.[4] We still lack definitive evidence, but the consensus seems to be that even though the conspiracy that Woodward unearthed actually existed, it is doubtful that it had a decisive effect on the outcome of the crisis because there were straightforward political incentives that were strong enough by themselves to have led Democrats to allow Rutherford B. Hayes to be sworn in as president.[5]

On the crucial question of whether continuity or discontinuity best describes the connection between Old and New South, there is convincing evidence that landownership did not change rapidly, nor did the agricultural basis of the economy. Furthermore, many of the New South entrepreneurs

---

4. C. Vann Woodward, *Reunion and Reaction: The Compromise of 1877 and the End of Reconstruction* (Boston, 1951).

5. Allan Peskin, "Was There a Compromise of 1877?" *Journal of American History,* 60 (June 1973), 63–75.

derived from the elite antebellum class and even continued to pay homage to the older values and aspirations.[6] Woodward responded in *Thinking Back,* and many historians agree, that even among persisting planters and other members of the elite in the New South there was a major shift in mentality or outlook. The ethos of the 1880s and 1890s was markedly different from the 1850s. Planters may have been engaged in their old tasks of growing staple crops for distant markets, but their plantations were organized differently, with tenant farmers and sharecroppers. Their managerial task was therefore different, and they displayed a new businesslike mind-set. Furthermore, economic roles were increasingly complex, so that planters were not only managers and landlords but also bankers and merchants, as well perhaps as lawyers in town and even promoters of the local cotton mill.[7]

Woodward's Redeemers were an unattractive lot, selfish and manipulative, but the more historians look at them, the more they seem to be representative of the cross section of humanity. Many were venal and self-serving, but there were those who thought they were pursuing their community's best interests as well as their own through industrialization. They look no worse than antebellum planters, perhaps, but that was the class that got the South into a disastrous war.

No one dissents from the idea that race was a central theme of the period, but increasingly historians are stressing the degree to which African Americans were active in their own behalf, resisting the fraud, intimidation, and violence that eventually led to their disfranchisement and segregation. This is a missing perspective in *Origins*. That there was widespread segregation, even going back to the antebellum period, is increasingly clear, some of it even initiated by freedpeople to assure access to public space, but it is also clear that race etiquette and roles were in flux throughout the period and that patterns of race relations varied enormously from one community to another. That was not changed decisively until the 1890s and 1900s by Jim

---

6. Jonathan M. Wiener, *Social Origins of the New South: Alabama, 1860–1885* (Baton Rouge, 1978); James Tice Moore, "Redeemers Reconsidered: Change and Continuity in the Democratic South, 1870–1900," *Journal of Southern History,* 44 (August 1978), 357–78 (109–30 in this volume).

7. Woodward, *Thinking Back,* 64–65 (148–49 in this volume); Gavin Wright, *The Political Economy of the Cotton South: Households, Markets, and Wealth in the Nineteenth Century* (New York, 1978); David L. Carlton, *Mill and Town in South Carolina, 1880–1920* (Baton Rouge, 1982).

Crow legislation that created a fixed, uniform, and universal system rooted in the law.[8]

Woodward has conceded that the Populists were not as altruistically equalitarian with regard to race as he implied in *Origins*. On the other hand, in the context of the times, even the segregated political pragmatism of the Populists was an advanced stance. Arguments still rage about which class or group was most responsible for disfranchisement, the conservative elite or the reform Democrats. Of that particular crime, the Populists were not guilty.[9]

No one today agrees with Richard Hofstadter's thesis in *The Age of Reform* that cast the Populists as backward-looking and socially marginal people, characterized by various unlovely traits.[10] In fact, the dominant treatment of Populism by Lawrence Goodwyn is more Woodwardian than Woodward himself, portraying the Populists not only as rationally aggrieved for economic reasons but as the last best hope for an effective democracy. Historians here and there suggest that the Populists may not have been the proto–New Dealers they are often portrayed as being, but that at the moment is a minority voice.[11] There are scholars, however, who disagree with Woodward about fusion with the Democrats in 1896. Even though it did not work out well in practice, these historians think fusion with the reform wing of the Democratic Party was a logical political step rather than a capitulation by the fainthearted.

We are still pondering the big question of why it took so long for the South to modernize. Woodward's answer was that the South became a colonial economy after the Civil War and that northern capitalists had an economic self-interest in keeping it that way. Some historians, however, are not at all sure that differential freight rates, for instance, had anything to do with slow industrialization. Some, in fact, wonder whether the rate of mod-

---

8. Leon F. Litwack, *Trouble in Mind: Black Southerners in the Age of Jim Crow* (New York, 1998); Joel Williamson, *The Crucible of Race: Black-White Relations in the American South since Emancipation* (New York, 1984).

9. J. Morgan Kousser, *The Shaping of Southern Politics: Suffrage Restriction and the Establishment of the One-Party South, 1880–1910* (New Haven, 1974); Michael Perman, *Struggle for Mastery: Disfranchisement in the South, 1888–1908* (Chapel Hill, 2001).

10. Richard Hofstadter, *The Age of Reform: From Bryan to F.D.R.* (New York, 1955).

11. Lawrence Goodwyn, *Democratic Promise: The Populist Moment in America* (New York, 1976); Elizabeth Sanders, *Roots of Reform: Farmers, Workers, and the American State, 1877–1917* (Chicago, 1999). See also Steven Hahn, *The Roots of Southern Populism: Yeoman Farmers and the Transformation of the Georgia Upcountry, 1850–1890* (New York, 1983).

ernization in the South cannot be explained by the depth of poverty after the Civil War, by the usual difficulties experienced by latecomers to the process of modernization, and especially by uncongenial cultural values growing out of plantation society and persisting across the Civil War. Furthermore, though the South did not close the economic gap appreciably during the period from Reconstruction to World War I, perhaps it is remarkable that it did not fall further behind, because the nation was making gigantic strides forward in industrialization and urbanization.[12]

The voices of women are inaudible in *Origins,* but a new sound track is being added at a great rate. Those female voices are not only found singing harmony on the front porch during family songfests; they are intruding into the public sphere, as in Glenda Elizabeth Gilmore's astute study of North Carolina, *Gender and Jim Crow.*[13]

Origins is focused relentlessly on the public sphere, on the actions of leaders and followers in political and economic arenas. For an appreciation of how ordinary people lived and of the popular culture they spawned, one should read *The Promise of the New South,* by Edward L. Ayers, a masterful telling from multiple points of view of the story of the South in the same period covered by *Origins.* Ayers finds more optimism in the New South than did Woodward, but in general his portrait is complementary rather than contradictory.[14]

The best guide to these various challenges and emendations is Woodward himself in *Thinking Back.* John Herbert Roper provides sympathetic biographical context and a comprehensive analysis in *C. Vann Woodward, Southerner,* as well as a sampling of the controversies in *C. Vann Woodward: A Southern Historian and His Critics.* Howard N. Rabinowitz, in *The First New South, 1865–1920,* and John B. Boles, in *The South Through Time: A History of an American Region,* can also be trusted as pathfinders through the Woodwardian thickets.[15]

---

12. See especially James C. Cobb, *Industrialization and Southern Society, 1877–1984* (Lexington, Ky., 1984).

13. Glenda Elizabeth Gilmore, *Gender and Jim Crow: Women and the Politics of White Supremacy in North Carolina, 1896–1920* (Chapel Hill, 1996).

14. Edward L. Ayers, *The Promise of the New South: Life After Reconstruction* (New York, 1992).

15. Woodward, *Thinking Back;* John Herbert Roper, *C. Vann Woodward, Southerner* (Athens, Ga., 1987), and Roper, ed., *C. Vann Woodward: A Southern Historian and His Critics* (Athens, Ga., 1997); Howard N. Rabinowitz, *The First New South, 1865–1920* (Arlington Heights, Ill., 1992); John B. Boles, *The South Through Time: A History of an American Region.* Vol. II (2d ed., Upper Saddle River, N.J., 2003).

One wonders, of course, what the subtext of *Origins* would be if Woodward were writing it today. The perspective would necessarily be different because the South is different. It has almost caught up with the non-South in income; it has disproportionate political power; and it watches with wry amusement as so many things southern attain a certain national cachet, from country music and NASCAR to the pampered self, as pictured in the magazine *Southern Living*.

More important, what could the story of the South in the late nineteenth century have to teach the nation in the wake of the terrorism of September 11, 2001, a nation shaken in its infatuation with materialism and radical individualism, a nation newly alerted to lasting values and to the importance of communities of mutual sacrifice, a nation conscious at last perhaps of the dangers of tolerating vast disparities in wealth and well-being either within American society or between first world and third world peoples?

I think the lesson should be that the costs of keeping the dispossessed down are significant and are borne by society as a whole. Local elites in the South, with a vested interest in keeping the labor force docile and cheap, myopically used racism to enforce conformity. The result was a society with an extremely limited ability to change itself or to respond adequately to an increasingly complex world. Education, transportation, public health, high-yield agriculture, and public services of all kinds received inadequate investment. Massive out-migration in the twentieth century was the marker of a failed public philosophy. It was not until the federal government put military bases and defense plants in the South during World War II that the southern economy achieved self-sustaining growth and began to close the gap with the rest of the nation in such indices as per capita income, not to mention education, health, and other indicators of "life chances." Outsiders had to instigate the economic change, just as they were crucial to the success of the efforts of black southerners to achieve full citizenship. The lesson is that when public policy is captured by an elite and focused on policies that serve the short-term interests of that elite, the long-term effect is that everyone suffers—even the favored elites. That is what happened in the South.

When I wrote my original assessment of Woodward's masterpiece in 1971, I could not have known that Woodward's greatest work was behind him. In the category of "great" I would place the books that restructured our way of thinking about the history of the South, especially for the period from the end of Reconstruction to World War I: *Tom Watson, Agrarian Rebel; Reunion and Reaction; Origins of the New South; The Strange Career of Jim Crow;* and the essays collected in *The Burden of Southern His-*

tory.[16] Woodward continued to produce wonderful work for another three decades, even winning the Pulitzer Prize in 1982 for editing *Mary Chesnut's Civil War,* but nothing that he did subsequently reoriented our understanding of a field as thoroughly as *Origins* and its early companions had done.[17] If for no other reason, *Origins* would be in our lives today because it is such an important part of the intellectual history of the field of southern history and of the story of America in the last half of the twentieth century.

16. Woodward, *Tom Watson, Agrarian Rebel* (New York, 1938); *The Strange Career of Jim Crow* (New York, 1955); *The Burden of Southern History* (Baton Rouge, 1960).

17. C. Vann Woodward, ed., *Mary Chesnut's Civil War* (New Haven, 1981).

Readers have long remarked that Origins of the New South *is a book filled with memorable passages, but none is more colorfully descriptive than Woodward's characterization of how the conservative Democratic Redeemers essentially sold out the interests of the southern masses and for self-serving reasons aligned themselves with eastern business interests: "It was plain that the road to reunion was a forked road, that the right fork led to the East and the left to the West. . . . It took a lot of hallooing and heading off by the conservative leaders to keep the mass of Southerners herded up the right fork. . . . [T]he right-forkers contrived to keep the South fairly faithful to the Eastern alignment—until the advent of the Populists." A quarter century after Woodward crafted that vivid image, Carl V. Harris, armed with new statistical techniques and assisted by a computer, subjected hundreds of congressional votes to sophisticated analysis. Lo and behold, practically no aspect of Woodward's famous interpretation in his chapter entitled "The Forked Road to Reunion" held up. Mostly the southern Democrats supported the western alignment, and mostly the masses of white southerners supported the general policies of their leaders. Woodward himself later seemed to acknowledge the correction offered by Harris when, in his essay "Origin of* Origins" *(reprinted below), he called Harris's article "one of the more effective" critiques of the book and accepted Harris's demonstration that "my metaphor of 'Right Fork, Left Fork' . . . was much too simplistic so far as congressional voting was concerned." Often Woodward genially responded to critics but artfully deflected their criticisms in such a way as to defend the basic outline of his argument; perhaps his phrase "so far as congressional voting was concerned" is another example of his low-key tenaciousness.*

Right Fork or Left Fork? The Section-Party Alignments of Southern Democrats in Congress, 1873–1897

During the 1870s the Democratic party rapidly redeemed the states of the American South from Radical Republican Reconstruction and began electing southern Democrats to Congress. The South held approximately one-third of the seats in each house of Congress, and by 1877 the southern Democrats, gaining control of those seats, outnumbered the northern Democrats and controlled the Democratic caucus. Indeed, the southern Democrats, often called the Redeemers, emerged as one of the three largest section-party blocs in Congress, comparable in size with the northeastern Republicans and the western Republicans. More than 90 percent of the southern Democratic congressmen had served in the Confederate government or army, and Republican propagandists charged that the returning "Rebel Brigadiers" in-

Reprinted from *Journal of Southern History,* 42 (November 1976), 471–506.

tended to "*control* the Union which they could not destroy," to "conquer by political strategy where they failed in open fight."[1] The Republicans exaggerated, but thoughtful citizens had good reason to ponder the impact of the resurgent Redeemers upon the congressional balance of power and upon the vast array of national legislation that had been enacted while the southern Democrats had been absent. It was obvious that the southern Democrats would oppose civil rights legislation and would seek to undermine federal protection of the Negro's right to vote. But how would they react to the new structure of national economic legislation created by the Republican party, legislation concerning money, banks, bonds, taxes, tariffs, railroads, and internal improvements? Some northern elements opposed portions of the Republican economic program. Would the southern Redeemers ally with the program's opponents or its defenders?

The most influential scholarly assessment of the Redeemers' alignment has been given by Professor C. Vann Woodward in *Reunion and Reaction: The Compromise of 1877 and the End of Reconstruction* and in *Origins of the New South, 1877–1913*. Woodward saw most of the opponents of the Republican economic program in the "agrarian" West and the supporters in the "conservative" East. And he argued that between 1876 and 1878 the South experimented with both conservative and agrarian alliances. First, according to Woodward, during the crisis over the disputed presidential election of 1876 conservatives spoke for the South. Hankering after the subsidies and grants of the Republican economic program and revolting against the antisubsidy stand of northern Democrats, the conservative southern Democrats negotiated the Compromise of 1877 with conservative northern Republicans. The Compromise placed Republican Rutherford Birchard Hayes in the White House, granted the South home rule on racial matters, and portended continued cooperation between northern and southern conservatives in support of "Whiggish" economic policies.[2] But suddenly in November 1877 "an irresistible tide of agrarian radicalism" disrupted the "Whiggish coalition." The agrarian tide temporarily swept "the South out of control of conservative leaders and into alliance with the agrarian West," voting in Congress for silver coinage, for repeal of the resumption of specie payments on greenbacks, and for federal regulation of

---

1. Chicago *Inter-Ocean*, January 13, August 17, 1876; *Biographical Directory of the American Congress, 1774–1971* (Washington, 1971), *passim.*

2. Woodward, *Reunion and Reaction: The Compromise of 1877 and the End of Reconstruction* (Boston, 1951), 51–67, 122–49, 166–85, 216–37; Woodward, *Origins of the New South, 1877–1913* (Baton Rouge, 1951), 23–50.

railroads. But in the congressional elections of 1878 the Republicans again vigorously waved the bloody shirt, and southerners, seeing that the West was still apparently "more responsive to the 'bloody shirt' than to appeals for agrarian unity," quickly became disillusioned with the western alliance. "It was plain," wrote Woodward, "that the road to reunion was a forked road, that the right fork led to the East and the left fork to the West. . . . In the end the counsel of the right-fork conservatives prevailed . . . . And the South did 'go with the East.' By dint of much hallooing and heading-off the Conservatives succeeded in herding the mass of Southerners up the right fork. . . . Agrarian mavericks were eternally taking off up the left fork. With the aid of the New South propagandists, however, the Redeemers managed to keep the South fairly faithful to the Eastern alignment—until the nineties." Of course, the southern Democrats did drop their brief flirtation with conservative northern Republicans, and they remained firmly in the Democratic party. But "They aligned themselves with the Conservative, Eastern wing of the party . . . a wing that was as devoted to the defense of the new economic order as the Republicans." Thus, "Under the regime of the Redeemers the South became a bulwark instead of a menace to the new order."[3]

Certainly, Woodward's right-fork thesis is consistent with the South's behavior in the quadrennial Democratic presidential nominating contests of the Gilded Age. Democratic conventions gave paramount consideration to candidates' ability to carry the swing state of New York, and the southern Democrats went down the line with Winfield Scott Hancock of Pennsylvania in 1880 and with Grover Cleveland of New York in 1884, 1888, and 1892. But what of the Congress, in which the South voted hundreds of times every year, rather than once every four years, and in which separate roll calls on a wide variety of issues permitted far more precise articulation of southern interests and alignments? It is the purpose of this article to test the Woodward thesis with regard to the congressional arena of sectional-political alignment. What was the impact of the Compromise of 1877 upon congressional alignments on economic issues? Did the southern Democrats shift as rapidly from conservative to agrarian to conservative alliances as Wood-

---

3. Woodward, *Reunion and Reaction*, 237–46; quotations appear in order on pp. 237, 243, 244, 245, and 246. A little-known earlier study by Hannah Grace Roach, "Sectionalism in Congress (1870 to 1890)," *American Political Science Review*, 19 (August 1925), 500–526, had analyzed sixty-four roll calls and described the southern voting pattern as usually "radical." However, her analysis did not identify roll calls precisely enough as to time and issue to provide either confirmation or refutation of Woodward's thesis.

ward argued? And did they finally adhere to a right-fork alliance with conservative eastern Democrats from the late 1870s to the 1890s?

To delineate the broad patterns of southern alignment this study has employed computer programs to calculate indices of cohesion and of likeness. The index of cohesion shows the extent to which a bloc, such as southern Democrats, was united. For any roll call the index is calculated by subtracting the percentage in the bloc minority from the percentage in the bloc majority. The index varies from zero (if the bloc is evenly split, 50 percent yea, 50 percent nay) to one hundred (if the bloc is 100 percent united). A split of 75 percent yea, 25 percent nay produces a cohesion score of 50, and in the American congressional system 50 is a relatively strong cohesion score. A bloc's cohesion scores for all roll calls on an issue can be combined to produce an average cohesion score for that issue.

The index of likeness measures voting agreement between pairs of blocs, such as southern Democrats and northeastern Democrats. For any roll call the index is calculated by taking the percentage in each bloc that voted yea, finding the point spread between these two yea percentages, and then subtracting that point spread from 100. Thus, if bloc A votes 80 percent yea and bloc B 40 percent yea, the point spread is 40, and the likeness score is 100 minus 40, or 60. Historians who have used the likeness index extensively suggest, as a rule of thumb, that any likeness score below 60 indicates substantial disagreement between two blocs. For any pair of blocs the likeness scores on all roll calls on a particular issue can be combined to produce an average likeness index for that issue.[4]

4. In computing the indices, announced pairs as well as votes actually cast were counted. This discussion of the indices is based on Lee F. Anderson et al., *Legislative Roll-Call Analysis* (Evanston, 1966), 31–45. Other historical studies that have employed these indices include Allan G. Bogue, "Bloc and Party in the United States Senate: 1861–1863," *Civil War History,* 13 (September 1967), 221–41; and William G. Shade et al., "Partisanship in the United States Senate: 1869–1901," *Journal of Interdisciplinary History,* 4 (Autumn 1973), 185–205. The Inter-University Consortium for Political Research, Ann Arbor, Michigan, supplied the roll-call data in partially proofed form. The consortium bears no responsibility for either the analyses or interpretations presented here. The indices were computed with a version of the ACCUM program described in Anderson et al., *Legislative Roll-Call Analysis,* 175–85. Curtis Mosso, supervisor of applications programming at the Computer Center, University of California, Santa Barbara, modified the program, greatly increasing its capabilities. Todd A. Shallat provided vital research assistance. The Research Committee of the Academic Senate of the University of California, Santa Barbara, funded the computer work as part of a larger study of Congress in the Gilded Age. For valuable suggestions and criticisms I am indebted to Professors Allan G. Bogue, W. Elliot Brownlee, Richard N. Current, J. Rogers Hollingsworth, Lynn L. D. Marshall, James T. Moore, and Raymond H. Pulley and to the late Professor William B. Hesseltine.

For this study indices of cohesion and likeness have been calculated for southern, northeastern, and western blocs of Democrats and of Republicans, and for the small handfuls of northern and southern Independents. Table 1 shows the number of men in each section-party bloc in the first session of each Congress from 1873 to 1897.[5]

For each Congress average indices were tabulated for all roll calls on all issues combined, and in these "total" indices the southern Democrats typically achieved much higher likeness scores with each northern Democratic bloc than with any Republican bloc, and they always achieved slightly higher likeness scores (ranging from 2 to 13 points higher) with western Democrats than with northeastern Democrats. But the diversity of issues included in such totals is so great that the historian can place little interpretive burden upon them. Indices for narrower issue catagories, defined according to traditional nineteenth-century congressional rubrics, are far more revealing.[6]

---

5. This study includes Maryland and West Virginia in the South, but Professor Woodward did not. These two states were among those most prone to vote with the Northeast, and including them in the South tends to bias the results in favor of the Woodward thesis. Professor Woodward did not specifically identify northeastern and western states, but he defined the East-West cleavage largely in terms of roll calls on money and regulation in 1878, and the Northeast and West as defined in Table 1 are consistent with that cleavage. In the Senate northeastern Democrats were often scarce, and their indices were often determined by the votes of only three or four men. But the Senate northeastern Democratic indices did not differ greatly from the House northeastern Democratic indices, which were based on substantial numbers of men. Any roll call on which all members of a particular bloc were absent was excluded from the bloc's cohesion and likeness scores. The northern Independent in Senates Forty-five to Forty-seven was David Davis of Illinois, and the Senate third-party members in the 1890s were Populists and Independents. In the Forty-fourth through the Fifty-first Houses the third-party members were Antimonopolists, Independents, or Greenbackers, and in the Fifty-second through the Fifty-fourth Houses they were Populists, Independents, and Farmers' Alliance men. Since the southern Independent blocs were always small, their indices were determined by the votes of a very few men, or even of one man. The data from the Inter-University Consortium for Political Research contains a party-affiliation code for each congressman, but for this study the party codes of a few men were changed to comply with information from the *Biographical Directory of the American Congress,* from Edward McPherson, *A Hand-Book of Politics* (Washington, biennially 1868 through 1894; reprinted in four volumes, New York, Da Capo Press, 1972), and, in the case of southern Independents, from Woodward, *Origins, passim.*

6. Each roll call was assigned to one issue category. This inevitably involved some subjective decisions, but most roll calls fell clearly into distinct categories. Many issue categories were not specifically considered in this study. Among them were private claims, civil service, education, the Agriculture Department, election disputes, contested seats, bankruptcy law, immigration, Indians, regulation of liquor, land law, relations with foreign countries, pensions, the government of Washington, D.C., the organization of territories and states, the ratification of nominations, the

TABLE 1

Number of Congressmen in Parties and Section-Party Blocs
Forty-Third to Fifty-Fourth Congress

Cong. Number	43	44	45	46	47	48	49	50	51	52	53	54
Opening Year	1873	1875	1877	1879	1881	1883	1885	1887	1889	1891	1893	1895
HOUSE												
SoDem	47	76	83	82	74	87	96	90	87	99	103	77
NeDem	17	50	37	23	26	42	32	34	29	53	44	8
WsDem	30	53	36	41	29	68	55	44	38	80	67	9
Dem (total)	94	179	156	146	129	197	183	168	154	232	214	94
SoRep	45	15	8	5	12	15	10	14	18	4	5	26
NeRep	78	45	59	68	65	51	62	61	66	43	55	92
WsRep	74	46	69	61	73	52	67	77	89	40	65	135
Rep (total)	197	106	136	134	150	118	139	152	173	87	125	253
SoInd	—	1	1	5	6	4	—	2	1	2	—	5
NoInd	—	7	—	8	8	6	3	3	—	9	12	3
SENATE												
SoDem	10	17	22	26	26	26	26	27	28	28	28	25
NeDem	3	7	8	7	3	3	3	4	3	4	5	4
WsDem	5	5	6	9	8	7	6	6	6	7	11	11
Dem (total)	18	29	36	42	37	36	35	37	37	39	44	40
SoRep	17	10	6	2	1	—	—	—	—	—	—	2
NeRep	17	13	12	13	17	17	17	16	17	16	15	15
WsRep	21	23	21	18	19	21	22	22	30	31	23	28
Rep (total)	55	46	39	33	37	38	39	38	47	47	38	45
SoInd	—	—	—	—	1	2	2	1	—	—	—	1
NoInd	—	—	1	1	1	—	—	—	—	2	3	3

The *Northeast* embraced New England plus New York, Pennsylvania, New Jersey, and Delaware.

The *South* included the eleven states of the former Confederacy plus Maryland, West Virginia, and Kentucky.

Before 1889 the *West* embraced Ohio, Michigan, Indiana, Illinois, Wisconsin, Minnesota, Iowa, Missouri, Kansas, Nebraska, Colorado, Oregon, California, and Nevada. In 1889 and 1890 the West gained the six new states of North Dakota, South Dakota, Montana, Wyoming, Idaho, and Washington, and in 1896 it gained Utah.

The congressional issue of greatest concern to southern Democrats was Negro rights, an issue which embraced civil rights, federal support for Radical Reconstruction regimes in the South, and federal enforcement of Negro voting rights. In Table 2, especially for the Senate, the Negro-rights likeness scores of southern Democrats with both northeastern and western Democrats were very high, often above 90, while southern Democratic likeness

annual appropriations for civil and military departments and services, treaties, and procedural matters. Often, however, specific amendments proposed for such measures or specific procedural maneuvers actually concerned either Negro rights or the economic issues analyzed in this study, and roll calls on such matters were included in the appropriate issue categories.

TABLE 2
Negro-Rights Indices

Cong. Number	43	44	45	46	47	48	49	50	51	52	53	54
Opening Year	1873	1875	1877	1879	1881	1883	1885	1887	1889	1891	1893	1895
HOUSE												
# Roll Calls	83	3	0	0	0	10	0	0	15	0	0	0
Likeness												
SoDem-NeDem	96	85				63			99			
SoDem-WsDem	93	89				74			99			
SoDem-NeRep	6	48				6			3			
SoDem-WsRep	6	48				9			3			
SoDem-SoRep	7	48				6			4			
SoDem-SoInd	—	83				69			1			
SoInd-NeRep	—	33				35			98			
NeDem-WsDem	92	96				89			99			
NeRep-WsRep	99	100				98			99			
NeDem-NeRep	5	63				43			2			
WsDem-WsRep	10	59				34			2			
Dem-Rep	8	55				22			2			
Cohesion												
SoDem	93	67				94			98			
NeDem	97	87				35			100			
WsDem	85	81				46			99			
Dem	91	74				64			98			
SoRep	93	100				95			94			
NeRep	96	100				94			97			
WsRep	96	100				89			97			
Rep	94	100				92			97			
SoInd	—	100				43			100			
SENATE												
# Roll Calls	19	42	22	46	0	4	5	2	30	0	0	0
Likeness												
SoDem-NeDem	100	96	82	100		97	99	100	95			
SoDem-WsDem	100	96	92	99		93	99	100	100			
SoDem-NeRep	21	1	15	1		3	1	0	1			
SoDem-WsRep	19	4	15	1		3	1	0	10			
SoDem-SoRep	16	9	17	0		—	—	—	—			
SoDem-SoInd	—	—	—	—		3	2	100	—			
SoInd-NeRep	—	—	—	—		100	100	0	—			
NeDem-WsDem	100	98	81	100		90	100	100	95			
NeRep-WsRep	90	97	99	100		100	100	100	91			
NeDem-NeRep	21	4	19	1		0	0	0	6			
WsDem-WsRep	19	7	7	0		10	0	0	10			
Dem-Rep	19	5	15	1		4	1	0	7			
Cohesion												
SoDem	100	98	80	99		94	98	100	99			
NeDem	100	96	90	99		100	100	100	100			
WsDem	100	96	92	100		80	100	100	100			
Dem	100	96	78	99		92	99	100	99			
So Rep	69	84	89	100		—	—	—	—			
NeRep	79	99	94	100		100	100	100	99			
WsRep	80	94	95	100		100	100	100	81			
Rep	75	93	94	100		100	100	100	88			
SoInd	—	—	—	—		100	100	100	—			

scores with various Republican blocs were extremely low, often below 20. In other words, the southern Democrats found all northern Democrats, whether from the Northeast or the West, to be consistent "doughface" allies, while Republicans of all sections were the clear-cut opponents.

However, in the Compromise of 1877 Republican president Hayes did make the momentous concession, not ratified directly in any congressional roll calls, that he would cease to use force to uphold Republican regimes in the southern states. After the compromise Congress no longer voted on the defunct Reconstruction regimes, but Democrats and Republicans continued to conflict sharply over the enforcement of the Thirteenth, Fourteenth, and Fifteenth Amendments to the United States Constitution, the authority to use the army and federal marshals at polling places, the carrying of deadly weapons at polling places, the registration of Negro voters, and the investigation of alleged outrages against Negro voters. This party conflict culminated in the Fifty-first Congress, 1889–1891, when the Republicans tried but failed to enact Henry Cabot Lodge's measure to create federal supervision of elections. Since both parties believed that southern Negroes, if given a truly free choice, would vote solidly Republican in national elections, such roll calls usually produced extremely intense polarization along sharp party lines. On most economic issues, by contrast, patterns were much more blurred, with neither the parties nor the section-party blocs typically attaining such tight unity within themselves or such sharp polarity vis-à-vis other parties or blocs.

The most intense economic controversy focused on monetary questions concerning greenbacks, gold, silver, treasury notes, and national-bank notes, and it was largely in terms of these issues that Professor Woodward discussed the South's right-fork, left-fork alternatives.[7] Table 3 shows that the monetary issue did tend to divide northern Democrats into an eastern right fork and a western left fork, but the divergence between the forks was not always sharp, and the separate trails not always clearly marked. Party affiliation exercised persistent influence throughout, and on occasion, as in the Forty-sixth, Forty-seventh, and Fifty-first Houses and in the Forty-seventh Senate, cleavages ran sharply along party lines, largely obliterating sectional alignments. Still, throughout the period the Northeast tended to

---

7. The monetary category embraced all roll calls that concerned the circulation of currency, including national-bank notes and their backing. Roll calls concerning bank charters and their duration were assigned to a separate "bank" category. The voting patterns in the two categories were very similar.

TABLE 3

Monetary Indices

Cong. Number	43	44	45	46	47	48	49	50	51	52	53	54
Opening Year	1873	1875	1877	1879	1881	1883	1885	1887	1889	1891	1893	1895
HOUSE												
# Roll Calls	35	32	29	45	9	6	9	5	18	30	66	6
Likeness												
SoDem-NeDem	60	70	52	75	62	65	55	62	80	41	49	78
SoDem-WsDem	92	93	95	93	95	95	87	91	97	80	92	95
SoDem-NeRep	62	37	26	14	19	50	41	41	8	41	25	26
SoDem-WsRep	66	61	55	19	22	73	66	56	18	64	71	37
SoDem-SoRep	67	42	55	26	21	64	67	38	8	30	59	43
SoDem-SoInd	—	86	97	83	82	80	—	84	55	88	—	92
SoInd-NeRep	—	32	21	21	22	31	—	54	46	39	—	18
NeDem-WsDem	56	75	54	80	61	64	59	53	79	57	56	83
NeRep-WsRep	64	76	70	92	94	75	58	84	90	77	67	89
NeDem-NeRep	71	66	73	37	58	84	74	66	27	72	65	48
WsDem-WsRep	68	67	56	24	21	69	71	53	17	74	76	42
Dem-Rep	71	59	54	21	27	68	66	51	17	66	72	36
Cohesion												
SoDem	63	75	88	88	84	47	64	33	94	83	85	83
NeDem	68	47	34	47	46	63	32	44	81	60	56	93
WsDem	60	65	83	79	84	57	52	49	98	56	77	73
Dem	51	57	68	79	73	41	45	25	89	48	71	79
SoRep	56	75	61	73	96	66	49	96	97	86	76	64
NeRep	34	85	70	87	87	76	59	91	97	73	93	94
WsRep	57	60	52	80	79	46	55	60	77	61	77	75
Rep	33	64	52	82	83	57	38	77	86	61	80	81
SoInd	—	100	100	70	78	78	—	0	100	93	—	100
SENATE												
# Roll Calls	60	2	51	10	8	10	13	5	19	22	67	9
Likeness												
SoDem-NeDem	44	34	45	44	36	75	60	34	54	49	60	58
SoDem-WsDem	80	79	85	85	89	80	79	97	97	75	86	88
SoDem-NeRep	45	18	30	25	15	54	60	25	18	22	58	59
SoDem-WsRep	83	64	80	40	24	68	77	71	56	54	79	92
SoDem-SoRep	79	86	82	43	7	—	—	—	—	—	—	74
SoDem-SoInd	—	—	—	—	13	55	63	100	—	—	—	53
SoInd-NeRep	—	—	—	—	98	77	39	0	—	—	—	7
NeDem-WsDem	56	33	31	36	24	62	53	31	51	73	71	56
NeRep-WsRep	56	54	47	85	91	74	69	54	60	67	71	64
NeDem-NeRep	70	83	81	77	80	69	75	76	60	71	91	90
WsDem-WsRep	75	63	69	32	13	56	73	68	55	71	85	93
Dem-Rep	83	64	78	42	21	63	75	60	46	54	81	87
Cohesion												
SoDem	50	64	69	74	74	46	33	68	93	68	57	59
NeDem	96	67	56	59	67	83	67	77	82	60	93	78
WsDem	39	67	97	90	96	59	61	74	98	35	51	43
Dem	32	51	48	59	70	40	27	57	87	52	49	48
SoRep	70	40	76	100	100	—	—	—	—	—	—	44
NeRep	69	100	79	96	97	71	74	82	78	88	91	88
WsRep	45	7	55	66	79	48	37	21	47	31	56	47
Rep	26	21	32	78	87	52	45	28	44	43	62	39
SoInd	—	—	—	—	100	71	85	100	—	—	—	100

vote more strongly for the gold standard and "hard money," which meant currency stability, or even contraction, and the West tended to vote for "soft money," which promised expansion of the nation's money supply.[8] And the likeness scores indicate that as early as the Forty-third Congress (1873–1875) the southern Democrats were voting in closer alignment with the soft-money western Democrats than with the hard-money northeastern Democrats. Most southerners believed that the South suffered from a currency shortage and that inflation would bring relief. The Redeemers' western soft-money orientation grew only slightly stronger in the Forty-fifth Congress during the South's asserted radical agrarian aberration of 1877 and 1878. And it continued at similar levels of strength, with southern Democrat–western Democrat likeness scores usually above 90 in the House and 80 in the Senate, right through the 1880s and 1890s. By contrast, the southern Democrat–northeastern Democrat likeness scores were consistently much lower, often dropping below 60.[9]

Beginning in the Forty-fourth House several southern hill-country Independent congressmen participated in the struggles over greenbacks, resumption, and silver. Professor Woodward has argued that the Independents, articulating a southern small-farmer interest, disagreed with the Redeemer Democrats. That may have been true on local issues, which were, as Woodward pointed out, at the heart of the Independent program, but on congressional monetary issues the Independents voted much like the Redeemers. In the Forty-fourth and Forty-fifth Houses the single southern Independent was Georgia's hill-country parson-doctor-farmer William Harrell Felton, who scored monetary likenesses of 86 and 97 with the Redeemers. And Felton's disagreement with hard-money northeastern Republicans, shown in his low likeness scores with them, was only slightly more intense than was the disagreement of southern Democrats with northeastern Republicans (see Table 3). The Forty-sixth House contained five southern Independents, and they scored a likeness of 83 with the Redeemers and were actually not quite

---

8. For discussions of monetary problems see Allen Weinstein, *Prelude to Populism: Origins of the Silver Issue, 1867–1878* (New Haven and London, 1970); and Irwin Unger, *The Greenback Era: A Social and Political History of American Finance, 1865–1879* (Princeton, 1964).

9. In many Congresses both the Democratic and Republican parties were deeply divided on the money issue, and the high interparty agreement on money issues in, for example, the Senates of the Forty-third, Forty-fifth, Forty-ninth, and Fifty-third Congresses does not indicate that strong majorities of the two parties voted in alliance but rather that both parties experienced similar divisions and had similar percentages voting yea. This situation is indicated by the relatively low monetary cohesion of the parties in these Senates.

as sharply in disagreement with the northeastern Republicans (likeness 21) as were the Redeemers (likeness 14). And until the 1890s the Redeemers usually (except for the Forty-eighth Congress) disagreed more sharply with the northeastern Republicans than did the Independents. In the Senate the only southern Independents in the 1880s were the Virginia Readjusters William Mahone and Harrison Holt Riddleberger, and in the Forty-seventh and Forty-eighth Senates they actually aligned strongly with the Republicans, even on the money issue (see Table 3). In short, southern Independents in Congress did not stake out an alternative left-fork inflationary position any more intense or consistent than that taken by the southern and western Democrats.[10]

To delineate monetary alignments more precisely it is necessary to examine key roll calls that defined and maintained basic monetary policies (see Table 4). In 1874, during the Forty-third Congress, the soft-money forces, getting their greatest strength from South and West, passed the so-called Inflation Act (Table 4, Roll Call 1), which would moderately increase the number of greenbacks and national-bank notes. President Ulysses Simpson Grant vetoed it, and soon the Republican party passed, by a tightly disciplined party vote, with nearly all Democrats in opposition, the Specie Resumption Act of 1875. The act committed the government to resume specie payments on greenbacks in January 1879, a policy that would result in currency contraction. Between 1875 and 1879 the southern and western Democrats voted frequently to repeal the resumption act. They failed, but they did exert enough pressure to get the Republican administration to leave $346 million, rather than the planned $300 million, of greenbacks permanently in circulation after resumption.[11]

---

10. On the southern Independents see Woodward, *Origins*, 75–106. The southern Independents in the Forty-sixth House were Felton, Emory Speer of Georgia, William Manning Lowe of Alabama, George Washington ("Wash") Jones of Texas, and Oscar Turner of Kentucky. A handful of northern Independent congressmen sat in the Forty-fourth House, 1875–1877, and on the monetary roll calls concerning greenbacks, specie resumption, and silver they and the southern Democrats scored a likeness of 82. The North elected no Independents to the Forty-fifth House, but to the Forty-sixth House it elected eight Independents, mostly Greenbackers, and they and the southern Democrats scored a monetary likeness of 89.

11. Unger, *Greenback Era*, 353–55, 371–73. The roll-call tabulations in Table 4 include announced pairs and announcements of how individual absent men would have voted if present. However, occasional pair announcements that failed to indicate which partners would vote yea or nay were omitted, and corrections were made for any duplication in pair announcements or changes in pairings during the voting. Also Table 4 omits the handful of third-party votes, but for some roll calls the text or the footnotes indicate how the third parties voted.

TABLE 4

Key Monetary Roll Calls

No. 1
Pass Inflation Act
43d House, April 14, 1874

	West	South	N. East	Total
		Republicans		
Yea	61	34	17	112
Nay	11	6	53	70
		Democrats		
Yea	14	24	0	38
Nay	11	13	17	41

Likeness: SoDem-NeRep 59
SoDem-NeDem 35 SoDem-WsRep 80
SoDem-WsDem 91 SoDem-SoRep 80
(*Cong. Rec.*, 43 Cong., 1 Sess., 3078)

No. 2
Remonetize and Coin Silver
44th House, July 24, 1876

	West	South	N. East	Total
		Republicans		
Yea	27	4	2	33
Nay	8	6	26	40
		Democrats		
Yea	33	40	11	84
Nay	5	5	18	28

Likeness: SoDem-NeRep 18
SoDem-NeDem 49 SoDem-WsRep 88
SoDem-WsDem 98 SoDem-SoRep 51
(*Cong. Rec.*, 44 Cong., 1 Sess., 4855)

No. 3
Pass Bland Silver Coinage Bill
45th House, November 5, 1877

	West	South	N. East	Total
		Republicans		
Yea	62	6	4	72
Nay	4	1	32	37
		Democrats		
Yea	33	68	9	110
Nay	0	4	11	15

Likeness: SoDem-NeRep 17
SoDem-NeDem 51 SoDem-WsRep 99
SoDem-WsDem 94 SoDem-SoRep 91
(*Cong. Rec.*, 45 Cong., 1 Sess., 241)

No. 4
Add Allison Amend. to Bland Bill
45th Senate, February 15, 1878

	West	South	N. East	Total
		Republicans		
Yea	18	3	12	33
Nay	2	2	0	4
		Democrats		
Yea	1	8	8	17
Nay	5	13	0	18

Likeness: SoDem-NeRep 38
SoDem-NeDem 38 SoDem-WsRep 52
SoDem-WsDem 79 SoDem-SoRep 78
(*Cong. Rec.*, 45 Cong., 2 Sess., 1076)

No. 5
Pass Bland-Allison Bill
45th Senate, February 15, 1878

	West	South	N. East	Total
		Republicans		
Yea	17	6	1	24
Nay	3	0	11	14
		Democrats		
Yea	6	18	2	26
Nay	0	4	5	9

Likeness: SoDem-NeRep 27
SoDem-NeDem 47 SoDem-WsRep 97
SoDem-WsDem 82 SoDem-SoRep 82
(*Cong. Rec.*, 45 Cong., 2 Sess., 1112)

No. 6
House Concur Allison Amend. to Bland
45th House, February 21, 1878

	West	South	N. East	Total
		Republicans		
Yea	65	8	56	129
Nay	1	1	3	5
		Democrats		
Yea	18	32	28	78
Nay	17	46	7	70

Likeness: SoDem-NeRep 46
SoDem-NeDem 61 SoDem-WsRep 43
SoDem-WsDem 90 SoDem-SoRep 52
(*Cong. Rec.*, 45 Cong., 2 Sess., 1284)

NOTE: Vote tallies include announced pairs. Third-party votes are omitted.

TABLE 4

(continued)

No. 7
Override Veto to Bland-Allison
45th House, February 28, 1878

	West	South	N. East	Total
		Republicans		
Yea	64	5	11	80
Nay	4	4	48	56
		Democrats		
Yea	34	76	12	122
Nay	1	2	19	22

Likeness:		SoDem-NeRep	21
SoDem-NeDem	41	SoDem-WsRep	97
SoDem-WsDem	100	SoDem-SoRep	58

(*Cong. Rec.*, 45 Cong., 2 Sess., 1420)

No. 8
To Suspend Silver Coinage
48th House, February 26, 1885

	West	South	N. East	Total
		Republicans		
Yea	15	5	44	64
Nay	25	5	2	32
		Democrats		
Yea	9	12	32	53
Nay ·	50	63	3	116

Likeness:		SoDem-NeRep	20
SoDem-NeDem	25	SoDem-WsRep	79
SoDem-WsDem	99	SoDem-SoRep	66

(*Cong. Rec.*, 48 Cong., 2 Sess., 2210)

No. 9
To Suspend Silver Coinage
49th House, April 8, 1886

	West	South	N. East	Total
		Republicans		
Yea	2	2	46	50
Nay	59	6	8	73
		Democrats		
Yea	1	7	27	35
Nay	48	76	4	128

Likeness:		SoDem-NeRep	23
SoDem-NeDem	21	SoDem-WsRep	95
SoDem-WsDem	94	SoDem-SoRep	83

(*Cong. Rec.*, 49 Cong., 1 Sess., 3300)

No. 10
Pass Bland Free Coinage Bill
49th House, April 8, 1886

	West	South	N. East	Total
		Republicans		
Yea	22	5	2	29
Nay	40	3	51	94
		Democrats		
Yea	37	57	1	95
Nay	12	28	30	70

Likeness:		SoDem-NeRep	37
SoDem-NeDem	36	SoDem-WsRep	68
SoDem-WsDem	92	SoDem-SoRep	95

(*Cong. Rec.*, 49 Cong., 1 Sess., 3300)

No. 11
Pass Silver Coinage Bill
51st Senate, June 17, 1890

	Far West	Mid West	South	N. East	Total
		Republicans			
Yea	16	0	—	1	17
Nay	3	9	—	16	28
		Democrats			
Yea	1	5	24	1	31
Nay	0	0	1	2	3

Likeness:		SoDem-NeRep	10
SoDem-NeDem	37	SoDem-MWRep	4
SoDem-WsDem	96	SoDem-FWRep	88

(*Cong. Rec.*, 51 Cong., 1 Sess., 6183)

No. 12
Repeal Sherman Silver Purchase Act
53d Senate, October 30, 1893

	Far West	Mid West	South	N. East	Total
		Republicans			
Yea	4	8	—	14	26
Nay	11	0	—	1	12
		Democrats			
Yea	0	6	11	5	22
Nay	3	2	17	0	22

Likeness:		SoDem-NeRep	46
SoDem-NeDem	39	SoDem-MWRep	39
SoDem-WsDem	85	SoDem-FWRep	87

(*Cong. Rec.*, 53 Cong., 1 Sess., 2958)

NOTE: Vote tallies include announced pairs. Third-party votes are omitted.

By the late 1870s the soft-money forces had switched their attention to silver. Indeed, as early as July 24, 1876, before the disputed presidential election, strong majorities of southern Democrats, western Democrats, and western Republicans—the same blocs that had voted most strongly for the 1874 Inflation Act—voted for a measure to remonetize silver and coin silver dollars (Table 4, Roll Call 2). Northeastern Republicans opposed it solidly 26 to 2, northeastern Democrats less solidly, 18 against, 11 for silver. In November 1877 a similar alignment passed the Bland silver-coinage bill in the House (Table 4, Roll Call 3), with the South and West strongly in favor. This South-West monetary alignment did not, therefore, suddenly come out in the open in late 1877, marking a radical turn away from the "Whiggish alliance of 1877," as suggested by Professor Woodward. Rather this alignment had steadily emerged and gained strength since 1874, and the electoral crisis and the Compromise of 1877 had only overshadowed rather than dismantled the alignment. The 1877 Bland vote did reveal right-fork–left-fork divergence, as suggested by Professor Woodward, but the distinction was blurred, since at this stage 9 out of 20 northeastern Democrats supported silver.[12]

In the Senate in 1878 Republican moderates, led by William Boyd Allison of Iowa, attached to the Bland bill a limiting amendment providing that each month the Treasury should coin not more than $4 million and not less than $2 million of silver. In the Senate northeastern Democrats and northeastern Republicans voted unanimously for the Allison amendment, and, crucially, western Republicans voted 18 to 2 for it (Table 4, Roll Call 4). The southern Democrats split, 13 against the Allison limitation, 8 for it. The Senate then passed the Bland-Allison measure, with the Northeast strongly against it even as amended, but with the crucial western Republicans overwhelmingly for it, as were the southern and western Democrats (Table 4, Roll Call 5), and the House concurred (Table 4, Roll Call 6). President Hayes vetoed the measure, but both houses overrode, with only the Northeast voting to uphold the veto (Table 4, Roll Call 7 for the House vote). The series of Bland-Allison roll calls thus defined three basic patterns. First, strong majorities of southern Democrats and western Democrats supported unlimited coinage, as did southern Independent William H. Felton. Second, strong majorities of western Republicans, joined by southern Republicans, supported the middle position, for coinage as limited by the Allison amendment. Third, a strong majority of northeastern Republicans and a weaker

12. Woodward, *Reunion and Reaction,* 239.

majority of northeastern Democrats were against any silver coinage and voted to defeat Bland-Allison even as amended. The moderate western Republicans held the balance of power and saw their silver program enacted.[13]

This Bland-Allison story is familiar and so far as 1878 itself is concerned basically consistent with Professor Woodward's account. Indeed, he seemed to define the right and left forks mainly in terms of the East-West cleavage on these roll calls. But the South-West monetary alignment had been emerging since 1874, as noted above, and after 1878 conservatives did not herd southern Democrats into a right-fork alliance with the Northeast as Woodward suggested. Rather the South-West monetary alliance continued, and the Bland-Allison section-party balance of power persisted and determined federal monetary policy right through the 1880s.[14]

Hard-money northeastern congressmen and such hard-money journals as Edwin Lawrence Godkin's *Nation* deplored the continuing moderate silver coinage required by the Bland-Allison Act and urged fervently that it be stopped. Senator John Sherman, the Republican financial expert, said in December 1884 that he considered limited coinage at the 16-to-1 ratio a temporary "experiment" which had been adequately "tested," which had clearly failed, and which should be suspended. But he acknowledged in great frustration that he lacked the congressional votes to stop it, because "You can not change this law, or speak of silver until a popular sentiment in this country demands it . . . ." Within two months, on February 26, 1885, the antisilver forces in the House did seek to suspend silver coinage (Table 4, Roll Call 8), but, as Sherman had warned, they met overwhelming defeat

---

13. No northern Independents sat in the Forty-fifth House which passed the Bland-Allison Act.

14. Woodward, *Reunion and Reaction*, 239. It is true that after 1879 the silver clamor temporarily subsided somewhat, partly because of the moderate currency expansion mandated by Bland-Allison, partly because of a general economic upturn, and partly because congressmen realized that neither the free-coinage nor the antisilver forces could mobilize enough votes to enact their programs. In the Forty-sixth and Forty-seventh Congresses, 1879–1883, monetary roll calls dealt mainly with less explosive technical questions concerning the deposit fees and mint fees on bullion, the circulation of subsidiary coins, the issuance of bullion certificates, and the regulation of national-bank-note circulation. But each monetary roll call had a clearcut inflationary-deflationary dimension, and southern and western Democrats voted persistently for inflation. On some mildly inflationary measures they invoked party discipline to get some northeastern Democrats to vote with the South and West. But on the fundamental question of continuing moderate silver coinage, the northeastern Democrats became more and more intensely opposed, while the South and West remained steadfastly in support. See Unger, *Greenback Era*, 406; Davis R. Dewey, *Financial History of the United States* (12th ed., New York, London, and Toronto, 1934), 407–11.

because of the continuing prosilver balance of power. And the *Nation* reported: "The principal strength of the silver faction, we regret to observe, is in the South."[15]

In 1885 Democratic president Grover Cleveland, who had been discreetly silent about silver until he was elected, came out against any coinage, and on April 8, 1886, his administration and the northeastern Democrats, who had become more united against silver, sponsored another bill to suspend silver coinage entirely, but they lost 86 to 203 (Table 4, Roll Call 9), including 1 northern Independent yea and 2 nay. Immediately the silver forces sought to enact unlimited coinage, and they lost 126 to 164 (Table 4, Roll Call 10), including 2 northern Independent yeas. In other words, the Bland-Allison section-party alignment had remained intact. Among southern Democrats, however, support for free coinage had dropped on Roll Call 10 to a 57-to-28 majority, a bare two-thirds for free coinage, its lowest point. Most of the other third of the southern Democrats had moved to limited coinage, the continuing position of the western Republicans, but only the 7 southern Democrats who voted yea on Roll Call 9, or the 12 who voted yea on Roll Call 8 had swung to suspension, the position of the northeastern right fork.[16]

The balance of power survived until 1889 and 1890, when it was upset by the admission of six new avidly silverite far western states, which cast twelve Senate votes, far out of proportion to their population. On June 17, 1890, the far western Republican senators joined the southern and western Democratic senators to pass an unlimited coinage bill over the nearly unanimous opposition of the Northeast and of the midwestern Republicans (Table 4, Roll Call 11). Again Republican moderates negotiated a compromise, the Sherman Silver Purchase Act, making it a party measure and enacting it by strict party vote, with the Democrats unanimously opposed. The act increased the coinage limit to four and one-half million ounces of silver per month, a measure of the new strength of the silver forces.[17]

---

15. *Congressional Record*, 48 Cong., 2 Sess., 244–47 (December 15, 1884; quotations on pp. 244 and 246); *Nation*, 40 (February 26, 1885), 172. The southern Independents cast no votes for suspension, two against. Northern Independents split, two for, two against.

16. *Nation*, 40 (March 5, 1885), 189, 194; *ibid.*, 42 (April 15, 1886), 307; H. Wayne Morgan, *From Hayes to McKinley: National Party Politics, 1877–1896* (Syracuse, 1969), 265–66. No southern Independents sat in the Forty-ninth House, which held Roll Calls 9 and 10. Northern Independents split on Roll Call 9, one for suspension, two against. On Roll Call 10 they cast two votes for free coinage.

17. Morgan, *Hayes to McKinley*, 343–45; *Cong. Record*, 51 Cong., 1 Sess., 7109, 7226 (July 10, 12, 1890).

In 1893 President Cleveland, blaming a gold drain and financial panic on the Sherman Act, demanded and obtained its repeal. Under the pressure of economic crisis and the patronage whip, 11 out of 28 southern Democrats in the Senate (Table 4, Roll Call 12) and 49 out of 101 southern Democrats in the House voted, many of them reluctantly, for repeal. But even in this crisis a majority of southern Democrats maintained their loyalty to silver coinage. The only other section-party blocs to cast majorities against repeal were the far western Republicans and the far western Democrats.[18]

During the years of silver coinage, 1879–1893, the total currency circulating outside the federal Treasury had roughly doubled, standing at $779 million in 1879 and adding another $741 million by 1893. And silver had been a major source of currency growth, adding $516 million to the circulating currency. This growth in silver, constantly opposed by the Northeast, was a measure of the political strength of the persistent silver-coinage alignment of southern Democrats, western Democrats, and western Republicans.[19]

Beginning in 1874 the southern Democrats had also sought to expand the currency by increasing the circulation of national-bank notes, but the bank-note circulation actually declined absolutely as the federal government paid off the bonds on which it was based. In 1881, therefore, when the Republicans proposed to recharter national banks, the southern Democrats in the House voted 10 yea, 38 nay, and western Democrats voted 1 yea, 18 nay, while northeastern Democrats voted for recharter, 13 yea, 2 nay. In the Senate the southern Democrats split 9 yea, 13 nay, while the western Democrats cast 6 nays and the northeastern Democrats all failed to vote.[20] Heavy majorities of southern Democrats also sought to expand the currency by relieving state banks of the prohibitive 10 percent wartime tax on state-bank notes, but they won support from only a few western Democrats and never came near success.[21]

---

18. J. Rogers Hollingsworth, *The Whirligig of Politics: The Democracy of Cleveland and Bryan* (Chicago and London, 1963), 12–18. For the House roll call see *Cong. Record,* 53 Cong., 1 Sess., 1008 (August 28, 1893).

19. Milton Friedman and Anna Jacobson Schwartz, *A Monetary History of the United States, 1867–1960* (Princeton, 1963), 128–34.

20. Unger, *Greenback Era,* 235; Richard Sylla, "Federal Policy, Banking Market Structure, and Capital Mobilization in the United States, 1863–1913," *Journal of Economic History,* 29 (December 1969), 663–65; *Cong. Record,* 47 Cong., 1 Sess., 4137, 5225–26 (May 19, June 22, 1882).

21. Atlanta *Daily Constitution,* June 20, 1878; *Cong. Record,* 45 Cong., 2 Sess., 3068–71, 3500 (May 1, 16, 1878); 52 Cong., 1 Sess., 5085 (June 6, 1892); 52 Cong., 2 Sess., 1781 (February 18, 1893); 53 Cong., 2 Sess., 5891–92 (June 6, 1894); Sylla, "Federal Policy," 664–65. By the time southern Democrats returned to Congress the Republican policy of repaying Union

A major cornerstone of the Republican economic program was the high protective tariff. The tariff tended to generate more consistent party-line voting than did the monetary issues, with southern Democratic likeness scores with northern Democrats of Northeast and West far above scores with any Republicans (see Table 5). But the Democrats were usually less cohesive than the Republicans, and the northeastern Democrats were especially divided. In the House in 1878, 1880, 1884, and 1886 about half the northeastern Democrats—a bloc of fifteen or twenty men led by Samuel Jackson Randall of Pennsylvania—aligned with the protectionist Republicans, providing the swing votes to defeat sporadic Democratic tariff-reduction proposals.[22] But the overwhelming majority of southern and western Democrats in the House continued the antebellum Democratic low-tariff tradition, claiming that the tariff was a sectional tax on agricultural producers for the benefit of monopolistic eastern industrialists. Voting consistently for tariff reduction, they generated much higher likeness scores along the left fork than along the right.[23]

The northeastern and southern Democrats did not unite on the tariff until 1887 and 1888, when Democratic president Grover Cleveland dramatically endorsed tariff reduction and whipped all his fellow northeastern Democrats into line with southern and western Democrats in support of the mildly reductionist Mills tariff bill. During the 1890s congressional tariff voting remained highly partisan, with the right-fork northeastern Democrats at last solidly in alliance with the South, but only after the northeasterners had united on an opening to the West (see Table 5).[24]

Civil War bonds in coin was well established, and the southerners did not oppose it. In 1878 a vast majority of them did vote with heavy majorities of western Republicans and western Democrats, and against the Northeast, to repay the bonds in silver as well as gold coin. And in 1881 all Democrats voted to use Treasury surpluses to retire the debt more rapidly and to use shorter term 3 percent refunding bonds, while the Republicans favored longer-term 3.5 percent bonds. See *Cong. Record,* 45 Cong., 2 Sess., 561, 628 (January 25, 28, 1878); 46 Cong., 3 Sess., 769–70, 773, 1733, 1750, 1788 (January 19, February 17, 18, 1881); Dewey, *Financial History,* 431–33; Albert S. Bolles, *The Financial History of the United States* (2d ed., 3 vols., New York, 1884–1886), III, 337–39.

22. *Cong. Record,* 45 Cong., 2 Sess., 4154–55 (June 5, 1878); 46 Cong., 2 Sess., 1383–84 (March 8, 1880); 48 Cong., 1 Sess., 3908 (May 6, 1884); 49 Cong., 1 Sess., 5830 (June 17, 1886).

23. *Ibid.,* 47 Cong., 1 Sess., 1118–25, 2674, 2709–14 (February 14, April 6, 8, 1882); 47 Cong., 2 Sess., 1642–44 (January 26, 1883).

24. *Ibid.,* 50 Cong., 1 Sess., 6660 (July 21, 1888). In 1894 the House Democrats passed the Wilson tariff-reduction bill, but in the Senate a few southern defectors, mainly spokesmen for Alabama and West Virginia coal and iron and for Louisiana sugar, joined with Senator

In the House southern Independents usually joined the southern and western Democrats in seeking tariff reduction, but after the Forty-fifth Congress the southern Independents were often less sharply in disagreement with the high-tariff northeastern Republicans than were the Redeemers. And in the Senate it was the southern Readjuster Independents, not the Redeemers, who galloped up the right fork on the tariff, generating high likeness scores with the northeastern Republicans (see Table 5).

To raise revenue for the Union cause the Republicans had levied, in addition to high tariff duties, numerous excise taxes, an income tax, and an inheritance tax. But by 1872 they had abandoned the income and inheritance taxes and had dropped the internal-revenue excise on most manufactured products except tobacco and alcoholic beverages, and in 1875 they increased the tobacco tax by 20 percent. In the eyes of southern Democrats these Republican actions perfected a brazenly sectional revenue system, which funneled profits from all consumers into the pockets of northeastern industrialists, while at the same time it directly taxed the product of the southern tobacco farmer and harassed him with obnoxious internal-revenue agents. Moreover, the whiskey tax and its agents, while not focused as uniquely on the South, were equally unpopular among southerners. To top it all, the Republicans had dropped the income tax, the one tax that would serve to equalize the sectional burden. In 1878 the Atlanta *Constitution* said, "The present revenue law might well . . . be entitled an act to plunder the producing sections of the country in the interest of its bond holding and rock-bound non-producing section. The income tax would equalize the burden—nothing more . . . ."[25]

In Congress the southern Democrats sought to reduce the tobacco tax and to enact exemptions and regulations that would protect distillers and tobacco farmers from the harassment of federal revenue agents. The southerners gave top priority to reducing the tobacco tax, and they had consider-

---

Arthur Pue Gorman of Maryland to create a protectionist balance of power and add over 630 amendments that scuttled meaningful tariff reduction. But this South-Northeast Democratic protectionist alliance did not occur until the mid-1890s, and it involved only a small balance-of-power minority of Democrats in each section. See Festus P. Summers, *William L. Wilson and Tariff Reform: A Biography* (New Brunswick, N.J., 1953), 187–208.

25. *Cong. Record*, 44 Cong., 1 Sess., 1579–80, 1727–29 (March 9, 15, 1876); Atlanta *Daily Constitution*, March 8, 1878. Though the tariff, the internal-revenue excise tax, and the income tax were clearly distinct, the three were often incorporated in separate sections of a single revenue bill. For such bills the roll calls on amendments have been carefully separated into the three categories of taxation. Since the tariff provisions predominated, the final votes of passage were assigned to the tariff category.

TABLE 5

Tariff Indices

Cong. Number	43	44	45	46	47	48	49	50	51	52	53	54
Opening Year	1873	1875	1877	1879	1881	1883	1885	1887	1889	1891	1893	1895
HOUSE												
# Roll Calls	7	2	10	7	22	3	2	8	23	14	12	0
Likeness												
SoDem-NeDem	86	41	54	45	66	56	51	86	98	99	86	
SoDem-WsDem	87	98	96	97	95	84	72	95	100	99	93	
SoDem-NeRep	23	3	26	13	6	16	21	16	2	31	24	
SoDem-WsRep	39	16	31	32	7	21	22	13	8	42	31	
SoDem-SoRep	36	10	59	32	8	11	19	8	4	0	31	
SoDem-SoInd	—	98	96	80	77	67	—	57	90	100	—	
SoInd-NeRep	—	1	23	24	28	39	—	74	10	31	—	
NeDem-WsDem	88	43	54	44	67	72	79	83	98	99	86	
NeRep-WsRep	84	87	88	81	97	93	97	88	94	86	90	
NeDem-NeRep	23	62	57	68	40	60	70	30	4	32	29	
WsDem-WsRep	35	18	31	31	8	37	50	11	7	43	32	
Dem-Rep	32	23	38	31	13	33	38	18	5	36	30	
Cohesion												
SoDem	84	97	90	79	92	81	63	86	97	100	80	
NeDem	77	22	42	64	57	12	35	77	99	98	78	
WsDem	84	93	90	80	90	49	49	91	93	98	83	
Dem	79	70	75	64	79	50	31	82	96	99	78	
SoRep	71	84	34	61	93	100	100	73	95	100	96	
NeRep	77	97	71	95	96	88	96	76	99	75	86	
WsRep	54	72	62	68	95	77	94	92	88	75	91	
Rep	64	85	60	75	95	84	95	84	93	69	85	
SoInd	—	100	100	63	53	67	—	75	100	100	—	
SENATE												
# Roll Calls	8	0	0	0	216	0	0	127	149	0	248	8
Likeness												
SoDem-NeDem	99				80			95	97		95	44
SoDem-WsDem	99				89			94	95		98	41
SoDem-NeRep	28				26			7	10		18	11
SoDem-WsRep	45				34			7	14		18	20
SoDem-SoRep	33				37			—	—		—	23
SoDem-SoInd	—				17			22	—		—	13
SoInd-NeRep	—				83			92	—		—	83
NeDem-WsDem	100				78			92	94		95	80
NeRep-WsRep	75				87			98	91		95	91
NeDem-NeRep	29				35			6	11		18	67
WsDem-WsRep	43				32			10	14		17	67
Dem-Rep	36				31			8	13		18	40
Cohesion												
SoDem	98				75			93	94		94	78
NeDem	100				76			95	95		90	42
WsDem	100				81			87	93		97	39
Dem	99				74			91	93		94	41
SoRep	58				100			—	—		—	100
NeRep	75				84			97	93		95	100
WsRep	29				69			96	84		90	83
Rep	50				74			97	86		91	87
SoInd	—				100			100	—		—	100

able success, cutting the rate by one-third in 1879, by another one-half in 1883, and by another one-fourth in 1890. This and other internal-revenue issues usually generated sharp party conflict, with most northern Democrats of right and left forks solidly endorsing the southerners' attack on the internal-revenue system, which had become identified with corrupt Republican spoilsmen of "whiskey ring" notoriety (see Table 6). Occasionally a few Republicans, embarrassed by treasury surpluses and unwilling to reduce the tariff, provided key votes for tobacco-tax reductions.[26]

But the southern Democrats also consistently advocated reinstatement of the income tax, voting overwhelmingly for it in 1874, 1878, and 1879, futilely introducing numerous income-tax bills during the 1880s, and finally, in 1894, successfully tacking an income-tax rider onto the Wilson-Gorman tariff bill, a rider which the United States Supreme Court promptly ruled unconstitutional. Southerners hoped an income tax would shift some of the revenue burden from the South and West to the East, and on income-tax roll calls the southern and western Democrats aligned in almost unanimous agreement, while the right-fork northeastern Democrats were always divided and usually cast strong majorities against the income tax.[27] In the House the southern Democrats generated the following income-tax likeness scores: on one roll call in 1874, 53 with northeastern Democrats and 89 with western Democrats; on one roll call in 1878, 48 with northeastern Democrats, 98 with western Democrats; on one roll call in 1879, 40 with northeastern Democrats, 98 with western Democrats; and on one roll call in 1894, 41 with northeastern Democrats, 100 with western Democrats. In the Senate the southern Democratic likeness scores were: on one roll call in 1889, 89 with one northeastern Democrat (who voted yea), 86 with western Democrats; and on 30 roll calls in 1894, 51 with northeastern Democrats, 97 with western Democrats. The southern Democratic income-tax likeness with southern Independents was always above 95, while with northeastern Republicans it was below 17 on all but one roll call, on which it was 40.

---

26. *Cong. Record,* 45 Cong., 3 Sess., 1521, 1527 (February 18, 1879); 47 Cong., 2 Sess., 2420–25 (February 10, 1883); Dewey, *Financial History,* 415–20, 438–40; Frederic C. Howe, *Taxation and Taxes in the United States Under the Internal Revenue System, 1791–1895* (New York, 1896), 165, 282–85; *The Statutes at Large of the United States of America,* XX (1879), 327–52; XXII (1883), 488–89; XXVI (1891), 618–20 (cited hereinafter as *Statutes at Large*).

27. In one exception during the Fiftieth Senate in 1889 only one northeastern Democrat voted on the income tax, and he voted favorably. *Cong. Record,* 45 Cong., 2 Sess., 744 (February 4, 1878); 46 Cong., 1 Sess., 1266–67 (May 12, 1879); 50 Cong., 2 Sess., 1094 (January 22, 1889); 53 Cong., 2 Sess., 6934 (June 28, 1894); 53 Cong., 3 Sess., 299–300 (December 13, 1894); Atlanta *Constitution,* January 26, 1894.

Table 6
Internal-Revenue Indices

Cong. Number	43	44	45	46	47	48	49	50	51	52	53	54
Opening Year	1873	1875	1877	1879	1881	1883	1885	1887	1889	1891	1893	1895
House												
# Roll Calls	3	2	24	7	8	7	8	3	2	2	1	0
Likeness												
SoDem-NeDem	92	66	72	86	79	93	67	91	92	86	19	
SoDem-WsDem	89	85	89	89	91	76	61	92	90	95	93	
SoDem-NeRep	12	2	16	35	21	63	24	18	8	8	9	
SoDem-WsRep	48	12	24	32	24	62	32	15	14	10	91	
SoDem-SoRep	68	25	65	77	29	64	41	12	9	88	*	
SoDem-SoInd	—	100	91	92	83	73	—	12	6	99	—	
SoInd-NeRep		2	11	35	36	45		94	98	7		
NeDem-WsDem	87	81	78	93	75	82	87	87	95	90	12	
NeRep-WsRep	64	89	91	93	91	88	92	96	94	98	0	
NeDem-NeRep	20	36	42	30	41	65	57	20	16	21	89	
WsDem-WsRep	57	28	30	32	26	64	71	7	24	15	98	
Dem-Rep	43	23	31	34	27	66	45	14	15	19	94	
Cohesion												
SoDem	98	100	81	78	82	45	59	76	88	99	83	
NeDem	82	69	50	87	62	41	40	73	71	73	79	
WsDem	79	69	78	78	79	65	61	92	68	89	97	
Dem	90	73	69	79	74	49	32	80	80	89	57	
SoRep	76	50	60	78	59	65	71	100	93	75	*	
NeRep	77	97	87	64	76	80	92	88	97	86	100	
WsRep	48	76	70	59	73	83	77	95	84	82	100	
Rep	43	82	72	60	72	72	83	93	90	73	45	
SoInd	—	100	100	83	56	100	—	100	100	100	—	
Senate												
# Roll Calls	5	0	25	2	53	5	1	10	4	1	8	5
Likeness												
SoDem-NeDem	92		90	100	68	85	100	87	69	100	83	63
SoDem-WsDem	98		91	100	83	88	100	89	94	100	97	57
SoDem-NeRep	13		39	10	36	18	0	11	24	0	8	18
SoDem-WsRep	27		45	24	49	16	0	14	27	0	22	44
SoDem-SoRep	33		76	50	51	—	—	—	—	—	—	18
SoDem-SoInd	—		—	—	44	46	0	*	—	—	—	67
SoInd-NeRep	—		—	—	68	71	100	*	—	—	—	20
NeDem-WsDem	93		85	100	62	78	100	81	75	100	83	89
NeRep-WsRep	86		79	86	84	99	100	96	86	100	83	73
NeDem-NeRep	21		44	10	52	11	0	17	49	0	22	50
WsDem-WsRep	28		45	24	37	28	0	24	21	0	19	81
Dem-Rep	25		51	18	41	17	0	15	29	0	15	53
Cohesion												
SoDem	90		79	100	64	70	100	88	88	100	94	65
NeDem	87		71	100	84	80	100	87	100	100	67	40
WsDem	87		72	100	86	84	100	65	100	100	100	46
Dem	86		75	100	65	67	100	84	88	100	94	32
SoRep	49		71	0	100	—	—	—	—	—	—	100
NeRep	84		75	80	86	97	100	100	89	100	90	100
WsRep	57		60	51	68	100	100	93	61	100	62	46
Rep	64		52	63	74	99	100	96	72	100	75	63
SoInd	—		—	—	100	80	100	*	—	—	—	100

*One bloc not voting on all roll calls.

During the 1870s the issue of federal regulation of railroads emerged, and in 1878 the House passed a regulation bill sponsored by Texas Democrat John Henninger Reagan, the former postmaster general in the Confederate cabinet. The bill's strongest support came from the southern Democrats (67 percent yea) and the western Democrats (70 percent yea); and Professor Woodward cited the vote as evidence of the 1878 "agrarian groundswell" that temporarily, in his view, linked South and West against the East. But railroad regulation did not create absolutely neat East-West cleavage; it struck northeastern interest groups in diverse ways, and the 1878 bill was supported by some northeastern businessmen and by significant minorities of northeastern Republicans (44 percent yea) and northeastern Democrats (27 percent yea). The Senate ignored the bill, but for the next nine years Reagan, usually chairman of the House Commerce Committee, pushed it tenaciously. His bill took a legalistic and moralistic approach, specifically outlawing railroad pools, rebates, and long-haul, short-haul discrimination, assigning enforcement to the courts. Though his approach was perhaps too simple for the complex railroad rate problem, Reagan developed the sternest antirailroad image of any congressman, and his bill provided a rallying point for advocates of tough regulation. And all through the early 1880s Reagan and his bill drew their strongest congressional support from united southern and western Democrats, with gradually a weaker majority of northeastern Democrats swinging behind him as well (see Table 7).[28]

In 1885 the Republican-controlled Senate, led by Shelby Moore Cullom of Illinois, developed a rival regulation plan, which the railroads preferred because it featured a regulatory commission but did not outlaw specific practices. Eventually in 1887 Reagan and Cullom compromised on the Interstate Commerce Act, which passed with bipartisan majorities from all sections. Many complex forces had led to the adoption of the act, but prominent among them had been the committed southern and western Reagan following, which had stuck together far beyond the agrarian uprising of 1878, keeping the issue alive and building pressure for the idea that corporations so powerful and useful as railroads must be subject to government control.[29]

---

28. Woodward, *Reunion and Reaction,* 240; Gerald D. Nash, "A Chapter from an Active Life: John H. Reagan and Railroad Regulation" (M.A. thesis, Columbia University, 1952), 15–68; *Cong. Record,* 45 Cong., 3 Sess., 101–2 (December 11, 1878); 48 Cong., 2 Sess., 554 (January 8, 1885).

29. Nash, "Chapter from an Active Life," 107–14; Albro Martin, "The Troubled Subject of Railroad Regulation in the Gilded Age—A Reappraisal," *Journal of American History,* 61 (September 1974), 339–71.

Table 7
Railroad-Regulation Indices

Cong. Number	43	44	45	46	47	48	49	50	51	52	53	54
Opening Year	1873	1875	1877	1879	1881	1883	1885	1887	1889	1891	1893	1895
HOUSE												
# Roll Calls	5	0	3	2	1	9	14	1	1	6	6	3
Likeness												
SoDem-NeDem	89		80	87	61	83	71	86	91	64	70	74
SoDem-WsDem	88		96	99	98	91	85	97	98	61	93	89
SoDem-NeRep	48		82	50	32	42	41	100	96	64	58	61
SoDem-WsRep	22		73	51	55	51	60	100	98	57	90	71
SoDem-SoRep	26		57	64	7	48	60	100	98	58	84	69
SoDem-SoInd	—		64	85	87	77	—	*	*	77	—	53
SoInd-NeRep	—		46	35	45	41	—	*	*	73	—	14
NeDem-WsDem	83		82	89	59	78	83	89	89	96	77	74
NeRep-WsRep	73		81	93	78	82	81	100	94	93	60	90
NeDem-NeRep	44		87	61	71	54	65	86	96	96	88	50
WsDem-WsRep	32		74	51	53	54	69	97	100	96	87	60
Dem-Rep	35		81	53	49	51	57	97	99	83	85	67
Cohesion												
SoDem	72		29	50	85	72	71	100	96	34	7	16
NeDem	78		31	72	8	54	47	71	79	83	57	67
WsDem	49		27	50	89	71	69	94	100	90	11	29
Dem	65		21	52	75	65	63	95	94	56	12	17
SoRep	77		81	25	100	47	58	100	100	75	60	26
NeRep	40		8	50	50	63	66	100	88	84	81	71
WsRep	88		39	48	5	59	66	100	100	98	14	52
Rep	65		25	47	28	56	61	100	95	88	40	57
SoInd	—		100	80	60	92	—	*	*	50	—	100
SENATE												
# Roll Calls	0	0	0	0	0	17	16	1	0	6	0	0
Likeness												
SoDem-NeDem						78	85	67		63		
SoDem-WsDem						75	89	83		80		
SoDem-NeRep						59	47	75		55		
SoDem-WsRep						68	60	90		61		
SoDem-SoRep						—	—	—		—		
SoDem-SoInd						70	26	*		—		
SoInd-NeRep						80	51	*		—		
NeDem-WsDem						60	82	50		49		
NeRep-WsRep						86	79	85		91		
NeDem-NeRep						64	48	92		40		
WsDem-WsRep						53	56	73		73		
Dem-Rep						63	56	84		64		
Cohesion												
SoDem						52	80	33		35		
NeDem						80	83	100		67		
WsDem						73	81	0		53		
Dem						53	79	36		34		
SoRep						—	—	—		—		
NeRep						73	65	83		97		
WsRep						71	69	54		78		
Rep						69	58	68		84		
SoInd						83	100	*		—		

*One bloc not voting on all roll calls.

The Republican economic program included generous federal appropriations to improve rivers and harbors, and on this issue alone the returning
southern Democrats truly became and remained a major bulwark of the Republican economic program, avidly supporting the appropriations and hun-
grily demanding their share. And precisely on this issue the right-fork
northeastern Democrats had by the mid-1870s become, as Woodward
pointed out, opponents of the new order, a position in which they persisted,
in opposition to the southern Redeemers, during the remainder of the century.[30]

River-and-harbor bills, classic logrolling agreements, were built in the
House by the chairman of the Commerce Committee. He carefully "included" the districts of a strong majority of the representatives, preferably
of a two-thirds majority who could suspend the rules and pass the bill without embarrassing debate and amendments. In the early 1870s midwestern
Republicans chaired the committee, and the appropriations heavily favored
the upper Mississippi Valley, the Ohio Valley, and the Great Lakes. The
1874 bill gave the fourteen states of the South only 22 percent of the total
appropriation, while the eight states of the Midwest (the Old Northwest
plus Missouri) received 46 percent.[31]

In the Forty-fourth Congress, 1875 to 1877, the Democrats controlled
the House for the first time since the Civil War and named Frank Hereford
of West Virginia chairman of the Commerce Committee. This provoked the
New York *Times* to observe, "It [the Commerce Committee] is apparently
made up in favor of the Southern schemes for rebuilding the commerce of
the South." Hereford certainly did include more southern Democrats than
ever before, and in the House on April 10, 1876, the southern Democratic
bloc contributed more votes to passage of the bill than did any other section-party bloc (see Table 8). But Republicans continued their traditional
support for rivers and harbors, with the western Republicans contributing
the second-largest bloc of House votes for the measure. In the Senate, still
under Republican control, the western Republicans cast the largest bloc for
the bill, and the southern Democrats the second largest. And the measure,
finally enacted in August 1876, apportioned the South 35 percent of the
total appropriation, the Midwest 38 percent.[32]

---

30. Woodward, *Reunion and Reaction*, 51–64.

31. Richard N. Current, *Pine Logs and Politics: A Life of Philetus Sawyer, 1816–1900*
(Madison, 1950), 75–82; sectional percentages of appropriations were calculated from the
river-and-harbor act, *Statutes at Large*, XVIII, Pt. I (1875), 237–44.

32. New York *Times*, December 21, 1875; *Statutes at Large*, XIX (1877), 132–39.

TABLE 8

River-and-Harbor Coalitions
Bloc Contributions to All River-and-Harbor Roll Calls for Final Passage of Bills, Adoption of Conference Reports, and Overriding Vetoes

Year	Action	Percentage Contributed by Each Bloc to Total Yea Vote						Percentage of Each Bloc Voting Yea					
		Ws Dem	Ws Rep	So Dem	So Rep	Ne Dem	Ne Rep	Ws Dem	Ws Rep	So Dem	So Rep	Ne Dem	Ne Rep
		HOUSE											
1874	Pass Bill	10	36	10	15	2	27	68	94	40	79	27	87
1875	Pass Bill	7	29	13	16	2	32	70	86	68	94	31	97
1876	Pass Bill	15	19	30	4	11	18	62	75	88	78	63	91
1876	Adopt Conf.	17	29	29	3	6	13	58	79	78	43	32	70
1878	Pass Bill	10	28	31	2	7	20	56	80	77	67	45	70
1878	Adopt Conf.	9	32	33	4	9	13	45	48	70	86	45	39
1879	Pass Bill	12	27	33	3	9	15	66	73	81	86	55	53
1879	Adopt Conf.	10	27	43	4	5	10	52	68	84	80	38	33
1880	Pass Bill	13	26	33	2	4	18	73	87	86	100	54	67
1881	Pass Bill	14	21	38	1	5	15	58	65	90	100	50	45
1881	Adopt Conf.	13	23	40	2	5	15	55	69	90	100	44	44
1882	Pass Bill	4	32	29	7	5	19	38	75	79	100	40	60
1882	Adopt Conf.	2	34	29	9	3	19	13	68	63	100	20	51
1882	Override Veto	4	32	36	4	4	17	36	75	82	100	31	56
1883	Pass Bill	5	27	40	10	3	11	26	56	90	92	17	26
1884	Pass Bill	21	18	44	4	3	8	60	64	87	70	14	35
1886	Pass Bill	16	22	42	6	3	12	55	65	84	89	17	34
1886	Adopt Conf.	15	13	48	6	3	15	48	40	89	88	19	39
1887	Pass Bill	19	18	45	3	3	12	67	51	91	71	27	39
1887	Adopt Conf.	15	20	41	4	7	13	58	62	90	80	52	45
1888	Pass Bill	12	19	42	6	6	14	70	52	90	79	50	53
1892	Pass Bill	23	15	34	1	9	14	69	85	77	100	47	93
1892	Adopt Conf.	24	16	37	1	8	13	63	87	76	100	33	84
1896	Override Veto	1	42	17	7	1	33	14	86	66	71	25	93
		SENATE											
1875	Not Table	7	28	34	28	0	3	68	57	91	89	0	10
1876	Pass Bill	6	41	29	6	9	9	66	88	83	100	75	38
1876	Adopt Conf.	5	41	27	8	8	11	66	94	83	100	60	44
1878	Pass Bill	5	41	32	14	0	8	50	79	63	100	0	30
1878	Adopt Conf.	8	33	33	13	5	8	60	81	68	100	25	38
1879	Pass Bill	9	25	38	16	3	9	100	62	80	100	20	30
1880	Pass Bill	15	23	49	0	0	13	86	90	86	0	0	63
1881	Pass Bill	14	14	58	6	0	8	71	50	91	100	0	43
1882	Pass Bill	13	30	45	0	0	13	83	67	78	0	0	33
1882	Adopt Conf.	7	28	40	0	2	21	60	80	77	0	100	69
1882	Override Veto	13	27	47	2	0	11	86	67	91	100	0	36
1886	Pass Bill	6	31	44	—	2	15	60	83	88	—	50	50
1892	Not Recommit	2	41	30	—	0	24	25	95	93	—	0	100
1896	Pass Bill	11	40	22	3	2	19	88	96	82	100	33	100
1896	Override Veto	10	39	27	3	0	19	78	96	86	100	0	87

NOTE: Announced pairs are included. Third-party members, not shown here, often contributed 1 to 5 percent of the yea votes.

The southern Democrats were eager to continue and increase such appropriations, and Professor Woodward has shown that in 1877 their acquiescence in the inauguration of Republican president Hayes was made easier by their awareness that Hayes and his fellow Republicans in Congress would cooperate on southern improvements. But such cooperation, already well underway by April 1876, would probably have developed and continued had there been no disputed election or compromise. In any case, it did continue in the Forty-fifth Congress, 1877 to 1879, under new Commerce Committee chairman John H. Reagan of Texas, who had served on the committee under Hereford in the Forty-fourth Congress. Reagan built the 1878 river-and-harbor bill around a core of western Republicans and southern Democrats, who together provided nearly two-thirds of the votes to pass the final conference version in the House and Senate (see Table 8). The South received 36 percent of the total appropriation, the Midwest 34 percent.[33]

Though the 1878 river-and-harbor bill included some northeastern Republican congressmen and projects, the Republican New York *Tribune* denounced it and warned that "The Hungry South" was seeking " 'to get even' at the public expense." But Republican senator William Windom of Minnesota defended the southern Democrats, saying "Now I think that they are becoming right on this point . . . . It is one of the most hopeful features I have seen of the democratic party for many years."[34]

And from the viewpoint of midwestern Republicans like Windom the southern wing of the Democracy stayed "right" on the river-and-harbor question throughout the remainder of the nineteenth century. For the period 1873 to 1897 Table 8 includes every river-and-harbor roll call on final passage, or adoption of a conference report, or overriding of a presidential veto. The left side of the table shows that in the Senate from 1876 to 1896 the southern Democrats and the western Republicans always contributed the two largest portions of the total river-and-harbor vote, with the southern Democrats most often providing the largest portion. In the House a similar pattern prevailed from 1876 through 1892, except that during a few years the western Democrats displaced the western Republicans as the second largest contributors. Thus the Redeemers found their most consistent river-and-harbor allies not in the Northeast but in the West, especially among western Republicans.

---

33. *Statutes at Large,* XX (1879), 152–63.

34. New York *Tribune,* March 14, 16 (quotation), 1878; *Cong. Record,* 45 Cong., 2 Sess., 4643 (June 15, 1878).

The southern Independents, though contributing only a tiny fraction of the votes for rivers and harbors, usually supported the appropriations as firmly as did southern Democrats. In the House southern Independents voted more than 75 percent yea on every final river-and-harbor roll call from 1876 to 1883. Only in the 1890s did the southern Independents fall as low as 50 percent support, and never below that. In the Senate the southern Independents voted on only two final river-and-harbor roll calls, once giving 100 percent support, once 50 percent.

During the 1880s the South continued to obtain river-and-harbor appropriations commensurate with its votes, receiving, for example, 39 percent of the 1880 bill. In 1879 the South-Midwest coalition also created a Mississippi River Commission, and in the 1882 river-and-harbor bill they granted the commission $5,468,000, with $4,123,000 designated for improvement of the lower Mississippi south of Cairo, Illinois. This boosted the South's portion to 51 percent of the bill, which the New York *Tribune* declared "the worst River and Harbor bill that was ever invented." It was the largest in history, and Republican President Chester Alan Arthur vetoed it. But the coalition overrode the veto, with the western Republicans and southern Democrats providing more than two-thirds of the overriding votes in each house (see Table 8).[35]

By the late 1880s and early 1890s passage of large river-and-harbor bills had become routine, often occurring on unrecorded voice votes. In the 1890s northeastern Republicans again became major contributors to the coalition. But the right-fork northeastern Democrats always ranked among the weakest supporters of rivers and harbors, usually contributing the smallest or next to smallest portion of the votes for passage, and during the 1890s they alone consistently cast majorities against this feature of the new economic order. The southern Democrats, however, continued to be one of the largest bulwarks of support for river-and-harbor bills, and the South continued to receive between 40 and 50 percent of the yearly appropriations.[36]

Concerning one other feature of the Republican economic program— land-grant subsidies to railroads—Woodward showed that by the mid-1870s northern Democrats of both the right and left forks had become opponents rather than defenders of the new order. But the resurgent southern

---

35. *Cong. Record,* 46 Cong., 1 Sess., 1730, 2103, 2281–84 (June 2, 18, 21, 1879); 47 Cong., 1 Sess., 6771, 6803 (August 2, 1882); New York *Tribune,* June 5, 1882; *Statutes at Large,* XXI (1881), 180–97; XXII (1883), 191–213.

36. *Statutes at Large,* XXIV (1887), 310–35; XXV (1889), 400–432; XXVI (1891), 426–65; XXVII (1893), 88–116.

Democrats, said Woodward, ardently supported railroad subsidies, especially a proposed new subsidy for Thomas Alexander Scott's Texas & Pacific Railroad, and they thereby provoked a "rift" in Democratic ranks. Such a rift is not evident, however, in the likeness scores on all railroad-subsidy roll calls from the Forty-third through the Forty-sixth Congresses, 1873 to 1881. The roll calls concerned sinking funds, the repayment of government loans by Pacific railroads, the extension of construction deadlines, and the adoption of resolutions opposing further subsidies; and southern Democrats supported the antisubsidy position of northern Democrats, consistently achieving higher likeness scores with northern Democrats than with Republicans (see Table 9).[37]

Of course, Table 9 embraces no Texas & Pacific roll calls, since the Texas & Pacific forces were never able to bring their proposed new subsidy to a congressional vote. Woodward does show convincing evidence of an impressive Texas & Pacific faction among southern Democrats, a faction whose disagreements with antisubsidy northern Democrats helped to lead the Redeemers into the Compromise of 1877. But no roll call revealed the actual showdown Texas & Pacific voting alignments of northern and southern Democrats. Moreover, President Hayes failed to supply decisive support, and, finally, Thomas A. Scott and the Texas & Pacific gave up. In 1881 the South did get its transcontinental railroad when Scott's rival, Collis Potter Huntington, completed the Southern Pacific Railroad without benefit of a new federal subsidy.[38] And southern Democratic support for railroad subsidies thereupon melted away.

During the 1880s Congress stopped considering new railroad subsidies and started forcing some railroads to forfeit unearned land grants. The forfeiture movement, led by Indiana Democrat William Steele Holman, consistently received its greatest support from Democrats of all sections, who found it popular to protest against the abuses of the Republican-originated railroad land grants. On many forfeiture roll calls a majority of Republicans

---

37. Woodward, *Reunion and Reaction*, 51–142. In documenting the Democratic rift Woodward analyzed only one roll call, the December 15, 1875, House roll call that passed 223 to 33 the resolution of Indiana Democrat William Steele Holman that Congress grant no more subsidies to corporations. Finding 19 southern Democrats and 7 southern Republicans among the 33 "nays," Woodward reported that the resolution passed "over Southern opposition" (*ibid.*, 62, 127), but in fact 44 southern Democrats (70 percent of the delegation) voted with northern Democrats for the resolution. See *Cong. Record*, 44 Cong., 1 Sess., 227 (December 15, 1875).

38. Woodward, *Reunion and Reaction*, 68–142, 234–37.

TABLE 9
Railroad-Subsidy Indices

Cong. Number	43	44	45	46	47	48	49	50	51	52	53	54
Opening Year	1873	1875	1877	1879	1881	1883	1885	1887	1889	1891	1893	1895
HOUSE												
# Roll Calls	5	8	10	0	2	18	12	5	4	9	4	0
Likeness												
SoDem-NeDem	72	90	80		88	92	85	89	91	91	70	
SoDem-WsDem	82	92	81		100	88	88	94	92	95	93	
SoDem-NeRep	56	58	70		33	62	70	75	10	22	23	
SoDem-WsRep	63	70	71		42	69	78	82	16	53	43	
SoDem-SoRep	59	76	59		36	69	81	75	12	42	67	
SoDem-SoInd	—	81	83		63	78	—	100	*	88	—	
SoInd-NeRep	—	49	60		63	66	—	89	*	20	—	
NeDem-WsDem	87	94	82		88	84	91	95	98	96	70	
NeRep-WsRep	84	85	89		91	89	82	90	95	68	79	
NeDem-NeRep	55	63	82		44	69	69	70	4	30	51	
WsDem-WsRep	63	65	78		43	67	84	77	8	58	42	
Dem-Rep	63	65	78		40	67	78	79	10	45	40	
Cohesion												
SoDem	44	61	54		60	64	71	66	84	85	66	
NeDem	72	60	44		36	53	64	72	96	81	46	
WsDem	62	68	69		60	71	64	77	100	78	69	
Dem	49	63	52		56	62	68	70	90	78	57	
SoRep	64	55	73		88	66	59	88	92	100	7	
NeRep	50	66	57		93	59	46	76	95	72	89	
WsRep	43	57	52		75	58	39	80	85	65	62	
Rep	36	59	54		83	58	36	79	90	50	64	
SoInd	—	100	100		67	87	—	100	*	89	—	
SENATE												
# Roll Calls	3	16	18	5	0	13	36	5	17	3	5	
Likeness												
SoDem-NeDem	83	71	77	86		75	71	74	98	97	78	
SoDem-WsDem	80	90	85	84		91	88	94	81	97	96	
SoDem-NeRep	54	48	48	26		44	51	35	47	3	56	
SoDem-WsRep	65	75	53	33		58	61	35	47	11	43	
SoDem-SoRep	59	65	47	6		—	—	—	—	—	—	
SoDem-SoInd	—	—	—	—		42	52	0	—	—	—	
SoInd-NeRep	—	—	—	—		73	75	58	—	—	—	
NeDem-WsDem	63	66	72	80		75	65	75	93	100	75	
NeRep-WsRep	89	62	78	87		78	84	94	95	91	85	
NeDem-NeRep	66	59	57	25		37	52	53	19	0	62	
WsDem-WsRep	85	78	58	39		53	60	41	39	9	44	
Dem-Rep	75	72	55	30		51	59	38	48	8	50	
Cohesion												
SoDem	67	58	63	85		70	59	68	87	95	56	
NeDem	100	61	57	87		95	75	67	100	100	73	
WsDem	40	65	63	73		86	64	63	73	100	53	
Dem	51	51	55	84		72	56	65	82	97	54	
SoRep	59	68	70	100		—	—	—	—	—	—	
NeRep	83	68	56	64		73	67	68	76	100	57	
WsRep	70	48	53	55		38	53	68	72	83	59	
Rep	65	39	51	57		51	56	68	74	88	47	
SoInd	—	—	—	—		100	79	100	—	—	—	

*One bloc not voting on all roll calls.

went along with the Democrats, generating several likeness scores above 60 between the two parties, especially in the House. But when the railroads sought amendments to provide delays or to reduce the amount of forfeitures, they found their strongest support among Republicans of all sections, especially in the Republican-controlled Senate.

In the Forty-eighth and Forty-ninth Congresses, 1883 to 1887, bipartisan congressional majorities forced specific defaulting railroads to forfeit 28 million acres, including the 15-million-acre Texas & Pacific grant. Party divergence came only on proposed Senate amendments to divert the forfeiture question to prorailroad circuit courts. Such an amendment to the Texas & Pacific forfeiture lost, with southern Democrats voting 6 yea, 14 nay; northern Democrats voting 1 yea, 7 nay; and Republicans 20 yea, 13 nay.[39]

In the Fiftieth and Fifty-first Congresses, 1887 to 1891, the House debated three general forfeiture measures concerning all remaining grants not earned within their time limits. On the most antirailroad proposal, which would forfeit 78.5 million acres, western Democrats voted 61 percent yea, northeastern Democrats 64 percent yea, southern Democrats 53 percent yea. All Republican blocs voted more than 85 percent nay. On a moderately antirailroad proposal which would forfeit 54 million acres western and northeastern Democrats voted 100 percent yea and southern Democrats 87 percent yea. Republicans voted 93 percent nay. On a prorailroad measure which would forfeit only 5.6 million acres western Democrats voted 92 percent nay, northeastern Democrats 90 percent nay, and southern Democrats 76 percent nay. Republicans voted 76 percent yea.[40] In the Fiftieth Congress the Democratic House and Republican Senate deadlocked, but in the Fifty-first Congress the Republicans, controlling both houses, enacted the prorailroad third proposal over sharp Democratic opposition. By the Fifty-first Congress the forfeiture alternatives had generated sharp partisan contention with little sectional cleavage. All northern Democrats sought stern forfeiture measures, and the southern Democrats, after recovering from their 1877 Texas & Pacific fever, had been only slightly less solid than northern Democrats in demanding tough forfeiture measures.[41]

---

39. *Cong. Record*, 48 Cong., 2 Sess., 1895 (February 19, 1885); David M. Ellis, "The Forfeiture of Railroad Land Grants, 1867–1894," *Mississippi Valley Historical Review*, 33 (June 1946), 27–60; John B. Sanborn, *Congressional Grants of Land in Aid of Railways* (Madison, 1899), 68–72.

40. Ellis, "Forfeiture," 52–56; Sanborn, *Congressional Grants*, 72–74; *Cong. Record*, 50 Cong., 1 Sess., 5933–34 (July 5, 1888); 51 Cong., 1 Sess., 7388 (July 17, 1890); 50 Cong., 1 Sess., 5935 (July 5, 1888).

41. Ellis, "Forfeiture," 51–56; Sanborn, *Congressional Grants*, 73–75.

To sum up, from 1873 to 1897 the congressional alignments of southern Democrats varied greatly from issue to issue, and so did their ability to win. They obtained significant river-and-harbor appropriations, and they helped sustain moderate silver coinage from 1879 until 1893. On both issues they relied crucially on alignments with western Republicans and western Democrats, overcoming opposition from northeastern Democrats. Southern Democrats joined western Democrats in persistently demanding tough railroad regulation, and their pressure helped to achieve passage of the mild bipartisan Interstate Commerce Act. Southern Democrats also joined western Democrats and opposed northeastern Democrats in seeking to reduce the tariff, to levy an income tax, and to create a more expansive banking system, but failing to find other allies, they lost. After 1887 the northeastern Democrats did join them in seeking tariff reduction, but they continued to lose. Many southern Democrats sought a new Texas & Pacific railroad subsidy in 1877, but no roll call recorded their support from other blocs, and the subsidy fell through. Otherwise, in 1877 they allied with the united northern Democrats in opposing new subsidies. After 1877 they joined all northern Democrats in seeking stern forfeiture of unearned railroad land grants, but the Republicans of all sections united in the Fifty-first Congress to hold forfeitures to a mild level. On internal-revenue issues the southern Democrats enjoyed consistent support from all northern Democrats, and this plus the occasional acquiescence of a few Republicans helped them lower the tobacco tax significantly. Finally, on the noneconomic issue of Negro rights the southern Democrats enjoyed unified support from all northern Democrats, and they finally won home rule when northern Republicans lost their resolve to uphold Republican Reconstruction regimes and Negro voting rights in the South.

How congruent is Professor Woodward's account with this record? Woodward depicted a redeemed South standing at a "forked road to reunion," facing fundamental choices between the economic policies of western agrarians up the left fork or of eastern conservatives up the right fork. And he portrayed southern Democrats swerving from right to left to right, creating a Whiggish alliance with conservative northern Republicans at the time of the disputed election of 1876 and the Compromise of 1877, swinging briefly into a radical agrarian western alliance during 1878, returning to a conservative right-fork northeastern alliance (with northeastern Democrats instead of Republicans) from 1879 until the 1890s, and then revolting against the East and embracing the West and William Jennings Bryan in the mid-1890s.[42]

Likeness and cohesion scores suggest a pattern at once more complex and more stable than that portrayed by Woodward, and, moreover, a pattern often directly at odds with his. First, the pattern was more complex than Woodward's. In Congress the distinction between the western left fork and the eastern right fork was often blurred. Radical agrarianism was not as neatly congruent with the West nor business conservatism with the East as the forked-road metaphor would suggest. On some issues, such as Negro rights, internal revenue, and the tariff after 1887, the major cleavage was along party lines, so that within each party the eastern and western wings largely agreed. Other issues, such as money, the income tax, the tariff before 1887, and, to some extent, railroad regulation, did produce some East-West conflict, but the sectional cleavage was always blurred by the party dimension, and the sectional polarity on these issues was never as sharp as was party polarity on such partisan issues as Negro rights.

Secondly, the indices suggest a pattern more stable than Woodward's. On each separate economic issue a basic section-party alignment had become evident before the Compromise of 1877, and it was not disrupted by the electoral crisis and the Compromise during the Forty-fourth Congress, by the asserted sudden "agrarian groundswell" during the Forty-fifth Congress, by the asserted reinstitution of a conservative right-fork alignment after the Forty-fifth Congress, nor by the revolt against the East in the 1890s.

Woodward's portrayal of rapid swings in southern alignment seems to have depended on a shift in his focus from one set of economic issues in the pre-Compromise period to other sets in later periods. For the period leading up to the Compromise of 1877 Woodward focused almost entirely on southern "home rule," railroad subsidies, and river-and-harbor improvements, using these to portray a rift in the Democratic party and an emerging southern Democratic alliance with northern Republicans. A Democratic rift and a Republican alliance do seem to characterize the unrecorded alignments on home rule and the Texas & Pacific subsidy, but not the recorded alignments on other railroad-subsidy questions. And certainly on rivers and harbors a southern Democratic–western Republican alliance did develop, as Woodward suggested. But the river-and-harbor alliance had already emerged

---

42. Woodward, *Reunion and Reaction*, 237–46.

full blown by April 1876, well before the disputed election, and it persisted, surviving the disputed election, the Compromise, the "agrarian ground-swell," and several shifts in party control of Congress. But Woodward, when describing an 1878 disruption of the "Whiggish" compromise coalition by the "agrarian groundswell," gave little attention to the continuing river-and-harbor coalition.

On the other hand, in his treatment of the developing "Whiggish" alliance before the Compromise Woodward almost completely ignored the section-oriented monetary issues of silver and the resumption of specie payments. But on roll calls during that period the South was in fact developing a persistent alignment with the western soft-money forces. Woodward turned to the monetary issues only in his treatment of the post-Compromise period, and he interpreted the South-West monetary alignment of November 1877 and early 1878 as evidence of a sudden agrarian tide which wrecked the conservative alignment that had negotiated the Compromise of 1877. These issues did indeed become more urgent in 1878, but the 1878 monetary alignment was quite similar to the monetary alignment in March and July 1876 before the disputed election. And that alignment was the culmination of a pattern that had been developing steadily since the Panic of 1873. The monetary likeness indices show no major deviations from the Forty-third through the Forty-fifth Congresses. Nor are there major deviations in indices on the income tax, railroad regulation, or the tariff. In fact, the patterns on all issues except the tariff persisted right through the 1890s. In short, the disputed election of 1876 and the Compromise of 1877 and its aftermath did little to disturb the established patterns of alignment on congressional economic issues.

Finally, on the economic issues that did generate East-West cleavage, the indices reveal that the southern Democrats persistently voted in close alliance with the left-fork western Democrats, a pattern directly at odds with Woodward's right-fork thesis. On such issues the northeastern Democrats sometimes moved close to the position of the South and West, but more often majorities of them opposed it. And almost never, from the early 1870s through the 1890s, did the southern Democrats vote in conservative right-fork alignment with northeastern Democrats against western Democrats.

But what, then, of the alleged southern Democratic "Revolt Against the East" in the 1890s as described by Professor Woodward in *Origins of the New South?*[43] In the 1890s the southern Democrats did revolt, but this did

---

43. Woodward, *Origins*, 264–90.

not involve any sudden realignment in congressional voting patterns. Rather, it consisted mainly of a sudden fierce southern Democratic denunciation of Democratic president Grover Cleveland and his silver and patronage policies. Southern Democrats revolted mainly because the president, under pressure of economic crisis, sought to coerce them to desert their long-standing western silver alliance, which he had previously tolerated, and to swing over to the northeastern antisilver position, a position he personally had long favored but had not previously insisted upon. Cleveland's sudden successful attack on silver, together with his patronage policies and his seemingly ineffectual efforts to cope with the depression, destroyed his political influence in the South and prepared the way for the southern Democrats to endorse William Jennings Bryan enthusiastically in the convention of 1896. But when they embraced Bryan the southern Democratic congressmen were not entering upon a new western alliance, they were simply reaffirming the long-standing congressional alliance from which President Cleveland had sought to divert them.

Professor Woodward, in describing a conservative eastern right-fork alignment for southern Democrats, indicated that it derived from the political dominance of commercial and industrial interests within the New South. If on the East-West issues the Redeemer congressmen in fact built a left-fork western alignment in Congress, does that mean that they were aligned against the business interests of the New South? Certainly, the Redeemers themselves did not think so. Most of them enthusiastically advocated rapid commercial and industrial development of a New South. To this end they sought not to overthrow the new economic order but rather to modify crucial portions of it so as to extend more of its benefits to the South. In 1874 Senator Augustus Summerfield Merrimon of North Carolina spoke for most of his Redeemer colleagues when he said: ". . . we must change the industrial and capital interests of the country so as to distribute them over the country in such a way as to produce an equilibrium of interests. . . . Our national policy ought to be to extend manufactures to the West and South . . . ." Urging a decentralization of the national banking system and an increase in bank-note circulation, he said, "that vast accumulation of capital and population in the Eastern States must in the end go to the South and West; and, so far as Congress can do it, Congress ought to inaugurate a policy that will lead to that result."[44]

Most southern Democratic congressmen considered their economic pro-

44. *Cong. Record*, 43 Cong., 1 Sess., 806 (January 21, 1874).

posals to be reasonable attempts to do just that, but northeastern Republicans and many northeastern Democrats denounced the southern programs, particularly the monetary proposals, as menacing attacks upon the new order. Therefore, on East-West issues most New South congressmen found congressional allies not in the Northeast but rather in the West among representatives of farmers and of expansive soft-money western commercial and industrial interests. Development-oriented western and southern congressmen could logically agree in advocating a more expansive national currency, a more decentralized and expansive national banking system, a system of federal improvements to extend water transportation, a system of federal regulation of railroads that were owned in the East but that were vital to developing areas, and a revision of the revenue system to shift the tax burden away from the South and West. Some southern Democrats even argued that tariff reduction, in addition to facilitating commercial expansion, would stimulate the rising southern textile industry, since it would unleash the winds of natural competition upon long-protected northeastern rivals and would help southern mills to conquer new foreign markets.[45]

Such policy goals, of course, were attractive not only to southern commercial and industrial interests but also to most southern planters and small farmers. Thus, the Redeemer congressmen enjoyed an enormous political luxury: on major national economic issues they found essential agreement among most economic interest groups within their constituency. Whatever the extent to which Redeemers in the southern statehouses may have provoked class conflict by governing against the interests of small farmers on state debts, state railroad bonds, legislative apportionment, lien laws, stock laws, state taxes, or schools, as Woodward argued, the Redeemers in Congress, dealing with the currency, the banking system, the tariff, the internal revenue, the development of waterways, and the regulation of monopolies, were often able to foster southern consensus by voting the common interests of southern farmers, planters, and businessmen. Indeed, the Redeemer Democrats would argue that the Independent revolt would only hurt the southern farmer since it would weaken the farmer's true defender, the national Democratic party, and would play into the hands of the high-tariff, currency-contracting Republicans. And such arguments gained credence

45. These basic southern economic-policy preferences, particularly those concerning banking, the tariff, and the income tax, persisted beyond the Gilded Age and continued to inform the actions of many southern congressmen during the administration of President Woodrow Wilson.

from the occasional tendency of a few prominent southern Independents to scamper up the right fork and join hands with the northeastern Republicans.

To conclude, from 1873 to 1897 the southern Democrats adhered to neither a simple eastern nor a simple western economic alignment in Congress; rather, they fashioned a unique alignment on each separate issue. Moreover, on each economic issue they did not waver from one alliance to another; instead, they found within the South a wide consensus upon which they could base a quite stable congressional alignment from Reconstruction through the Populist era. Thus, the disputed election of 1876 and the Compromise of 1877, important as they were for Negro rights and southern home rule, had little impact on established southern congressional alignments on economic issues. On some issues these alignments followed party lines closely, with the major cleavages separating Democrats from Republicans rather than East from West. But from the era of redemption to the end of the nineteenth century some crucial economic issues did pit an eastern right fork against a western left fork, and on those issues the southern Democrats consistently maintained a left-fork western alignment.

Redeemers versus Agrarians?

In *Thinking Back* Professor C. Vann Woodward affirmed that he had built *Origins of the New South, 1877–1913,* upon the Beardian framework of interregional conflict among a capitalistic Northeast, an agrarian West, and a planting South. But Woodward emphasized his "significant departure" from Charles and Mary Beard's *Rise of American Civilization.* They had seen essential unity within each antebellum region, and they had seen southern farmers "under the dominion of the planting interest." But within the postwar South Woodward had concentrated upon intraregional conflict that pitted Whiggish business-oriented Redeemers against agrarian masses.[1]

---

1. C. Vann Woodward, *Thinking Back: The Perils of Writing History* (Baton Rouge, 1986), 66 (first quotation, 149 in this volume); Charles A. Beard and Mary R. Beard, *The Rise of American Civilization* (2 vols., New York, 1927), I, 556–57, II, 20 (second quotation); Woodward, *Origins of the New South* (Baton Rouge, 1951), 24. Page numbers for subsequent references to *Origins* in this essay are inserted parenthetically in the text.

A pre-1920s historical interpretation had celebrated heroic Democratic *redemption* of the South from Republican Reconstruction and had described the New South of the *Redeemers* as harmonious, virtuous, and continuous with a glorious Old South. But since 1920, revisionists had been at work, and as James Tice Moore puts it in his article in this volume, Woodward "brilliantly synthesized" the revisionists. He posed classic Beardian questions—"Who is in control and what are they after?"—and he gave irreverent answers that demolished the heroic interpretation of the Redeemers. His creative demolition cleared the way for the next half century of New South scholarship and placed generations of southern historians deeply in his debt.[2]

Woodward found evidence of much conflict within the New South, and as Sheldon Hackney noted, he tended to define it in dualistic Beardian (and Populistic and Progressive) terms: "the classes versus the masses or business versus the people." In chapter 2 Woodward explicitly inserted his innovative theme of Redeemers suppressing agrarians into the traditional Beardian interregional framework. Focusing upon the national monetary issues of greenbacks, silver, and banks, and invoking congressional voting patterns, as had the Beards (and Frederick Jackson Turner) before him, Woodward argued that in 1877–78, in the aftermath of the Compromise of 1877, the South confronted a "Forked Road to Reunion" (p. 23).[3] The masses of southern people sought to revive an antebellum agrarian "left-fork" soft-money alliance with the West, wrote Woodward, but they were headed off by the Whiggish Redeemers, who had just finished conspiring with northern Republicans and capitalists to load the Compromise of 1877 with secret mutual payoffs. Redeemers resorted to "repressive or demagogic devices" (p. 50) to herd the leftward-veering agrarians into an enduring "right-fork" congressional alliance with the hard-money conservative Democrats of the capitalistic Northeast, an alliance directly at odds with the agrarians' true

---

2. James Tice Moore, "Redeemers Reconsidered: Change and Continuity in the Democratic South, 1870–1900," *Journal of Southern History*, 44 (August 1978), 359 (112 in this volume). Sheldon Hackney formulated the "Beardian" questions in "*Origins of the New South* in Retrospect," *Journal of Southern History*, 38 (May 1972), 196 (30 in this volume). See also James C. Cobb, " 'On the Pinnacle in Yankeeland': C. Vann as a [Southern] Renaissance Man," *Journal of Southern History*, 67 (November 2001), 715–40 (161–88 in this volume).

3. Hackney, "*Origins of the New South* in Retrospect," 194–96 (28–30 in this volume); Beard and Beard, *Rise of American Civilization*, I, 552, 556–57, 569–71, 579–80, II, 4, 29–31, 54, 99; Frederick Jackson Turner, *Rise of the New West, 1819–1829* (1906; reprint, New York, 1962), 112–13, 164, 172–73, 203–5, 219.

self-interest. The dramatic episode of right-fork herding became the climactic event in Woodward's brilliant account of the sordid Compromise of 1877, and it set the stage for the next chapters of *Origins,* which, in Hackney's apt summary, portrayed the history of the New South as "largely the story of how the Redeemers ruled in a manner that was against the interests of the mass of common people."[4]

Origins, published in 1951, was masterful, and in 1962 when I showed up as a graduate student in the seminar of Professor William B. Hesseltine at the University of Wisconsin, my seminar colleagues and I revered it as the bible of New South history. When we read Hesseltine's *Confederate Leaders in the New South,* published one year before *Origins,* we were intrigued to discover that he had anticipated Woodward's theme of a conservative alignment. Hesseltine had highlighted high-ranking ex-Confederates who "sat in the legislative halls of their conquerors," who were derisively labeled "rebel brigadiers," but who fostered connections with northern capitalists, who helped negotiate the Compromise of 1877, and who upheld the economic "results of the war"—the "protective tariff, the national banking system, the grants to railroads, and all the other war-borne gifts to the disciples of Alexander Hamilton and Henry Clay."[5]

Accordingly, when Professor Hesseltine recruited my help to retrieve his old "rebel brigadier" notes from his attic and suggested that I take a new look at them, I was puzzled. There seemed to me no conceivable nuance to add to the story of the northeastern alignment. But Hesseltine saw a gleam of something new and led me into a master's thesis on the rebel brigadiers. After his untimely death in 1963, I completed the thesis with Professor Richard N. Current. Current had been part of a previous generation of Hesseltine seminarians, and he had collaborated with two fellow seminarians, T. Harry Williams and Frank Freidel, to write the widely used textbook *A History of the United States,* which featured a comprehensive and sophisticated synthesis of the Turner/Beard interregional conflict framework.[6]

Thus surrounded by Wisconsin variations on Beardian tradition, I read the *Congressional Record* and counted votes. For help with the daunting

---

4. Hackney, "*Origins of the New South* in Retrospect," 194 (28 in this volume).

5. William Best Hesseltine, *Confederate Leaders in the New South* (Baton Rouge, 1950), 138–43 (all quotations on p. 140).

6. T. Harry Williams, Richard N. Current, and Frank Freidel, *A History of the United States,* Vol. I (1959; reprint, New York, 1962), 286–87, 302, 332–33, 382, 415–17, 425, 444, 457–59, 464, 464–71, 473–94. The three authors dedicated the book to their common mentor, William Best Hesseltine.

task of counting I turned to Professors J. Rogers Hollingsworth, Allan G. Bogue, and Eric E. Lampard. They introduced me to rigorous quantitative methods and to the computer, and they instilled in me the idea that systematic counting and rigorous analysis of complex quantitative data could often reveal significant underlying patterns that eyeball inspection had missed.

While tallying roll calls I wrote a dissertation on Birmingham, Alabama, and took a job at the University of California, Santa Barbara. There my new colleague Lynn Marshall had launched computer analysis of antebellum congressional roll calls, and I learned from his methods and employed his computer programmers. I also learned from my colleague and economic historian W. Elliot Brownlee, a fellow alumnus of the Current and Lampard seminars at Wisconsin. I ordered data tapes from the Inter-University Consortium for Political Research at Ann Arbor, Michigan, I classified congressional roll calls into categories, and I launched a comprehensive counting exercise.

The results formed the core of the article "Right Fork or Left Fork? The Section-Party Alignments of Southern Democrats in Congress, 1873–1897." Congressional roll call analysis demonstrated that in the 1870s the fundamental Beardian pattern of hard-money Northeast versus soft-money West had reemerged, although the sectional cleavage was not entirely neat. East-West conflict also emerged on the issues of the income tax, the tariff before 1887, and to some extent on railroad regulation, but on other issues more complex patterns of congressional cleavage prevailed.[7]

But what about Woodward's central departure from the Beards—his innovative right-fork Redeemer-versus-agrarian theme? It received absolutely no support from congressional roll call analysis. During the post-1877 conflict between a deflationist hard-money East and an inflationist soft-money West, Woodward's Whiggish southern conservatives did not herd southern congressmen into a right-fork eastern alliance. Actually ever since 1873 most southern Redeemer congressmen, including former Whigs, had on monetary issues coalesced in support of a firm alliance with the left-fork western Democrats, and they would steadily maintain the western agrarian alliance all the way through the 1890s.

Were the Redeemer Democrats in Congress therefore antibusiness opponents of the New Economic Order? Neither the Redeemers nor their western

---

7. Carl V. Harris, "Right Fork or Left Fork? The Section-Party Alignments of Southern Democrats in Congress, 1873–1897," *Journal of Southern History,* 42 (November 1976), 471–506 (59–95 in this volume).

allies thought so. They sought not to overthrow the new order, they said, but rather to modify crucial portions so as to distribute more of its benefits to the South and West. Western and southern farmers, planters, and businessmen could agree that they would all benefit from currency expansion, banking decentralization, federal subsidization of internal improvements, and federal regulation of railroads. Thus, I concluded, "the Redeemer congressmen enjoyed an enormous political luxury: on major national economic issues they found essential agreement among most economic interest groups within their constituency," and they "were often able to foster southern consensus by voting the common interests of southern farmers, planters, and businessmen."[8]

But where I saw southern white consensus on national economic issues (though not on all matters), Woodward saw in the 1878 congressional silver votes and their aftermath the first dramatic episode of intrasouthern class conflict in which Redeemers suppressed white agrarian opponents. In his detective work on the Compromise of 1877 Woodward had found Whiggish Redeemer congressmen conspiratorially linked with a "Who's Who" of northeastern capitalists and railroad tycoons, not to speak of a coterie of powerful conservative editors and a swarm of mercenary Republican Party hacks. Moreover, his research had shown that in the aftermath of the compromise many venal business-oriented Redeemers would use machine politics, fraud, violence, regressive taxation, and severe retrenchment to construct reactionary southern state regimes that would produce disgraceful embezzlement, defalcation, and scandal (pp. 1–74). In this volume Barbara J. Fields summarizes his portrait with superb concision: "From the moment Woodward introduces the Redeemers, discusses their social provenance, and characterizes their political program, he makes clear that the central issue for their regimes was how to forestall democracy."[9]

The Redeemers' forestalling of democracy became the central plot line of Origins. But just who were the forestalled white agrarian opponents of the Redeemer regimes? Woodward had no computer to help him tally the 80 congressional monetary roll calls during 1877 and 1878, or the 129 monetary calls before 1877, or the 357 monetary roll calls after 1879. He misidentified the 1878 southern silver-coinage advocates as the South's oppositional white agrarians who had suddenly but temporarily "stam-

---

8. *Ibid.*, 505 (94 in this volume).

9. Barbara J. Fields, *"Origins of the New South* and the Negro Question," *Journal of Southern History*, 67 (November 2001), 814 (264 in this volume).

peded" on stage in rebellion against the conservative right-fork policies of the Redeemers and their dubious Compromise of 1877. Thus Woodward's vivid account of the conspiratorial compromise reached its climax with "repressive" Redeemers "hallooing" and "heading off" the stampeding "droves" of "Agrarian mavericks," using "demagogic devices" to keep them "herded up the right fork" (p. 50).

The metaphors of domination—clamorous cowboys driving maverick agrarians like cattle—transformed the 1878 silver episode into an allegoric drama of democracy forestalled, an action-packed parable that propelled Woodward's readers and his theme of Redeemers suppressing agrarians forward into the next chapters. Without such propulsion the theme would have been much less robust, for nowhere else in *Origins* did Woodward narrate an episode so compelling in rhetorical support of it.

But comprehensive counting revealed that the Whiggish southern hallooers were few and their herding quite futile. In the Senate they actually consisted of a small but famously eloquent trio: Lucius Q. C. Lamar of Mississippi, Benjamin H. Hill of Georgia (the only real Whig among them), and Matthew C. Butler of South Carolina. Their valiant antisilver "hallooing" was recorded by sympathetic newspaper editors and became part of the evidence upon which Woodward relied.

But the hallooing herded nobody. The hallooers were no commanding cavalry of cowboys. Rather, as Todd A. Shallat wrote in a penetrating seminar paper, they were a nagging "thorn of hard-money opposition in the soft-money South." Despite occasional thorn pricks, the southern Democrats remained from 1873 to 1897 the largest and most tenacious prosilver section-party bloc in Congress, and they formed the bulwark of the South-West coalition that kept the government coining silver dollars until 1890.[10]

In *Thinking Back* Woodward graciously acknowledged that my roll call analysis had demonstrated that his "Right Fork, Left Fork" metaphor "was much too simplistic so far as congressional voting was concerned." But his acknowledgment resembled a Woodwardian pattern that Harold D. Woodman has described in this volume—he had formulated it in a "manner that leaves the basic structure of his work intact." Actually a bit of "hallooing" deserved to remain intact, but none of the "herding" (p. 50).[11]

---

10. Todd A. Shallat, "Old Whigs in the New South: Section-Party Alignments in Congress, 1873–1881" (unpublished seminar paper, University of California, Santa Barbara, and University of Wisconsin), 11.

11. Woodward, *Thinking Back*, 69 (first quotation, 152 in this volume); Harold D. Woodman, "The Political Economy of the New South: Retrospects and Prospects," *Journal of Southern History*, 67 (November 2001), 789 (239 in this volume).

The absence of herding suggested that historians should reevaluate Woodward's entire "core" argument. According to Woodman, "this core economic argument that informs *Origins* as well as Woodward's analysis of Populism" was that "the resistance of the lower classes of small farmers and workers to the domination of the business-oriented Redeemers" was "at the center" of 1880s Independent disaffection and of 1890s Populism and "that class could and sometimes did overwhelm racial differences, at least temporarily."[12]

Woodward did identify reactionary Redeemer state policies of the 1880s, and he did find struggles over state economic issues like debts, taxes, and schools. But he acknowledged that such issues did not provoke sharply defined class-oriented opposition from agrarians. White farmers "did not, during the decade following Redemption, seriously question the philosophy of the New Order" (p. 176), and the Independents "never developed . . . keen, interest-conscious realism" (p. 82). Instead "chaotic" party lines produced Machiavellian coalitions, and during the 1880s the confused "average Southerner" tended to retreat "into some form of political nihilism" (pp. 94, 102, 105).

For the 1890s Woodward constructed a more assertive, but still qualified, portrait of "agrarian resurgence" (p. 235) by the Farmers' Alliance and the Populist movement. But neither at the national level, on which most Populist rhetoric and platforms focused, nor at the state level have historians actually nailed down clear-cut classlike Populist revolution against the economic policies of business-oriented Redeemer Democrats. In state politics, with a partial exception in North Carolina, Populists matched Democrats in insisting on low taxes and minimal government. In a few industrial districts Populists did support organized labor during specific strikes. In several state platforms Populists did oppose the convict lease system and did endorse mild pro-labor reforms, but in pertinent state legislative showdowns they equivocated. Populists persistently demanded state electoral reform, but they did not formulate comprehensive state economic policy alternatives that fundamentally challenged the Redeemer economic order.[13]

---

12. Woodman, "Political Economy of the New South," 790, 792, 807–8 (240, 241, 258 in this volume).

13. Barton C. Shaw, *The Wool-Hat Boys: Georgia's Populist Party* (Baton Rouge, 1984), 124–39; Sheldon Hackney, *Populism to Progressivism in Alabama* (Princeton, 1969), 48–76; Dwight B. Billings Jr., *Planters and the Making of a "New South": Class, Politics, and Development in North Carolina, 1865–1900* (Chapel Hill, 1979), 140–42, 153, 175–76, 183; Donna A. Barnes, *Farmers in Rebellion: The Rise and Fall of the Southern Farmers' Alliance and People's Party in Texas* (Austin, 1984), 136–59; Helen G. Edmonds, *The Negro and*

Delineating the class standing of Populists is difficult. Typically they were more numerous in the predominately white and relatively less wealthy counties outside the plantation black belt. But Barton C. Shaw's research indicates that within specific Georgia counties Populists were only marginally less wealthy than their Democratic counterparts and were similarly situated within the rural class structure. In North Carolina Dwight Billings found Populist class standing ambiguous, with a fundamental class antagonism between Populist tenants and relatively large Populist landowners.[14]

Woodward vividly described the hardships of the "Unredeemed Farmer" (title of chapter 7) under the crop lien system, but he outlined no state-level lien reform program. Instead he wrote that impoverished farmers demanded change in national policies regarding money, banks, tariffs, trusts, and railroads. Woodward saw the demands pitting farmers against the policies of the conservative "right-fork" Redeemer alignment that he had erroneously posited. But in fact the farmers were essentially embracing the venerable policies of the Redeemers' left-fork western alliance (pp. 175–86). In the 1890s the Farmers' Alliance did produce one new radical national agrarian program to combat the lien system—the subtreasury plan that would extend federal credit to farmers and greatly expand paper currency. Agrarian advocates like Thomas E. Watson championed the subtreasury, and when Redeemers opposed it, he smote them with words as piercing as "the thrust of a bowie knife."[15]

Historian Lawrence Goodwyn also championed the subtreasury. He saw the "politics of the sub-treasury" as a "sword that cut the ancestral bonds to the party of the fathers." In late 1890 the "far-flung Alliance lecturing system" set out to recruit a grassroots Populist army to wield the sword. But Goodwyn's own meticulously reported research revealed that by 1892 there were only three southern states—Georgia, Texas, and Alabama— where "the politics of the sub-treasury had been brought home, with varying degrees of organizational thoroughness, to the farmers." In all other southern states, for many complex reasons, said Goodwyn, the lecturing ef-

---

Fusion Politics in North Carolina, 1894–1901 (Chapel Hill, 1951), 41, 53, 62–63; Albert D. Kirwan, Revolt of the Rednecks: Mississippi Politics, 1876–1925 (Lexington, Ky., 1951), 93–102; Roger L. Hart, Redeemers, Bourbons and Populists: Tennessee, 1870–1896 (Baton Rouge, 1975), 155–78, 200–223.

14. Shaw, Wool-Hat Boys, 96–101; Billings, Planters and the Making of a "New South," 184–85.

15. Robert C. McMath Jr., American Populism: A Social History, 1877–1898 (New York, 1993), 157.

fort had fallen short and "the People's Party had only a shadow presence," which meant that ultimately third-party leaders would champion silver rather than the subtreasury.[16]

In *American Populism* Robert C. McMath Jr. summed up the failure of subtreasury lecturing. In the 1892 elections "Fraud, intimidation, and outright violence accounted for part of the poor showing, but more importantly, the Alliance's educational campaign failed to convert the great mass of rural white Southerners to the third-party cause." Briefly during 1891 and 1892 the subtreasury had loomed as a sword with which a grassroots third-party army might sever small farmers from Democrats and silver. But in the 1892 elections the army failed to materialize, and abruptly the Alliance collapsed and subtreasury energy dissipated. By 1894 even in Georgia and Alabama the third-party gubernatorial candidates dropped the subtreasury and championed silver and fair elections. Altogether during the mid-1890s southern farmers cast more votes for candidates supporting the vintage Redeemer-Democratic left-fork silver program than for candidates swinging the subtreasury sword.[17]

Woodward capped his story of 1890s agrarian resurgence with an entire chapter devoted to the southern "Revolt Against the East" (pp. 264–90). But the "Revolt" was an internal Democratic Party phenomenon, and it actually involved no realignment of the monetary voting patterns of southern Democratic congressmen. Rather, Redeemer congressmen revolted specifically against Democratic president Grover Cleveland and warmly embraced William Jennings Bryan precisely because Cleveland had suddenly dropped his toleration of the Redeemers' long-standing western prosilver alignment and had aggressively attempted to divert them from it.[18]

Such analysis supports Charles L. Flynn Jr.'s argument that all late-nineteenth-century southern white politicos, whether Democratic, Independent, or Populist, subscribed to a conspiracy theory of national politics. It blamed the South's poverty upon Republican Reconstruction and upon Republican corruption, tariffs, pensions, hard-money policy, and support of monopo-

---

16. Lawrence Goodwyn, *Democratic Promise: The Populist Moment in America* (New York, 1976), 243, 242, 314; see also 213–43, 323–43.

17. The Georgia candidate was James K. Hines, the Alabama candidate Reuben F. Kolb. McMath, *American Populism*, 177–78 (quotation on p. 177), 196; Goodwyn, *Democratic Promise*, 402–7. On the collapse of the Alliance and the decline of subtreasury energy, see McMath, *American Populism*, 180–211; and Goodwyn, *Democratic Promise*, 387–514.

18. Harris, "Right Fork or Left Fork?" 503–4 (92–93 in this volume).

lies. Accordingly southern white small farmers saw the Democratic Redeem-ers' national left-fork congressional program, which had a host of allies, as the best strategic attack upon their economic problems. In light of such con-sensus Independent and Populist conflict with Democrats involved little sub-stantial dissent over federal or state economic policy, but rather featured sharp out-group hostility to Democratic Party organizational strategies, cliques, courthouse rings, machine politics, and rigged elections.[19]

Sheldon Hackney had briefly speculated about southern white consensus in his 1972 assessment of *Origins*. Asking why the twentieth-century South did not develop a two-party political system, Hackney suggested, "It may be that a homogeneity of economic interests and culture among whites was the real perpetuator of the Solid South." Perhaps, he continued, "with the defeat of populism and the success of disfranchisement there were few bases of political division left in the predominantly agricultural South except per-sonal popularity, family loyalties, intrastate sectionalism, moral questions such as prohibition, and similar ephemeral alignments." But perhaps al-ready in the nineteenth century the homogeneity of economic interests in the predominantly agricultural South had fostered underlying white consensus on economic issues and had been a key factor that had contributed to the fragility and brevity of the Populist moment and to the success of disfran-chisement.[20]

Harold D. Woodman and Robert C. McMath Jr., the 2001 symposium authors who deal extensively with Populism, both sympathetically outline Woodward's core Redeemer-versus-agrarian theme, but neither staunchly defends it. Both propose to update and salvage Woodward's analysis, but their proposed amendments actually undermine the core theme.[21]

McMath proposes that scholars revise Woodward's periodization and extend his view of Populism into "a long agrarian moment stretching at least from the 1860s through the rise of southern Progressivism and reach-ing the peak of its national influence during the presidency of Woodrow

19. Charles L. Flynn Jr., "Procrustean Bedfellows and Populists: An Alternative Hypothe-sis," in Jeffrey J. Crow, Paul D. Escott, and Charles L. Flynn Jr., eds., *Race, Class, and Politics in Southern History: Essays in Honor of Robert F. Durden* (Baton Rouge, 1989), 81–105.

20. Hackney, "*Origins of the New South* in Retrospect," 205–6 (quotation on p. 206, 39–40 in this volume).

21. Woodman, "Political Economy of the New South," 789–810 (238–60 in this volume); McMath, "C. Vann Woodward and the Burden of Southern Populism," *Journal of Southern History*, 67 (November 2001), 741–68 (189–217 in this volume).

Wilson." McMath's move would boost Woodward by reaffirming Populism's vibrancy, durability, and long-term impact.[22]

But it undermines Woodward's "core" Redeemer-versus-agrarian argument. McMath derives the concept of "a long agrarian moment" from Elizabeth Sanders's powerful 1999 book, *Roots of Reform: Farmers, Workers, and the American State, 1877–1917*. He notes that "Sanders pays close attention to congressional legislative histories," and he reports that "Sanders analyzes voting patterns along regional lines and reaches an overall conclusion about the shared economic interests of the 'periphery' (South and West) that Tom Watson himself could have applauded."[23]

True. But Sanders also affirms that from 1873 to 1897 the Redeemers embraced the very same set of southern economic interests. Sanders bases her analysis of nineteenth-century congressional voting patterns upon Harris's "Right Fork or Left Fork," and her concept of a "long agrarian moment" builds directly upon Harris's concept of an enduring 1873–1897 southern left-fork agrarian coalition. Both concepts contradict Woodward's dramatic portrayal of fundamental intrasouthern congressional conflict between right-fork and left-fork strategies. Both also negate Woodward's use of 1878 right-fork "hallooing" and "herding" as allegoric for pervasive Redeemer suppression of white agrarians and Populists.[24]

Moreover, as McMath notes, to construct the "long agrarian moment" Sanders adopts definitions that, quite contrary to Woodward, lump together "under one 'agrarian' banner" the South's dispossessed farmers and possessing farmers, "along with the South's emergent commercial interests." That move invites attention to Harold Woodman's "Woodwardian" reanalysis of the southern rural class structure. Woodman sees black plantation sharecroppers becoming a proletariat while landowning white yeoman commercial farmers became small businessmen and members of the business class. Accordingly, diverging material class interests reinforced the color line that separated white yeomen from black proletarians. Accordingly also, any conflict between white yeomen and merchants was not fundamental class conflict but rather a blurry "struggle *within* the business class." Woodman's

---

22. McMath, "C. Vann Woodward and the Burden of Southern Populism," 758 (207 in this volume).

23. *Ibid.*, 762 (211 in this volume).

24. Elizabeth Sanders, *Roots of Reform: Farmers, Workers, and the American State, 1877–1917* (Chicago, 1999), 112–15; see Table 4.6. Like Sanders, Harris, in "Right Fork or Left Fork?" pointed to the persisting impact of the left-fork coalition during the Progressive era. See p. 505 n. 45 (94 in this volume).

revision effectively reinforces Woodward's theme of discontinuity between Old South and New South, and it can help to account for the failure of the Populist effort to build a black-white coalition. But it further undermines Woodward's core argument about the centrality and classlike intensity of white agrarian political opposition to dominating business-oriented Redeemers.[25]

Woodman's reemphasis on the intensity of the color line points to one of the most enduring strengths of Woodward's *Origins*. As Barbara Fields points out, "Never at any point in *Origins* is Woodward unaware of Afro-Americans' entire implication within the vital questions of the New South." Woodward saw clearly that a "Negro Problem" existed only because whites set about to replace slavery with a system that would continue to subordinate freedpeople, and he recognized that different white groups sought different benefits from the subordination. Woodward dealt with blacks as "active subjects of history," and he pointed the way toward understanding that race was not natural and was not identity, but rather was a badge of identification peremptorily assigned by others who were intent upon forcing the people so identified "to ride Jim Crow."[26]

Congressional roll calls provide robust evidence of the centrality and the partisan intensity of the nineteenth-century "Negro Problem," a problem to which Elizabeth Sanders fails to do justice, as McMath rightly observes. On issues of "Negro Rights" southern Redeemers encountered not an East-West fork but a sharp partisan division. Republicans from East, West, and South persistently supported black rights, but from 1866 to 1900 no Democrat from East, West, or South voted for civil rights legislation.[27]

This essay does not seek to revive the pre-1920s interpretation of heroic Redeemers building a harmonious and virtuous New South. It affirms several Woodwardian points. In the New South ordinary farmers suffered extreme hardship. Many Redeemer state policies were reprehensible and counterproductive. Redeemer Democrats were tenacious partisans who did manipulate black votes and did rig elections against opposition factions and

---

25. McMath, "C. Vann Woodward and the Burden of Southern Populism," 763 (212 in this volume); Woodman, "Political Economy of the New South," 789–810 (quotations on pp. 808 and 805, pp. 259 and 255 in this volume).

26. Fields, "Origins of the New South and the Negro Question," 811–26 (quotations on pp. 811, 823, and 818; 261–62, 274, and 268 in this volume).

27. Harris, "Right Fork or Left Fork?" 477 (64–66 in this volume); J. Morgan Kousser, *Colorblind Injustice: Minority Voting Rights and the Undoing of the Second Reconstruction* (Chapel Hill, 1999), 38–39.

parties. Redeemers did subordinate and segregate blacks and did oppose federal intervention on behalf of black rights.

But historians have not demonstrated that southern white small farmers steadfastly opposed Redeemer economic and social policies or that most white agrarians persistently advocated sharply focused class- or interest-oriented alternatives that Redeemers ruthlessly crushed. Agrarians embittered by hardship directed most of their political energy toward the federal arena, espousing a left-fork western alignment to intensify a soft-money policy. Redeemer Democrats embraced soft money rather than suppressing it, and thereby they won white agrarian support that ultimately blunted the subtreasury sword. At the state level white agrarians did not advocate any comparably comprehensive and coherent economic policy alternative. Southern white agrarians did object to Redeemer manipulation of black votes and did oppose specific suffrage restrictions that would undermine non-elite whites' own capacity to vote. But southern agrarians typically collaborated with Redeemers to subordinate and segregate blacks, particularly in schools, and to oppose federal intervention on behalf of black rights.

The ongoing debate on these matters reveals that historians have not come close to exhausting the mighty agenda set by *Origins*. Historians still have much to do to delineate fully the postbellum southern process by which 60 percent of the people reconfigured and reinforced antebellum color boundaries and used them to continue to define the other 40 percent of people as black, unworthy, and deeply subordinate. Historians still struggle to explain fully why most southern white agrarians and non-elites embraced color boundaries that separated them from potential political allies and that helped to construct a twentieth-century southern political landscape in which non-elite whites would have little standing.

Woodward's *Origins* brilliantly posed all these issues. A half century later scholars continue to engage his agenda, and their efforts testify vividly to the deep significance of the questions he posed and to the enduring resonance of the answers he ventured.

One of the major themes of Woodward's Origins of the New South, 1877–1913, *was that the South's history had been marked by major discontinuities, an argument that flew in the face of much accepted wisdom that portrayed the South as largely unchanging in its essential values and leadership. Woodward had a number of interpretative agendas, not simply revising the uncritically positive way many white southerners had portrayed the so-called Redeemers who took political leadership of the South after Reconstruction. He portrayed these Redeemers as betrayers of the real interests of most southerners, white and black—false leaders who aligned themselves with the eastern financial establishment and feathered their own nests. But Woodward also took pains to describe these Redeemers as new men taking charge of the South, not the prewar planter elite and their sons. Woodward's thesis that these new men who climbed to power represented a real break with Old South traditions is a key part of his influential reinterpretation of southern history, and his theme of discontinuity has significantly shaped the writing of southern history. But in 1978 a young scholar, James Tice Moore, revisited that interpretation and examined very carefully every aspect of Woodward's argument in the light of both earlier and more recent scholarship, and Moore's findings strongly suggested that Woodward had exaggerated both the newness of the post-Reconstruction southern leadership and the extent of its repudiation of the interests of the mass of southerners. Neither Woodward nor his disciples particularly welcomed Moore's revisionist view, but it stands a quarter century later as an important corrective.*

Redeemers Reconsidered: Change and Continuity in the Democratic South, 1870–1900

The political leaders of the post-Reconstruction South have experienced a curious fate at the hands of historians. Variously known as "Bourbons," "Redeemers," or "New Departure Democrats" (*Redeemers* is used in this essay), these men were lionized by scholars well into the twentieth century— only to suffer a sharp decline in their reputations from the 1920s to the 1950s.[1] The sources of their initial popularity are readily apparent, for they had expelled the hated carpetbag governments from the South, reestablished white supremacy on the wreckage of a defunct Radicalism, and put an end

Reprinted from *Journal of Southern History,* 44 (August 1978), 357–78.

1. Insight into these historiographical trends is provided by Dewey W. Grantham Jr., "The Southern Bourbons Revisited," *South Atlantic Quarterly,* 60 (Summer 1961), 286–95; and George B. Tindall, *The Persistent Tradition in New South Politics* (Baton Rouge, 1975), 8–13.

to the humiliating military occupation of the region. Reflecting this favorable climate, historians in the first four or five decades after Reconstruction rarely questioned the motives or personal integrity of the Democratic leaders. Instead, scholars generally contented themselves with eulogies on the Redeemers' Confederate war records, their heroism and sagacity in the struggles against "Negro rule," and their ties in blood and sentiment to the chivalric aristocracy of antebellum days.[2]

Occasional criticisms crept into these early analyses, to be sure; students of the period sometimes suggested that the region's Gilded Age Democrats had been too parsimonious in their spending policies and too conservative in their political outlook, too resistant to new men and new ideas.[3] Even so, historians excused these shortcomings because of the politicians' service on the battlefields and in the legislative halls. Repeatedly hailed as the heirs and equals of the patriots of 1776, the Redeemers' place in history seemed assured.[4] They were—in the eyes of scholars and public alike—the patrician saviors of their homeland, the natural leaders of the South.

This exalted image has not survived. Attacks on the post-Reconstruction leadership began to appear in the 1920s and became increasingly vitriolic for a generation. Inspired by Charles Austin Beard and other reformist historians of the Progressive era, scholars tended to reinterpret the southern past from the perspective of the lower classes of the backwoods and farms and referred often to the region's Gilded Age dissidents—the Greenbackers, Republicans, Readjusters, and Populists who had attempted to overthrow

---

2. These laudatory tendencies are apparent in Hilary A. Herbert et al., *Why the Solid South? Or, Reconstruction and Its Results* (Baltimore, 1890), *passim;* Claude G. Bowers, *The Tragic Era: The Revolution After Lincoln* (Cambridge, 1929), *passim;* Philip A. Bruce, *The Rise of the New South* (Philadelphia, 1905), 440; Holland Thompson, *The New South: A Chronicle of Social and Industrial Evolution* (New Haven, Toronto, and London, 1920), 12–13, 25; William W. Ball, *The State That Forgot: South Carolina's Surrender to Democracy* (Indianapolis, 1932), 59, 150, 170, 183–84, 207; William A. Percy, *Lanterns on the Levee: Recollections of a Planter's Son* (New York, 1941), 62–74.

3. Walter L. Fleming, *The Sequel of Appomattox: A Chronicle of the Reunion of the States* (New Haven, Toronto, and London, 1920), 280–81, 302; Albert B. Moore, *History of Alabama and Her People* (3 vols., Chicago and New York, 1927), I, 646, 656; J. G. de Roulhac Hamilton, *North Carolina Since 1860* (Chicago, 1919), 169, 214, 218; Thompson, *New South,* 26, 46–47.

4. For examples of analogies drawn between the Redeemers and the American Revolutionaries see Edward L. Wells, *Hampton and Reconstruction* (Columbia, S.C., 1907), 108–9; David D. Wallace, *The History of South Carolina* (4 vols., New York, 1934), III, 313; Alfred B. Williams, *Hampton and His Red Shirts: South Carolina's Deliverance in 1876* (Charleston, S.C., 1935), 41; and John G. Fletcher, *Arkansas* (Chapel Hill, 1947), 264.

the Democratic hegemony.[5] These historians emphasized the negative aspects of the Redeemer establishment, and an image of the Democratic elite took shape that was far different from the heroic vision of previous years. Where an earlier generation had perceived courage, self-sacrifice, and a sincere devotion to good government, the revisionist historians of the 1930s and 1940s by and large saw only intolerance, avarice, and a shocking indifference to popular needs. Many historians examined long-forgotten Democratic financial scandals and conflicts of interest, and they attacked the Redeemers' inadequate funding for schools, asylums, and prisons.[6] Most important of all, students of the period questioned the social and economic origins of the post-Reconstruction leadership. Rejecting the previous emphasis on the Redeemers' "good blood" and patrician heritage, hostile scholars described the Democratic politicians of the 1870s and 1880s as an essentially new class of money-hungry townsmen, as upstart capitalists who had muscled their way to prominence in the turbulent post–Civil War era.[7] This revisionist trend culminated in the 1951 publication of C. Vann Wood-

---

5. Between 1917 and 1955 historians published books concerning Gilded Age agrarian unrest in Georgia, Mississippi, South Carolina, Tennessee, Texas, and Virginia, and biographies of such prominent anti-Redeemer dissidents as Thomas E. Watson, Benjamin R. Tillman, William Mahone, and Leonidas L. Polk appeared during the same period. These years also witnessed the publication of articles which probed the activities of Greenbackers, Republicans, and anti-Redeemer "Independents" in Alabama, Florida, Georgia, Mississippi, North Carolina, South Carolina, and Texas. For a full treatment of this historiographical trend see Allen J. Going, "The Agrarian Revolt," in Arthur S. Link and Rembert W. Patrick, eds., *Writing Southern History: Essays in Historiography in Honor of Fletcher M. Green* (Baton Rouge, 1965), 362–82.

6. For examples of these exposés see Fletcher M. Green, "Some Aspects of the Convict Lease System in the Southern States," in Fletcher M. Green, ed., *Essays in Southern History Presented to Joseph Gregoire de Roulhac Hamilton . . .* (Chapel Hill, 1949), 112–23; Allen W. Moger, "Railroad Practices and Policies in Virginia After the Civil War," *Virginia Magazine of History and Biography,* 59 (October 1951), 423–57; Garnie W. McGinty, *Louisiana Redeemed: The Overthrow of Carpet-bag Rule, 1876–1880* (New Orleans, 1941), 125, 138, 142, 146, 203, 228–33, 247–48; C. Vann Woodward, *Tom Watson, Agrarian Rebel* (New York, 1938), 52–72; William A. Sheppard, *Red Shirts Remembered: Southern Brigadiers of the Reconstruction Period* (Atlanta, 1940), 231, 246–47, 253–54, 291, 315–16.

7. Alex M. Arnett, *The Populist Movement in Georgia: A View of the "Agrarian Crusade" in the Light of Solid-South Politics* (New York, 1922), 23, 32–33; Albert D. Kirwan, *Revolt of the Rednecks: Mississippi Politics, 1876–1925* (Lexington, Ky., 1951), 3, 8–9; Woodward, *Tom Watson,* 65; William D. Sheldon, *Populism in the Old Dominion: Virginia Farm Politics, 1885–1900* (Princeton, 1935), 60; Charles C. Pearson, *The Readjuster Movement in Virginia* (New Haven and London, 1917), 23; Benjamin B. Kendrick and Alex M. Arnett, *The South Looks at Its Past* (Chapel Hill, 1935), 108–12.

ward's *Origins of the New South,* a work that brilliantly synthesized the findings of the preceding decades.

According to Woodward, the collapse of the carpetbaggers neither restored the South's prewar leaders to office nor revitalized the region's traditional values and beliefs. The secessionist firebrands of the planter class never regained their old preeminence, and the powers of government gravitated inexorably into the hands of urban-oriented parvenus, men who had enjoyed little influence in the antebellum years. Railroad executives, corporation lawyers, and speculators of various kinds set the political tone in Professor Woodward's New South. Revisionist historians also emphasized the importance of erstwhile Whigs in the Democratic hierarchy, and Woodward exploited this theme with particular effectiveness. He insisted that probusiness Whigs monopolized public offices in the Redeemer period, displacing the old-line adherents of Jefferson and Jackson. He described a Democratic elite that allegedly ignored the farmers' demands, lavished favors on the corporate interests, and aligned itself with northeastern capital on the great economic issues of the Gilded Age. In Woodward's opinion, therefore, the Redeemer hegemony represented fundamental, irreversible change. Parvenus presumably gained power over traditionalists, Whigs over Jacksonians, capitalists over agrarians. New men with new ideas clearly held sway in the revisionist South.[8]

Iconoclastic, even cynical in tone, this revisionist interpretation rapidly supplanted the earlier pro-Redeemer assessments. Graphic proof of this change is apparent in textbooks on southern history published from the 1950s to the 1970s. Analyses of the post-Reconstruction era in these works are often little more than paraphrases of Woodward's conclusions. Such surveys generally stress negative characteristics of the Redeemer hegemony, and their pages offer few if any favorable comments on the Democratic leadership.[9] In spite of its wide acceptance by historians, the revisionist ap-

---

8. C. Vann Woodward, *Origins of the New South, 1877–1913* (Baton Rouge, 1951), 1–22 and *passim.* For an assessment of the continuing impact of Woodward's synthesis of the revisionist argument see Sheldon Hackney, "*Origins of the New South* in Retrospect," *Journal of Southern History,* 38 (May 1972), 191–216 (25–49 in this volume).

9. Monroe L. Billington, *The American South: A Brief History* (New York, 1971), 212–15; Thomas D. Clark and Albert D. Kirwan, *The South Since Appomattox: A Century of Regional Change* (New York, 1967), 53–60; William B. Hesseltine and David L. Smiley, *The South in American History* (2d ed., Englewood Cliffs, N.J., 1960), 416–25; John S. Ezell, *The South Since 1865* (2d ed., New York and London, 1975), 102–5, 111–12. A more critical view of the revisionist thesis is offered in Francis B. Simkins and Charles P. Roland, *A History of the South* (4th ed., New York, 1972), 311–15, 318.

praisal, dominant for at least three decades, is now itself in need of revision. This claim is supported by the marked increase in historical research and writing on the Redeemer years since the publication of *Origins of the New South*. At the time Woodward and others constructed their interpretations in the 1930s and 1940s, the actual performance of the Gilded Age Democratic regimes had received little attention. Instead, scholars had been attracted to the dramatic political clashes of Reconstruction or (as in the case of the revisionists themselves) to the Populist upheavals of the 1890s. The Democratic leaders of the 1870s and 1880s were either idolized or vilified—but rarely studied—during the first half of the twentieth century. Since 1950 the Redeemer interlude has attracted considerable scholarly interest. Inspired by Woodward's provocative findings, historians have produced an array of detailed monographs on the period. Book-length studies of post-Reconstruction politics in Alabama, Louisiana, South Carolina, Tennessee, Texas, and Virginia have appeared, along with incisive articles on other states and biographies of such prominent Redeemers as John Brown Gordon, David McKendree Key, John Henninger Reagan, and Zebulon Baird Vance.[10] This abundant new information should make possible a reassessment of the revisionist argument. Were the Democratic leaders in fact townsmen instead of farmers? Did parvenus take the place of aristocrats? Were old-line Jacksonians overshadowed by erstwhile Whigs? Did the Redeemers actually abandon antebellum traditions and favor industry and

---

10. Allen J. Going's book, *Bourbon Democracy in Alabama, 1874–1890* (University, Ala., 1951), was published the same year as Woodward's *Origins of the New South*. Subsequent studies include: Alwyn Barr, *Reconstruction to Reform: Texas Politics, 1876–1906* (Austin and London, 1971); William J. Cooper Jr., *The Conservative Regime: South Carolina, 1877–1890* (Baltimore, 1968); William I. Hair, *Bourbonism and Agrarian Protest: Louisiana Politics, 1877–1900* (Baton Rouge, 1969); Roger L. Hart, *Redeemers, Bourbons, and Populists: Tennessee, 1870–1896* (Baton Rouge, 1975); Jack P. Maddex Jr., *The Virginia Conservatives, 1867–1879: A Study in Reconstruction Politics* (Chapel Hill, 1970); Allen W. Moger, *Virginia: Bourbonism to Byrd, 1870–1925* (Charlottesville, 1968); James T. Moore, *Two Paths to the New South: The Virginia Debt Controversy, 1870–1883* (Lexington, Ky., 1974); William W. Rogers, *The One-Gallused Rebellion: Agrarianism in Alabama, 1865–1896* (Baton Rouge, 1970); Judson C. Ward Jr., "The New Departure Democrats of Georgia: An Interpretation," *Georgia Historical Quarterly,* 41 (September 1957), 227–36; Edward C. Williamson, "The Constitutional Convention of 1885," *Florida Historical Quarterly,* 41 (October 1962), 116–26; David M. Abshire, *The South Rejects a Prophet: The Life of Senator D. M. Key, 1824–1900* (New York, 1967); Ben H. Procter, *Not Without Honor: The Life of John H. Reagan* (Austin, 1962); Allen P. Tankersley, *John B. Gordon: A Study in Gallantry* (Atlanta, 1955); Glenn Tucker, *Zeb Vance: Champion of Personal Freedom* (Indianapolis, Kansas City, and New York, 1965).

commerce at the expense of agriculture? The extent of change in the South's Gilded Age ruling class is obviously at issue, and this essay will attempt to gauge the strength of the contending forces of continuity and discontinuity, tradition and innovation.

As noted previously, revisionist scholars have concluded that the Redeemers were much more urban in occupation and attitude than were the prewar elite. Analysis of this claim suggests, however, that the evidence supporting it is too narrowly based to be conclusive. In 1922 Alex Mathews Arnett demonstrated that townsmen controlled the Georgia legislature and held almost all of the state's congressional seats in the 1870s and 1880s,[11] but subsequent investigations have offered only the most tenuous proof of similar developments elsewhere. Revisionist arguments on this point have by and large been founded more on untested assumptions and sweeping generalizations than on substantive research.[12]

C. Vann Woodward attempted to bolster the case for Redeemer urbanism, but his evidence was insufficient. Although Woodward cited examples of urban Democratic spokesmen throughout the region, including a number of governors and senators, he offered no systematic proof that these men were representative of the Redeemer leadership.[13] On the contrary, much of the pertinent statistical data supports the concept of a continuing and potent agricultural influence. Publishing his findings in 1926, Francis Butler Simkins noted that farmers occupied most of the seats in South Carolina's legislature in the mid-1880s (several years before the upsurge of Tillmanite "agrarianism"), and Willie D. Halsell's 1945 analysis of Mississippi's "Bourbon" regime documented the predominance of rural lawmakers in that state as well.[14] William Best Hesseltine in his 1950 survey of the post-

---

11. Arnett, *Populist Movement in Georgia*, 31–32.

12. Arnett and those influenced by his work have shown a marked tendency to assume (without additional systematic research on Redeemer urbanism) that his Georgia findings were valid for the entire South. For examples of this approach see Kendrick and Arnett, *The South Looks at Its Past*, 108–10; and Daniel M. Robison, "From Tillman to Long: Some Striking Leaders of the Rural South," *Journal of Southern History*, 3 (August 1937), 294.

13. Woodward, *Origins of the New South*, 2–22.

14. Francis B. Simkins, *The Tillman Movement in South Carolina* (Durham, 1926), 65 n. 16; Willie D. Halsell, "The Bourbon Period in Mississippi Politics, 1875–1890," *Journal of Southern History*, 11 (November 1945), 524, 528–31. In other states statistics concerning the agriculturalists' legislative representation are less clear in their implications. North Carolina's 50-member state senate, for example, contained 17 farmers and 5 part-time farmers in 1877—an agricultural bloc composing almost half the membership; see Stuart Noblin, *Leonidas LaFayette Polk: Agrarian Crusader* (Chapel Hill, 1949), 106. In Alabama farmers appear

Civil War careers of 656 former Confederate leaders—men whose activities shaped the economic and political life of the Gilded Age South— acknowledged that many of these prestigious individuals pursued new opportunities in the business world, but he also showed that the percentage of agriculturalists among them increased from 20 percent in the antebellum era to almost 30 percent after the war. The number of lawyers in the group, by contrast, actually declined, further indicating that the urban ascendancy over the countryside may have been less pronounced than historians have assumed.[15] The argument that rural interests were eclipsed should be modified.

Approaching Redeemer urbanism from another direction, it is inaccurate to argue (as revisionists typically do) that the presence of a sizable group of lawyers or businessmen in a postwar southern legislature or congressional delegation constitutes *prima facie* evidence of a sharp break with antebellum or agrarian ideals, attitudes, or even personnel. Definitive statistical evidence on this point is lacking, but some of the "urban-oriented" Redeemer leaders may have emerged from the old plantation elite and borne its impress on their personal values and intellectual heritage. A planter or his son could move to the city and begin a new career with relative ease, but abandoning the ideological trappings of a lifetime was undoubtedly more difficult. Perhaps an even larger number of the postwar Democratic leaders lived in crossroad hamlets or courthouse towns. Although they were no longer planters, these Redeemer "urbanites" depended on rural constituencies for their livelihood and political preferment and were only little more independent of agricultural interests than the antebellum leadership had been. Such circumstances offer as great, if not greater, support for notions of continuity as for change in Gilded Age political patterns. To complicate the issue still further, Ralph Ancil Wooster has demonstrated that nonfarm occupational groups, especially lawyers, were already assuming dominant governmental roles in the upper South before the Civil War and held a smaller (though sizable) number of positions in the antebellum cotton states also.[16] Develop-

---

to have dominated the state legislature during the 1870s, but lawyers had gained the ascendancy by the end of the 1880s; see Going, *Bourbon Democracy in Alabama,* 47.

15. William B. Hesseltine, *Confederate Leaders in the New South* (Baton Rouge, 1950), 19–23.

16. Ralph A. Wooster, *Politicians, Planters, and Plain Folk: Courthouse and Statehouse in the Upper South, 1850–1860* (Knoxville, 1975), 33, 63, 66, 69, 119; of particular interest is Wooster's demonstration (page 63) that 23 of the 30 governors of the upper South in the 1850s were lawyers. In the lower South farmers outnumbered lawyers in state legislatures by two-to-one in the 1850s, but many of the farmer-legislators also had interests in law or business; see

ments in the 1870s and 1880s consequently represented, to some extent at least, a continuation of long-established trends. In other words, evidence concerning Redeemers' occupations does not appear adequate in and of itself to sustain the concept of a sharp break with the prewar regime.

The revisionist case for discontinuity, of course, went beyond this occupational analysis to incorporate other arguments, notably the oft-recurring theme that the Redeemer leadership comprised too many new and unfamiliar faces to constitute a "Bourbon" restoration of the antebellum ruling class. Here Professor Woodward and his compatriots touched upon an obvious truth: no full-fledged restoration of the old elite was possible in the Gilded Age. The period of war and Radical rule, lasting as much as sixteen years in some of the states, had inevitably winnowed the ranks of the traditional elite through death, old age, and disillusionment. The passage of time created vacancies in the South's power structure, naturally enough, and the Redeemers compensated for some of these losses by elevating outsiders, parvenus, and adventurers of various stripes to public office. Democrats in Florida and Virginia elected immigrants from the North (George F. Drew and Gilbert Carlton Walker respectively) to gubernatorial terms in the 1870s, while unsettled conditions in Louisiana allowed the unscrupulous Edward A. Burke, a man of uncertain antecedents at best, a free field for his manipulations.[17] Similar accessions occurred elsewhere, weakening the aristocratic pretensions of the Democratic regimes. Even so, it is possible to carry this emphasis on the parvenu aspects of the Redeemer elite too far. Restorations of traditional ruling classes in the aftermath of wars and revolutions are rarely complete or undiluted; deaths and sociopolitical dislocations undoubtedly created opportunities for new men in the England of Charles II or the France of Louis XVIII, yet there can be no denying that restorations of a sort took place in those countries. The same is true of the Redeemer South.

In spite of the impact of the newcomers, a large number of prewar lead-

---

Ralph A. Wooster, *The People in Power: Courthouse and Statehouse in the Lower South, 1850–1860* (Knoxville, 1969), 33, 35, 40.

17. Burke, who claimed for himself the title of "Major," played a shadowy role in the famous Hayes-Tilden election compromise in 1877. He subsequently became the state treasurer of Louisiana and exerted a powerful influence over that state's political life, especially through his ties with gambling and convict-labor syndicates. He absconded to Honduras late in the 1880s, leaving his state treasury accounts in arrears by almost two million dollars. Joy J. Jackson, *New Orleans in the Gilded Age: Politics and Urban Progress, 1880–1896* (Baton Rouge, 1969), 38–39, describes Burke as a man of "humble origin."

ers successfully reasserted their influence, in many instances gaining greater power after the conflict than they had enjoyed before it. Antebellum congressman Lucius Q. C. Lamar, the author of Mississippi's ordinance of secession, won a Senate seat in the 1870s, and Tennessee's secession governor Isham Green Harris captured a Senate post during the same decade. George S. Houston, a nine-term prewar congressman from Alabama, accomplished a similar comeback. Heading the Democratic state ticket in a bitter campaign, Houston wrested the Alabama governorship from the Republicans in 1874. Wade Hampton, one of the wealthiest planters in the United States during the slavery era, dominated South Carolina politics for more than a decade after Redemption, and erstwhile Confederate postmaster general John H. Reagan achieved national prominence as a senator from Texas in the Gilded Age. Texans also manifested their loyalty to the old elite by choosing Oran Milo Roberts, the president of their state secession convention, for consecutive gubernatorial terms in 1878 and 1880. Further exemplifying this trend, former Confederate vice president Alexander Hamilton Stephens gradually rebuilt his political fortunes and won elections to the United States House of Representatives and the Georgia governorship before his death in 1883. North Carolina's Confederate governor, Zebulon B. Vance, captured a Senate seat in 1879, moreover, and Georgia's controversial wartime executive, Joseph Emerson Brown, did the same in 1880. The continuing influence of these men, and of many others like them, did not constitute anything approaching a complete restoration of the old order, but it did set a tone which lent credence to the concept of a "Bourbon" triumph in the post-Reconstruction era.[18] Once again, the case for continuity with the antebellum period is perhaps as strong as that for change.

The revisionists' stress on the emergence of new men in the Redeemer leadership appears at first glance to contradict another, more vital tenet of their interpretation—their emphasis on the continuing importance of Old Whigs in the southern Democratic regimes of the 1870s and 1880s. The

---

18. Hesseltine, *Confederate Leaders,* 16, 23, 95–96, provides the most graphic evidence of this restorationist trend. On page 16 he notes that of 656 prominent ex-Confederate leaders who survived an appreciable length of time after the war, "only 71 failed to recover a substantial portion of the position and prestige they had enjoyed at the Confederacy's peak." The ex-Confederates' political standing in the immediate post-Reconstruction era was particularly striking. On page 23 he points out that during the heyday of Redemption (1875–1885) some 128 of the ex-Confederate leaders held office as state officials. On page 95 he observes that, of the 585 top civilian and military leaders of the Confederacy who survived the war, 418 held public office at some time during the postwar years.

Whigs had been a vigorous political force in the antebellum South, battling the Democrats on relatively even terms for a generation before the Civil War. The presence of many erstwhile Whigs in the Gilded-Age Democratic ranks (their own party having collapsed in the 1850s) would seem, therefore, to provide yet another link between antebellum and postbellum days, another evidence of continuity with the past. Accentuating change, however, Woodward and like-minded scholars have contended that former Whigs not only survived into the New South era but actually achieved a dominant role in the politics of the period—successfully imposing their nationalistic, capitalistic views on their old-line Democratic rivals. This dramatic upsurge of Whigs and Whiggery, according to the Woodward appraisal, thus further differentiated the New South from the Old.

This "Old Whig" thesis, like other aspects of the revisionist interpretation, is not altogether convincing. The impact of Whig views on Redeemer economic policies will be considered later, but at this point some assessment of the extent to which former Whigs were overrepresented in the councils of the post-Reconstruction Democracy is essential. Did Old Whigs actually receive a disproportionate share of the offices in the 1870s and 1880s? Again, few statistics are available, and conclusions involving prewar political affiliations of Redeemers must necessarily be tentative. Still, some criticisms of the revisionist appraisal are in order. For one thing, this "Old Whig" approach can be almost completely discounted with reference to Texas and South Carolina. Whigs had exerted relatively little influence in either of those states during the prewar years, and the same was true in the post-Reconstruction era.[19] The states that Woodward and others cite most often to illustrate the Whiggish character of the Redeemers—notably North Carolina and Tennessee—had been bastions of Whig strength before the war.[20] The election of many former Whigs in those states after Redemption

---

19. Barr, *Reconstruction to Reform*, 22; Cooper, *Conservative Regime*, 17, 133 n. 68. John V. Mering in "Persistent Whiggery in the Confederate South: A Reconsideration," *South Atlantic Quarterly*, 69 (Winter 1970), 127, offers a more striking criticism of Woodward's "Old Whig" thesis. Mering notes that of thirty-one prominent Redeemer politicians whom Woodward delineates to exemplify the Whig takeover of the post-Reconstruction Democracy in his *Reunion and Reaction: The Compromise of 1877 and the End of Reconstruction* (Boston, 1951), nine had actually been Democrats in the antebellum years.

20. The Whig party in Tennessee and North Carolina had been devastated by the sectional upheavals of the 1850s, but prior to that decade the party had exerted a potent influence in both states. Between 1835 and 1853, for example, Whigs controlled the Tennessee governorship for twelve of the eighteen years. In North Carolina Whigs monopolized the governorship from 1836 to 1850. For Woodward's emphasis on rejuvenated Whiggery in North Carolina and Tennessee see *Origins of the New South*, 1–4.

is neither surprising nor conclusive proof that the remaining advocates of Whiggery exerted a disproportionate influence.

The notion of an aggressive, unrelenting, and uncompromising Whig takeover is also undermined by the rapid subsidence of traditional Whig-Democrat antagonisms after Reconstruction. Although Woodward described the Redeemer coalition as a *"mésalliance"* of natural enemies, a Whiggish hegemony where old-line Jacksonians could find no place,[21] the evidence suggests that cooperation between the groups was more typical than conflict. Only in Tennessee did persisting antebellum party feuds seriously disrupt a Redeemer government, exacerbating disagreements over state finances at the start of the 1880s. And the outcome of this struggle appears to contradict the "Old Whig" thesis: Isham Harris's traditionalist Democrats soon gained the upper hand in the state, further impeding the Whig resurgence.[22] Elsewhere, by contrast, a spirit of compromise, a willingness to subordinate old quarrels to new realities, generally prevailed, and the Redeemers' (Old Whigs and Democrats alike) were willing to continue the Reconstruction-born practice of referring to themselves as "Conservatives"—thus deemphasizing their prewar party allegiances and stressing instead their common opposition to the so-called radical Republicans.[23]

Pragmatic politics, to be sure, played a role in this reconciliation, but other more fundamental forces were at work, in particular the inexorable passage of time. More than twenty-five years separated the Redeemer period from the classic Whig-Democrat confrontations of the 1830s and 1840s, and the old antagonisms had lost much of their fervor. The rise of a new generation of southerners too young to have participated in the antebellum party battles helped to dilute the old rivalries. Professor Jack Pendleton Maddex Jr.'s 1970 study of the Virginia Redeemers analyzes prewar political affiliations of members of the Conservative Party Executive Committee and indicates that the influence of the Old Whigs and Democrats was roughly equal through the early 1870s. By 1873, however, the thirty-one-man group included some fourteen members with no discernible antebellum party ties at all—a circumstance Maddex attributes to the increasing influence of the younger generation in Virginia politics.[24] Studies of other states are necessary to determine whether similar developments occurred else-

---

21. *Ibid.*, 2, 77.

22. Hart, *Redeemers, Bourbons, and Populists,* 37, 46, 55, 58.

23. Woodward, *Origins of the New South,* 2–3, notes the popularity of the "Conservative" party label in the Redeemer South.

24. Maddex, *Virginia Conservatives,* 284–87.

where, but there is little reason to doubt that such was the case. This trend further undermines the "Old Whig" thesis.

Professor Woodward's revisionist interpretation of Redeemer origins is itself in need of revision. City dwellers, parvenus, and persistent Whigs undoubtedly participated in Democratic politics in the 1870s and 1880s, but there is little evidence that they were numerically dominant in the party councils. Indeed, historical scholarship for the past three decades strongly supports the opposite conclusion. Recent state studies for the most part suggest that traditionalist, agriculturally oriented elites grasped the New South as firmly as they had the Old. William James Cooper provided the most forceful statement of this viewpoint in his analysis of Wade Hampton's South Carolina, but support for it can be found in other works as well. Allen Johnston Going and William Warren Rogers stressed the influence of black-belt planters in Redeemer Alabama, and Roger L. Hart wrote about the return to power of a similar group in Tennessee at the start of the 1880s. C. Alwyn Barr Jr. emphasized the preeminence of cotton farmers, cattlemen, and other rural interests in post-Reconstruction Texas. William Ivy Hair and Edward Charles Williamson noted the continuing power of old-line "Bourbons" in Louisiana and Florida respectively, and Willie D. Halsell documented the influence of agricultural representatives in Mississippi's Redeemer government, especially in the state legislature.[25] Jack P. Maddex Jr. broke with the prevailing trend by accentuating the capitalistic, entrepreneurial character of Virginia's ruling elite in the 1870s. But Allen Wesley Moger argued instead that antebellum attitudes and values permeated the Old Dominion's Conservative regime.[26]

These developments were paralleled in the other states. Indeed, only in the case of Georgia has the revisionist interpretation been fully sustained. In that state, according to Judson Clements Ward Jr., the corporate interests set the political tone and controlled the operations of the Democratic ma-

---

25. For evidence of this concern with traditionalist and agrarian elements in the Redeemer hierarchy see Cooper, *Conservative Regime,* 17, 39, 139, and *passim;* Going, *Bourbon Democracy in Alabama,* 44, 92, 110; Rogers, *One-Gallused Rebellion,* viii, 46; Hart, *Redeemers, Bourbons, and Populists,* xv, 55–57, 84, 228; Barr, *Reconstruction to Reform,* 9, 13, 22, 52; Hair, *Bourbonism and Agrarian Protest,* 21, 24, 30, 226; Williamson, "Constitutional Convention of 1885," 117; Edward C. Williamson, "Independentism: A Challenge to the Florida Democracy of 1884," *Florida Historical Quarterly,* 27 (October 1948), 131; Halsell, "Bourbon Period in Mississippi Politics," 528–30.

26. Maddex, *Virginia Conservatives,* xii, 33, 121, 164–65, 276–79; Moger, *Bourbonism to Byrd,* 4, 24–25, 44–45. See also Moore, *Two Paths to the New South,* 27–44, for additional criticisms of Maddex's assessment.

chine.[27] Elsewhere in the Redeemer South, by contrast, Whiggish innovators apparently continued to function as subordinate elements or junior partners—just as they had before the Civil War. Such findings necessarily point to the need for a reassessment of other aspects of the revisionist interpretation. If traditionalist groups dominated most of the post-Reconstruction Democratic regimes, it seems unlikely that those governments actually adopted the one-sidedly pro-urban and pro-industrialist approach to the region's problems that Woodward describes. A new appraisal of Redeemer economic policies is, therefore, essential to a more accurate reinterpretation of the period.

Revisionist historians have devoted considerable attention to Redeemer economic programs, and, as noted previously, their findings have done little to enhance the image of the South's Democratic regimes. Exposés of pro-business bias fill their pages, and the evidence they advance to support their accusations is impressive. Seeking to attract capital investments, five of the post-Reconstruction state governments granted tax exemptions to new manufacturing enterprises.[28] Legislatures and state constitutional conventions granted monopolies to such companies as the infamous Louisiana State Lottery, and the convict-lease system provided cheap labor for ambitious entrepreneurs, especially for owners of railroads, mines, and lumber camps. Railroads, in particular, became prime beneficiaries of Redeemer largesse. Democratic regimes in North Carolina and Virginia sold state-owned railroad properties to private interests at bargain prices, and the governments of Texas and Florida encouraged the construction of new lines with massive grants of governmental land.[29] Further exploiting this Redeemer

---

27. Ward, "New Departure Democrats of Georgia," 228, 231–33.

28. Arkansas, Florida, Louisiana, Mississippi, and South Carolina granted tax exemptions to manufacturers during the 1870s and 1880s. See Hair, *Bourbonism and Agrarian Protest,* 101; Cooper, *Conservative Regime,* 120; Dunbar Rowland, *History of Mississippi: The Heart of the South* (2 vols., Chicago and Jackson, 1925), II, 224; David Y. Thomas, ed., *Arkansas and Its People: A History, 1541–1930* (4 vols., New York, 1930), I, 166; Woodward, *Origins of the New South,* 60.

29. The best source on the Louisiana State Lottery is Berthold C. Alwes, "The History of the Louisiana State Lottery Company," *Louisiana Historical Quarterly,* 27 (October 1944), 964–1118. Business exploitation of convict labor is noted in Green, "Convict Lease System," 112–23; Maddex, *Virginia Conservatives,* 225–27; and Mark T. Carleton, *Politics and Punishment: The History of the Louisiana State Penal System* (Baton Rouge, 1971), *passim.* For evidence of state aid to railroads see Moger, *Bourbonism to Byrd,* 13–18; Hugh T. Lefler, *History of North Carolina* (4 vols., New York, 1956), II, 668; Barr, *Reconstruction to Reform,* 77, 111; and Charlton W. Tebeau, *A History of Florida* (Coral Gables, Fla., 1971), 281–82.

generosity, speculators purchased millions of additional acres of timber and mineral lands from state and federal governments at extremely low prices.[30] Such developments, according to the revisionists, constituted nothing less than a southern-style "great barbecue," a wholesale plundering of the region's resources by avaricious capitalists.

This indictment of Redeemer economic policies is damning in tone and, for the most part, convincing in its main thrust. The Democratic regimes undoubtedly made numerous errors in their quest for economic growth. They squandered resources with little or no thought for the future and frequently confused private greed with public good. Even so, the revisionist argument is misleading in several significant respects. For one thing, the Woodward school employs this evidence of probusiness activity to support the concept of a radical break between New South and antebellum attitudes toward economic growth—a highly questionable assumption. Working essentially within the interpretive framework established by Charles A. Beard, the revisionists view the Redeemer program as marking the ascendancy of industry over agriculture in the region, the collapse of pre–Civil War agrarianism before the onslaughts of triumphant capitalism.

Analysis of the South's financial history suggests instead that the break with antebellum values and policies was much less extensive than this approach implies. Land speculation was certainly no stranger to a region that had known the Yazoo frauds of the 1790s and the "flush times" of the burgeoning cotton kingdom, and southern states had made their initial railroad land grants during the prewar period. The Old South's state governments were not reticent about expending public funds to encourage the establishment of banks and the construction of turnpikes, canals, and railroads. Indeed, by 1860 the slave states had amassed debts of more than a hundred million dollars by supporting such projects. These activities established precedents that were followed on an even grander scale during Reconstruction; the conservative "Johnson" regimes and their Radical Republican successors funneled still more funds into internal improvements, boosting the region's public indebtedness to roughly a quarter of a billion dollars and creating bonanzas for unscrupulous financial manipulators.[31]

---

30. Paul W. Gates, "Federal Land Policy in the South, 1866–1888," *Journal of Southern History*, 6 (August 1940), 313–25; Williamson, "Independentism in Florida," 132–33; Robert L. Brandfon, *Cotton Kingdom of the New South: A History of the Yazoo Mississippi Delta from Reconstruction to the Twentieth Century* (Cambridge, Mass., 1967), 51, 61–62.

31. Benjamin U. Ratchford, *American State Debts* (Durham, 1941), 73–134, 162–83, surveys the growth of antebellum and Reconstruction debts in the southern states.

Viewed from the perspective of earlier activities, therefore, the Redeemers' aid to business was not a radical departure. In some respects, in fact, the Gilded Age Democrats were less generous toward the corporate interests than the antebellum or Reconstruction leaders had been. Direct state investments in business enterprises practically ceased after Redemption. Shocked by the extravagance of the Radical regimes, Democratic state constitutional conventions in the 1870s and 1880s uniformly banned future bond issues or public expenditures for internal improvements.[32] The Redeemers re-enforced this trend by taking an even more drastic step: they repudiated more than half of the South's inflated governmental debt burden. All the states of the former Confederacy except Texas and Mississippi scaled down their debts during the period, alienating European and northern investors for decades to come and closing the door still further against additional bond issues.[33] Instead, the Redeemers' help to business primarily took the form of the aforementioned land grants and tax incentives—methods which paled in comparison with the freewheeling cash outlays of previous years. The post-Reconstruction elite held a "barbecue" of sorts for the corporate interests, to be sure, but the fare was relatively meager and the hosts more frugal than in the past.

In addition to exaggerating the innovative character of the Redeemer program, the dominant Woodward interpretation of New South economic policies suffers from another significant defect: the revisionists' stress on Democratic favoritism toward business led them for the most part to neglect Redeemer attempts to exact concessions from the corporate interests, to tap their financial resources for the public benefit. The post-Reconstruction politicians' efforts along these lines are evident in their revenue policies. Railroad magnates and other businessmen made handsome profits from the convict-lease system, as noted previously, but they also had to pay hundreds of thousands of dollars into southern state treasuries each year in return for the privilege.[34] Louisiana derived forty thousand dollars annually from lottery interests in compensation for gambling rights, and South Carolina

---

32. Ward, "New Departure Democrats of Georgia," 231; Going, *Bourbon Democracy in Alabama*, 24; Hart, *Redeemers, Bourbons, and Populists*, 7–8; Williamson, "Constitutional Convention of 1885," 122; Thomas, ed., *Arkansas*, I, 162; T. R. Fehrenbach, *Lone Star: A History of Texas and the Texans* (New York, 1968), 435–36.

33. Ratchford, *American State Debts*, 183–229.

34. Green, "Convict Lease System," 117; Carleton, *Politics and Punishment*, 42; Going, *Bourbon Democracy in Alabama*, 86; Rowland, *History of Mississippi*, II, 236; Lawrence D. Rice, *The Negro in Texas, 1874–1900* (Baton Rouge, 1971), 245–46.

reaped even greater profits from its abundant phosphate beds. Allowing private contractors to mine the rich deposits, the state siphoned off mineral royalties which amounted to over $250,000 a year by 1890.[35] Public-land sales, even at bargain prices, provided another source of funds for the Democratic regimes. Florida's Redeemer administration obtained a million dollars from one such sale during the 1880s, while Texas officials employed half the state's land receipts to support the public school system.[36]

Revenues from these sources, however trifling by modern standards, constituted major windfalls at a time when a typical southern state's budget ranged from one to two million dollars a year. Carrying this approach still further, the Democratic leaders also demonstrated a willingness to exact license fees, sales taxes, and property taxes from the business community. Although liberal in their treatment of new factories and the railroads (many of which continued to enjoy tax exemptions under their original antebellum charters), the Redeemers showed much less consideration for the mercantile and professional classes. Southern legislatures imposed a bewildering variety of levies on storekeepers, insurance agents, traveling salesmen, liquor dealers, expressmen, money lenders, and other urban occupational groups.[37] The enactment of such measures suggests a significant conclusion: the Redeemers were less subservient to business than has generally been assumed. They granted important concessions, but they expected those interests to pay part of the cost of providing public services.

The Democrats' pragmatic attitude toward businessmen was also expressed in their penchant for retracting privileges they had previously bestowed. The opportunism of South Carolina politicians in this respect is particularly notable. After witnessing the rapid expansion of the state's textile industry at the start of the 1880s, the Redeemers in 1885 repealed the tax exemption for new factories. Tax incentives in South Carolina rapidly gave way to tax levies.[38] Southern Democrats also retreated from favoritism toward the railroads, especially after many of the lines fell under the control of Wall Street financiers during the depression of the 1870s. This northern

---

35. Alwes, "History of Louisiana State Lottery Company," 1001; Cooper, *Conservative Regime*, 125.

36. Tebeau, *History of Florida*, 278; Barr, *Reconstruction to Reform*, 77, 80.

37. In Virginia these levies boosted business tax revenues from 15.99 percent of state tax receipts to 36.75 percent of the total during the 1870s; see Maddex, *Virginia Conservatives*, 147, 171. See also Thomas, ed., *Arkansas*, I, 206; Going, *Bourbon Democracy in Alabama*, 86, 112; and Rogers, *One-Gallused Rebellion*, 92.

38. Cooper, *Conservative Regime*, 120–21.

takeover reignited old sectional antagonisms, and antirailroad sentiment surged through the former Confederacy. Responding to this unrest, Redeemer legislatures passed laws requiring the rail corporations to maintain adequate depots, to fence their rights-of-way, and to compensate farmers for livestock killed by trains.[39] Democratic regimes in Arkansas and Florida manifested the new hostility by defeating the rail lines in the courtroom, enabling them to raise the tax assessments on railroad property early in the 1880s—in the Florida case abolishing tax exemptions granted in 1855.[40] Most important of all, the Redeemers joined with western politicians in pioneering the practice of governmental railroad regulation. Between 1877 and 1891 all the states of the former Confederacy except Arkansas and Louisiana established regulatory commissions of one sort or another. Significant rate cuts ensued, even though the commissions were frequently hampered by corporate intransigence and judicial conservatism.[41] Not satisfied with these efforts, the region's Democrats played prominent roles in the struggle for federal railroad regulation as well. Texas senator John H. Reagan led the fight to establish the Interstate Commerce Commission, and Alabama Redeemer Walter Lawrence Bragg, another champion of the regulatory cause, served as one of the original members of the new agency.[42]

Paralleling these developments, moreover, Democratic attitudes toward the public lands underwent a similar transformation. Eager for economic growth, southerners had generally favored liberal land policies at the start of the Redeemer era. Northern lumber interests had bought timber tracts in the South in order to forestall potential competition, and other capitalists had purchased large acreages for purely speculative purposes, making no immediate effort to promote the region's prosperity. Misgivings arose about the land boom, and in 1888 southern congressmen led a successful movement to suspend cash sales of federal land, a maneuver that paved the way for reorganization of the entire public-land system along conservationist

---

39. Moger, *Bourbonism to Byrd,* 56; Going, *Bourbon Democracy in Alabama,* 132–35; Rowland, *History of Mississippi,* II, 229; Barr, *Reconstruction to Reform,* 113–21.

40. Thomas, ed., *Arkansas,* I, 193–94; Tebeau, *History of Florida,* 277.

41. Arthur S. Link, "The Progressive Movement in the South, 1870–1914," *North Carolina Historical Review,* 23 (April 1946), 183–88, provides a good survey of southern efforts at railroad regulation. For insight into the achievements and problems of one of these state railroad commissions, Alabama's in this case, see James F. Doster, *Railroads in Alabama Politics, 1875–1914* (University, Ala., 1957), 9–36.

42. Procter, *Not Without Honor,* 217, 231, 239, 258–60, 270; Going, *Bourbon Democracy in Alabama,* 137–39.

lines.[43] Two Redeemers in Grover Cleveland's cabinet also worked to improve the management of natural resources. Secretary of the Interior Lucius Q. C. Lamar of Mississippi and Attorney General Augustus Hill Garland of Arkansas took action against illegal encroachments on the federal domain, and together they expelled speculators, ranchers, and railroads from an estimated 45,000,000 acres in the South and West.[44] In land policies as well as railroad regulations, therefore, southern Democrats manifested an increasingly sophisticated attitude toward Gilded Age capitalism. Skepticism gradually supplanted gullibility; restrictions accompanied and sometimes overshadowed concessions.

Abounding in such ambiguities, the Redeemer economic program offered uncertain and tenuous encouragement for the entrepreneurial classes. Indeed, a case can be made that the Democratic elite provided more consistent and reliable support for farmers than for businessmen. Gathering most of their electoral strength from the countryside, Redeemer politicians generally reflected agrarian biases on such issues as debt scaling and railroad regulation, and their tax policies followed a similar pattern. As noted previously, they veered from one direction to another in their revenue demands on business. But they pursued a much more uniform and straightforward course with reference to property taxes—the exactions which fell most heavily on rural areas. Appalled by the high property levies of the Reconstruction years, Democratic leaders moved in the 1870s and 1880s to prevent the recurrence of such abuses. They wrote strict limits on property taxes into their state constitutions, severely curtailing the revenue-gathering authority of local as well as state governments.[45] Southern legislatures accelerated this trend with numerous tax cuts, and the results were impressive. Mississippi set the pace for the entire region by slashing its state property levy from 14 mills in 1874 to 2.5 mills in 1882, a reduction of more than 80 percent. Alabama's less drastic adjustment from 7.5 mills in 1874 to 4 mills in 1889 was more typical, but substantial reductions occurred in state after state.[46]

---

43. Gates, "Federal Land Policy," 327–30.

44. Wirt A. Cate, *Lucius Q. C. Lamar: Secession and Reunion* (Chapel Hill, 1935), 427, 444–48, 457; see also Carl V. Harris, "Right Fork or Left Fork? The Section-Party Alignment of Southern Democrats in Congress, 1873–1897," *Journal of Southern History*, 42 (November 1976), 499–501 (87–89 in this volume).

45. Hair, *Bourbonism and Agrarian Protest*, 100–101; Thomas, ed., *Arkansas*, I, 162; Fehrenbach, *Lone Star*, 435; Going, *Bourbon Democracy in Alabama*, 24.

46. Rowland, *History of Mississippi*, II, 213, 224; Going, *Bourbon Democracy in Alabama*, 83, 86. Thomas, ed., *Arkansas*, I, 198–99, indicates that by 1885 Arkansas's state prop-

These cuts, together with the South's traditionally low assessments of property values, offered massive tax savings for the agricultural population. The impact of these reforms was readily apparent, for millions of acres which had been forfeited for delinquent taxes during Reconstruction were reclaimed by farmers in the Redeemer era.[47]

Applying political pressure through the Grange and Alliance, the rural interests derived many additional benefits from the Democratic regimes. Agricultural and mechanical colleges received increased funding, and the Redeemer established new land-grant schools in the Carolinas, Mississippi, and Virginia.[48] Government-supported agricultural experiment stations proliferated as well. North Carolina pioneered the development of experimental farms in the 1870s, setting a pattern that the rest of the South followed during the next decade.[49] Democratic legislatures provided another recognition of the farmers' importance by creating state departments of agriculture. Although hampered by inadequate budgets, these new agencies became increasingly innovative and efficient. By the 1880s state agriculture departments were inspecting commercial fertilizers, analyzing soil samples, conducting geological surveys, encouraging immigration, providing veterinary services, dispatching speakers to farm meetings, and collecting statistics on crop yields.[50] In Alabama the Department of Agriculture eventually

---

erty levy amounted to only 4 mills, half of which was earmarked for support of the public schools. In Florida the millage was reduced from 12.5 in 1877 to 4 in 1884; see Tebeau, *History of Florida,* 276–77. North Carolinians demonstrated their attitude toward the property tax in 1881. Receiving $600,000 from the sale of state-owned railroad properties, the North Carolina legislature used the money for current state expenses and abolished the property tax for that year; see Lefler, *History of North Carolina,* II, 648. Georgia, the state which most closely conformed to the Woodward model of Redeemer behavior, broke from the prevailing pattern by raising its property tax millage from 2.5 in 1883 to 4 in 1890 and 6.2 in 1898, as noted in Arnett, *Populist Movement in Georgia,* 73.

47. C. Vann Woodward, in one of his few positive comments on Redeemer policies, acknowledged this trend in *Origins of the New South,* 59–60.

48. For evidence of Redeemer support for agricultural education see Cooper, *Conservative Regime,* 166; Maddex, *Virginia Conservatives,* 214–15; Rowland, *History of Mississippi,* II, 213; Going, *Bourbon Democracy in Alabama,* 165–67; Lefler, *History of North Carolina,* II, 655; Theodore Saloutos, *Farmer Movements in the South, 1865–1933* (Berkeley, 1960), 41.

49. Samuel A. Ashe, *History of North Carolina* (2 vols., Raleigh, N.C., 1925), II, 1182; Moger, *Bourbonism to Byrd,* 85; Wallace, *History of South Carolina,* III, 340; Going, *Bourbon Democracy in Alabama,* 166–67.

50. These activities are noted in Sheldon, *Populism in the Old Dominion,* 62; Cooper, *Conservative Regime,* 122–23, 139–40; Ward, "New Departure Democrats of Georgia," 232; Rogers, *One-Gallused Rebellion,* 110–11, 120; Going, *Bourbon Democracy in Alabama,* 104–5; Noblin, *Polk,* 106–12; and Tebeau, *History of Florida,* 292.

became the second most powerful agency in the state, enjoying an influence exceeded only by that of the governor.[51]

Southern Democrats also demonstrated their support for farmers by sponsoring agricultural societies. Legislatures appropriated thousands of dollars each year to subsidize these groups (primarily to enable them to hold state fairs).[52] Further belying the notion of the Redeemers' indifference to rural needs, the region's legislators passed hundreds of laws regarding the crop-lien system, the maintenance of fences and roads, and the conservation of fish and wildlife—all issues of concern to farm areas.[53] These activities reflected an essential fact: the agriculturalists still constituted the most important interest group in the South, and they received due consideration from the Democratic elite.

The Redeemers' favoritism toward farmers also influenced developments at the national level, undermining another facet of the revisionist interpretation. According to Professor Woodward, investment-hungry southern congressmen generally subordinated the needs of their section and its people to the demands of the capitalistic, conservative Northeast. If this in fact was the case, the Democratic leaders manifested their subservience in an extremely curious way—by opposing the northern business interests on almost all the great economic issues of the Gilded Age. Southern crusades for federal railroad regulation and the conservation of the public domain have been noted previously, but the Redeemers assumed anticorporate stands in other national controversies as well. The great majority of the region's political leaders denounced protective tariffs and for decades battled to reinstitute the low duties of the antebellum years. Gaining particular prominence in these struggles, newspaper editor Henry Watterson of Kentucky, together with Senator Lamar of Mississippi, formulated the famous "tariff for revenue only" pledge in the 1880 Democratic platform, and House Ways and Means chairman Roger Quarles Mills of Texas led the unsuccessful congressional fight for tariff reform in 1888.[54]

---

51. Rogers, *One-Gallused Rebellion,* 110.

52. Cooper, *Conservative Regime,* 140–41; Going, *Bourbon Democracy in Alabama,* 105.

53. For evidence of such legislation see Maddex, *Virginia Conservatives,* 176–78; Noblin, *Polk,* 112–14; Rogers, *One-Gallused Rebellion,* 15–20; Wallace, *History of South Carolina,* III, 328; Cooper, *Conservative Regime,* 136–39; Going, *Bourbon Democracy in Alabama,* 97–99; and Barr, *Reconstruction to Reform,* 81–82.

54. Isaac F. Marcosson, *"Marse Henry": A Biography of Henry Watterson* (New York, 1951), 139–40; Barr, *Reconstruction to Reform,* 105. See also Procter, *Not Without Honor,* 270–71; May S. Ringold, "Senator James Zachariah George of Mississippi: Bourbon or Lib-

Other aspects of the federal revenue system sparked additional Redeemer criticisms during the 1870s and 1880s. Although they clamored for the repeal of the punitive, war-inspired excises on whiskey and tobacco, most southern Democrats favored the reimposition of the federal income tax, a levy which would fall most heavily on the capitalists of the North.[55] The Redeemers displayed a similar bias in their approach to the perennially troublesome "money question." Responding to the appeals of the debt-laden agricultural and commercial classes, the South's political leaders (with a relative handful of exceptions) consistently endorsed proposals for an expanded currency supply. Two-thirds of the Redeemer congressmen flirted with the Greenback movement by voting for the controversial "Inflation Bill" in 1874, and Democratic state conventions throughout the former Confederacy endorsed the paper-money craze later in the decade. Silver coinage received even greater support. The region's Democratic senators and representatives joined with western lawmakers to pass the Bland-Allison Act in 1878 and the Sherman Silver Purchase Act in 1890. Alienated by Grover Cleveland's insistence on the gold standard, southern politicians carried their inflation campaign still further; they aligned themselves with the silverite West to back William Jennings Bryan's abortive presidential bid in 1896.[56]

The Redeemers' commitment to an increased money supply also led them to criticize the restrictive policies of the national banking system. They opposed the rechartering of many of the national banks in the 1880s, and they urged the repeal of the federal government's prohibitive tax on state bank notes.[57] Far from endorsing the Hamiltonian financial structure that had emerged during the Civil War, as revisionist historians have maintained, the southern Democrats were instead among the more persistent critics of that structure. Only with reference to federal aid to internal improvements did

---

eral?" *Journal of Mississippi History,* 16 (July 1954), 170; Cate, *Lamar,* 395–96; and Harris, "Right Fork or Left Fork?" 488–89 (76–77 in this volume).

55. Harris, "Right Fork or Left Fork?" 489–93 (77–80 in this volume).

56. *Ibid.,* 478–86 (66–75 in this volume), analyzes southern congressional support for inflation. The "hard money" anti-inflation cause attracted support from such prominent Redeemers as Wade Hampton, Lucius Q. C. Lamar, and Benjamin H. Hill, but they failed to rally the bulk of the Redeemer leadership to their side. See Cate, *Lamar,* 309–10; Halsell, "Bourbon Period in Mississippi Politics," 526; and Manly W. Wellman, *Giant in Gray: A Biography of Wade Hampton of South Carolina* (New York and London, 1949), 309.

57. Harris, "Right Fork or Left Fork?" 486–88 (75 in this volume). See also James W. Garner, "Senatorial Career of Gen. J. Z. George," Mississippi Historical Society, *Publications,* 7 (1903), 254, 257.

they find themselves in harmony with the prevailing system. Having witnessed the destruction of their ports, railroads, and levees by federal power during the war years, southerners requested federal money for rebuilding them. Even on this issue, surprisingly enough, the Redeemers' stand placed them in opposition to northern sentiment. Northeastern congressmen—Democrats and Republicans alike—had turned against government-financed internal improvements after the scandals of the Grant era, and the southerners were only able to vote the funds for their projects with the help of the West.[58] On issue after issue, therefore, the Redeemers took sides against, not with, the masters of capital.

These national developments, together with similar trends at the state level, clearly point up inadequacies in the revisionist interpretation of Redeemer origins and views. Parvenus, urbanites, and persistent Whigs made their way into the Democratic leadership during the post–Civil War years, as Woodward and others have argued, but these potentially innovative groups proved either unable or unwilling to alter the entrenched patterns of southern government. Traditionalist forces enjoyed too much strength in both the electorate and the party hierarchy to permit any wholesale departure from established practices and policies. As a result the southern Democrats neither abandoned the farmers nor embraced Whiggery in the aftermath of Reconstruction. Indeed, their economic programs were more congruent with the ideals of Jefferson, Jackson, or even Calhoun than with those of Clay or Webster. Although they promoted limited industrial growth, the Redeemers continued to acknowledge and reward the primacy of agriculture in their region's life. Although they accepted the defeat of secession and the collapse of the slave system, most of them also continued to regard the capitalistic North with a deep-seated antagonism. Recognizing political realities (in particular the need to win the electoral votes of New York and other key states), southern Democrats cast their presidential ballots for northeastern candidates such as Samuel Jones Tilden and Grover Cleveland in the 1870s and 1880s—just as they had voted for northerners Franklin Pierce and James Buchanan before the war. In the decisive economic clashes of the Gilded Age, however, the Redeemer South consistently joined forces with the other great agricultural section of the United States, the West. Such facts lend further support to the notion of continuity between the Old and New Souths. All things had not changed with Appomattox, much less with the Compromise of 1877.

---

58. Harris, "Right Fork or Left Fork?" 495–99 (83–86 in this volume).

The Historical Context for "Redeemers Reconsidered"

The lot of most academic historians is a far from distinguished one. Laboring for decades in relative obscurity, they achieve (at best) a local or narrowly specialized reputation—manifested primarily in footnote references to their work by a handful of other, like-minded drudges. In death, these run-of-the-mill scholars are apt (unlike the fabled "old times" in the lyrics of "Dixie") to be soon forgotten, their books and articles either ignored or relegated to the "see also" portions of reading lists and bibliographical essays for a short while before vanishing from sight, and mind, for eternity.

Such was not the fate of C. Vann Woodward. Instead, as the author of four pathbreaking studies (all of which appeared within the remarkably brief span of seventeen years), he quickly vaulted into the front rank of the profession. *Tom Watson, Agrarian Rebel* (1938) sparked a reassessment of the role and significance of southern Populism that has continued to this day; *Reunion and Reaction* (1951) provided a radically new perspective on the Compromise of 1877; *Origins of the New South, 1877–1913* (1951) rapidly gained recognition as a classic work of historical iconoclasm, shattering an array of long-prevalent stereotypes concerning the Redeemer Democratic hegemony of the post-Reconstruction era. And, last but by no means least, *The Strange Career of Jim Crow* (1955) achieved popular as well as academic acclaim for its timely, succinct, and incisive account of the beginnings of racial segregation. Not surprisingly, prestigious academic appointments and leadership roles in professional organizations accompanied these successes, and additional honors accumulated during the long, less productive remainder of Woodward's career. In the decade before his death he was, according to one authority, the "undisputed dean of the country's historians."[1] Renown, not obscurity, thus characterized his professional endeavors from start to finish—an enviable record indeed!

There was, however, one arguably less desirable feature of this much-deserved eminence. Woodward's boldly venturesome interpretations soon became lightning rods for controversy, and as the years passed, criticisms (and critics) proliferated on a number of fronts. During the 1950s so-called consensus historians, most notably Richard Hofstadter, offered analyses of the Populist movement that differed in significant ways from the reformist vision enunciated in *Tom Watson*.[2] By the end of the 1960s, *Strange Career,* too, had come under attack (at least inferentially) in the works of Leon Litwack and Joel Williamson, with Howard N. Rabinowitz joining the revisionist hue and cry during the 1970s.[3] The latter decade witnessed other assaults on Woodward's arguments as well. Allan Peskin challenged the central premises of *Reunion and Reaction* in a 1973 article, and Carl V. Harris's "Right Fork or Left Fork? The Section-Party Alignments of Southern Democrats in Congress, 1873–1897," first published in 1976 and reprinted in the present volume, mustered column after column of statistics about

---

1. John Herbert Roper offered this assessment in the introduction to his edited volume, *C. Vann Woodward: A Southern Historian and His Critics* (Athens, Ga., 1997), 1. The full citations for Woodward's various books are *Tom Watson, Agrarian Rebel* (New York, 1938); *Reunion and Reaction: The Compromise of 1877 and the End of Reconstruction* (Boston, 1951); *Origins of the New South, 1877–1913* (Baton Rouge, 1951); and *The Strange Career of Jim Crow* (New York, 1955).

2. Richard Hofstadter, *The Age of Reform: From Bryan to F.D.R.* (New York, 1955), 23–130.

3. Leon F. Litwack, *North of Slavery: The Negro in the Free States, 1790–1860* (Chicago, 1961); Joel Williamson, *After Slavery: The Negro in South Carolina during Reconstruction, 1861–1877* (Chapel Hill, 1965); Howard N. Rabinowitz, *Race Relations in the Urban South, 1865–1890* (New York, 1978).

congressional voting patterns to refute *Origins*'s contention that the Redeemer Democrats had been obsequiously subservient to the demands of the industrialized Northeast.[4] Meanwhile, Jonathan M. Wiener and Dwight B. Billings were crafting book-length studies—which appeared in 1978 and 1979, respectively—that contradicted *Origins*'s emphasis on the allegedly bourgeois, parvenuish character of Dixie's Gilded Age economic elite. According to Wiener and Billings, the region's dominant class during the period had borne a closer resemblance to the antebellum planter aristocracy or even (as Wiener maintained) to the Junker landlords of Bismarckian Germany than to the relentlessly acquisitive entrepreneurs of Grover Cleveland's America.[5] And, while this diverse cadre of revisionist scholars was proceeding up the "Left Fork" or down the "Prussian Road," I was attempting to chart yet another pathway through—and perhaps beyond—the interpretive landscape that Woodward had created in *Origins*.

My first steps toward involvement in this burgeoning cottage industry of Woodward criticism occurred while I was a graduate student at the University of Virginia from 1966 to 1970.[6] As might have been expected, the two professors at that institution who dealt extensively with the New South era in their classes both emphasized the need for thorough familiarity with the Woodward canon. Paul M. Gaston was (and, to my knowledge, still is) a determined advocate of Woodward's views and, as such, bears no responsibility for my subsequent deviations from the true faith. By contrast, Edward Younger, who ultimately directed my dissertation, may be more culpable in that regard, since he tended to keep his own counsel on interpretive issues and encouraged his students to decide such matters for themselves.[7] In any

4. Allan Peskin, "Was There a Compromise of 1877?" *Journal of American History,* 60 (June 1973), 63–75; Carl V. Harris, "Right Fork or Left Fork? The Section-Party Alignments of Southern Democrats in Congress, 1873–1897," *Journal of Southern History,* 42 (November 1976), 471–506 (59–95 in this volume).

5. Jonathan M. Wiener, *Social Origins of the New South: Alabama, 1860–1885* (Baton Rouge, 1978); Dwight B. Billings Jr., *Planters and the Making of a "New South": Class, Politics, and Development in North Carolina, 1865–1900* (Chapel Hill, 1979).

6. After accepting an appointment as a history instructor at Virginia Commonwealth University in 1970, I completed work on my doctoral dissertation two years later.

7. To my recollection, Dr. Younger never offered any overt assessment of *Origins* in the seminar that I took with him or during our many talks while he was directing my dissertation. After Dr. Younger's death in 1979, his widow, Barbara Younger, gave me a large number of books from his personal library, including a hardbound copy of *Origins* that had obviously seen extensive use. I still have that volume, which on the inside back cover contains several paragraphs of commentary in Dr. Younger's handwriting (perhaps in preparation for a prospective review of the book). These notes were fulsome in their praise of Woodward.

case, it was soon evident that I had a great deal of reading to do and that the works of one particular historian would occupy a considerable portion of my time during the months and years to come.

At the distance of a third of a century I cannot recall the precise order in which I grappled with Woodward's major books, but I do remember my initial reactions to them. *Tom Watson* was—and remains—my favorite, perhaps because (as the son of a vocational agricultural teacher in a rapidly urbanizing part of the South Carolina Piedmont) I could empathize with the protagonist of that splendid biography as he waged his valiant but foredoomed struggle to arrest the decline of the rural civilization that he loved. My response to *Strange Career* was likewise positive, although I was uncertain whether that brief, unfootnoted volume could fully support the weight of its thesis. *Reunion and Reaction* impressed me as a brilliant case study in historical detective work; nevertheless, my innate skepticism led me to wonder how, for so many years, the true story of the Compromise of 1877 had been hidden from view, especially since so many presumably loquacious newsmen and politicians had participated in one phase or another of the backstage shenanigans that Woodward had described.

As for *Origins,* my admiration for the breadth of its coverage and the literary flare of its prose was tempered by a marked ambivalence toward some of its other characteristics. I appreciated the author's willingness to challenge the conventional wisdom about Dixie's past, but I also wondered if the earlier generation of New South chroniclers (Holland Thompson, Broadus Mitchell, Philip Alexander Bruce, et al.) had really been so purblind and inept as *Origins* seemed to imply. In addition, the relentlessly negative tone of Woodward's account gave rise to concerns about its balance and objectivity. Were there *no* significant features of the region's economic, political, or cultural life between 1877 and 1913 that merited praise—other than the "middle-of-the-road" radicalism of Tom Watson's wing of the Populist movement?[8] I must confess that I took considerable pleasure in Woodward's adept use of irony and sarcasm to skewer the assorted corporate, governmental, and journalistic malefactors who populated his narrative, but on reflection I began to doubt that all of the targets of these barbs— including virtually the entire Democratic leadership in the South—could ac-

---

8. According to Woodward, the most radical southern Populists had been correct in opposing "fusion" with the Bryanite, "Free Silver" Democrats in the 1896 presidential race. Watson had unsuccessfully urged the People's Party to hold to the "middle of the road," maintaining its independence from both of the old parties. For Woodward's account of these developments, see *Origins of the New South,* 264–90.

tually have been so self-interested in their motives, so destructive in their conduct, and so indifferent to the long-term consequences of their acts. To be sure, there must have been at least a few men of character, integrity, and foresight among them, but, judging by Woodward's account, their number could not have greatly exceeded that of the godly inhabitants of Sodom. Perturbed by these evidences of bias, I soon concluded that *Origins* was a truly great polemic, a masterful indictment of a region and of an era, but I was dubious as to whether it was, in fact, very good history.

Other developments only served to fuel these doubts. My professors' allusions to an evidently still controversial (albeit deceased) historian named Charles A. Beard inspired me to peruse several of the books that he had authored, and while doing so I recognized the influence that they must have exerted on Woodward—specifically through their unabashed economic determinism and their almost obsessive emphasis on struggles between capitalistic and agrarian forces in the United States from the 1780s to the 1890s.[9] As my graduate studies wore on, moreover, I learned that Beard's interpretations had come under withering fire from scholars since World War II and that his views with reference to the early national period, the Jacksonian era, and the Civil War and Reconstruction years were no longer widely accepted. Instead, his dualistic, even Manichaean accounts of rapacious financiers and oppressed, rebellious farmers had been supplanted by more complex analyses that stressed the importance of schisms *within* economic classes and that paid much greater heed to the ideological, psychological, and ethnocultural dimensions of political behavior.[10] And, I reasoned, if support for Beard's arguments had waned among American historians at large, why should the warmed-over Beardianism of *Origins* continue to hold sway as the overarching interpretive motif for the New South?

For better or worse, I brought these recently acquired perspectives to bear in my doctoral dissertation and the book that soon evolved from it,

---

9. If I recall correctly, I read—or at least scanned—significant portions of Charles Beard, *Economic Origins of Jeffersonian Democracy* (New York, 1915); and Charles A. and Mary R. Beard, *The Rise of American Civilization* (2 vols., New York, 1927).

10. For examples of books that were then enjoying a considerable vogue, see Louis Hartz, *The Liberal Tradition in America: An Interpretation of American Political Thought since the Revolution* (New York, 1955); Robert E. Brown, *Charles Beard and the Constitution: A Critical Analysis of "An Economic Interpretation of the Constitution"* (Princeton, 1956); Lee Benson, *The Concept of Jacksonian Democracy: New York as a Test Case* (Princeton, 1961); and Robert P. Sharkey, *Money, Class, and Party: An Economic Study of Civil War and Reconstruction* (Baltimore, 1959).

Two Paths to the New South: The Virginia Debt Controversy, 1870–1883.[11] My portrayal of the clash between the Old Dominion's repudiationist Readjusters and their Funder opponents paralleled *Origins*'s account in some ways but differed significantly in others. Like Woodward, I offered a favorable assessment of the Readjusters and of the social and economic reforms that they had implemented during their brief ascendancy from 1879 to 1883.[12] I perceived little merit, however, in *Origins*'s Beard-style depiction of the debt revolt as an agrarian movement imbued with distinctively Jeffersonian attitudes and values.[13]

To be sure, the Readjusters had leveled many rhetorical blasts against "bloated bondholders" and Wall Street "Shylocks," but my survey of their editorials and personal correspondence disclosed neither a pervasive hostility toward the capitalist system nor a desire to restore Virginia to some prelapsarian condition of pastoral innocence.[14] Indeed, quite the opposite had been the case. After 1877 (when erstwhile railroad executive William Mahone had taken charge of the insurgent cause), the Readjusters' words and actions had become increasingly attuned to the entrepreneurial ethos of the Gilded Age. Insurgent spokesmen had trumpeted their commitment to industrial and commercial growth—and had argued that partial repudiation of the state's burdensome debt would hasten, not hamper, economic recovery. Tax cuts, enhanced financing for public schools, and a more egalitarian political climate would further accelerate this revitalization, they had argued, by attracting not only immigrants but also the investment capital needed to transform Virginia into a land of mines and factories, enterprise and initiative. Securing control of the commonwealth's legislature in 1879 and again 1881, the insurgents had approved scores of new corporate charters, and Mahone's Richmond *Whig* had proclaimed that the state's interests were now aligned with the "progressive" North and not with Dixie's impoverished and reactionary cotton belt. Under the circumstances, the debt revolt's 1881 alliance with national and state Republicans had been, if not inevitable, at least predictable, and the same was true of the Readjusters'

---

11. James Tice Moore, "Two Paths to the New South: Funders, Readjusters, and the Virginia Debt Controversy, 1870–1883" (Ph.D. dissertation, University of Virginia, 1972), later published as *Two Paths to the New South: The Virginia Debt Controversy, 1870–1883* (Lexington, Ky., 1974).

12. Compare Woodward, *Origins*, 94–98, with Moore, *Two Paths*, 83–108.

13. Woodward, *Origins*, 88–89.

14. Moore, *Two Paths*, 45–53.

prompt declaration of support for protective tariffs.[15] These developments (in my opinion, at least) could not be readily explained within a Beardian interpretive framework. Even debt repudiators, it appeared, had displayed a host of markedly Hamiltonian inclinations, and the line between the advocates of capitalism and agrarianism was sometimes difficult to discern.

My analysis of the Funders contradicted the interpretive thrust of *Origins* as well, albeit in more nuanced fashion. Woodward had made little effort to disguise his contempt for the state-credit wing of Virginia's Conservative (i.e., Democratic) Party. According to his account, the Funder creed had been championed by an unprepossessing assortment of scheming mountebanks and laissez-faire ideologues, bourgeois men-on-the-make and reactionary scions of the old plantation elite—none of whom had taken any particular interest in the problems and needs of the rural masses. With such individuals in charge of public affairs throughout most of the 1870s, it was only a matter of course, Woodward implied, before large quantities of state-owned stock in local transportation companies would be sold (at bargain-basement prices) to the railroad magnates of Baltimore and Philadelphia; that the so-called Funding Bill of 1871 would be enacted, committing the commonwealth to exorbitant interest payments on a holdover antebellum debt of more than $30 million; or that the budget of the newly established school system would be slashed in order to line the pockets of coupon-clipping bondholders in New York and London. More sensitive to the balance sheets of outside capitalists than to the exigencies of ordinary Virginians, the Funders (as described in *Origins*) had allowed the public credit to take precedence over the public good. The result had been a bitter harvest of public antagonism, culminating in Readjuster successes at the polls that had threatened, for a time, to demolish Democratic power in the state.[16]

This was a compelling story, and I echoed considerable portions of it in *Two Paths to the New South*.[17] Nevertheless, during the course of my research I became aware of certain anomalous aspects of the Funders' performance in the political clashes of the 1870s and 1880s that, in my opinion, required explanation. I was perplexed, for example, by the large amount of popular support that the anti-repudiationists had received. (Given their evidently abysmal record in office, it had seemed reasonable to assume that no one would have voted for them—with the possible exception

---

15. *Ibid.*, 49–53, 56–57, 69–92.
16. Woodward, *Origins*, 4–5, 61, 89–90, 93–95, 97–98.
17. Moore, *Two Paths*, 12–26.

of close relatives and personal friends.) Instead, I discovered that they had run neck-and-neck with the Readjusters in the 1879 legislative elections, had soundly defeated them in a bizarre contest for control of the state's electoral votes in the 1880 presidential race, had conducted a strong—if unsuccessful—campaign for the governorship and other state offices in 1881, and had captured half of Virginia's congressional seats in 1882, an outcome that had set the stage for decisive triumphs over the Readjuster-Republican coalition in subsequent years. More striking still, analysis of the election returns suggested that substantial majorities of Virginia's white voters had supported the Funders in 1880, 1881, and 1882 and that a narrow majority had, in all likelihood, done so in 1879 as well.[18]

Why had so many of the commonwealth's white citizens rallied behind a political faction whose leaders had raised taxes and closed schools so that an onerous prewar debt could be repaid? Woodward's answer to this question was brief and Beardian; he characterized the Funders' popular appeal as having been limited, for the most part, to urban areas where, presumably, the electorate had been susceptible to the influence of railroad money, financial rings, venal journalists, and officeholding cliques.[19] The election returns, however, told a different and decidedly more complex story. To be sure, the state-credit advocates had dominated a number of cities (most notably Richmond and Lynchburg), but their victory margins in those locales had been counterbalanced by significant defeats in Norfolk, Petersburg, and Danville. The voting statistics contained another surprise as well: the Funders had compiled their most consistent successes in the rural counties of the central and northern Piedmont, the ancestral heartland of Jeffersonian republicanism.[20] Perhaps there was some way that these findings could be reconciled with the Beard/Woodward interpretive model, but if so, I was unable to discern it.

Attempting to make sense of this data, I ultimately concluded that political culture had outweighed agriculture as the prime determinant of partisan allegiances during the debt controversy. The Funders, I argued, had commanded the support of the bulk of the white electorate, urban and rural, in the more patrician-dominated, socially conservative areas of the state, particularly in the counties and municipalities east of the Blue Ridge. Shaken by the upheavals of the Civil War–Reconstruction years, these traditionalist

18. *Ibid.*, 64, 75–76, 82, 109, 112–13.
19. Woodward, *Origins*, 93–95.
20. Moore, *Two Paths*, 28, 50.

voters had feared that the debt revolt would plunge the commonwealth into yet another abyss of economic instability, political turmoil, and racial unrest.[21] By contrast, the Readjusters had attracted adherents from a diverse array of groups that had cherished few (if any) ties to "Old Virginia" attitudes and values. Recently enfranchised freedmen had flocked to the repudiationist cause, I noted, as had long-restive upland whites, laboring-class immigrants in the cities, and ambitious, upwardly mobile newcomers from the North.[22] Thus, as I saw it, Woodward had erred in characterizing the debt struggle as a clash between the countryside and the town, the agrarian and the capitalist. A more viable approach, I contended, would be to envision the Readjuster-Funder schism as a split between those who had welcomed change and those who had opposed it, between those who had embraced the prospect of an economically dynamic, socially fluid, and politically egalitarian commonwealth and those who had hoped that the Old Dominion of the future would continue to bear a close resemblance to that of the past.[23]

When *Two Paths to the New South* was published in 1974, I contemplated no additional interpretive forays against *Origins* or its distinguished author. On the contrary, environmental issues had attracted my attention, and I had begun to collect data that would, I hoped, eventually result in a book about Virginia's nineteenth- and twentieth-century efforts to regulate oyster harvesting—a subject that, so far as I was aware, had failed to elicit Woodward's notice in any way, shape, or form.

As research on that project started to gain momentum, however, an unexpected development redirected my efforts back to familiar haunts. A letter from Jack Temple Kirby arrived, inviting me to prepare a historiographical essay for a volume that he and L. Moody Simms Jr. wanted to publish as a tribute to Edward Younger. Although I was glad to assist in the completion of this much-deserved festschrift, I could summon up little enthusiasm for the topic that had been provisionally assigned to me: a rehash of the already stale debate over Woodward's "Jim Crow" thesis. Instead, perceiving a chance to elaborate on several themes that I had briefly explored in *Two Paths*, I suggested an alternative submission that would examine the extent to which *Origins*'s portrayal of the Redeemer Democrats had been sustained or undermined by the findings of post-1951 scholarship.

21. *Ibid.*, 27–44.
22. *Ibid.*, 44–53.
23. *Ibid.*, 27–53.

Kirby and Simms concurred with this proposal, and during the months that followed, I took copious notes on scores of books and articles dealing with southern politics and government from the 1870s to the 1890s.[24] Ultimately, the prospective festschrift for Younger failed to materialize,[25] but my research nonetheless culminated in two articles, one of which appeared in *Southern Studies* and the other in the *Journal of Southern History*.

The *Southern Studies* piece (somewhat mischievously entitled "Origins of the Solid South") advanced the heretical concept that the Democrats' post-Reconstruction hegemony had been based as much on the popular appeal of their rural-oriented economic policies as it had on the fraud, violence, and intimidation that Woodward had chronicled.[26] The *Journal of Southern History* article, "Redeemers Reconsidered" (which is here reprinted), was, if anything, even more subversive, challenging several of *Origins*'s bedrock analytical postulates. Where Woodward had emphasized the role of self-seeking adventurers and bourgeois parvenus in the Democratic leadership, I stressed instead the continuing prominence of many political chieftains whose careers in public service had begun during the antebellum period. Where Woodward had delineated an alleged takeover of Dixie's Gilded Age Democratic organizations by erstwhile Whigs, I perceived little evidence that such a coup had occurred or, for that matter, had even been attempted. Where Woodward had characterized the Redeemers as sedulously attentive to the demands of northeastern capital and conspicuously deaf to those of southeastern agriculture, I argued that, in fact, the reverse had been closer to the truth. And where Woodward had assailed the region's Democrats as opportunistic, unprincipled front men for a new, Yankee-inspired economic order, I strove (with my usual contrariness) to document their ongoing allegiance to the traditional values of the white

24. These notes, inscribed in more than a dozen spiral notebooks, are on deposit in the James Tice Moore Papers, Virginia Historical Society, Richmond, Virginia.

25. Dr. Younger had, in the mid-1970s, solicited many of his former graduate students to prepare essays for a volume dealing with the lives of Virginia's governors since 1861. Consequently, the Kirby-Simms project never came to fruition because prospective contributors were involved in Dr. Younger's project; Jack Temple Kirby and I, for example, were among several former students recruited to serve as associate editors of what we called the "governors book," which was ultimately published in 1982: Edward Younger and James Tice Moore, eds., *The Governors of Virginia, 1860–1987* (Charlottesville, 1982).

26. James Tice Moore, "Origins of the Solid South: Redeemer Democrats and the Popular Will, 1870–1900," *Southern Studies,* 22 (Fall 1983), 285–301.

South. "All things had not changed with Appomattox," I concluded, "much less with the Compromise of 1877."[27]

What was the impact of these two articles? Both have frequently been cited, and I believe that, if nothing else, they achieved the worthwhile result of calling added attention to the broad-based critique of *Origins* that Carl V. Harris, Dwight B. Billings, and others had formulated in the 1970s.[28] I would argue as well that my essays contributed to a number of evident and, in my opinion, significant shifts in the post-Reconstruction era's historiographical terrain. For the last two decades researchers have, I think, been much less inclined to parrot Woodward's claim that the South's Gilded Age Democrats were an essentially new ruling class, and the once common use of "persistent Whiggery" as an explanation of the Redeemers' conduct has also diminished to a marked extent.[29] Meanwhile, published references to Redeemer initiatives on behalf of agriculture have proliferated, although I must note that the authors of post-1978 analyses have, almost as a rule, felt obliged to bewail the benefits that large landowners had derived from the Democrats' reforms, presumably at the cost of the countryside's yeomen, share tenants, and hired hands.[30] (In the Redeemers' defense, it might be

---

27. James Tice Moore, "Redeemers Reconsidered: Change and Continuity in the Democratic South, 1870–1900," *Journal of Southern History,* 44 (August 1978), 357–78 (109–30 in this volume). The quotation is from the last page. The *Journal's* visiting managing editor at the time, John B. Boles, suggested the article's primary title, a change from "Redeemers in Retrospect" (which was my original notion).

28. See the following essays in John B. Boles and Evelyn Thomas Nolen, eds., *Interpreting Southern History: Historiographical Essays in Honor of Sanford W. Higginbotham* (Baton Rouge, 1987): Harold D. Woodman, "Economic Reconstruction and the Rise of the New South, 1865–1900," 270 n. 29; and Richard L. Watson Jr., "From Populism through the New Deal: Southern Political History," 329 n. 46. See also John Herbert Roper's introduction to "Redeemers Reconsidered" in Roper, ed., *C. Vann Woodward: A Southern Historian and His Critics,* 95.

29. For evidence of these trends, see Michael Perman, *The Road to Redemption: Southern Politics, 1869–1879* (Chapel Hill and London, 1984), 178–277; Laurence Shore, *Southern Capitalists: The Ideological Leadership of an Elite, 1832–1885* (Chapel Hill and London, 1986), 149–68; Howard N. Rabinowitz, *The First New South, 1865–1920* (Arlington Heights, Ill., 1992), 80–86; and Edward L. Ayers, *The Promise of the New South: Life after Reconstruction* (New York and Oxford, 1992), 34–54. In connection with the last of these works, it is significant, I believe, that Ayers does not even have a "Whig" listing in his index.

30. Examples of this practice may be found in Perman, *Road to Redemption,* 221–63; Rabinowitz, *First New South,* 89–91; Ayers, *Promise of the New South,* 44–45; and Gavin Wright, *Old South, New South: Revolutions in the Southern Economy since the Civil War* (New York, 1986), 47–50. For a particularly harsh critique of southern Democratic farm legis-

observed that their "farm program" was not the first such effort in American history that had been marred by this perceived defeat—nor would it be the last.)

On the whole, I have been very pleased by the response to "Redeemers Reconsidered" and "Origins of the Solid South." Still, as Woodward noted in the subtitle of his memoirs, the writing of history is not without its "perils," and while venturing along the byways of scholarly revisionism, I have come to appreciate the truth of that sentiment.[31] From the outset of my stint as an *Origins* critic, I was struck by the attitudes that the book's defenders manifested and by the tactics that they employed. For example, Paul M. Gaston informed me in 1979 that a conference paper that I had just presented had been "brilliant" but that I needed to recognize that "history has to have a moral point." I appreciated the prefatory compliment, of course, but I was unable to fathom how my advocacy of an alternative viewpoint with reference to the Redeemers had subverted the public good.[32]

In *Thinking Back,* published in 1986, Woodward adopted a similar approach in his chapter entitled "Origin of *Origins*" (reprinted in the present volume). After classifying several of those who had disagreed with *Origins,* including myself, as (horrors!) closet conservatives, he devoted one of his pages to "Redeemers Reconsidered." Although he gave brief notice to a few of my arguments concerning political linkages between the Old and New Souths, he expressed no opinion at all about their validity. Instead, zeroing in on a tangential part of my narrative, he proceeded to call me up short for displaying insufficient interest in—and, I suppose, outrage about—the "absconding Redeemer treasurers" and the Democrats' oft-discussed failure to aid the "propertyless and the freedmen."[33] Evidently, when it came to appraisals of the South's post-1877 leadership, analytical moderation was no virtue, and interpretive redundancy no vice.

Irked by the tenor of Gaston's and Woodward's observations, I was utterly mystified by some of the other pronouncements that emanated from

---

lation during the Gilded Age see Michael R. Hyman, *The Anti-Redeemers: Hill-Country Political Dissenters in the Lower South from Redemption to Populism* (Baton Rouge, 1990), 98–166.

31. C. Vann Woodward, *Thinking Back: The Perils of Writing History* (Baton Rouge, 1986).

32. This episode took place after I had presented a paper entitled "Beyond the Woodward Synthesis" at the Southern Historical Association convention in Atlanta on November 15, 1979. That paper was later published in *Southern Studies* as "Origins of the Solid South."

33. Woodward, *Thinking Back,* 70–71 (153–54 in this volume).

the anti-revisionist camp. Near the end of an otherwise insightful 1981 essay about the *Origins* debate, Dan T. Carter proposed that scholars might do well "to forget the whole dichotomy of change and continuity" (an idea that, if implemented, would doubtless have led to some very peculiar—and pedestrian—historical works).[34] And, during the next year, J. Morgan Kousser and James M. McPherson weighed in with their collective opinion that Woodward's assessment of the Redeemers had been "more often confirmed than revised" by later accounts.[35] Although I had no cause to doubt the sincerity of those two accomplished researchers, there was, I thought, very good reason to question their judgment. The clouds surrounding the upper reaches of academia's "ivory tower" were, it appeared, very thick indeed.

In the mid-1980s, weary of moralistic posturing and evasive bombast, I withdrew from firsthand participation in what might be termed the "Woodward wars." Since that time my aforementioned articles have, however, continued to perform good service on the interpretive front and have, I believe, held up surprisingly well. I take particular pride in "Redeemers Reconsidered." Cited more frequently, and more favorably, than anything else that I have written, it was reprinted in a 1997 book edited by Jack Roper.[36] And, early in 2001, John B. Boles asked if the essay could be published yet again in a volume commemorating the fiftieth anniversary of *Origins of the New South*.

How could I refuse? After all, I have long cultivated an appreciation for the ironies of southern history—and of southern historical writing.

---

34. Dan T. Carter, "From the Old South to the New: Another Look at the Theme of Change and Continuity," in Walter J. Fraser Jr. and Winfred B. Moore Jr., eds., *From the Old South to the New: Essays on the Transitional South* (Westport, Conn., and London, 1981), 30.

35. J. Morgan Kousser and James M. McPherson, eds., *Region, Race, and Reconstruction: Essays in Honor of C. Vann Woodward* (New York and Oxford, 1982), xxix.

36. Roper, ed., *C. Vann Woodward: A Southern Historian and His Critics*, 95–117.

In 1984 and 1985 C. Vann Woodward gave a series of lectures at Baylor University and at Louisiana State University, and from these lectures grew his insightful book of reflections on his career, Thinking Back: The Perils of Writing History *(Baton Rouge, 1986). His purpose was to recall the state of southern history—and the state of mind of most southern historians—in the decade of the 1930s, to claim that* Origins *was a conscious effort of "revisionary subversion," and to show how the views of professional historians had changed over the years. Of course, much of that change was inspired by his own writings, so to a fascinating degree* Thinking Back *is an intellectual history both of one historian and the historiography of the South. Woodward modestly suggests that one reason his emphasis on change in southern history found wide acceptance in 1951 and thereafter was because that generation of readers had personally witnessed enormous change over the past several decades, thereby problematizing arguments for continuity in southern history. In 1951 neither the South nor its historians were as they had been in 1935. The chapter that follows first appeared in that book, and it is placed here, after two earlier appraisals and two noted critiques, and before the fifty-year appraisals that conclude this volume. Hence Woodward does not have the last word, but this chapter does help the reader understand both the context of the book and some of the reasons for its instant and lasting acclaim.*

Origin of *Origins*

"How can you possibly write so long a book," asked a friend, only half humorously, "about a period in which nothing happened?" He was referring to the book I had undertaken to write on the period of Southern history between Reconstruction and the First World War. We were sitting on the steps of the Library of Congress and the conversation went on till closing time. His question, however serious, reflected a prevailing popular impression about the post-Reconstruction era that was stuck with the name New South. Historians had so far done relatively little to correct the idea that nothing happened and that there was really not much to say about what did happen. Compared with shelves upon shelves of books that lined the Library of Congress stacks in the sections on the Cotton Kingdom of slavery,

---

Reprinted from *Thinking Back: The Perils of Writing History* (Baton Rouge: Louisiana State University Press, 1986), 59–79.

the rise and fall of the Confederacy, and the Reconstruction period, the existing bibliography of the period following was, apart from a few monographs, discouragingly short, thin, primitive, and immature.

My reply to my friend's question about nothing happening was that the shortness of the shelf was no measure of the period's significance and no indication that little had happened worthy of note. Taking the offensive and turning the tables, I contended that, in fact, the three previous periods mentioned had received an altogether disproportionate amount of time and attention from historians. After all, the antebellum Cotton Kingdom, the Confederate nation, and Radical Reconstruction were a succession of lost causes, ephemeral experiments of relatively brief duration. The Confederacy lasted only four years, and the Radicals less than an average of three and a half in the states involved. Taken all together from the beginning of the Cotton Kingdom to the end of Reconstruction, the three lost causes spanned only about three quarters of a century. That was the number of years already covered by the era whose foundations were laid in the 1870s by the so-called Redeemers, and as things turned out, still had a few years to go. Granted that all causes are lost in the end, did the longest and most durable one not deserve somewhat more attention than it had received?

In addition to the prejudice of low esteem for the period and the deficiency of scholarship on which to build, there were other problems. The title for the book, because it was to be one of a series, had been assigned or inherited—*Origins of the New South,* followed in monograph fashion by the dates, 1877–1913. I was glad to see the definite article before the word *Origins* dropped, and I very reluctantly accepted the *New South* and the coercive dates in the prescribed title. But I was also stuck with the term *Origins.* The word recalled a brief essay entitled "The Idol of Origins" by a martyred hero of the time, Marc Bloch of the French Resistance, foremost French historian of his generation. One trouble with *origins,* wrote Bloch, was the unavoidable ambiguity of the term—whether it meant *beginnings* or *causes* or was a "cross-contamination of the two meanings." Bloch continued, "In popular usage, an origin is a beginning which explains. Worse still, a beginning which is a complete explanation. There lies the ambiguity, and there the danger!" In his time, said Bloch, he had seen *origins* grow from a *preoccupation* to an *obsession* and in many cases a *demon,* which was "perhaps, only the incarnation of that other satanic enemy of true history: the mania for making judgments."

What an incubus of fallibility and temptation I had fallen heir to! How could I cope with it? One solace at least was the knowledge that Marc Bloch himself had used the forbidden term in the title of his greatest book, *Les caractères originaux de l'histoire rurale française*. His essay on "The Idol of Origins" was, in fact, a sort of apology. He began it with a memorable sentence: "It will never be amiss to begin with an acknowledgement of our faults." With the humility of the master in mind, I reflected that neither could it be amiss to begin forewarned of fallacies to be avoided. It was perfectly obvious that Bloch's "satanic enemy of true history" was still at work upon my own generation and that I enjoyed no immunity from "the mania for making judgments." I was even dimly aware of a personal propensity for it. Moreover, the very subject I was addressing seemed in a peculiar way to cry out for the making of judgments and thereby to compound the temptation. How much could I, or should I, resist the "satanic enemy"?

I have pointed out earlier some ways in which the legitimacy of the New South regime—and in my view the legitimacy of the social order still in place in the 1950s—was dependent upon a special reading of history. I would go so far as to say that the cornerstone of the New South—to borrow a figure from Alexander Stephens about the Old South—rested upon historical assumptions that constituted a veritable credo of the region. To question those assumptions at any point was not only to make judgments about history, but to pass judgment on the legitimacy of the social order sustained by the assumptions questioned. Yet that seemed precisely what my researches and my convictions disposed me to do.

Among the significant tenets of the New South's historical credo, first in importance was an image of Reconstruction as betrayal, humiliation, and horror; as the work of radicals, carpetbaggers, scalawags; and as Negro rule that resulted in corruption, misrule, and degradation. Following this came the flattering image of Redemption, the overthrow of the Radical regimes, and restoration of Home Rule. The evils and excesses of Reconstruction not only justified the violence and fraud by which Redemption was achieved, but also the repudiation of all principles of Reconstruction, or as many as possible. Since Redemption was seen as salvation, the Redeemers were viewed as heroes. And since they proclaimed their work a restoration, the new leaders were assumed to represent a return to power of antebellum leaders of the old type. In contrast to the corrupt regimes of the Reconstruction period, the governments of the Redeemers were held to be beyond reproach, impeccable in their purity. Gratefully, the once-divided whites rallied around their old Confederate captains, put aside all differences, and became a Solid South—one in politics, one in credo, and one in all matters of race. Rising above logic, they professed to be equally loyal to the Old

South of the Lost Cause and to the New South of Yankee ideals and business and nationalism. The contentment and acquiescence of the Negro and the corrupt abuse of his votes justified his disfranchisement and segregation. The South's enthusiasm for the war with Spain proved that reconciliation and reunion had been achieved. The South was at last in step with the U.S.A. in patriotism, progressivism, and prosperity. In the meantime, obliging Northern capitalists were seeing to the industrialization and modernization of the regional economy to the benefit of all, but especially Southerners.

According to the orthodox historical credo, these marvelous and beneficient developments had come about without any significant break with the past. Properly understood, they were to be thought of as the fulfillment and continuation of ideals, convictions, folkways, and institutions deeply rooted in tradition. These roots were tested by Civil War and Reconstruction but held firm in the passing storms. Henry W. Grady put the dogma succinctly in the 1880s when he said the New South was "simply the Old South under new conditions." The same view was sustained in various ways later by professional historians such as Ulrich B. Phillips and Broadus Mitchell. Wilbur J. Cash in 1941 gave the doctrine its most popular and influential expression in *The Mind of the South*. The Civil War, he declared, left the old mentality "entirely unshaken" and instead "operated enormously to fortify and confirm that mind and will." This meant that "the Old South was preserved virtually intact," and "the pride of the old ruling class was not weakened but even distinctly enhanced." The new political leaders and industrialists came from "the old ruling class, the progeny of the plantation," and the common folk "never departed in the least from their ancient allegiance."

Within the historical guild of professionals, the orthodox views of continuity held predominant sway through the 1940s and received their most eloquent and extreme expression at the end of that decade in the presidential address of Robert S. Cotterill before the Southern Historical Association. "In no phase of the economic life," declared Cotterill, "was the New South new. . . . It was merely a continuation of the Old South. And not only in its economic life: the New South inherited, also, the *spirit* of the Old. It inherited the racial pride, and if anyone wants to call it racial prejudice, there can be no objection. . . . There is, in very fact, no Old South and no New. There is only The South. Fundamentally, as it was in the beginning it is now, and, if God please, it shall be evermore."

Merely to state in bare outline the tenets put forth in *Origins of the New South,* published in 1951, would be to repeat the orthodox credo backward or turn it upside down—a sort of historiographical black mass in the eyes of true believers. The blasphemy included the replacement of continuity with discontinuity, unity with disunity, and harmony with conflict. I do not mean to say that all historians of the period were true believers or rigidly orthodox, nor that I was the only one suspected of heresy. Nor would it be accurate to suggest that I was so simplistic as to believe there was no continuity, unity, or harmony at all and no truth in any of the dominant views then held. At issue, as in most historical problems of importance, were questions of emphasis and degree—not the existence of the phenomena under discussion. Although I did not set out with the deliberate intent of challenging all predominant views, I should have to acknowledge that the end product might reasonably suggest to some minds such an unworthy suspicion.

To start with the founding fathers of the new order, the Redeemers, who overthrew and replaced the Reconstruction regimes, they were denied the identity implied by the term *restoration*. Of course nearly all of the new rulers were old enough by 1877 to have established some roots in the old order, but it was my contention that, "In the main they were of middle-class, industrial, capitalistic outlook, with little but nominal connection with the old planter regime." In political antecedents, the combination of old parties under the Conservative name brought the Whigs into prominence, and in policies the Redeemers leaned to business, wealth, and commercial sympathies. The Redeemers thus represented more innovation than restoration, more break than continuity with the past.

Instead of the orthodox record of scrupulous honesty attributed to Redeemer governments and contrasted so sharply with the corrupt record of Reconstruction, I found these new administrations disgraced by numerous state treasury embezzlements and defalcations, sordid deals, public land scandals, and blatant favoritism. More continuity, at least with Reconstruction, was ironically manifest along these lines than along others. Most disgraceful was the common practice of leasing state prisons and convicts to favored politicians for exploitation as a private labor force. Instead of the white loyalty and political solidarity supposedly inspired by Redeemers, third-party rebellions and bitter division over economic and political issues faced the new administrations from the start. After a brief suspension of revolt in the 1880s, more powerful and widespread rebellions erupted under Populist party organization in the 1890s.

Instead of industrialization and cotton-mill construction under the benevolent paternalism of old planter types as pictured in New South historiography, the new Southern captains of the cotton-mill industry were found to be predominantly hard-nosed entrepreneurs bent on large profits and distressingly indifferent to the well-being of their white labor force, largely women and children. Much the same genus presided over the new fortunes in mining, lumber, heavy industry, tobacco, and railroads. The New South creed, intoned in the chorus led by Henry Grady, proclaimed a gospel of reconciliation between estranged races, classes, and sections, a miraculous melding of Old and New South ideals. But it proved in fact to constitute a capitulation, a celebration of the values, standards, aims, and interests of the new masters. *Reconciliation* was only a code word. As the editor of the *Industrial South* put it in 1885, the New South message was a belated acknowledgment and a cordial submission that the South, like the rest of the country, was destined "to be peculiarly a community of business men."

In this vein the revisionary subversion was repeated throughout *Origins*. The reconciliation of the farmer meant subordination to the status of tenant or sharecropper and the degradation of poverty. The reconciliation of the black freedmen meant their submission to the demands of white supremacy, including disfranchisement, segregation, and loss of civil rights. The reconciliation of labor meant the lowest wages and most degraded standards in the country. The reconciliation of the sections meant local control for the Southern elite and the South's political subordination in many federal matters to the Northeast. Investment, development, and modernization by Northern capital, more fruits of reconciliation, meant a colonial status for the Southern economy. For the region as a whole per-capita wealth in the first decade of the new century was about half the national average, and per-capita income about 40 percent lower than the national average. Distribution of the better things of life—health, education, and the standard of living—in the colonial economy reflected not only these gross disparities between the South and other regions but also appalling inequities within the region itself.

This summary has not paused for elaboration or minimal concessions to opposing views, nor has it suggested the numerous cautionary reservations and exceptions and hedgings inserted to guard against charges of extremism. Without them it sounds more dogmatic and polemical than it was. If it revives the familiar charge of relapse into quaint and outdated Beardian patterns, I should point out a significant departure I made from that path. Beard had framed his classic economic and political conflicts in interregional terms—North versus South, industrial versus agrarian, free labor versus slave labor, and so forth. My picture included in the frame large components of intraregional conflicts—strife within the South itself, discord between forces that were equally Southern on both sides. This alteration, of course, served to sharpen rather than blunt my assault upon orthodox views.

The reception of *Origins* when it finally appeared late in 1951 brought surprises and puzzlement. Was I rightly understood? Or had I subdued and qualified my tone too much? Instead of voicing expected indignation and protest, predominant responses ranged from tolerance and respect to un-qualified applause. This was even true of the later reviews in learned jour-nals. Perhaps I had misjudged my professional colleagues. There were exceptions, to be sure, such as the regrets of one reputable member of the guild that I had not "shown a greater measure of sympathy for Southern traditions and for the essential goodness of long-suffering people." Or an-other who felt I had gone "to the other extreme" and emphasized "eco-nomic and racial conflict to the exclusion of everything else." But these were relatively rare exceptions to the rule.

A source of continued puzzlement and some concern was the silence of negative critics and the failure of serious criticism to appear for years fol-lowing. The absence of criticism, if it lasts long enough, can be as disturbing as being ignored—though admittedly in a different way. It can mark the su-perannuation of a book. The critical silence continued ominously for some two decades. In a preface to a new edition published in 1971, twenty years after the first and entirely unrevised, save for an updated bibliography by Charles B. Dew, I remarked that revision "must be the task of others," very likely a historian with "another world view, fresher insights, and perhaps a different philosophy of history." I added that "it would already appear to be time for him to be about his work." Instead, I was confronted the next year with a full-length reappraisal of the book in the *Journal of Southern History* by Sheldon Hackney, a former student then in his more impression-able years. It was his conclusion in 1972 that "the pyramid still stands," that there had been "no major challenge," that the book had "survived rela-tively untarnished through twenty years," and that most monographs in the field since 1951 "reinforce much more than they revise about *Origins of the New South*." He went so far as to suggest the highly tentative explanatory hypothesis that, "One possible answer is that Woodward is right about his period."

I wish it were possible for me to go along with such an attractive hypoth-esis, even to embellish it with the theory that the evidence was so massive, the logic so conclusive, and the writing so persuasive that the conclusions were irresistible. Quite apart from the questionable tenability of such theo-ries, however—as Hackney himself pointed out, "revisionists have never been noticeably deterred by the absence of serious flaws in the body of knowledge they wished to revise"—there is an alternative if less-flattering explanation that I find more persuasive. The period of Southern history from 1877 to the 1950s, despite changes within it, was the longest era of reasonable stability in the nineteenth and twentieth centuries. Toward the end of that long period, in the 1930s and 1940s, it is not surprising to find historians and laymen alike taking much stock in the predominance of continuity and unity in Southern history. The assumption was that basically things had always been pretty much that way. It was only in such a period that Cash could have come forth in 1941 with his remarkable summation of the prevailing consensus, or that Robert Cotterill could have set his words to the meter of the doxology in 1949.

Given such firm commitments to the old doctrine of continuity, what happened to delay for so long criticism of a book that took the very opposite line? What happened, I think, was less the persuasiveness of the book than a change in the times, a series of drastic changes. In the 1940s the South suddenly entered a period of nearly three decades filled with more shocks of discontinuity than any period of its history, with the possible exception of the 1860s. Part of them are caught in the familiar litany—cotton moving west, cattle moving east, blacks moving north, Yankees moving south, everybody moving to town, and towns and industries growing faster than ever before. Old monuments of continuity disappeared in rapid succession: one-party politics, one-crop agriculture, one-horse farmers, the white primary, the poll tax, Jim Crow signs, disfranchisement laws. Out they went. In their place came the *Brown* decision of 1954 against segregated schools, the Civil Rights movement and black nationalism, the collapse of massive resistance, and at the demand of a Southerner in the White House a new and comprehensive Civil Rights Act and a Voting Rights Act. With all that pandemonium of contemporaneous upheaval and daily change of the "unchangeable" during the fifties, sixties, and into the seventies, what was there left to say about continuity? I know the present is not supposed to affect our reading of the past, but in this instance I think it did. In fact I think it had much to do with the charmed immunity from criticism that *Origins* enjoyed for so long.

At any rate the old chorus of continuity fell silent, and 1951 turned out by chance to be a fortunate time to gain a hearing for a different tune. The old orthodoxy of continuity yielded much ground to revisionists who emphasized the importance of change in Southern history. It was even possible in 1955 to begin a book on the Jim Crow system by writing that "the people of the South should be the last Americans to expect indefinite continuity of their institutions and social arrangements," that while others had "less reason to be prepared for sudden change and lost causes," the South's historical experience was different and distinctive.

It was an intellectually exciting experience to be restoring the neglected third dimension of change to the relatively flattened two-dimensional picture of Southern history. The oncoming younger generations joined eagerly in the enterprise, and their new monographs poured from the presses. It was great while it lasted, but I knew that it could not continue in health and vigor without the stimulus and challenge of genuine criticism. That was not to come on in full cry until the 1970s—certainly soon enough to forestall premature superannuation of *Origins*.

In the meantime it was gratifying to witness the beginnings of criticism around my own seminar table as early as the 1950s. To mention a few examples, there was Robert Sharkey, *Money, Class, and Party* (1959), who upset the Beardian concept of Republican economic motives that I inherited. Earlier criticism did not derive from ideological but from methodological, mainly quantitative, techniques that had been unavailable to me. Applying these techniques as well as conventional sources, Sheldon Hackney's *Populism to Progressivism in Alabama* (1969) offered a more realistic view of both movements; and J. Morgan Kousser, *The Shaping of Southern Politics* (1974), corrected errors of mine as well as some of V. O. Key's. Quantifying critics were at work at other seminar tables as well. One example of the more effective was Carl V. Harris, who demonstrated in the *Journal of Southern History* that my metaphor of "Right Fork, Left Fork" to characterize the South's sectional politics was much too simplistic so far as congressional voting was concerned.

The main thrust of criticism in the 1970s and 1980s, however, was ideologically oriented, whether quantified or not. This orientation was not tied to right or left. Instead it embraced representatives of points across the whole political spectrum who reflected in some degree a common return to the old pre-1950 orthodox ideology of continuity. Some were more orthodox than others, but in spite of sharp differences between them I shall lump them all together as the New Continuitarians. The return to continuity is perhaps not so clearly related to a change in the times as was its temporary abandonment. But as soon as the hurricane of social, political, and economic change had subsided in the 1970s, as soon as the Civil Rights Movement and the Second Reconstruction were ended and repudiation begun, a new orthodoxy in race relations was established, and something like social stability was restored—the chorus of continuity took up where it had left off a generation before. The discontinuity of Continuitarianism had only been temporary—*continuity interruptus*. The New Continuitarians often sounded much like the old, cited the same works and used many of the same arguments. So numerous are their contributions to the critical literature on the thesis of discontinuity that it is impractical to treat them all and only possible to sample them.

Since continuity nurtures tradition, minimizes change, and fosters respect for the past, it has a natural appeal for conservatives. It is significant that a new organization of conservative historians in 1980 should have given their journal the title *Continuity*. Conservatives of the guild are generally less ready than radicals to proclaim their leanings. With no desire to apply unwanted tags to individuals, I shall confine my comments to specific works and *their* leanings. One early critique from this side is William J. Cooper Jr., *The Conservative Regime* (1968), a low-keyed and civil reminder that the Redeemers of South Carolina, at least, as represented by Wade Hampton, would have liked nothing better than to have restored the old order with some concessions. Which was true enough, if a bit impractical. Cooper does concede that "the Conservative regime welcomed industry and capitalists," and he even acknowledges that cooperation was pretty close between Conservatives and industry, and that their chief editorial voice, F. W. Dawson, equaled Grady as a New South tub-thumper.

A bolder and more direct attack was an essay called "Redeemers Reconsidered: Change and Continuity in the Democratic South, 1870–1900," by James Tice Moore in 1978. Weighing "the contending forces of continuity and discontinuity, tradition and innovation," he comes down firmly on the side of continuity and tradition, dismissing departures from the old order as superficial. He contends that the Redeemers represented no change of guard and that the old "traditionalist, agriculturally oriented elites grasped the New South as firmly as they had the Old." Granting that they recruited a few "outsiders, parvenus, and adventurers," so did "the England of Charles II or the France of Louis XVIII, yet there can be no denying that restorations of a sort took place in those countries. The same is true of the Redeemer South." While Moore concedes that the indictment of Redeemer economic policies and pro-business bias in *Origins* is "convincing in its main thrust," he feels that the book is much too hard on the Redeemers and deplores its interpretation as "iconoclastic, even cynical in tone." The stress on the infamies of the convict-lease system, public-land and railroad swindles, tax exemptions for business, favors to speculators, and monopolies to the

Louisiana State Lottery overlooks the rewards of economic development, public benefits, and large state revenues derived from these sources. Also overlooked were the blessings of huge cuts in tax rates, more than 80 percent in one state, and "massive tax savings" for property owners generally. Benefits for the propertyless and the freedmen are not explored, nor are losses to state treasuries from defaulting and absconding Redeemer treasurers.

One entirely new dimension of continuity, incidental to the subject, comes from the conservative journal *Continuity* in the spring of 1981, an essay by Grady McWhiney entitled "Continuity in Celtic Warfare." Since the "Celts constituted an overwhelming majority in the South," they managed to carry on down to the Civil War folkways first noted by the Romans at a battle in 225 B.C. The Rebel yell lifted at Shiloh and Gettysburg, it seems, was first heard by the Roman legions more than two millennia ago.

Critics on the left, with no apparent awareness of a common cause with allies on the right (and with other fish to fry), also enlisted under the banner of continuity. The two examples noted are of the Marxist persuasion, and both are fellow-travelers of the continuity line, though they arrive at quite different destinations. They differed from each other as well as from travelers on their right. The quotation marks in the title of Dwight B. Billings Jr.'s *Planters and the Making of the "New South"* (1979) anticipate his conclusion that it was "hardly new at all." How could it be if, as he finds, the old planters took charge after the war and largely planned, owned, and managed the industrial South on into the twentieth century? The sample on which his finding is based is North Carolina, with emphasis on the cotton textile industry. Since the old aristocracy took the lead in industrializing the economy, North Carolina, like some European countries, took the "Prussian Road" of modernization by aristocratic elites. Billings finds support in the old-school Continuitarians Broadus Mitchell and Wilbur Cash. He quotes Mitchell and his brother approvingly as saying that in the South "the pioneers of industry were generally gentlemen. Not operatives or mechanics as in England, they did not see themselves as seizing mean advantage," but were instead "moved by the spirit of noblesse oblige" much as were "manorial lords of the early middle ages." While the governing law of industry "outside the South was the impersonal market," writes Billings, Southern industry "by contrast, stressed communal values. Its image for social relationships in mill villages was not the market but the paternalistic family." He takes special pleasure in quoting Cash on the identity of Old and New South and the continuity of the one with the other. Historians who emphasize change and discontinuity are snared in "the romantic tradition," while Cash, he declares, was "right on target."

Also from the left comes Jonathan Wiener, *Social Origins of the New South: Alabama, 1860–1885* (1978), and he too finds that the old planters not only survived but prospered and dominated the New South as they had the Old South. Still in the saddle, booted and spurred and armed with hegemony, the Alabama planter elite, however, charged off in the opposite direction from that supposedly taken by North Carolina planters. Instead of taking the lead in modernization and industrial development, they took a socially reactionary line and proved an obstacle to growth in manufactures, industry, and commerce. Wiener's most interesting and scholarly contributions to the ongoing discussion are the statistical data he dug out at great pains about the "persistence" of landholding among the large planters in five counties of the western half of the Alabama black belt from 1850 to 1870. Of the 236 planters with the greatest wealth in landholdings in 1860, 43 percent "remained in the elite in 1870," as compared with a "persistence rate" of 47 percent in the previous decade. Moreover, the wealthiest among the wealthy persisted in larger percentage. This is all based on retention of acreage of land. Granting devastating losses among all landowners in the South, he finds that "the planter elite in 1870 was relatively wealthier than it had been in 1860." That may have been cold comfort to the "relatively" blessed in view of the 67 percent decline in the average value of land per acre in Alabama, and the total loss of capital invested in slaves, or the 60 percent loss of all capital invested in agriculture, not to mention all investments in Confederate bonds and paper, and the huge debts concealed by land titles. But it is on this basis that Wiener contends that "war and Reconstruction did not significantly alter the antebellum pattern of elite persistence and social mobility."

Although much remains to be cleared up—how typical is the Alabama sample, for example, and how reliable was 1870 as a stopping point (with 1873 coming up) for measuring persistence—I nevertheless think Jonathan Wiener was justified in challenging Roger Shugg's phrase, "revolution in land titles," and my quoting it to describe "the downfall of the old planter class." I still believe something that can be called a revolution occurred and that in the process the planter class took a terrific tumble. The question becomes how significant are land titles, many of them heavily debt-encumbered, in measuring the persistence of wealth and power. If one is interested in "relationships to the means of production," as Marxists regularly are, I think other questions will arise. For example, how many of the old planters who hung onto or inherited land and prospered are known to have moved to town, opened stores, run gins, compresses, and banks, invested in railroads and mills, and played the speculative markets? My suggestion is that those members of the old planter families who made it to the top in the new order very likely took that course. And in becoming businessmen they transformed themselves into members of the new class that was creating a commercial revolution and fostering an industrial revolution. They might still call themselves planters, as might any townsman who foreclosed on land for debt. Most towns boasted a "Merchants and Planters Bank." But land at depressed values, crops at depressed prices, and labor with 30 percent lower productivity were not the real sources of power, nor were celebrated genealogies.

Wiener is not entirely blind to these realities. He notes that the percentage of large landholders listing their identifying occupations as other than "planter" multiplied five-fold in one sample, and he speaks, for example, of John B. Gordon and Alfred H. Colquitt as being "secret industrialists." They certainly made no secret of it, though, for Gordon's numerous ventures in railroads, manufactures, mining, and real estate were advertised, not concealed. Together with Colquitt, Gordon and his brothers cleared $1,000,000 in speculations in less than a year. To describe General Gordon as "the living incarnation of the aristocracy of the Old South" misconceives his antebellum origins as well as his postbellum career. On all these matters the neo-Continuitarians of the left would profit from thoughtful reconsideration.

Between the left and the right are those of the center who have shifted back toward the old orthodoxy of continuity or become fellow travelers of the neo-Continuitarian line. Like the radicals and conservatives, the liberals also return for support to the old classics of the tradition, but for the most part they have been content to correct what they take to be recent overemphasis on change and discontinuity. For example, George B. Tindall, *The Persistent Tradition in New South Politics* (1975), announces as his "central theme" the idea that "a thread of continuity ran through the transition from Bourbonism to Progressivism in the New South," with Populism linking the two. But it is only "a thread" and not a hempen rope that he chooses for his metaphor, and his thread is knotted into a Hegelian triad of thesis, antithesis, and synthesis. The last is supplied by the Progressives, who "built into their synthesis" of Bourbonism and Populism "the persistent tradition of community in the South." Even then, he modestly declares that this is only the theme of his book, not "that it is the central theme of southern political history, nor that it will resolve the complexities of the subject."

A more explicit example of a return to the old orthodoxy of continuity from the centrist position is found in Carl N. Degler, *Place Over Time: The Continuity of Southern Distinctiveness* (1977). As the title of his book indicates, he is addressing two themes, that of distinctiveness as well as that of continuity. But he makes it clear at the start that the latter is his main concern and that distinctiveness is incidental to it. "I want to emphasize," he writes, "that my purpose in discussing distinctiveness is to demonstrate the essential continuity of southern history." More specifically, he writes, "My intention in this book is to demonstrate the continuity in southern history that has been either explicitly or implicitly denied by recent historians of the South like Woodward, Genovese, and Gaston."

Degler's premise is that continuity is "closely related to the question of distinctiveness" and that he can "show the continuity of southern history" by proving that the South became distinctive quite early and has remained so all along. If his premise is correct his case is proved. Few historians of the South, and certainly not those just named, would deny the region's distinctiveness. Without it there would be little point in writing of the South separately from the rest of the nation. The question is the logic linking distinctiveness with continuity. The fact is that the former can and has been maintained without the latter and that difference can and has been enhanced by change—by discontinuity.

After elaborating upon the standard constants of climate, soil, and geography, about which there can be little argument, Degler settles upon slavery as "the basis of southern difference." Since it was slavery "that made the plantation possible," the two institutions "laid the foundation for the South's distinctiveness" and assured the continuity of Southern history. Did the abolition of slavery, then, not mark a break of discontinuity? He seems to be of divided mind on this question. First he says that "the ending of slavery did not mark a major break in the continuity of southern history," but a few pages later he writes, "One must admit that the abolition of slavery marked a significant change in the lives of southerners, white as well as black. Certainly it was a discontinuity in southern history." He manifests the same indecisiveness about the Civil War and its consequences. In a previous book, *The Other South,* published in 1974, he writes that "out of that war came not only devastation, but also the destruction of slavery and the society that rested on it." It might be assumed that the destruction of a society and its foundations could be the occasion of some historical discontinuity. Three years later, however, in *Place Over Time,* after saying, "The Civil War was certainly a discontinuity in the United States," he can write in the same paragraph, "It is my contention that the end of the Old South did not mark a significant break in the flow of southern history; it was only a minor disruption, with limited effects." Apparently it was the Old North instead of the Old South that bore the brunt of discontinuity. While admitting "the undoubted contribution of Reconstruction to southern distinctiveness," he contends that this "should not cause us to overlook the continuity between the antebellum years and those after Appomattox."

Like fellow travelers of the continuity line on his right and on his left, Degler derives support for his thesis from older Southern prophets ranging from Grady to Cash. Citing Henry W. Grady, Daniel Augustus Tompkins, and Richard H. Edmonds, he quotes the last as saying in 1903, "The South of today, the South of industrial and railroad activity, is not a new South, but a revival of the old South." It was perhaps inevitable that Degler should also cite Ulrich B. Phillips and that he should conclude triumphantly with a quotation from Wilbur J. Cash.

On the other hand, the incoming tide of continuity historiography already shows signs of turning. The criticism of the thesis of discontinuity and change has not all been negative and some of it lends strong support. For example, Harold D. Woodman in a forthcoming paper speaks of "massive changes following the Civil War" as "a revolutionary transformation" of the South's economy. "I use the term 'revolutionary' advisedly," he writes. "I mean a fundamental, radical transformation in Southern history." He has little patience with the advocates of "planter persistence" and planter dominance in the development and industrialization of the New South.

While Gavin Wright regrets that the controversy has been defined as continuity versus change (as do I), he leaves no doubt about his own views. In *The Political Economy of the Cotton South* (1978), he emphasizes not only the massiveness but the suddenness of change as well. "The South," he writes, "was wrenched out of one historical epoch and into another during the decade of the Civil War." The transition "involved a basic change in the character of human relations" and "the loss of financial independence" on the part of farmers. Changes of this extent have happened "elsewhere in history," to be sure, "but they represent the kind of long-run development" that is associated "with basic legal, institutional changes evolving over decades and centuries. In the South, it happened overnight, historically speaking." His conclusions have been greeted as emphasizing "the basic coherence and continuity of Southern economic history," but they do not sound that way to me.

Similar conclusions about the revolutionary character of post–Civil War change in agriculture are reached by Michael Wayne, *The Reshaping of Plantation Society* (1984), a study of the rich Natchez district where there occurred "a profound break between the plantation regime of the old order and the plantation regime of the new." Barbara Fields, *Slavery and Freedom on the Middle Ground* (1985), discloses revolutionary alterations in the lives of Maryland freemen and freedmen, as well as the old master class. Numerous other studies point toward similar conclusions. One that addresses the question of the old planters' role in industrialization deserves attention. David Carlton, in *Mill and Town in South Carolina* (1984) and elsewhere, challenges the thesis of "continuing planter hegemony" in the New South industry as "a serious misinterpretation of postbellum Southern history." In South Carolina, the prime exhibit of Old South continuity, he shows by detailed statistics that planters and farmers "played distinctly minor roles in mill development" and could be said to dominate in only two of a hundred firms. New men, mainly small-town businessmen with vital Yankee help, ran the industrial show.

No end to the debate seems yet in sight, though it threatens the exhaustion of patience. Monographs, articles, published debates and rebuttals, conferences, symposia and their collected papers continue to proliferate. No comprehensive treatment of them is possible here. *Origins of the New South* is cited frequently as the take-off point of controversy or the source of misguided theses. Nowhere in the 1951 volume, so far as I recall, however, are the terms *continuity* and *discontinuity* counterposed to announce or frame a thesis. Admittedly the issue arises repeatedly, with emphasis usually falling on change, but the emphasis derives from substance rather than theory. In the preface to the 1971 edition, in speaking of changes that had overwhelmed the South during the two decades since 1951, I did remark that the South had been "long unique among the regions of the nation for abrupt and drastic breaks in the continuity of its history." Perhaps the provocation derives as much from that as from the substance of the book. Of course, I do not shoulder or claim all the blame, for other historians, including economic and econometric historians, have pitched in freely. They are free to share what consolation may be had (besides that of being "right") from the belief that stirring up controversy can be an incidental service to scholarship.

But could not this debate have been shortened by some such reflection as those found in Carl Degler's concession that "all questions of continuity are relative," and that "all history is a combination of varying degrees of continuity and change"? It probably will be in the end, as banal as that solution is. But that does not dismiss the significance or deny the value of the controversy. For most of the important debates over history, as I have remarked earlier, have not been about absolute but about relative matters, not about the existence but about the degree or extent of the phenomenon in question. Evidently there have existed deep differences of opinion over questions of that sort in Southern history that needed airing.

"On the Pinnacle in Yankeeland": C. Vann as a [Southern] Renaissance Man

A decade after *Origins of the New South* appeared, University of Georgia historian E. Merton Coulter heartily concurred with a friend's assessment that C. Vann Woodward's book had been written "to please Gunnar Myrdal, the Civil Rights advocates and all the Northern Left-Wingers." "As one of the editors of the [History of the South] series," Coulter explained, "I would have objected to the MS, if there had been any way to bring it more into line with the facts; but the point of view permeated the whole. And so we could not afford to reject the MS, which by the way, put C. Vann on the pinnacle in Yankeeland."[1]

Reprinted from *Journal of Southern History,* 67 (November 2001), 715–40, the Woodward symposium issue.

1. C. Vann Woodward, *Origins of the New South, 1877–1913* (Baton Rouge, 1951); J. Fred Rippy to E. Merton Coulter, October 24, 1961, Folder 5, Box 34 (first quotation); Coulter to Rippy, October 25, 1961, Folder 5, Box 48 (second quotation); both in E. Merton

Headed to Yale University as Sterling Professor of History, Woodward had also reached the pinnacle of his profession in 1961, having in scarcely two decades not only "revolutionalized the established views of Southern history from the end of the Civil War to World War I" but actually introduced what Richard H. King called "a new paradigm"—"a new way of looking at Southern history." As the story of the origins of *Origins of the New South* reveals, Woodward's revolutionary new approach to the study of southern history was actually grounded in the same appreciation of the power of the past and its oneness with the present he had found in the works of William Faulkner, Robert Penn Warren, Thomas Wolfe, and other major writers of the Southern Literary Renaissance.[2]

Although he had majored in philosophy at Emory University, as an undergraduate Woodward's closest companions were Ernest Hartsock, a brilliant but ill-fated young poet who published the avant-garde literary magazine *Bozart,* and Woodward's lifelong friend Glenn W. Rainey, who was also an aspiring poet at the time. Although Woodward had apparently toyed with the idea of writing a novel, either on his own or in cooperation with Rainey, under Hartsock's tutelage at Emory he concentrated primarily on perfecting a "literary style" in his writing. After graduation Woodward and Rainey immersed themselves in literature of all sorts, including the works of Marcel Proust and James Joyce. Woodward had trouble at first with William Faulkner, whose *Sound and the Fury* he did not finish, but both he and Rainey immediately devoured anything written by Thomas Wolfe.[3]

Needless to say, when the twenty-five-year-old Woodward enrolled for

Coulter Papers (Special Collections Division, University of Georgia Library, Athens, Ga.). The author wishes to thank Dr. Fred A. Bailey and Dr. Anne Firor Scott for sharing their insights and information with him. He is also indebted to Mr. Stephen A. Berrey and Mr. Jonathan A. Haws for their assistance in research for this article.

2. Richard H. King, *A Southern Renaissance: The Cultural Awakening of the American South, 1930–1955* (New York and Oxford, 1980), 257.

3. Interviews with C. Vann Woodward by John Herbert Roper, July 18, 1978, and April 13, 1979, transcripts in Folder 10, John Herbert Roper Papers #4235 (Southern Historical Collection, Wilson Library, University of North Carolina at Chapel Hill; hereinafter SHC); Interview with LeRoy E. Loemker by John Herbert Roper, August 11, 1979, transcript in Folder 6, Roper Papers (quotation); John Herbert Roper, *C. Vann Woodward, Southerner* (Athens, Ga., and London, 1987), 38–44; C. Vann Woodward to Glenn W. Rainey, July 17, 1934, and October 2, 1938, Folder 1; Rainey to Woodward, September 16, 1929, May 1, 1936, and May 15, 1939, Folder 2; all in Box 22, Glenn W. Rainey Papers (Special Collections Department, Robert W. Woodruff Library, Emory University).

graduate study in history at the University of North Carolina in 1934, at "the peak and crest of the Southern Literary Renaissance," he was sorely disappointed to find "[n]o renaissance here, no surge of innovation and creativity, no rebirth of energy, no compelling new vision." Instead, he discovered that, in Chapel Hill and elsewhere, the masters of southern history were simply recycling the "received wisdom" that had long sustained "the system founded on the ruins of Reconstruction called the New South."[4]

By the middle of the twentieth century, the term *New South* connoted a thoroughgoing regional transformation, but in its original, late-nineteenth-century incarnation, the "New South Creed," as Paul M. Gaston called it, promised immediate and sweeping economic change without the sacrifice of racial, political, and cultural autonomy or continuity. Espousing a powerful mixture of myths about the past, illusions about the present, and fantasies about the future, the architects of the New South succeeded in constructing a new regional identity, one so enduring that, as Michael O'Brien observed, "the New South helped to make permanent the very idea of a South."[5]

Regional, national, or otherwise, new group identities often come equipped with an appealing vision of instant and dramatic progress toward a bounteous future, but an inspiring and unifying past is an even more essential feature. Thus, as Woodward put it, the "nostalgic vision" of a glorious and genteel Old South became "[o]ne of the most significant inventions of the New South," and "[t]he deeper the . . . commitments to the New Order, the louder the protests of loyalty to the Old."[6]

Because Henry W. Grady and his New South apostles blamed the unsettled racial conditions in the late-nineteenth-century South on the tragically misguided policies of Reconstruction, the perception of that era as a time of untold horrors and suffering became another fundamental element of the New South Creed's version of southern history. The most crucial ingredient of all, however, was a celebration of the heroic Redeemers, who had rescued the white South from the living hell of Reconstruction and embraced a new vision of industrial progress without discarding the benevolent and honor-

---

4. C. Vann Woodward, *Thinking Back: The Perils of Writing History* (Baton Rouge, 1986), 21–23 (first, second, and third quotations on p. 23; fourth quotation on p. 22).

5. Paul M. Gaston, *The New South Creed: A Study in Southern Mythmaking* (New York, 1970); James C. Cobb, "From 'New South' to 'No South': The Southern Renaissance and the Struggle with Southern Identity," in Cobb, *Redefining Southern Culture: Mind and Identity in the Modern South* (Athens, Ga., and London, 1999), 150–56; Michael O'Brien, *The Idea of the American South, 1920–1941* (Baltimore and London, 1979), 6.

6. Woodward, *Origins of the New South*, 154–55.

able traditions passed down from their planter-aristocrat ancestors. With the Redeemers representing an umbilical connection between the two, propagandists could reassure white southerners that the New South was "simply the old South under new conditions."[7]

The construction of new group identities also requires the "invention of tradition." In the case of the New South, this obviously meant both the greatly embellished vision of the Old South and the ritualistic trotting out of the old captains of the Lost Cause to convey their blessings on the new captains of industry and commerce. Invented traditions typically serve pragmatic as well as symbolic ends, however. In the New South both segregation and disfranchisement were cases in point. While both reinforced and enhanced white power and prestige, segregation, which John W. Cell described as nothing less than "an organic component of the New South creed," promised a more stable urban labor climate for prospective employers. Meanwhile, disfranchisement guaranteed political stability by purging the electorate of black voters and a great many lower-class white ones as well, thereby institutionalizing the Democratic Party's right to rule through the invention of yet another New South tradition—one-party politics.[8]

Armed with the New South Creed's seamless and seductive vision of a glorious yesterday, a dynamic today, and a glittering tomorrow, its champions became the defenders of past, present, and future, while its challengers represented threats not only to the status quo but to progress and tradition as well. When southern governors of the 1950s courted northern industrialists with assurances of cheap labor and low taxes while defending the New South's racial legacy of Jim Crow and disfranchisement as the "Southern Way of Life," they merely confirmed the remarkable durability of what Woodward called a "New South fraud papered over by an Old South myth."[9]

---

7. Henry W. Grady, "The New South" [1899], *The New South: Writings and Speeches of Henry Grady* (Savannah, Ga., 1971), 107 (quotation); Thomas Nelson Page, *The Old South: Essays Social and Political* (Chautauqua, N.Y., 1919), 5.

8. Eric Hobsbawm and Terence Ranger, eds., *The Invention of Tradition* (Cambridge, Eng., and other cities, 1983); Charles Reagan Wilson, *Baptized in Blood: The Religion of the Lost Cause, 1865–1920* (Athens, Ga., 1980); John W. Cell, *The Highest Stage of White Supremacy: The Origins of Segregation in South Africa and the American South* (Cambridge, Eng., and other cities, 1982), 181; J. Morgan Kousser, *The Shaping of Southern Politics: Suffrage Restriction and the Establishment of the One-Party South, 1880–1910* (New Haven and London, 1974).

9. C. Vann Woodward, "New South Fraud Is Papered by Old South Myth," *Washington Post*, July 9, 1961, p. E3, c. 5.

Because the New South identity depended on a rigid scripting of both the region's distant and recent past, its orthodoxy weighed so heavily on those who wrote the region's history that, as William E. Dodd pointed out in 1904, "many subjects" of interest to historians might "not with safety be even so much as discussed." Certainly, "to suggest that the revolt from the union in 1860 was not justified, was not led by the most lofty minded of statesmen," was "to invite not only criticism but an enforced resignation."[10]

Southern historians inclined either to objectivity or candor were forced to do battle not just with the romance of the Lost Cause but also with the uncritical boosterism of the New South Creed and its insistence on the region's miraculous self-resurrection, omnibeneficent economic progress, and racial and class harmony. As Gaston summarized it, the "central theme" of the writings of early-twentieth-century New South historians such as Philip Alexander Bruce and Holland Thompson was "the concept of triumph over adversity, of steel will and impeccable character overcoming staggering problems, often against what seemed impossible odds."[11]

In the hands of many writers, the history of the New South was every bit as romantic as that of the Old. Broadus Mitchell's *The Rise of Cotton Mills in the South* even promised readers "not only an industrial chronicle, but a romance, a drama as well." As Daniel J. Singal explained, Mitchell's portrayal of the early mill builders as the philanthropic descendants of the antebellum cavaliers demonstrated "the extraordinary power that could be wielded by the New South ideology over one of the most intelligent, learned, and compassionate southerners of his era."[12]

Trinity College (now Duke University) historian John Spencer Bassett had insisted in 1897 that any historian in the South who had ever departed from traditional views was "denounced as a traitor and a mercenary defiler of his birthplace." Proceeding to prove his own point, after showing the temerity to challenge the New South's racial and political institutions, Bassett

---

10. William E. Dodd, "Some Difficulties of the History Teacher in the South," *South Atlantic Quarterly*, 3 (April 1904), 119.

11. Paul M. Gaston, "The New South," in Arthur S. Link and Rembert W. Patrick, eds., *Writing Southern History: Essays in Historiography in Honor of Fletcher M. Green* (Baton Rouge, 1965), 321. See, for example, Philip Alexander Bruce, *The Rise of the New South* (Philadelphia, 1905); Holland Thompson, *From the Cotton Field to the Cotton Mill: A Study of the Industrial Transition in North Carolina* (New York and London, 1906); and Thompson, *The New South: A Chronicle of Social and Industrial Evolution* (New Haven, 1919).

12. Broadus Mitchell, *The Rise of Cotton Mills in the South* (Baltimore, 1921), vii; Daniel Joseph Singal, *The War Within: From Victorian to Modernist Thought in the South, 1919–1945* (Chapel Hill, 1982), 81.

eventually found it prudent to head north to Smith College in 1906. He explained to colleagues that "[i]t was the conviction that I could not write history and direct public sentiment too that made me willing to come North" and predicted that it would be "another generation before [the South] will be ready for the scholar or the writer of serious books."[13]

Bassett's prediction proved remarkably accurate, although a bit too optimistic where professional historians were concerned. Singal pointed to the influence of the New South Creed as the principal obstacle to the arrival of intellectual modernism in the region.[14] In fact, a move to unravel the tangle of myth and inconsistency that lay at the heart of the New South identity did not coalesce until the post–World War I intellectual awakening of the Southern Renaissance.

As the 1920s began, tensions between the New South's myths and its realities seemed to be reaching the snapping point. Events such as the Leo Frank lynching, the resurgence of the Ku Klux Klan, the wave of postwar racial violence, and the Scopes trial drew unprecedented attention to the South's problems and deficiencies and raised a multitude of questions about the New South Creed's vision of progress in the region. For the most part, however, the critical commentators on the South in the 1920s seemed too astonished by its ongoing panorama of ignorance and depravity to reflect seriously on the historical context from which this sorry state of affairs had evolved. Only with the onset of the Great Depression did a significant number of white southerners finally begin to grapple with the fundamental contradiction that, as Louis D. Rubin put it, "[t]he South has not always been this way; it has become this way. The image of the heroic past renders the distraught present so distasteful, just as it is this very same heroic past that has caused the present."[15]

Rubin's words suggest that, except for the stifling impact of the New South Creed on any impulse toward critical, detached historical analysis, historians might well have played a pivotal role in the Southern Renais-

13. Wendell Holmes Stephenson, "John Spencer Bassett: Trinity College Liberal," in Stephenson, *Southern History in the Making: Pioneer Historians of the South* (Baton Rouge, 1964), 102 (first quotation); Bruce Clayton, *The Savage Ideal: Intolerance and Intellectual Leadership in the South, 1890–1914* (Baltimore and London, 1972), 90–101 (second and third quotations on p. 101). See also Peter Novick, *That Noble Dream: The "Objectivity Question" and the American Historical Profession* (Cambridge, Eng., and other cities, 1988), 79.

14. Singal, *War Within*, 9.

15. Cobb, "From 'New South' to 'No South,'" 159–60; Louis D. Rubin Jr., "The Historical Image of Modern Southern Writing," *Journal of Southern History*, 22 (May 1956), 159.

sance. As it was, however, Donald Davidson's observation in 1937 that the most important contemporary writers were asking "the historian's question—what the South was?—and the related question—what the South is?"—simply meant that many of the key figures of the Southern Renaissance were practicing history without a license.[16]

Ellen Glasgow, whose 1913 novel, *Virginia,* was set in the 1880s when "[t]he smoke of factories was already succeeding the smoke of battlefields," had shown both a significant historical consciousness and a certain skepticism of the New South Creed in her writing well before World War I. By 1928 Glasgow herself was praising "an important group of Southern novelists" who were re-evaluating "both the past and the present, and subjecting the raw material of life to the fearless scrutiny and the spacious treatment of art."[17]

Glasgow's profile of the new breed of southern writer clearly foreshadowed the work of Thomas Wolfe and William Faulkner, both of whom made the paradox of family and community decline in the midst of New South progress a dominant theme in their novels. In Faulkner's *Sound and the Fury,* for example, an aristocratic pedigree only fuels the anger and frustration of the mercenary but luckless and neurotic Jason Compson, who has been reduced to clerking in a hardware store. Woodward insisted that the New South "means the Compsons going to work for the Snopeses," and for Faulkner himself, the disintegration of the Compsons and their displacement by the Snopeses was but one aspect of the rise of what he characterized in 1933 as "a thing known whimsically as the New South . . . ."[18]

When Glasgow updated her list of southern literary rebels in 1943, it included not only Wolfe and Faulkner but, perhaps surprisingly to some, Margaret Mitchell. Mitchell's challenge to the New South Creed was largely lost in the rush to romanticize her best-selling book into a blockbuster movie, but her literary portrayal of a war-hardened Scarlett O'Hara's metamorphosis from flighty Old South coquette to ruthless New South lumber baroness offered readers a healthy dose of the same greed, materialism,

---

16. Donald Davidson, "Expedients vs. Principles—Cross-Purposes in The South," in Davidson, *The Attack on Leviathan: Regionalism and Nationalism in the United States* (Chapel Hill, 1938), 323; originally published in *Southern Review,* 2 (Spring 1937), 647–69.

17. Ellen Glasgow, *Virginia* (New York, 1913), 13 (first quotation); Ellen Glasgow, "The Novel in the South," *Harper's Magazine,* 158 (December 1928), 98 (second quotation), 99 (third quotation).

18. Woodward, "New South Fraud," p. E3, c. 5; William Faulkner, "An Introduction to *The Sound and the Fury,*" *Mississippi Quarterly,* 26 (Summer 1973), 411.

brutality, and forsaken tradition that would eventually pervade *Origins of the New South*. Despite its generally dismissive treatment at the hands of historians, Willie Lee Rose noted *Gone With the Wind*'s almost Beardian economic realism and observed, as Mitchell herself acknowledged, that Scarlett's "sheer greed" and "shabby dealings in business" were "meant as a personal characterization of the city of Atlanta itself, and by extension the New South." For Mitchell the story of the New South lay not so much in Atlanta's rising from the ashes as in Scarlett's rising from the garden at Tara and heading off to Atlanta to make good on her vow never to be hungry again.[19]

Those who recall that Scarlett made this vow after regurgitating a dirt-encrusted radish will find it a striking coincidence that C. Vann Woodward claimed to have suffered a "violent muscular contraction in the esophagus" while trying to read Mitchell's story "about how a tart little bitch gets all the men in North Georgia in rut." Woodward's admission that he gave up on *Gone With the Wind* after 118 pages suggests that his views on the New South were probably not shaped by Margaret Mitchell. Despite her orthodox views on race, slavery, and Reconstruction, however, Mitchell's treatment of the New South actually put her closer to Woodward than most of his contemporaries in southern history as of the mid-1930s.[20]

The same was true of W. J. Cash, who, like Woodward and other nonfiction writers of the Southern Renaissance, harbored his own literary ambitions. Admitting in 1936 that he wanted "above everything else to be a novelist," Cash confessed that in his early years as a journalist he had written "a subjective novel . . . a blood and thunder romance which I disposed of in the same fashion." At various points, Cash also toyed with writing a novel about "the Old South as it was," focusing on a young Irishman named Angus Carrick who rose from the yeomanry to end his career as "a major in the Southern hierarchy" (sound familiar?), as well as "a huge novel of the Civil War." He even described *Mind of the South* as "creative writing" of a sort, and he won a Guggenheim fellowship in 1941 by proposing a novel centered on Andrew Bates, scion of a wealthy North Carolina textile family,

19. Ellen Glasgow, *A Certain Measure: An Interpretation of Prose Fiction* (New York, 1943), 147; Margaret Mitchell, *Gone With the Wind* (New York, 1936); [Willie Lee] Rose, *Race and Region in American Historical Fiction: Four Episodes in Popular Culture* (Oxford, 1979), 25–28 (quotations on p. 26).

20. C. Vann Woodward to Glenn W. Rainey, July 12, 1936, Folder 1, Box 22, Rainey Papers.

and the larger story of his family's role in "the rise of an industrial town in the South after the introduction of the idea of Progress after 1880."[21]

Likewise, though he was no great admirer of either Cash or Mitchell, Woodward arrived in Chapel Hill for graduate school with considerably more interest in literature than history and certainly more of a literary sensibility than a historical one. After graduating from Emory and teaching English at Georgia Tech for a year, he headed off in 1931 to earn a master's degree from Columbia University "without the vaguest notions of what I was going to do." Put off by the only three classes in sociology that he attended, after flirting briefly with anthropology he eventually gravitated toward political science. Woodward's master's thesis on Alabama senator Thomas E. Heflin led him to ponder a book, which he planned to call "Seven for Demos," that would focus on seven southern demagogues, including Heflin, Huey Long, Ben Tillman, James K. Vardaman, and Tom Watson. His growing fascination with Watson, the fiery Populist advocate of biracial political activism who degenerated into a malicious racial and religious bigot of the worst sort, eventually dictated an entire book on him alone.[22]

Concerned less with historical analysis than with literary style, Woodward began writing the Watson biography after reading Proust and proclaiming him "infallible" and "god like," his every sentence "a *tour de force.*" In contrast, Woodward struggled mightily to write his own first few pages, complaining to his friend Rainey that he was suffering from "a severe attack of the Faulknerian galloping-hooves." "The poor, poor Old South," he wrote, "I write and snatch a blotter to save the MSS from the briny ruin of a heart wrung sob. . . . [N]obody should write anything about the South right here in the middle of it all. . . . Goddammit, I say, how can you *help* sounding like Thomas Nelson Page and Al Jolson? It all makes me suspect the redoubtable Bill Faulkner of being bemused on tobacco juice and dipping his pen in the garbage can."[23]

---

21. Alfred A. Knopf, Incorporated, "Authors Form A, 4-29-36," Folder 56 (first quotation); "Application for a John Simon Guggenheim Memorial Fellowship," [October 1936], Folder 56 (second, third, and fourth quotations); W. J. Cash to Alfred A. Knopf, September 8, 1940, Folder 59 (fifth quotation); "Application for a John Simon Guggenheim Memorial Fellowship," [October 1940], Folder 59 (sixth and seventh quotations); all in Box 5, Joseph L. Morrison Papers #3787, SHC. See also W. J. Cash, *The Mind of the South* (New York, 1941).

22. C. Vann Woodward to Glenn W. Rainey, October 20, 1931, Folder 1 (quotation); Woodward to Rainey, n.d., Folder 3; both in Box 22, Rainey Papers; Roper, *C. Vann Woodward,* 52, 76.

23. C. Vann Woodward to Glenn W. Rainey, n.d., Folder 3, Box 22, Rainey Papes.

After researching for a year and writing four chapters, Woodward's depleted finances forced him to admit that "the best hope of completing the book seemed to lie in getting a fellowship for graduate work in history and offering the book as a dissertation." With the assistance of sociologists Howard W. Odum, whose family's farm was near the town of Oxford, Georgia, where Woodward's parents then lived, and Rupert B. Vance, whose parents had been Woodward's neighbors when his family had lived in Morrilton, Arkansas, Woodward secured a Rockefeller Foundation grant for his Ph.D. studies at the University of North Carolina. North Carolina was the "logical university" for his purposes because its library held Watson's private papers. Woodward had begun his book on Watson with "no academic purpose in mind" and only "the faintest formal preparation in American history" acquired in an exceedingly dull course at Emory that had "been more than enough to discourage further curiosity." For him southern history was not so much a chosen field but one dictated by his choice of a dissertation topic, and he was forced therefore to accept the fact that "a Southern historian I must be—or somehow become . . . ."[24]

This realization became even more sobering when he found the secondary historical literature that he was expected to master so bland and poorly written: "Plodding through volume after volume, I began to wonder if I had ever encountered prose so pedestrian, pages so dull, chapters so devoid of ideas, whole volumes so wrongheaded or so lacking in point." Wholly focused on completing his biography of Watson, Woodward resented the "rigamarole" of classes and note-taking that was required of him, and he admitted that he repeatedly "stole from graduate class work" to work on the Watson project.[25] Complaining that his writing had "about come to an impasse" because "courses take up all my time," Woodward threatened to minimize his course work thereafter by signing up only for enough classes to retain his grant. "History, I find, is a collection of facts," he wrote to Rainey in the fall of 1934. "Should have looked into that before going so far. Nothing but contempt for facts! Opinion all that matters. Proper attitude." Typically, even as he complained of having "7⁶/₇ volumes to go" in a dreary eight-volume history of England in the eighteenth century, Wood-

24. Woodward, *Thinking Back*, 20 (first and second quotations), 21 (third, fourth, and fifth quotations), 22 (sixth quotation). On the Rockefeller grant see C. Vann Woodward to Glenn W. Rainey, June 17, [1933?], Folder 3, Box 22, Rainey Papers.

25. Woodward, *Thinking Back*, 21 (first quotation); Interview with C. Vann Woodward by James Green, July 3, 1983, transcript in Folder 26, Roper Papers (second quotation); Woodward interview, July 18, 1978, transcript in Folder 10, Roper Papers (third quotation).

ward recommended that Rainey read a two-volume set on English literature and a *Saturday Review* essay on Faulkner's *Sanctuary.* As his first year of Ph.D. study drew to a close, the frustrated biographer, who at one point had considered transferring to the University of Chicago, wearily concluded that "since in all seriousness I can say that I have not gleaned a single scholarly idea from any professor here, I would be no more likely to fare any better with the professors who taught these professors."[26]

The day after his Ph.D. orals, Woodward judged that he had "performed adequately, of course, but not brilliantly. There is simply nothing in the idea of examinations that challenges my temperament. I seldom rise to them more than sufficiently." His mediocre showing notwithstanding, Woodward admitted to Rainey that he was "indulging myself the dubious pleasure of some extravagant forgetting. No niggardly date here and a dictator there, but whole dynasties at a time—Poof, there go the Hapsburgs, poof, the Hohenzollerns. (I made the mistake of forgetting the Hanoverians before the orals.) A continent or two, an ocean of diplomacy, and a library of books—alcohol proves an excellent solvent for the unused impedimientia [sic] of information after examinations."[27]

However cleverly Woodward's words may have expressed the sentiments of generations of history graduate students, his fellow Ph.D. candidates at North Carolina might not have thought them terribly exaggerated in his case. As one of his closest friends from that era put it, little in graduate school "really influenced" Woodward, who had come to Chapel Hill "with a definite point of view and a definite project—the Tom Watson study." Observed another, "He borrowed notes and crammed for exams, [and he] was totally uninterested in history except for the post–Civil War South." If Woodward had been little impressed by the faculty at North Carolina, the feeling was mutual among some of them who were "unhappy that [Woodward] simply did not know many facts of history."[28]

The only member of Woodward's examining committee who seemed un-

26. C. Vann Woodward to Glenn W. Rainey, October 27, [1934], Folder 3 (letter dated by reference to the essay on *Sanctuary*: Lawrence S. Kubie, "William Faulkner's 'Sanctuary,'" *Saturday Review of Literature,* 11 [October 20, 1934], 218, 224–26); Woodward to Rainey, April 29, 1935, Folder 1; both in Box 22, Rainey Papers.

27. C. Vann Woodward to Glenn W. Rainey, May 17, 1936, Folder 1, Box 22, Rainey Papers.

28. Interview with J. Carlyle Sitterson by John Herbert Roper, November 10, 1979, transcript in Folder 7, Roper Papers (first and third quotations); Interview with Bennett H. Wall by John Herbert Roper, April 11, 1979, transcript in Folder 9, Roper Papers (second quotation).

troubled by his somewhat lackadaisical approach to the facts was the recently arrived Howard K. Beale. Like Woodward, the erratic and eccentric
Beale had a record of activism, especially on civil rights, and from the start
their relationship was less that of mentor-student than kindred spirits and
friends. Beale arrived only in the second of Woodward's three years in
Chapel Hill. Woodward had already drafted most of his manuscript at that
point, and in early July 1937, scarcely a year after Beale had agreed to direct
it, the carbon of his unrevised dissertation was on its way to Macmillan.
Woodward learned of its acceptance for publication in early September
1937. He hurriedly inserted fifteen pages, "mostly dealing with Watson's
personal life and feelings," and was reading page proofs by the end of the
year.[29]

Woodward would later praise Beale for giving him "a sense of the demands and rigor of historical scholarship," and their correspondence after
Woodward left Chapel Hill affirms this judgment. Still, Woodward's gra-
cious attempt in his memoir, *Thinking Back,* to credit his mentor for mini-
mizing the time "between dissertation and published book" hardly accords
either with his admission that "[b]ecause Beale was the director, I was allowed much more latitude than otherwise" or with his revelation that he
had yielded "only when I had to" when Beale urged him to provide more of
the "transitions, summaries, etc." that would assist readers in grasping the
broader historical and historiographical implications of his study. Woodward's magnanimity is legendary, but his lavish praise of Beale obscured the
reality that, at the time it was written, the gifted young author of *Tom Watson, Agrarian Rebel* still saw himself more as a storyteller or biographer
than as a professional historian.[30]

The same was true of Woodward's effort, a half century after the fact,
to characterize his dissertation as a fledgling scholar's attempt to launch an
"oblique" assault on "the ramparts of the establishment in Southern histori-

---

29. Roper, *C. Vann Woodward,* 98, 108–9; C. Vann Woodward to "Jack" [?], July 15,
1937, Folder 4; Woodward to Glenn W. Rainey, September 11, 1937, Folder 1; Woodward to
Rainey, October 27, 1937, Folder 1 (quotation); all in Box 22, Rainey Papers.

30. Woodward interview, July 18, 1978, transcript in Folder 10, Roper Papers (first quotation); Woodward, *Thinking Back,* 38 (second quotation); C. Vann Woodward to Glenn W.
Rainey, May 7, 1937 (third quotation); Woodward to Rainey, January 10, 193[8] (this letter
is mistakenly dated 1937, probably because it was written so early in the new year); and Woodward to Rainey, December 4, 1942 (fourth and fifth quotations); all in Folder 1, Box 22,
Rainey Papers. See also Comer Vann Woodward, "The Political and Literary Career of
Thomas E. Watson" (Ph.D. dissertation, University of North Carolina at Chapel Hill, 1937).

ography" in the 1930s. Though he had chosen the topic and written much of the book with no such purpose in mind, his biography of Tom Watson "seemed made to order in many respects" for such an undertaking: "Not only was it a fascinating story in itself, but it plunged the historian into all the dark, neglected, and forbidden corners of Southern life shunned by the New South school."[31]

Woodward's reference to Watson's "fascinating story" is instructive because, as he struggled to complete his dissertation, he seemed less intent on making a historiographical statement than in telling Watson's personal story in a smooth and engaging literary style. Cramming for his Ph.D. exams, he had complained, "I still believe in the *story* strong. But, hell, I can't call the choice of an adjective my own until I have that cursed degree behind me." Woodward had gained access to Watson's papers through Watson's granddaughter, Georgia Watson, who wanted to "do a novel of her family." He readily agreed that "[i]t would make as powerful stuff" as Wolfe's *Look Homeward, Angel*—"drunken, raw, and full of passion." Although Woodward promised that his book would be "a better read than Huxley's new novel," his effort to do justice to Watson's story simply confirmed for him "the sheer inadequacy of biography vs. fiction." As his manuscript went to press, he worried that "the book would have been better . . . if I had been prey to all the pangs of a literary conscience—instead of sometimes mearly [sic] the Ph.D. conscience which is something else."[32]

As it turned out, readers consistently praised the literary style in which Woodward told Tom Watson's story or, as one put it, allowed Watson "to speak for himself . . . with a minimum of comment," without "overanalyzing him in a Freudian manner" or "expanding the sectional issues with which he was so completely identified." In hindsight it seems clear enough that in taking Populism, especially southern Populism, seriously, and in showing that white unity and Democratic hegemony had not gone unchallenged in the wake of Reconstruction, *Tom Watson, Agrarian Rebel* was a work with revisionist implications for New South historiography, broadly

---

31. Woodward, *Thinking Back*, 29 (first and second quotations), 30 (third and fourth quotations).

32. C. Vann Woodward to Glenn W. Rainey, April 13, 1936, Folder 1 (first quotation; emphasis added); Woodward to Rainey, October 7, 1933, Folder 1 (second, third, and fifth quotations); Woodward to Rainey, August 24, [?], Folder 3 (fourth quotation); Woodward to Rainey, November 6, 1937, Folder 1 (sixth and seventh quotations); all in Box 22, Rainey Papers.

defined. Yet Woodward's scattered generalizations about southern Populism were based almost exclusively on events and conditions in Georgia.[33]

In a critique of an article taken directly from Woodward's forthcoming book, *Journal of Southern History* editor Wendell Holmes Stephenson advised the young author that if he could "clarify somewhat your explanation of how Watson arrived at his liberal views by 1892 and then how he came to reverse them in later years, I think it might be a distinct improvement." Woodward declined to do this either in his article or in his book, conceding years later that he had "avoided explicit analysis of his [Watson's] change" because, at the time, it had seemed sufficient simply to describe Watson's tragic career, punctuating the narrative with occasional interpretative suggestions.[34]

Only in the book's preface did Woodward venture the opinion that Watson was not so much an agent as a victim of " 'the sinister forces of intolerance, superstition, prejudice, religious jingoism, and mobbism' " that gripped the South in the era after Reconstruction. "Although I have not sought to impose the view on the reader," he added, "I might confess here my private feeling that his story is also in many ways the tragedy of a class, and more especially the tragedy of a section." At the end of the book, however, quoting a popular ballad called "The Thomas E. Watson Song," Woodward simply described Watson as a man who " 'fought and struggled' and, in the end, failed."[35]

Not surprisingly, reviewers read *Tom Watson* in a variety of ways. Journalist Gerald W. Johnson saw its "true importance . . . as a case history of a Southern liberal" and made no mention of Populism whatsoever in his critique. Fellow southern historians Alex M. Arnett and Frank L. Owsley also focused almost entirely on Woodward's treatment of Watson's life and bifurcated career. Only John D. Hicks, whose recent study, *The Populist Revolt,* had greatly influenced Woodward, seemed to appreciate some of the

---

33. Anne Behrens to C. Vann Woodward, July 16, 1938, Folder 1, Box 1, C. Vann Woodward Papers (Manuscripts and Archives, Yale University Library); C. Vann Woodward, *Tom Watson, Agrarian Rebel* (New York, 1938). On Woodward's generalizations about the South as a whole drawn from Georgia sources, see *Tom Watson,* 122–25, 217–19. Note that the index contains no entries for any other southern state.

34. C. Vann Woodward, "Tom Watson and the Negro in Agrarian Politics," *Journal of Southern History,* 4 (February 1938), 14–33; Wendell Holmes Stephenson to C. Vann Woodward, October 6, 1937, Box 1, Woodward Papers (first quotation); Woodward interview, July 18, 1978, transcript in Folder 10, Roper Papers (second quotation).

35. Woodward, *Tom Watson,* viii, 486.

historiographical contributions of this "understanding portrayal of a man, a movement, and a section . . . ."[36]

In his 1932 biography of Grover Cleveland, Allan Nevins had dismissed Watson as "a voluble hothead who made political demagogy and the editorship of a Populist weekly pay well." Woodward admitted to Rainey that "if there was any one contemporary biographer that I had in mind as in a measure 'answering,' it was Nevins." Yet, after reading Woodward's manuscript for Macmillan and heartily endorsing its publication, Nevins went on in a glowing New York *Times* review to suggest that the book's primary contribution was the revelation that "popular ignorance and the race question" had given the "Populist movement in the South . . . a bitterness, violence and crudity that never stamped the Northern movement." Stunned by this apparent misreading of his message, Woodward found it ironic that Nevins's endorsement "should have sold the book to Macmillan," and after anticipating criticism from him, he confessed to feeling "a little dashed at being taken into his [Nevins's] school and just a little resentful. Maybe I wasn't forceful enough."[37]

Whether it was interpreted precisely as Woodward intended, the Watson biography brought its author sufficient notice that, less than a year after its publication, he was invited to write one of the volumes in the recently announced History of the South series. Ironically, this project had grown out of the same New South insistence on historical orthodoxy that Woodward had encountered when he arrived in Chapel Hill. A joint effort of the University of Texas and Louisiana State University Press, this series had actually evolved from the pre–World War I efforts of wealthy banker and former Confederate officer George W. Littlefield to prevent historians at the University of Texas from assigning textbooks that struck him as too critical of white southerners. The enterprising head of the Texas history department, Eugene C. Barker, ultimately yielded to Littlefield's pressure, but he

---

36. Gerald W. Johnson, "Vinegar Tree," *New Republic*, 94 (April 20, 1938), 338 (first quotation). See also the reviews of *Tom Watson* by Alex Mathews Arnett in *American Historical Review*, 44 (April 1939), 661–62; by Frank L. Owsley in *Mississippi Valley Historical Review*, 25 (December 1938), 431–32; and by John D. Hicks in *Journal of Southern History*, 4 (November 1938), 538–39 (second quotation on p. 539). See also John D. Hicks, *The Populist Revolt: A History of the Farmers' Alliance and the People's Party* (Minneapolis, 1931).

37. Allan Nevins, *Grover Cleveland: A Study in Courage* (New York, 1932), 594 (first quotation); C. Vann Woodward to Glenn W. Rainey, January 10, 193[8], Folder 1, Box 22, Rainey Papers (second, fourth, and fifth quotations); Nevins, "Tom Watson and the New South: Crucial Economic, Social and Political History Is Reflected in His Career," *New York Times Book Review*, April 3, 1938, pp. 1, 26 (third quotation on p. 26).

later persuaded the well-heeled ex-Confederate to finance the creation of an archival collection that would lead to the publication of a "History of the United States with the plain facts concerning the South . . . fairly stated in order that the children of the South may be truthfully taught . . . ."[38]

Through the collaboration of University of Texas historian Charles W. Ramsdell, a William A. Dunning student, and Wendell Holmes Stephenson, a U. B. Phillips student who was then teaching at Louisiana State University, this plan was reshaped into what was initially projected as a ten-volume "History of the South" beginning with the colonial period and coming forward to 1940. When Ramsdell died in 1942, he was succeeded as co-editor by the aforementioned E. Merton Coulter, who, in addition to his own nearly completed volume on Reconstruction, also agreed to write what was to have been Ramsdell's volume on the Confederacy.[39]

The agreement between the University of Texas and Louisiana State University Press softened the language of the original Littlefield proviso to a "full and impartial History of the South and of its part in the building of the Nation," but there were few names on the initial list of prospective authors for the series that would have distressed the champions of the New South Creed. Paul H. Buck, whose *Road to Reunion* had recently won the Pulitzer Prize, was raised as one of the possibilities for the post-Reconstruction volume. Despite his sympathetic take on the New South, however, Buck had never lived, taught, or been taught in the region and therefore lacked the firsthand acquaintance with the South that the co-editors considered "absolutely essential."[40] When the eventual choice, Benjamin B. Kendrick, withdrew unexpectedly in January 1939, the most suitable replacement seemed to be Francis Butler Simkins. However, Simkins's boldly revisionist writings on Reconstruction included a recent paper that urged fellow south-

---

38. Fred Arthur Bailey, "Free Speech and the 'Lost Cause' in Texas: A Study in Social Control in the New South," *Southwestern Historical Quarterly*, 97 (January 1994), 465–68; "Littlefield Fund for Southern History, Second Grant, Quotations from Major Littlefield's Will," Folder "Correspondence, Classified, 1945–1952 and undated," Box 2B104, Eugene C. Barker Papers (Center for American History, University of Texas at Austin; hereinafter UT) (quotation).

39. "A Prospectus of A History of the South," Folder "Correspondence: Classified, Littlefield 1952," Box 2B104, Barker Papers. For the announcement of the series see "Project for a Co-operative History of the South," *Journal of Southern History*, 4 (May 1938), 263–64.

40. "Project for a Co-operative History of the South," 263 (first quotation); Wendell Holmes Stephenson to Charles W. Ramsdell, May 20, 1938; Ramsdell to Stephenson, May 25, 1938 (second quotation); both in Box 3N292, Charles W. Ramsdell Papers, UT; Paul H. Buck, *The Road to Reunion, 1865–1900* (Boston, 1937).

ern historians to rethink their assumptions about "the innate inferiority of the blacks" and to reject "the gloomy generalization" that southern blacks must continue to play their "present inferior role." Conceding that Simkins was "quite familiar with the field," Stephenson nonetheless warned that Simkins's inclinations "toward sensationalism . . . would undoubtedly tend to prevent a judicious handling of certain important questions, especially the race issue."[41]

Although Woodward remained largely an unknown quantity to many leading southern historians, both Kendrick and Rupert Vance, Woodward's Chapel Hill mentor who had recently agreed to write the final volume in the series, gave him a strong endorsement. (Kendrick did express some concern that Woodward "likes his liquor quite a little better than he should," although he added that so far as he knew, Woodward "indulges over much only when he is on some sort of excursion.") Hoping to find an author who could be "genuinely objective" without becoming "too much of an advocate," Ramsdell was leery of Woodward and wondered "whether so young a man can have the maturity of judgment and acquaintance with the broad field." When Stephenson sought his appraisal of the "youngster," E. Merton Coulter responded that Woodward "could do it, but he is still quite young and has some distance to go yet."[42]

Rather than the "evidently brilliant" thirty-year-old Woodward, Ramsdell and Stephenson actually preferred the clearly failing sixty-six-year-old Holland Thompson. Thompson had published an academic but nonetheless admiring history of the New South some twenty years earlier, and as Coulter advised, "he certainly has the background and mellowed knowledge about the period which is not given to many." Judging from Thompson's earlier work, had his declining health not settled the matter, Volume IX of the History of the South series might now be offering its third generation of readers such decidedly un-Woodwardian insights as "No governments in American history have been conducted with more economy and

---

41. Francis B. Simkins, "New Viewpoints of Southern Reconstruction," *Journal of Southern History*, 5 (February 1939), 58; Wendell Holmes Stephenson to Charles W. Ramsdell, January 23, 1939, Box 3N303, Ramsdell Papers.

42. Benjamin B. Kendrick to Charles W. Ramsdell, February 11, 1939 (first quotation); Ramsdell to Kendrick, February 7, 1939 (second, third, and fourth quotations); both in Box 3N303, Ramsdell Papers; Wendell Holmes Stephenson to E. Merton Coulter, February 12, 1939, Folder 16, Box 7, Coulter Papers (fifth quotation); Coulter to Stephenson, February 15, 1939, Box 55, Wendell Holmes Stephenson Papers (Rare Book, Manuscript, and Special Collections Library, Duke University) (sixth quotation).

fidelity than the governments of the Southern States during the first years after the Reconstruction period."[43]

Only after almost two months of agonizing did Ramsdell, with "still a small measure of doubt in my mind," finally contact Woodward about replacing Kendrick. There was no doubt in Woodward's mind, however. He promptly accepted Ramsdell's invitation, thanking him profusely for the "unusual honor" bestowed on him. By now Woodward was married and in his second year at the University of Florida, where he taught only interdisciplinary freshman-sophomore courses on the western heritage. He realized that his best hope for a lighter teaching load and the opportunity to teach (at Florida or elsewhere) upper-level courses in southern and United States history lay in writing the kind of book that would establish him as a specialist in the field he had entered initially only as a means of becoming a biographer. Forced to admit that "it is from my teaching and not my writing that I am going to have to make my living," he explained to Rainey that the History of the South volume was "more important professionally than anything I could write just now . . . ." Perhaps acknowledging as well that the historical implications of *Tom Watson* had eluded readers caught up in his well-told story of personal tragedy, he shelved plans for a biography of Eugene V. Debs and leaped at the chance to have "my say on the period. . . . to lay down the main lines of interpretation and to do something fairly definitive . . . ."[44]

Woodward's contract called for a completed manuscript in three years. Realizing that the New South era "had hardly been opened to research" in 1939, he left the University of Florida for a temporary appointment at the University of Virginia, which offered "more time and better library facilities." His move the following year to California's Scripps College promised access to the Huntington Library, and he hoped to capitalize on a sabbatical leave to complete his research before the end of 1941. Owing to other events at the end of 1941, however, in January 1945 Lieutenant C. Vann Woodward was advising Stephenson that, depending on how long it took him to

---

43. Charles W. Ramsdell to Wendell Holmes Stephenson, January 31, 1939, Box 3N303, Ramsdell Papers (first quotation); E. Merton Coulter to Stephenson, February 15, 1939, Box 55, Stephenson Papers (second quotation); Thompson, *The New South*, 25 (third quotation).

44. Charles W. Ramsdell to Wendell Holmes Stephenson, March 8, 1939 (first quotation); Ramsdell to C. Vann Woodward, March 6, 1939; Woodward to Ramsdell, March 11, 1939 (second quotation); all in Box 3N303, Ramsdell Papers; Woodward to Glenn W. Rainey, March 26, 1939, Folder 1, Box 22, Rainey Papers (third, fourth, and fifth quotations).

complete his final assignment for the navy, he might be able to get him a manuscript by September.[45]

Despite this and several subsequent promises, the full and final version of *Origins of the New South* would not be in Stephenson's hands until April 1950. Soon after his release from the navy, Woodward realized that "notes taken four and five years ago, some of them six and seven years ago, are not nearly as usable as I had imagined." This discovery meant numerous repeat visits to various archives which, in turn, yielded new sources. These led to revision and rewriting of existing chapters and finally, in 1949, to a decision to expand what would have been the second chapter of *Origins* into a separate book, *Reunion and Reaction,* that Woodward promised would present "an entirely new story of the Compromise of 1877" and "an interpretation of its implications."[46]

Not all of Woodward's energies after his release from the navy were devoted to his writing, however. As his reputation grew, he launched a campaign to wrest the Southern Historical Association (SHA) from the grip of New South orthodoxy. The SHA had been formed in 1934 in order to encourage the " 'study of history in the South, with particular emphasis on the history of the South,' " but many of its founders saw its primary goal as defending the region's past rather than interpreting it. Its first president was E. Merton Coulter, whose inaugural presidential address in 1935 rebuked white southerners for their failure to gather and preserve the records necessary to rebut the South's northern antagonists. Five years later, former Nashville Agrarian Frank L. Owsley, whose essay in *I'll Take My Stand* had offered a vision of freedmen "who could still remember the taste of human flesh," used the presidential pulpit to insist that the "egocentric sectionalism" of the South's northern critics had caused the Civil War. (Hardly mellowing with age, twelve years later, as Woodward was preparing his own SHA presidential address, Owsley privately condemned the Democratic Party as a "conglomeration of minorities—'Big Labor,' 'Big Nigger,' [and] 'Big Jew.' ") Other SHA presidents in the 1940s blamed the contemporary

---

45. C. Vann Woodward to Glenn W. Rainey, March 26, 1939, Folder 1, Box 22, Rainey Papers (first quotation); Woodward to Wendell Holmes Stephenson, May 30, 1939 (second quotation), and August 24, 1940, Box 74; Woodward to Stephenson, January 23, 1945, Box 36; all in Stephenson Papers.

46. C. Vann Woodward to Wendell Holmes Stephenson, September 14, 1946 (first quotation), and July 23, 1949 (second quotation), Box 36, Stephenson Papers; C. Vann Woodward, *Reunion and Reaction: The Compromise of 1877 and the End of Reconstruction* (Boston, 1951).

South's problems on Reconstruction or on its colonial exploitation by the North.[47]

Needless to say, Woodward sent shock waves through the organization when, as program chair in 1949, he invited his friend John Hope Franklin to be the first black scholar to read a paper at an SHA meeting, a move that foreshadowed the group's first integrated dinner three years later on the occasion of Woodward's presidential address. Seeking "fresh approaches, revisions, [and] ideas" for the 1949 program, Woodward commissioned his former Emory classmate David M. Potter to dissect the contents of all the previous volumes of the *Journal of Southern History*. He also invited political scientist H. C. Nixon to present a paper based on a critical composite analysis of all the presidential addresses delivered during the first fifteen years of the group's existence. In his paper, which a delighted Woodward described as "a real mickey finn," Nixon noted the reluctance of the SHA's past presidents to acknowledge "anything inherently wrong with the South" and deplored the strident sectionalism of the orations, many of which were either "polemics" or "pretty well spiked with the hard liquor of polemics."[48]

---

47. Joseph J. Mathews, "The Study of History in the South," *Journal of Southern History,* 31 (February 1965), 15 (first quotation); E. Merton Coulter, "What the South Has Done About Its History," *Journal of Southern History,* 2 (February 1936), 3–28; Frank Lawrence Owsley, "The Irrepressible Conflict," in Twelve Southerners, *I'll Take My Stand: The South and the Agrarian Tradition* (New York and London, 1930), 62 (second quotation); Frank L. Owsley, "The Fundamental Cause of the Civil War: Egocentric Sectionalism," *Journal of Southern History,* 7 (February 1941), 3–18 (third quotation); Frank L. Owsley to Wendell Holmes Stephenson, October 6, 1952, Box 23, Stephenson Papers (fourth quotation); A. B. Moore, "One Hundred Years of Reconstruction of the South," *Journal of Southern History,* 9 (May 1943), 153–80; B. B. Kendrick, "The Colonial Status of the South," *Journal of Southern History,* 8 (February 1942), 3–22. The presidential addresses of the early years of the SHA are conveniently reprinted in George Brown Tindall, ed., *The Pursuit of Southern History: Presidential Addresses of the Southern Historical Association, 1935–1963* (Baton Rouge, 1964).

48. Sarah Newman Shouse, *Hillbilly Realist: Herman Clarence Nixon of Possum Trot* (Tuscaloosa, 1986), 164–65 (first Woodward quotation), 166 (second Woodward quotation); H. C. Nixon, "Paths to the Past: The Presidential Addresses of the Southern Historical Association," *Journal of Southern History,* 16 (February 1950), 37 (third quotation), 35 (fourth quotation); David M. Potter, "An Appraisal of Fifteen Years of the *Journal of Southern History,* 1935–1949," *Journal of Southern History,* 16 (February 1950), 25–32. On the 1949 Southern Historical Association program see C. Vann Woodward to Howard K. Beale, May 18, 1949, Folder 3, Box 26, Howard K. Beale Papers (Archives Division, State Historical Society of Wisconsin, Madison); and C. Vann Woodward, "The Fifteenth Annual Meeting of the Southern Historical Association," *Journal of Southern History,* 16 (February 1950), 40–47 (Franklin's participation on p. 43).

Woodward's almost gleeful crusade to shake up the SHA establishment doubtless did not sit well with History of the South co-editor E. Merton Coulter, a University of Wisconsin Ph.D. whose fundamental views on southern history had actually been shaped in his undergraduate years by the unapologetically racist J. G. de Roulhac Hamilton of the University of North Carolina. Although even Dunning protégé Charles Ramsdell had advised that "a general revision of that period is due," in *The South during Reconstruction,* which in 1947 became the first volume in the series to be released, Coulter warned that "[n]o amount of revision can write away the grievous mistakes made in this abnormal period of American history." Not surprisingly, Coulter's volume proved to be what David Donald mocked as "an impartial history from the Southern point of view" and what T. Harry Williams even less charitably called a " 'godawful book . . . based on race prejudice and distortion of the sources.' " Privately, Woodward found it "too bad the Reconstruction volume had to come out first" and worried that "the tone of extreme conservatism" might well "prevail in other volumes of the series."[49]

Woodward's relationship with Coulter could hardly have benefited from the actions of his mentor, Howard K. Beale, who had trounced directly on Coulter's toes in a 1940 article urging "a younger generation of Southern historians" to reject the Dunning/New South view of Reconstruction and "cease lauding those who 'restored white supremacy.' " Woodward's friend John Hope Franklin not only wrote a scathing review of Coulter's book but mailed copies of the review to a number of historians around the country. Coulter in turn sourly dismissed Franklin as "an exhibit in our counter moves against the Communists showing how much we appreciate our colored people" and suggested that "had Franklin not been a Negro, he would likely never or little been heard of."[50]

---

49. Charles W. Ramsdell to E. Merton Coulter, September 8, 1939, Folder 3, Box 17, Coulter Papers; E. Merton Coulter, *The South during Reconstruction* (Baton Rouge, 1947), xi; David Donald, "The Southern Memory," *New Leader,* July 31, 1947, clipping in Coulter Folder, Box 7, Stephenson Papers; T. Harry Williams to William B. Hesseltine, n.d., quoted in Novick, *That Noble Dream,* 349 n. 45; C. Vann Woodward to Manning J. Dauer, March 2, 1948, Box 2, Woodward Papers. On Coulter see Michael Vaughn Woodward, "Ellis Merton Coulter and the Southern Historiographic Tradition" (Ph.D. dissertation, University of Georgia, 1982).

50. Howard K. Beale, "On Rewriting Reconstruction History," *American Historical Review,* 45 (July 1940), 808 (first and second quotations); John Hope Franklin, "Whither Reconstruction Historiography?" *Journal of Negro Education,* 17 (Autumn 1948), 446–61; Novick, *That Noble Dream,* 349 n. 45; E. Merton Coulter to H. B. Fant, June 29, 1955, Folder 5, Box 47, Coulter Papers (third and fourth quotations).

Hoping to steer Woodward back onto the New South school's historio-graphical straight and narrow, Coulter had actively discouraged archival in-vestigation, pointing out that books in the series were "to represent a riper scholarship than a purely research project." Most of the secondary sources that Woodward had found were a bit too "ripe" for his taste, however. He explained that the paucity of "substantial monographs" on his period had forced him to do a great deal of original, primary research. Just as Coulter had feared, all this digging, Woodward confessed with considerable under-statement, had led him "to some revisionist interpretations that are depar-tures from certain views of older and better established historians."[51]

Woodward also fought back editorial efforts to set the starting date for his volume at 1880, knowing that such a break between his and Coulter's books would leave not only the Compromise of 1877 but the rise of political insurgency solely at the mercy of the ultraorthodox Coulter. Coulter had seen the outline for Woodward's book, however, and was determined to get in his licks. In the final chapter of *The South during Reconstruction,* he praised a "New South in the making" by virtue of the heroic efforts of Henry W. Grady and others, blamed the emergence of the one-party South on Reconstruction, and concluded that while the freedman might actually have been happier as a slave, he was still "vastly better off than the mass of his race in its native Africa" and the beneficiary of "a closer and friendlier feeling of his employer toward him than capitalistic Northerners showed their workmen."[52]

Coulter's conclusions affirmed Woodward's insistence that, as a book fairly reeking of "revisionary subversion," *Origins of the New South* repre-sented "a sort of historiographical black mass in the eyes of true believers." As his first heresy, Woodward advanced what would become for many his-torians the book's most disputable contention: the argument that the Re-deemers were " 'of middle-class, industrial, capitalistic outlook, with little but nominal connection with the old planter regime.' " This point was par-ticularly crucial to Woodward's revisionist agenda because it undermined

---

51. C. Vann Woodward to E. Merton Coulter, February 9, 1945, Woodward Folder, Box 36, Stephenson Papers.

52. C. Vann Woodward to Glenn W. Rainey, October 28, 1942, Folder 1, Box 22, Rainey Papers; Woodward to Wendell Holmes Stephenson, July 2, 1947, Box 36, Stephenson Papers; Coulter, *The South during Reconstruction,* 377–82 (first quotation on p. 382; second and third quotations on p. 381).

the claims of the Redeemers and their New South descendants to ancestral legitimacy through their roots in the old cavalier order.[53]

After questioning the Redeemers' bloodlines, Woodward went on to assail their behavior, showing that their governments were neither more scrupulously honest nor more fiscally responsible than those of the Reconstruction era. Shamelessly insensitive to the exploitation of the South's human and natural resources, the Redeemers had willingly shackled the region with a colonial economy. They had also overseen the brutal repression of the South's black population and the wholesale relegation of its rural labor force of both races to the seemingly endless and hopeless cycle of tenancy, dependency, and debt that was the sharecropping and crop lien system.

Foreshadowing the argument that he would develop more fully a few years later in *Strange Career of Jim Crow*, Woodward described in *Origins* a period of uncertainty and flux in southern race relations prior to the passage of the segregation statutes of the 1890s. Acutely sensitive to the symbolic as well as functional importance of the New South's invented traditions of Jim Crow and disfranchisement, Woodward explained that "[i]t took a lot of ritual and Jim Crow to bolster the creed of white supremacy in the bosom of a white man working for a black man's wages."[54]

As the foregoing and countless other passages reveal, *Origins of the New South* reflected Woodward's triumphant discovery that his affinity for literary artistry need not dilute and could actually enhance the interpretive power of his work. Woodward came to this realization only after wrestling with his own predilections, however. Despite his initial enthusiasm for the project, he was soon yearning "for a return to the beautiful simplicity of the biographer's job." Convinced that this approach was "much better suited as a vehicle of expression *for me* than the straight history that I am now struggling on," some two years after he had received his contract for *Origins*, he signed another one with Little, Brown and Company for a volume of biographical essays focused on "Henry Grady and the Makers of the New South."[55]

53. Woodward, *Thinking Back,* 65 (first quotation), 63 (second quotation), 64 (third quotation) (149, 147–48 in this volume).

54. Woodward, *Origins of the New South,* 211 (quotation); C. Vann Woodward, *The Strange Career of Jim Crow* (New York, 1955).

55. C. Vann Woodward to Howard K. Beale, February 18, 1941, Folder 2, Box 26, Beale Papers (first quotation); Woodward to William G. Carleton, March 1940, Folder 3, Box 7, William G. Carleton Papers (Special Collections and University Archives, George A. Smathers

The cancellation of this contract a few years later indicated that Woodward had finally gotten the biography monkey off his back, but he was also forced to admit that if he were truly going to have his "say" about the New South, he would have to eliminate the interpretive ambiguities that many readers had found in Tom Watson. Although he still believed that "sometimes there is virtue in lack of clarity" and that "the reader should do some of the work . . . and appreciates more *what* is not spoonfed," he wanted to avoid "intentional obscurity" in *Origins,* and he invited those who read his manuscript to "give me hell for it."[56] Several readers obliged, particularly Rainey and Beale. The former thought Woodward's "thread of thought was somewhat tangled" and called for "clear summaries of intent and accomplishment at the start and the close, and plain unadorned transitions within the chapters!" Meanwhile, Beale chided him for repeatedly assuming "too much intelligence and imagination on the part of the reader" and pointed to specific passages where "you could state it [your argument] much more explicitly than you do without spoiling the artistic effect of it as it is."[57]

Woodward's greater receptivity to such criticism paid off handsomely. Reviewers of Tom Watson had failed to acknowledge what Woodward thought were obvious continuities in plight and prospects between "the Okies and the Arkies" of the 1930s and the "rednecks," "lintheads," and "Samboes" of the 1890s. In contrast, Origins all but defied readers to miss the connection between the contemporary South's multitude of problems and deficiencies and the racial, political, and economic transgressions of the Redeemers, whose political heirs continued to thwart the region's material and human development as the second half of the twentieth century began. Reviewer David Donald praised Woodward's "realistic reappraisal of basic social and economic forces in the South" and concluded that "[t]oday's Southern problem is the result of the historical processes which Professor Woodward so admirably analyzes."[58]

Library, University of Florida, Gainesville) (second quotation); Stanley Salmen to Woodward, March 26, 1948, Box 2, Woodward Papers (third quotation).

56. Stanley Salmen to C. Vann Woodward, March 26, 1948, Box 2, Woodward Papers; Woodward to Glenn W. Rainey, November 6, 1937 (first quotation), and December 8, 1942 (subsequent quotations), Folder 1, Box 22, Rainey Papers.

57. Glenn W. Rainey to C. Vann Woodward, November 14, 1942, Folder 2, Box 22, Rainey Papers (first and second quotations); Howard K. Beale to Woodward, August 4, 1939, Box 1, Woodward Papers (third quotation); Beale to Woodward, December 3, 1942, Folder 1, Box 26, Beale Papers (fourth quotation).

58. Woodward, *Thinking Back,* 42 (first quotation); David Donald, "After Reconstruction," *The Nation,* 174 (May 17, 1952), 484 (second quotation), 485 (third quotation).

As Donald's comments implied, the persuasive power of *Origins* reflected not just the prodigious research that lay behind Woodward's revisionist interpretations but his conviction, affirmed in the works of Wolfe, Warren, and Faulkner, that "[t]he past is indeed an essential dimension of the present." Woodward felt such "warmth of affection" for Wolfe that his death in 1938 had caused him "personal grief," and shortly after *Origins* appeared, he described himself as "not only an admirer but an envyer" of the "historical talents" of Warren, to whom he would later dedicate *The Burden of Southern History.*[59]

On the other hand, Woodward admitted that he had initially struggled with Faulkner, "not understanding a fraction of what I read." Hence, he had merely been "parroting" the dismissive sentiments of the New York critics in 1938 when he disparaged his soon-to-be hero as a writer who "seemed to draw most of his subjects out of abandoned wells." Four years later, however, as he eagerly sought a copy of the recently published *Go Down, Moses,* Woodward described its author as "tops of contemporaries—a high sense of tragedy and humor as rich as W. Shakespeare and more so than Mark Twain's." By the end of World War II, Woodward was reading Faulkner with both empathy and understanding. He was soon quoting him in his essays and eventually hung Faulkner's portrait behind his desk, telling an interviewer, "He was always a powerful influence on me, although I didn't always know it."[60]

Pointing out that *"Origins of the New South* would provide a familiar context" for many of Faulkner's characters, Sheldon Hackney suggested that the book actually blended a less fatalistic but still decidedly Faulknerian vision of history as a constant burden to the present with a less optimistic but still decidedly Beardian vision of history as the story of an ongoing struggle over economic self-interest. To this blend, Woodward added his

59. C. Vann Woodward, "Why the Southern Renaissance?" *Virginia Quarterly Review,* 51 (Spring 1975), 236 (first quotation); Woodward to Glenn W. Rainey, October 2, 1938, Folder 1, Box 22, Rainey Papers (second and third quotations); Woodward to Thomas P. Govan, November 30, 1951, Folder "Southern Historical Association, 1951–1952," Box 2, Woodward Papers (fourth and fifth quotations); Woodward, *The Burden of Southern History* (Baton Rouge, 1960).

60. Woodward interview, July 18, 1978, transcript in Folder 10, Roper Papers (first and fifth quotations); C. Vann Woodward, *The Future of the Past* (New York and Oxford, 1989), 203 (second quotation); Woodward, "The South in Search of a Philosophy," *Phi Beta Kappa Addresses delivered at the University of Florida,* No. 1 (Gainesville, Fla., 1938), 15 (third quotation); Woodward to Glenn W. Rainey, October 19, 1942, Folder 1, Box 22, Rainey Papers (fourth quotation).

personal conviction that "education . . . besides teaching people what to hate and what [to] cherish . . . should equip them with proper heroes and proper villains."[61]

Since his undergraduate days, Woodward had delighted in villainizing prominent representatives of the New South order, particularly Emory's principal benefactors, the Candlers. During his year at the University of Virginia, he encountered a "primness and formality and smug tradition" that was "pretty hard to stomach," but whenever Virginia's "stuffiness" began to remind him of Emory, he had only to "lift up mine eyes to Monticello and reflect that these colonnades were not constructed on the profits of Coca-Cola stock." (Ironically, he seemed untroubled by the fact that those colonnades had probably been built by slave labor.) Likewise, Woodward found Duke University, with its "middle Gothic in cellophane" ambience, "a case of loathe at first sight," unlike Chapel Hill, which was "unraped by Coca-Cola or Chesterfield."[62]

Accordingly, as he proceeded in *Origins* "to repeat the orthodox credo backward," Woodward offered a radically re-scripted version of the New South drama. By celebrating the Redeemer/New South elite and scorning or simply ignoring their challengers, he suggested, white southerners had actually been applauding the villains and booing the heroes. The result, historian Avery O. Craven observed, was a book that "wrecks most of the old notions that have grown up about southern life after the Civil War."[63]

However rewarding or necessary, notion-wrecking can be a risky business. As Daniel Singal pointed out, in their zeal to correct the excesses of their predecessors, intellectuals often wind up committing excesses of their own. Critiquing the *Origins* manuscript in 1949, Rupert Vance worried that his protégé held "such high ideals that nobody ever reaches them" and that his study conveyed "the impression that no progress was made throughout the period." Vance's associate Harriet L. Herring praised Woodward's reve-

---

61. Sheldon Hackney, "*Origins of the New South* in Retrospect," *Journal of Southern History*, 38 (May 1972), 216 (49 in this volume); C. Vann Woodward to Glenn W. Rainey, July 12, 1936, Folder 1, Box 22, Rainey Papers.

62. C. Vann Woodward to Glenn W. Rainey, October 27, 1939 (first, second, and third quotations), and October 7, 1933 (fourth, fifth, and sixth quotations), both in Folder 1, Box 22, Rainey Papers. The author is indebted to Anne F. Scott for sharing her observation about the colonnades at the University of Virginia.

63. Woodward, *Thinking Back*, 63 (147 in this volume); Avery O. Craven, "The South in Critical Days After Civil War—Debunking Some Legends," Chicago *Tribune*, January 20, 1952, pt. 4, p. 5.

lation that the Redeemers were not "the saviors and the haloed saints which political speakers in my youth would have led us to think," but she also felt that his treatment of retrenchment in the Redeemer era was "pretty hard on those old boys," given that there was "not too much to tax" nor "too much to pay taxes with." Conceding that he might have been a bit overzealous in his campaign against New South orthodoxy, Woodward explained many years later that " 'the familiar line of Southern historiography was the one I was trying to overthrow, so I had to speak out rather forcibly to be heard. In such circumstances it's perhaps natural to overemphasize some points, and I think I did that.' "[64]

Not surprisingly, the excesses Woodward committed in his assault on the New South Creed—denying the Redeemers' connections to the planter regime and insisting that segregation was an invented, rather than a naturally evolved, tradition—eventually became the most inviting and vulnerable targets for those seeking to revise Woodward's interpretations. That these critics enjoyed a measure of success is noteworthy, but perhaps less so in revealing the weaknesses in Woodward's scholarship than in confirming the strength of his scholarly example. In Woodward's "new paradigm" for the study of southern history, revisionism was not an unnatural act but an integral, even indispensable, part of the process.[65] Like Wolfe, for whom "[e]ach moment is the fruit of forty thousand years," and Warren, whose Jack Burden moves "out of history into history and the awful responsibility of Time," Woodward believed that "the past is always a part of the present, shaping, haunting, duplicating, or reflecting it." Therefore, changing perspectives on the past were inevitable either as cause or as consequence of changing perspectives on the present.[66]

Woodward's fascination with the major figures of the Southern Literary

---

64. Singal, *War Within*, 374; Rupert B. Vance to C. Vann Woodward, August 1, 1949, and Harriet L. Herring to Woodward, September 17, 1949, in Folder 12, Rupert B. Vance Papers #4014, SHC; Jan DeBlieu, "A Past Apart," *Emory Magazine*, 61 (October 1984), 10 (Woodward quotation).

65. On criticism of Woodward's work, see Woodward, *Thinking Back*, 39–42, 67–79, 94–99; John Herbert Roper, ed., *C. Vann Woodward: A Southern Historian and His Critics* (Athens, Ga., and London, 1997), esp. 95–202; and James C. Cobb, "Beyond Planters and Industrialists: A New Perspective on the New South," *Journal of Southern History*, 54 (February 1988), 45–68.

66. Thomas Wolfe, *Look Homeward, Angel: A Story of the Buried Life* (New York, 1929; reprint, New York, 1957), 1 (first quotation); Robert Penn Warren, *All the King's Men* (New York, 1946; reprint, San Diego, New York, and London, 1974), 438 (second quotation); Woodward, "Why the Southern Renaissance?" 236 (third quotation).

Renaissance is crucial to our understanding of his role in revolutionizing a field he had entered more or less by default. Inspired by their literary artistry, he also recognized that in their treatment of the present as merely "a fleeting segment of the cumulative past," the writers he so admired "had something special to say to the historian." In *Origins of the New South* he not only demonstrated why southern historians should listen to their literary contemporaries, but in doing so, he found the voice that would secure his place beside the giants of southern fiction as one of the modern South's most eloquent and influential interpreters. As it matured, that voice spoke neither as stridently nor as definitively as it had in *Origins,* but softly and suggestively, like the novelist humbled by the inexplicable "chaos and irony of history." Yet, it also spoke earnestly and insistently because Woodward understood that if, as Faulkner wrote, "yesterday today and tomorrow are Is: Indivisible," then for those who write history no less than for those who make it, "tomorrow night is nothing but one long sleepless wrestle with yesterday's omissions and regrets."[67]

---

67. Woodward, "The Historical Dimension," in *Burden of Southern History,* 37 (first quotation), 30 (second quotation), 38 (third quotation); William Faulkner, *Intruder in the Dust* (New York, 1948), 194 (fourth quotation), 195 (fifth quotation).

ROBERT C. McMATH JR.

C. Vann Woodward and the Burden of
Southern Populism

In the spring of 1939 C. Vann Woodward was basking in the glow of critical
acclaim for his book, *Tom Watson, Agrarian Rebel,* and casting about for a
new subject.[1] He had already done some reconnaissance on a biography of
Eugene V. Debs but had decided to lay that project aside for "at least three
years, perhaps longer." In a letter to his friend and confidant, Glenn W.

Reprinted from *Journal of Southern History,* 67 (November 2001), 741–68, the Woodward symposium issue.

1. C. Vann Woodward, *Tom Watson, Agrarian Rebel* (New York, 1938). I would like to
thank William F. Holmes, Anne Firor Scott, and Bertram Wyatt-Brown for their comments
and suggestions and also to thank our hosts at Rice University for making the Woodward symposium such an enjoyable and productive experience. For providing me with a collegial forum
in which to develop some of these ideas at an earlier stage, I thank Chancellor John A. White
and Professor Jeannie Whayne of the University of Arkansas.

Rainey, Woodward explained that a new opportunity had just presented itself: "Then came an invitation from Prof. Ramsdell of the Univ. of Texas asking me to agree to write volume nine, 'The Origins of the New South' for the series, 'The History of the South, 1607–1940,' that he and Stephenson of [Louisiana State University] are editing." The thirty-year-old Woodward, who was just two years out of graduate school, recognized that this was too good an opportunity to pass up and accepted Ramsdell's offer immediately. "After all I don't see how I could hope for a better chance of having my say on the period. . . . It seems to me then that there is a chance to lay down the main lines of interpretation and to do something fairly definitive rather than merely summarizing or condensing."[2]

Those "main lines of interpretation" have defined a field and shaped its debates for half a century. Beyond those specific points of interpretation, as Drew Gilpin Faust has said, "Woodward's achievement rests on the central place he established for Southern history in our understanding of the nation's identity and moral character. The Southern past appeared to Woodward as burden and opportunity, the key to injustices, delusions, and oppressions of his own time."[3] That vision of southern history as burden and opportunity and as somehow bound up with his own time was already discernible in *Tom Watson*, a story of contingency and choice, a history of the awful commingling of good and evil within one tribe and within the soul of one human being.

Writing at a moment when the seemingly timeless South was poised on the brink of massive transformation, Woodward told stories of long-forgotten southerners, black and white, who struggled to create better futures for themselves and their people. In Woodward's skillful telling, even their failures allowed modern-day Americans to imagine alternatives to the segregated status quo and to envision a biracial coalition of working people capable of reclaiming the democratic promise of Populism. No wonder that his writings inspired many of us to believe that "[t]heirs is a legacy waiting to be fulfilled."[4]

Woodward's eye toward the here-and-now led some library-bound histo-

2. C. Vann Woodward to Glenn W. Rainey, March 26, 1939, Folder 1, Box 22, Glenn W. Rainey Papers (Special Collections Department, Robert W. Woodruff Library, Emory University).

3. Drew Gilpin Faust, "C. Vann Woodward: Helping to Make History," *Chronicle of Higher Education*, January 14, 2000, p. B7.

4. Robert C. McMath Jr., *American Populism: A Social History, 1877–1898* (New York, 1993), 211.

rians to fling at him the epithet "presentist"—an odd criticism coming from scholars who would presumably wish the past to speak wisely to our present needs, but a slur nevertheless. Reflecting decades later on this criticism and the related charge of believing the historian's craft was more closely tied to literature than to science (which he freely acknowledged), Woodward feigned alarm that he might be remembered as "a presentist, . . . a chronicler with a weakness for history-with-a-purpose and . . . [worse,] a historian, presumably dedicated to fact, who is inspired by fiction."[5]

The young Woodward could not have avoided "history-with-a-purpose" even if he had tried. In 1928 he left his native Arkansas for Atlanta, where he completed his undergraduate studies at Emory University and then briefly taught at Georgia Tech. In Atlanta Woodward came under the influence of progressive thinkers who were striving to pull the region out of poverty and social reaction and, in the process, to create a more humane South. In those desperate years he came face-to-face with grinding rural poverty in ways he had never before witnessed. Moving on to Chapel Hill to write Watson's biography (and, incidentally, to pick up a Ph.D.), Woodward watched the general strike of 1934 unfold before his eyes.[6] The desperation of embattled textile workers and down-and-out sharecroppers seemed to converge in his mind with the struggles of Watson's Populists, all of them tied up somehow with the world of politics and state power.

Indeed, politics and the power that office could bestow were never far from the center of Woodward's thinking about the South. From *Tom Watson,* through *Origins of the New South,* to the reflections of his later years, Woodward revisited political themes that had captured his attention in the 1930s, themes that had followed strange careers of their own in the intervening decades. So while our immediate focus is on *Origins,* the sum of Woodward's intellectual legacy requires us to broaden our perspective to

---

5. C. Vann Woodward, *Thinking Back: The Perils of Writing History* (Baton Rouge, 1986), 146.

6. John Herbert Roper, "The City: Youthful Activism and Revolt, 1928–1934," chap. 2 in *C. Vann Woodward, Southerner* (Athens, Ga., and London, 1987), 31–60; Woodward, *Thinking Back,* 11–14. From Chapel Hill Woodward wrote to Rainey, "I followed the strike pretty closely, making some trips. I learned little, except that the only way to learn anything about American labor is through first-hand observation. [Communist organizer] Don West [is] now traveling for the C.P. under the name of Weaver (warrants for his arrest in three southern states), and I helped him organize some protests of terrorism, etc. Wounded strikers had retreated to Chapel Hill, met with sympathetic students, and 'ruffled some feathers' . . . . I suppose every method of fascism was used in the South. What happened in Georgia?" Woodward to Rainey, September 24, 1934, Folder 1, Box 22, Rainey Papers.

include his ongoing dialogue with himself and with his critics about the politics of the New South and especially about southern Populism.[7]

That dialogue has produced such a mountain of scholarship and commentary that one must ask whether it is possible to say anything new about Woodward's Redeemers, Populists, and Progressives. It is too late for me to answer in the negative, so here is what I propose: With regard to Woodward's famous triad, I will touch lightly on the Redeemers, the study of whom, as our colleagues in the sciences would say, is a "mature field," meaning "nothing much left here, time to move on." (Of course we should not be surprised if even now some enterprising scholar is breathing new life into those dry bones.) I will say a good deal about the Populists because I *like* to talk about the Populists. And besides, when approached from certain angles, they still have much to tell us. The story of southern Progressives is the least developed part of Woodward's political narrative and is thus ripe for further discussion. At this particular juncture, moreover, reflections on the course of southern Progressivism and its relation to earlier political movements can enrich an important discussion now developing among historians and political scientists about the emergence of the modern state.

While acknowledging my own enormous professional debt to Professor Woodward, here are the new perspectives that I find most useful:

1. While the pivot of *Origins* was the "Populist moment" of the 1880s and 1890s, we may profitably view the entire period from the 1870s to the 1910s as a "long agrarian moment" during which a populistic spirit and agenda had always to be reckoned with in the South. This vibrant populism helped define the South's substantial influence on national Progressivism.[8]

2. Although the main focus of *Origins* is on struggles within the South between the new industrial order and the "unredeemed farmer" (p. 175), we may usefully inquire about the region's role in national partisan realignments and in the formation of the modern American state.

---

7. C. Vann Woodward, *Origins of the New South, 1877–1913* (Baton Rouge, 1951). Page numbers for subsequent references to *Origins* in this essay are inserted parenthetically in the text. The first edition's pagination is retained in later reprint editions.

8. The phrase "Populist moment," while thoroughly Woodwardian, is from Lawrence Goodwyn, *Democratic Promise: The Populist Moment in America* (New York, 1976), xiii. The phrase "Long Agrarian Moment" is borrowed from Robert D. Johnston, "Peasants, Pitchforks, and the (Found) Promise of Progressivism," *Reviews in American History*, 28 (September 2000), 394.

3. Although Woodward's account of Populism centers on Tom Watson's Georgia, we may explore to our benefit the varieties of southern populism, including that of Woodward's native Arkansas, to better understand the complexity and long sweep of agrarian protest.

4. Though years of jousting with critics have almost reified Woodward's Populists into an affirmation of all that is noble in American politics, we must nevertheless confront the possibility that there was one Tom Watson, not two. And at the beginning of this new century, as at the beginning of the last one, we must acknowledge the awful commingling of good and evil within the soul of that one Populist and within the tribe to which he belonged.

Now to the main characters.

Beginning with the Redeemers, it is sufficient for my purposes to point to Woodward's famous detour on the road to *Origins* that led to the publication, also in 1951, of *Reunion and Reaction: The Compromise of 1877 and the End of Reconstruction*. That short book was summarized in *Origins* in a chapter entitled "The Forked Road to Reunion" (pp. 23–50). Here Woodward's topic is not so much the disputed election of 1876 as the role played by certain southerners in resolving the presidential succession crisis in a manner beneficial to themselves and their political and economic allies, both in the South and in the Northeast. So I will take only the briefest mention, without presentist comparisons, of his conclusion in *Origins* that "[t]he consensus of recent historians is that [Samuel J.] Tilden deserved the 4 electoral votes of Florida and was therefore elected" (pp. 24–25).[9]

The significance and even the facts of the Compromise of 1877 have long been a matter of debate between Woodward and his critics, but let us focus on what Woodward believed to be at stake and consider what his position reveals about his understanding of New South politics.[10] A Republican defeat in 1876 would have put at risk legislative victories protecting the new economic order of the Northeast—and this at a time when the privileged

---

9. In the opening chapter of *Reunion and Reaction*, Woodward briefly sketches the work of Zachariah Chandler, national Republican chairman, in snatching victory from the jaws of defeat in the three contested southern states: "Flagrantly partisan and arbitrary decisions of the Florida [returning] board converted an apparent Tilden majority into Hayes votes." C. Vann Woodward, *Reunion and Reaction: The Compromise of 1877 and the End of Reconstruction* (Boston, 1951), 17–19 (quotation on p. 19).

10. Woodward himself fairly summarizes the points at issue regarding the Compromise of 1877 in *Thinking Back*, 52–55.

position of industrialism was already threatened by eastern labor violence and western agrarian radicalism. "And now," writes Woodward, "the South, kept at bay for sixteen years, presented a third threat to the New Order" (p. 24). The South was a threat, that is, unless an opportunistic band of New Order southerners were prepared first to strike a bargain with the Yankees and then to corral their more militant countrymen into submission or acquiescence. (Enter southern neo-Whigs, stage right.) "It took a lot of hallooing and heading off by the conservative leaders to keep the mass of Southerners herded up the right fork," Woodward concludes. "Agrarian mavericks were eternally taking off up the left fork followed by the great droves that they had stampeded" (p. 50).

The end of politics for these Redeemers, as Woodward calls the southern conservatives, was to forge a political and economic alliance with the East that would foster an industrial New South and, by the way, enhance their own well-being. The means of building the regional political consensus that was required to make this alliance work was "hallooing" of all sorts: promises of southern prosperity, appeals to the Lost Cause and to white solidarity, and even—when necessary—the resort to force of arms to keep the lower sorts from following their own best interests into alliances with western radicals. For their part, agrarian mavericks, political Independents, and the nascent labor movement—black and white together with their backs against the same wall—hewed stubbornly to the left fork, at least, Woodward argues, until the climactic national campaign of 1896 and the multitude of local campaigns for disfranchisement that preceded and followed it.

In *Origins,* as in *Tom Watson,* these down-home agrarian radicals are viewed in a positive light, and their political aspirations receive a respectful hearing. Here, in a nutshell, is what Woodward has to say about the Populists in *Origins:*[11]

Above all, they and their fellow travelers were honest farmers and laborers beaten down by the long depression of the 1870s–1890s; shackled by monopolists who controlled transportation, finance, and commerce; impoverished by the crop lien system that stole the fruits of their labor; and robbed of their political birthright by scheming Redeemer Democrats.

---

11. Commentary on the conclusions of *Tom Watson* and *Origins* is voluminous, but much of it is fairly summarized in Woodward, *Thinking Back,* chap. 2 and chap. 4. Handy summaries of the historiographical debates are also found in Sheldon Hackney, "*Origins of the New South* in Retrospect," *Journal of Southern History,* 38 (May 1972), 191–216 (25–49 in this volume); William F. Holmes, "Populism: In Search of Context," *Agricultural History,* 64 (Fall 1990), 26–58; and Howard N. Rabinowitz, *The First New South, 1865–1920* (Arlington Heights, Ill., 1992).

In the 1880s and 1890s southern farmers and their allies from within what they called the "producing classes" took matters into their own hands. They created grassroots democratic organizations like the Texas-based Farmers' Alliance and the Arkansas-based Agricultural Wheel to establish cooperative economic institutions and to press the ruling Democratic Party for legislative relief. When those efforts failed, many white farmers reluctantly left the party of their fathers and, in league with African Americans, created a new People's Party. In concert with farmers and laborers from the western plains, they launched a heroic but short-lived campaign to wrest national political power from the equally corrupt Democratic and Republican Parties.

This great southern crusade unfortunately came to a sad and quick end, destroyed at the hands of Democrats through election fraud, racial hysteria, and force of arms. (Scores died during southern elections in 1892 and 1894, and in 1898 a duly elected government in Wilmington, North Carolina, was overthrown in what the history books would call a *coup d'etat* had it happened in another country.) Populists hastened the demise of their own movement, Woodward concedes, when some of them yielded to temptation and aligned themselves at the state level with Republican machines and nationally in 1896 with the Democratic Party of William Jennings Bryan. In the end, the terrible pressure for white solidarity within the Democracy proved irresistible for many.

Despite its sad end, Woodward's narrative is driven forward by a sense of hopeful contingency. The alternative world that his southern Populists imagined—in which producers received the fruits of their labor, the power of monopolists and the crop lien were broken, and political power was returned to the people—that world *could* have been realized. Ultimately, the Populists were counted out, beaten down, and tripped up by their own internal divisions, but amid the economic turmoil and political fluidity of the 1890s, Woodward suggests, the story might have turned out differently.

Allow me a brief digression on the construction of Woodward's political narrative and the historiographical context of *Origins*. Although the book appeared in print in 1951, major portions, including several of the early chapters, were first drafted between 1939 and 1942, and many of its key themes are foreshadowed in *Tom Watson*.[12] *Origins* was a remarkable accomplishment, for Woodward's eagerness "to do something fairly definitive

---

12. See especially Woodward, *Tom Watson*, chaps. 4–5, 8–9, 13, and 16, which contain the main outlines of Woodward's later treatment of the Redeemers and their ideology and of his explanation for the rise and fall of the Farmers' Alliance and People's Party.

rather than merely summarizing or condensing" belied the sobering reality that in 1939 there was not much secondary literature on his subject worth summarizing and condensing. "Where . . . is the monograph output of a generation of seminars on the period?" he asked series editor Charles W. Ramsdell. In its place stood the required shelf of standard works on southern and American history, works that had left Woodward the graduate student wondering "if I had ever encountered prose so pedestrian, pages so dull, chapters so devoid of ideas, whole volumes so wrongheaded or so lacking in point."[13]

When it came to Populism, however, all was not desert. *The Populist Revolt* by John D. Hicks, which was published in 1931, gave Woodward a national context and a western foil for his tale. Two excellent studies illuminated the movement in key southern states: Roscoe C. Martin's *The People's Party in Texas* and Alex M. Arnett's *The Populist Movement in Georgia*. Woodward's own *Tom Watson* was arguably the best of the lot.[14]

The point of this historiographical digression is that, whatever the limitations of the literature overall, Woodward took up his labors on *Origins* with a Beardian framework for Populism already in place, one that highlighted interregional and intraregional conflict over the role of the state in economic life. Woodward refined the position, giving pride of place to southern rather than western Populists, privileging those who made common cause with neither major party but stuck to the middle of the road, and arguing—contra

---

13. Woodward to Rainey, March 26, 1939, Folder 1, Box 22, Rainey Papers (first quotation); Woodward, *Thinking Back,* 45 (second quotation), 21 (third quotation). Woodward's disdain for the arcane practice of the comprehensive examination based on "mastering" a body of secondary literature is well known, though the graduate student legend that he initially failed his own exam is without basis. The day after his orals Woodward wrote to Rainey that they were "rather formidable, as expected. I performed adequately, of course, but not brilliantly. There is simply nothing in the idea of examinations that challenges my temperament." Then this confession: "I am indulging myself the dubious pleasure of some extravagant forgetting. No niggardly date here and a dictator there, but whole dynasties at a time—Poof, there go the Hapsburgs, poof, the Hohenzollerns . . . ." Woodward to Rainey, May 17, 1936, Folder 1, Box 22, Rainey Papers.

14. John D. Hicks, *The Populist Revolt: A History of the Farmers' Alliance and the People's Party* (Minneapolis, 1931); Roscoe C. Martin, *The People's Party in Texas: A Study in Third Party Politics* (Austin, 1933); Alex Mathews Arnett, *The Populist Movement in Georgia* (New York, 1922). This list does not include the sprawling and never finished Northwestern University dissertation on the Negro and Georgia's Independent movement by Glenn W. Rainey, Woodward's Emory debate coach, Georgia Tech colleague, and great friend. The correspondence of these two men during the 1930s and early 1940s illuminates a dialogue in which many of the big themes of *Origins* took shape.

Hicks and Arnett—that there was a sharp break between Populism and Progressivism. The framework he received and made his own would go largely unchallenged until after the publication of *Origins*.

In his later essays (especially those in which Woodward responds to authors who viewed the Populists differently or used the term more loosely than he), this framework was "codified" in a set of propositions that can be summarized as follows:

1. Populists were members of an economic interest group who shared legitimate grievances: "Populism was hardly 'status politics,' " Woodward argued in 1959, opposing Richard Hofstadter, "and I should hesitate to call it 'class politics.' It was more nearly 'interest politics,' and more specifically 'agricultural interest politics.' "[15]

2. Finding themselves in a situation where the institutions of commerce and politics seemed not only unresponsive but downright hostile to their needs, farmers and laborers took matters into their own hands by creating alternative institutions. Community-based farmers' organizations gave agricultural workers space within which to affirm each other and launch ambitious programs of cooperative enterprise and issue-based politics. These "little platoons," to borrow Edmund Burke's apt description of early voluntary associations, formed the vanguard of the People's Party.

3. The Populists' commitment to a coalition of black and white farmers who were stuck in the same economic ditch was genuine, if not perfect. "[P]erhaps," Woodward writes with conviction, "the most remarkable aspect of the whole Populist movement was the resistance its leaders in the South put up against racism and racist propaganda and the determined effort they made against incredible odds to win back political rights for the Negroes, defend those rights against brutal aggression, and create among their normally anti-Negro following, even temporarily, a spirit of tolerance in which the two races of the South could work together in one party for the achievement of common ends."[16]

---

15. C. Vann Woodward, "The Populist Heritage and the Intellectual," *The Burden of Southern History* (3d ed., Baton Rouge, 1993), 153 (quotation); Richard Hofstadter, *The Age of Reform: From Bryan to F.D.R.* (New York, 1955). Woodward's essay originally appeared in *American Scholar*, 28 (Winter 1959), 55–72.

16. Woodward, "The Populist Heritage and the Intellectual," 156–57.

4. The southern branch of Populism, though aligned with that of the West, was distinct from it. Furthermore, "the more radical wing of the agrarian revolt of the nineties was Southern rather than Western" (p. 200). This comment from *Origins* refers to the economic and political program of the "southern" Farmers' Alliance, but in other contexts Woodward also argues that in confronting the racial issue, however imperfectly, southern Populists took a more radical step than their western counterparts and were more committed to the cause: "Having waged their revolt at such great cost, the Southern Populists were far less willing to compromise their principles than were their Western brethren."[17]

5. Populism, like the Democratic Party of the Redeemers, lived in a moment of sharp discontinuity in southern political history. The institutions that these aggrieved farmers created, while not without roots in the past, were new, even as the Redeemers themselves "represented more innovation than restoration, more break than continuity with the past."[18] Similarly, the demise of Populism after 1896 marked the end of agrarian reform, and the southern version of Progressivism that followed had little to do with it.

To begin an assessment of these propositions let me propose the following thought experiment. What if, instead of centering his study of Populism on Tom Watson and Georgia, Woodward had looked first and in greatest detail at his native state? What does the story of the farmer-labor movement in Arkansas (and by extension the varieties of southern populism) suggest to us about Woodward's version of the movement as a whole?

Turn for a moment to Plumerville, Arkansas, a hamlet in Conway County, where in January 1889 one John M. Clayton was murdered in cold blood while investigating the theft of a ballot box that had cost him a congressional election. Clayton, a Republican, and Louis Featherston, president of the State Agricultural Wheel, had been robbed of congressional victories in 1888 by Democrats desperate to turn back the combined challenge of Republicans and the populistic Union Labor Party.[19]

In a riveting account of political violence centering on John Clayton and

---

17. *Ibid.*, 151.

18. Woodward, *Thinking Back*, 64 (148 in this volume).

19. Kenneth C. Barnes, *Who Killed John Clayton? Political Violence and the Emergence of the New South, 1861–1893* (Durham and London, 1998), 68–71, 74–78.

his world, Kenneth C. Barnes notes, "Some of the men who engineered the Democratic victory were still running county government three decades later, in the early 1920s, when C. Vann Woodward passed through adolescence in Morrilton, the county seat of Conway County." None of those men were ever tried for Clayton's murder, which remained a "mystery." Plumerville, though less than ten miles from Morrilton, was a world apart from the middle-class town life of Woodward's adolescence, and his family were newcomers from the plantation districts near Memphis; his apparent ignorance of these matters, therefore, is not altogether surprising.[20]

Yet Woodward's native state had witnessed a remarkable flourishing of populism, springing from the "little platoons" of the Brothers of Freedom, the Agricultural Wheel, the Knights of Labor, the short-lived Union Labor Party, and in something of an anticlimax, the People's Party. Even though the high point of Arkansas populism came in 1888 rather than 1894 or 1896, John Clayton's story and the story of farmer-labor politics in Arkansas confirm parts of Woodward's telling of southern Populism while suggesting some modifications.[21]

The histories of the Brothers of Freedom and Agricultural Wheel support Woodward's conclusions that Populism was a rational interest group movement of rural men and women who had some personal stake in the market economy and that this movement was grounded in community-based membership organizations that were energized not only by cooperative enterprises but also by the familiar forms of fraternal and religious organizations—rituals, secret handshakes, picnics, hymn singing, camp meetings, and the like. The characterization by some social scientists of American Populism as an irrational mass movement of socially dysfunctional individuals—a representation so passionately contested by Woodward—is not borne out by the Arkansas evidence. Nor does that claim, which was adopted from European models of something else called "popu-

---

20. *Ibid.*, 4 (quotation); Roper, *C. Vann Woodward*, 6–8, 15–21.

21. The story of Arkansas farmer-labor politics is well summarized in Carl H. Moneyhon, *Arkansas and the New South, 1874–1929* (Fayetteville, Ark., 1997), chap. 5. Fuller accounts are given in several dissertations and journal articles including Berton E. Henningson Jr., "Northwest Arkansas and the Brothers of Freedom: The Roots of a Farmer Movement," *Arkansas Historical Quarterly*, 34 (Winter 1975), 304–24; F. Clark Elkins, "Arkansas Farmers Organize for Action, 1882–1884," *Arkansas Historical Quarterly*, 13 (Autumn 1954), 231–48; Thomas S. Baskett Jr., "*Miners Stay Away!* W. B. W. Heartsill and the Last Years of the Arkansas Knights of Labor, 1892–1896," *Arkansas Historical Quarterly*, 42 (Summer 1983), 107–33; and John McDaniel Wheeler, "The People's Party in Arkansas, 1891–1896" (Ph.D. dissertation, Tulane University, 1975).

lism," square with what we know in general about the great mobilization of nineteenth-century Americans into democratic voluntary associations.[22]

Woodward depicts the rich social life of local Alliances and farmers' clubs with empathy. He acknowledges the religious fervor of the agrarian organizations. But the associational form of the movement plays little or no role in Woodward's explanatory framework. He accepted leading participants' accounts of how the Alliance's army of organizers spread the Populist spirit like wildfire from Texas across the South without asking how such a conflagration could move so quickly and with such ease from one isolated community to another. These accounts come largely from the Alliance's "official histories," published in the 1880s and early 1890s, whose purpose was to persuade a skeptical public of the power of the movement's economic platform and to rouse rural southerners to action (pp. 189–92). Had Woodward not been so singularly focused on the economic agenda of the agrarian movement, he might have asked different questions about these community-based organizations. For Woodward, the social features of Populism are interesting, even a bit of a curiosity to be described to modern readers (a task for which he was superbly equipped), but they do not help *explain* the phenomenon.

Call it Beardian or what you will, Woodward's explanation of Populism is economical as well as economic, requiring only these elements: great financial distress and inequity; an ideology and program that interpret this distress to the sufferers and offer remedies; charismatic leaders like Tom Watson, Charles W. Macune, and James H. "Cyclone" Davis to do the explaining; and just enough instability or competition in the political system to give agrarian radicalism a chance of electoral success. The notion that voluntary associations in the South, whether part of or in opposition to the farmers' movement, could have influenced the course of a "movement culture" or conversely have undercut this new force does not appear in Woodward's scheme.[23]

Today there is evidence from many quarters that voluntary associations

---

22. Harvard University's Civic Engagement Project is cataloging American participation in such membership organizations in the nineteenth and twentieth centuries. For an introduction to its findings, see Theda Skocpol et al., "How Americans Became Civic," in Theda Skocpol and Morris P. Fiorina, eds., *Civic Engagement in American Democracy* (Washington, D.C., and New York, 1999), 27–80. The role of fraternal organizations in the direct delivery of services is well summarized in David T. Beito, *From Mutual Aid to the Welfare State: Fraternal Societies and Social Services, 1890–1967* (Chapel Hill and London, 2000).

23. Goodwin, *Democratic Promise*, xiii.

did help shape and define the political culture of reform throughout North America, not just in the southern United States. A persuasive new study of Virginia's biracial Readjuster movement by Jane Dailey finds that in this precursor to Populism "a dense network of community associations and religious organizations enabled the political activism of black men and women in the postwar South."[24] Anne Firor Scott, summarizing her findings on women's associations, contends that such organizations "lay at the very heart of American social and political development."[25] And one of the best new studies of populism in the prairie provinces of Canada concludes that community-based social and religious institutions in Alberta "made the agrarian revolt possible."[26] Historians with presentist tendencies will notice a resonance with the contemporary "civil society" debate, which grapples not only with the issue of how community-based organizations influence political mobilization but also with the question of what role such organizations, including religious ones, should play in the delivery of services in the "post–welfare state" era.[27]

I believe that unless we remain open to the possibility that voluntary associations played a causative role, our broader understanding of populism and its conceptualization of state and society will be deficient, and we will miss an opportunity to use that history wisely for our present needs. The same is true for the role of the family, which does not figure in Woodward's

---

24. Jane Dailey, *Before Jim Crow: The Politics of Race in Postemancipation Virginia* (Chapel Hill and London, 2000), 49.

25. Anne Firor Scott, *Natural Allies: Women's Associations in American History* (Urbana and Chicago, 1991), 2. See also Scott, "Most Invisible of All: Black Women's Voluntary Associations," *Journal of Southern History*, 56 (February 1990), 3–22. For a perceptive analysis of the ways in which "those who are relatively weak or disadvantaged by a particular set of political rules can change those rules," see Elisabeth S. Clemens, "Organizational Repertoires and Institutional Change: Women's Groups and the Transformation of American Politics, 1890–1920," in Skocpol and Fiorina, eds., *Civic Engagement in American Democracy*, 81–110 (quotation on p. 82).

26. Bradford James Rennie, *The Rise of Agrarian Democracy: The United Farmers and Farm Women of Alberta, 1909–1921* (Toronto, 2000), 87. In the interest of full disclosure I will acknowledge a long-term interest in this aspect of populism: see my book, *Populist Vanguard: A History of the Southern Farmers' Alliance* (Chapel Hill, 1975), esp. chap. 5, "Brothers and Sisters: The Alliance as Community," 64–76; and my more recent article, "Populism in Two Countries: Agrarian Protest in the Great Plains and Prairie Provinces," *Agricultural History*, 69 (Fall 1995), 517–46.

27. For a useful introduction to the civil society debate, see the essays in E. J. Dionne Jr., ed., *Community Works: The Revival of Civil Society in America* (Washington, D.C., 1998); and Skocpol and Fiorina, eds., *Civic Engagement in American Democracy*.

story of Populism at all. As the foundational social institution, as a crucial economic unit, and as the place where gendered relationships were reconceptualized and new definitions of manliness and womanhood were worked out, the family *must* figure in any effort to situate Populism within its social context.[28] Attention to social institutions—whether the rural family or the voluntary associations that formed the social fabric of the countryside—will also make visible southern Populist women who, though less likely than their western counterparts to assume roles as leaders and spokespersons, played a vital role in the movement.[29]

One notable exception to the lower visibility of women in the southern agrarian movement was Rebecca Latimer Felton of Georgia, Tom Watson's contemporary and sometime confidante. Though not a Populist in the strictest sense, she was a force in Georgia politics for over half a century, first as political counselor and speechwriter for her husband, William H. Felton, who was elected to Congress as an Independent Democrat three times in the 1870s, and then as a champion of reform causes in her own right. As a critic of the Redeemer ideology and program, she was the equal of Watson. As a champion of women's rights within the context of agrarian reform, she was the equal of Mary Elizabeth Lease and any of the other better-known western Populists. Upon the death of Tom Watson in 1922, she was appointed to assume temporarily Watson's seat in the United States Senate, becoming

---

28. Useful starting points for such an understanding include Laura F. Edwards, *Gendered Strife and Confusion: The Political Culture of Reconstruction* (Urbana and Chicago, 1997); Stephanie McCurry, *Masters of Small Worlds: Yeoman Households, Gender Relations, and the Political Culture of the Antebellum South Carolina Low Country* (New York and Oxford, 1995); Glenda Elizabeth Gilmore, *Gender and Jim Crow: Women and the Politics of White Supremacy in North Carolina, 1896–1920* (Chapel Hill and London, 1996); Stephen Kantrowitz, *Ben Tillman and the Reconstruction of White Supremacy* (Chapel Hill and London, 2000); and Kantrowitz, "Ben Tillman and Hendrix McLane, Agrarian Rebels: White Manhood, 'The Farmers,' and the Limits of Southern Populism," *Journal of Southern History,* 66 (August 2000), 497–524.

29. The classic article on this subject is Julie Roy Jeffrey, "Women in the Southern Farmers' Alliance: A Reconsideration of the Role and Status of Women in the Late Nineteenth-Century South," *Feminist Studies,* 3 (Fall 1975), 72–91. See also Marion K. Barthelme, ed., *Women in the Texas Populist Movement: Letters to the Southern Mercury* (College Station, Tex., 1997). On the role of women within specific community-based farm organizations, see Robert C. McMath Jr., "Agrarian Protest at the Forks of the Creek: Three Subordinate Farmers' Alliances in North Carolina," *North Carolina Historical Review,* 51 (Winter 1974), 41–63.

the first woman to serve in that body.[30] We shall return to Mrs. Felton in another context.

Woodward's proposition that southern Populism was distinct from and more radical than its western counterpart has attracted considerably more notice from other historians of the movement than has his attention or lack thereof to the movement's social and institutional dimensions. As to the distinctiveness there can be no doubt; focusing again on farmer-labor movements in Woodward's native state and in neighboring Texas, we might argue even for a distinctly southwestern variant—one more closely tied to the national Greenback movement and to the Knights of Labor than was the case in much of the Southeast.

What of Woodward's claim that southern Populism was also more radical than the western kind? When encountering such claims in his writing one is tempted to dismiss them as another of Woodward's masterful rhetorical devices, this one designed to persuade skeptical southerners in the middle third of the twentieth century that these exotic forebears were truly southern and their ideas still relevant to the pursuit of social justice. But, on closer examination, I am convinced that for Woodward the distinctly southern voice of radical Populism was part and parcel of the burden of southern history itself—the history of poverty and defeat that had set the region apart had also raised up prophets in the land like Jeremiah of old to hurl down anathemas on monopolists and plutocrats. For Woodward, in all seriousness, those southern prophets were a breed apart.

This was an important message to hear at the time, as was Woodward's message to white southerners about "forgotten alternatives" to de jure segregation.[31] But how useful and even how accurate is it to dwell on regional distinctiveness within Populism?[32] Certainly Tom Watson, like more than a

---

30. John E. Talmadge, *Rebecca Latimer Felton: Nine Stormy Decades* (Athens, Ga., 1960), 40, 46–48, 51–54, 59, 140.

31. C. Vann Woodward, *The Strange Career of Jim Crow* (3d rev. ed., New York, 1974), 31.

32. Norman Pollack argues that such claims for "more radical than thou" are not useful: "Ever since the distinguished southern historian C. Vann Woodward presented this view in 1951, it has become an article of faith . . . . The issue is a false one. No one should really care about the comparative radicalism of the different regional expressions of Populism, unless it furthers some analytical purpose, because it is self-evident that both regions were important to the movement and that each region faced its own peculiar problems, drew upon its own historical and cultural experiences, and confronted its own specific obstacles in advancing a position of political and economic dissent. Populism was not an interregional beauty contest to determine who was most radical . . . ." Pollack, *The Just Polity: Populism, Law, and Human Welfare*

few of Woodward's southern contemporaries in the 1930s, raged against the economic colonialism that held the South in thrall to northern monied interests, but those arguments were frequently couched in terms of the shared exploitation of the South and West and in terms of a national market economy. This larger field of vision among southern Populists is evident in Arkansas through both the collective biography of their leaders and the national focus of their ideology and platform. Southern regional distinctiveness hardly explains agrarianism in a state where Isaac McCracken, the founder of the Brothers of Freedom and leader of the Wheel, was Canadianborn and had lived much of his life outside the South, or where its principal publicist, W. Scott Morgan, was Ohio-born and widely traveled in national antimonopoly and reform circles. Nor, for that matter, does southernness explain Wisconsin-born and Illinois-raised Charles Macune, who presided over the expansion of the Farmers' Alliance, or even Leonidas L. Polk, Tarheel born and bred, who as national president of the Farmers' Alliance worked tirelessly to unify southern and western farmers. Free trade in reform ideas extended not only across the Mason and Dixon line but across the Canadian border and the Atlantic as well.[33]

Of course there were regional emphases and even regional cleavages within American Populism, but the Populists' appeal was intensely nationalistic and manifested itself, among other ways, in a critique of the nation's history as it was then most commonly presented. The right to interpret American history to the public, Populists claimed, had been usurped by the "textbook trust," the popular press, the universities, and even the pulpits of America's great urban churches, all controlled by big business. Those reactionary forces purveyed a whiggish version of the national story that "celebrated the rise of industrial capitalism, denied the loss of economic and political liberties among farmers and laborers, and ignored the erosion of traditional family and community values."[34] Populists from all regions sought to redeem *America* and reclaim its history for the producing classes. The solutions they proposed were predominantly national in scope and required an expanded national state for their implementation.

It was, of course, the race issue that brought Woodward to view southern

(Urbana and Chicago, 1987), 220–21. The fact that Pollack makes just such claims for *western* Populism does not negate his criticism.

33. W. Scott Morgan, *History of the Wheel and Alliance and the Impending Revolution* (St. Louis, 1891; reprint, New York, 1968), 306–8; Wheeler, "The People's Party in Arkansas," 157; McMath, *Populist Vanguard*, 28.

34. McMath, *American Populism*, 149.

Populists as exceptional and exceptionally courageous. Years after the last Populist battle, Tom Watson, who had by that point sunk into a sour racism and bizarre xenophobia, complained that his nemesis William Jennings Bryan had *"no everlasting and overshadowing Negro Question to hamper and handicap his progress:* I HAD."[35]

No part of Woodward's interpretation of Populism has drawn closer scrutiny than what he has said about racial inclusiveness within the movement, particularly with regard to Tom Watson. Some of his critics have refuted claims Woodward never made (white Populists, with few exceptions, never practiced or even advocated social equality with blacks), and others have ignored the qualifications that Woodward was careful to make. For all the challenges there is still much to commend Woodward's nuanced claim about Populist leaders' efforts to resist racism, defend the political rights of African Americans, and "create among their normally anti-Negro following, even temporarily, a spirit of tolerance in which the two races of the South could work together in one party for the achievement of common ends."[36]

Where I find it difficult to follow Woodward's lead is on what he refers to as the "Dr. Jekyll–and–Mr. Hyde problem" of Tom Watson and by extension the problem of what happened to the supposed inclusiveness of white Populists once the political tide had turned decisively against them. The Watson who in his Populist youth appealed eloquently for solidarity among producers, black and white, became a champion of white supremacy, anti-Semitism, and anti-Catholicism. Critics like Charles Crowe and Barton C. Shaw have found signs of continuity in word and in deed between the young and the old Watson on matters of race. Shaw uncovered evidence of Populist violence against black Democratic voters in the heat of Georgia election campaigns—certainly not a surprising finding, but one that led Woodward to concede that "Populist gains in interracial cooperation 'were limited and that their significance is easily exaggerated.' "[37]

The Arkansas story affirms Woodward's basic point about Populism and race but also underscores the need to qualify it. Biracial Populism in Arkansas was real, even heroic, but suspicion and factionalism among both black

---

35. *Jeffersonian Weekly,* January 20, 1910, quoted in Woodward, *Tom Watson,* 220.

36. Woodward, "The Populist Heritage and the Individual," 157.

37. Woodward, *Thinking Back,* 33 (first quotation), 36 (second quotation); Charles Crowe, "Tom Watson, Populists, and Blacks Reconsidered," *Journal of Negro History,* 55 (April 1970), 99–116; Barton C. Shaw, *The Wool-Hat Boys: Georgia's Populist Party* (Baton Rouge, 1984).

and white adherents rendered such cooperation precarious even before the election laws of 1891 made it next to impossible. Furthermore, the limits of economic cooperation across the racial divide came sharply into view in the Arkansas cotton-pickers strike of 1891, when black farm laborers struck for a living wage and white farmers opposed their efforts. These conflicting interests drove another nail in the coffin of "agricultural interest politics." In the new business plantations of the Southwest and Mississippi Delta, as Harold D. Woodman has noted, many African Americans "were gradually transformed in law and in practice into a proletariat" with little or no interest in the producerist agenda of Populism.[38]

But something else in the culture of John Clayton's Arkansas suggests the conditions under which interracial cooperation might have survived. The Republican–Union Labor coalition that would have given Clayton the congressional victory in a fair fight was not a new thing. Barnes tells us (and others agree) that this alliance was foreshadowed in opposition to secession in the Ozarks and Conway County, formed organizational expression in the biracial Republicanism of Reconstruction, and remained vibrant in the relatively open political world of the 1880s.[39]

Such continuities, though unusual, do turn up elsewhere in the South. Lawrence Goodwyn reconstructed the dramatic story of a biracial Populist coalition in Grimes County, Texas, that could only be destroyed by force of arms in 1898. It was "the story of a black-white coalition that had its genesis in Reconstruction." In the Tennessee Valley of northern Alabama, Wheelers and Knights of Labor built a biracial coalition with remarkable staying power. And in Granville County, North Carolina, in the heart of the bright leaf tobacco belt, the Knights of Labor picked up the Republicans' Reconstruction agenda and provided a new organizational home for biracial politics. From Arkansas, Texas, Alabama, and North Carolina comes evidence that, at its strongest points, biracial Populism in the South had been fired in the crucible of local struggles for decades. Just as Woodward's explanation of the Populist experience can be enriched by a broader understanding of the local organizations that undergirded it, so can his interpreta-

---

38. William F. Holmes, "The Arkansas Cotton Pickers Strike of 1891 and the Demise of the Colored Farmers' Alliance," *Arkansas Historical Quarterly*, 32 (Summer 1973), 107–19; Harold D. Woodman, "The Political Economy of the New South: Retrospects and Prospects," *Journal of Southern History*, 67 (November 2001), 806 (256 in this volume).

39. Barnes, *Who Killed John Clayton?* 2–3, 15–23; Henningson, "Northwest Arkansas and the Brothers of Freedom," 306–7.

tion be reaffirmed by following the origins of a movement culture back to the 1860s and beyond.[40]

To trace agrarian reform back to a time before Woodward's discontinuous New South is to understand that American populism is broader than its Alliance and People's Party manifestations and that its roots were deeply embedded in the culture of nineteenth-century America.[41] If that is so, then we might also imagine that populism, in its larger meaning, would have survived the demise of the People's Party. I believe the evidence now warrants a reconsideration of Woodward's periodization of southern Populism. Instead of discontinuity fore and aft, we may profitably consider a long agrarian moment stretching at least from the 1860s through the rise of southern Progressivism and reaching the peak of its national influence during the presidency of Woodrow Wilson.

40. Lawrence C. Goodwyn, "Populist Dreams and Negro Rights: East Texas as a Case Study," *American Historical Review,* 76 (December 1971), 1436 (quotation); Paul Horton, "Testing the Limits of Class Politics in Postbellum Alabama: Agrarian Radicalism in Lawrence County," *Journal of Southern History,* 57 (February 1991), 63–84; and Edwards, *Gendered Strife and Confusion,* 218–54. The Granville story, as told by Laura F. Edwards, bears out another fact about biracialism, one that Stephen Kantrowitz has also confirmed for Ben Tillman's South Carolina: "not simply race, but a racialized conception of manhood" was a powerful tool in the hands of Populism's foes. Kantrowitz, "Ben Tillman and Hendrix McLane," 498. While John Clayton was winning a majority of the votes cast, if not of those counted, in his Arkansas congressional district, Ben Tillman co-opted an incipient agrarian radicalism by channeling it into a racialized conception of "the farmer" and thereby smothered South Carolina's Greenback Labor Party in its crib. "[N]ot simply race, but a racialized conception of manhood" trumped class yet again. The work of Kantrowitz, Edwards, Gilmore (*Gender and Jim Crow*), and others on the contested terrain of gender and politics in the New South has added an important new dimension to our understanding. But it is important, as Woodward reminds us, to balance that perspective with the economic conditions under which this terrain is contested. It is also important to remember that biracial Populism could itself appropriate themes of family, manliness, and womanhood and put a different spin on them from Tillman and his ilk. Finally, such contests need to be understood within the larger national context of party politics and party discipline in the nineteenth century, in which gendered language was widely used to discredit reformers who lacked party loyalty. As Paula Baker notes, "Party politicians often spoke of reformers . . . in terms that questioned the reformers' masculinity," viewing them as "politically impotent" and referring to them as "the 'third sex' of American politics, 'man-milliners,' and 'Miss-Nancys.'" Baker, "The Domestication of Politics: Women and American Political Society, 1784–1920," *American Historical Review,* 89 (June 1984), 628 n. 27.

41. I have argued elsewhere that the Populist movement of the 1880s and 1890s was part of a larger culture of protest dating to the 1860s with cultural and political roots in the antebellum period. McMath, *American Populism,* chap. 2.

To propose such a reconsideration is to call into question not only Wood-ward's interpretation but also a large body of scholarship published since *Origins* that finds fundamental differences between Populism and Progress-ivism.[42] A persuasive engagement with that body of work is beyond the scope of this essay, but instead I will address two more modest questions: Why did Woodward draw such a sharp line between Populism of the 1880s–1890s and agrarian reform of the Progressive era? And what kind of evidence might indicate that the long agrarian moment was a major factor in what we have known as Progressivism?

At a somewhat superficial level, in *Origins* Woodward was constrained chronologically by the series editors who determined that the dividing line between his volume and the "final" volume by George Brown Tindall (who took over the assignment from Rupert B. Vance) was 1913. While Demo-crats regained control of the House of Representatives in 1910, southern congressmen and senators did not reach the height of their influence in Washington until after the elections of 1912.[43] But even if *Origins* had con-tinued through the Wilson administration, I doubt that Woodward's analy-sis would have changed.

The shadow of the latter-day Tom Watson loomed over Woodward's post-Populist New South, and the burden of Woodward's Populism— defined as a biracial political movement of hardworking folk whose griev-ances justified their collective action—made it difficult to relate the agrarian movement of the 1880s and 1890s to other forms of white popular protest in the following decades, which at their worst were violently racist. *Origins,* like *Tom Watson,* posits a sharp break in reform politics in the first decade of the century, when over the issue of race, "[white] Southern agrarianism . . . became isolated and went reactionary." Furthermore, the rise of share-cropping widened the economic chasm between blacks and whites: "The trend toward increasing tenancy [after 1900] was fraught with fatal implica-tions for the ideology of Populist agrarianism. Yet it was a trend that Tom

---

42. Although it interprets Populism quite differently than Woodward, one of the best of these studies is by one of his students: Sheldon Hackney, *Populism to Progressivism in Ala-bama* (Princeton, 1969).

43. Tindall's treatment of southern congressmen during the first Wilson administration places considerable emphasis on the role of southern "radical 'agrarians'" in Congress, partic-ularly Robert Henry and Joseph Eagle of Texas, Claude Kitchin of North Carolina, Willard Ragsdale of South Carolina, and James K. Vardaman of Mississippi. George Brown Tindall, *The Emergence of the New South, 1913–1945* (Baton Rouge, 1967), 10–11.

Watson's logic never took into account. . . . The dichotomy between dispossessed farmers and possessing farmers was one he chose to ignore."[44]

While Woodward's own thorough research informed his treatment of the Redeemer-Populist era in *Origins*, for the Progressives he relied heavily on an emerging secondary literature. Most importantly, the work of Arthur S. Link was becoming available between 1945 and 1947, just as Woodward was returning to civilian life and to the completion of his great project.[45] From Link, Woodward took examples of southern innovation in municipal and state reform that confirmed his own view of Progressivism as essentially urban and pro-business. But Woodward ignored Link's evidence (and that of Alex Arnett before him) of continuities between the late-nineteenth-century agrarian agenda and southern Democratic progressivism. Even in his account of the South in the presidential election of 1912, which relied heavily on Link, Woodward seems mainly to be listening for echoes of earlier compromises between eastern Democrats and southern Redeemers going back to 1877 (pp. 470–81).

Although Woodward describes the South of the early twentieth century as "the most thoroughly Bryanized region in the country" (p. 469), one gets little sense from *Origins* of southerners' leading role in a Bryanized national Democratic Party after 1906, by which time Bryan himself had embraced some of the most radical demands of the Populists. Southern congressional Progressivism is almost invisible in *Origins*. Its stalwarts, most of whom now wore the "agrarian" label if uncomfortably in some cases, included not only former Populists and their fellow travelers but also pro-business progressives who had been sworn enemies of the People's Party in the 1890s.[46]

As a result, Woodward's story of southern political culture in the Progressive era—set within the context of segregation, disfranchisement, and racial violence as well as a widening economic gulf between blacks and

---

44. Woodward to Rainey, March 9, 1937, Folder 1, Box 22, Rainey Papers (first quotation); Woodward, *Tom Watson*, 404 (second quotation). Woodward suggested the same point in *Origins* (pp. 413–15), but not as emphatically as this passage from the biography, which followed a discussion on the rise in cotton prices after 1900 and the increase in Watson's own wealth and landholdings, mainly in the form of tenant plantations.

45. Arthur Stanley Link, "The South and the Democratic Campaign of 1912" (Ph.D. dissertation, University of North Carolina at Chapel Hill, 1945); Link, "The Progressive Movement in the South, 1870–1914," *North Carolina Historical Review*, 23 (April 1946), 172–95; and Link, *Wilson: The Road to the White House* (Princeton, 1947).

46. David Sarasohn, *The Party of Reform: Democrats in the Progressive Era* (Jackson, Miss., 1989), 17–19, 35–86.

whites—becomes two stories: one of elite-led municipal and state reform that sounds like a replay of the Redeemers' modernizing agenda and the other of isolated and reactionary agrarians howling their support for the demagogues and rabble-rousers.

Another version of the story, however, predates Woodward's and has never been without its champions in the half century since the publication of *Origins*. That version provides a reference point for scholars seeking to re-democratize Progressivism and to reopen questions about roads not taken along the way to the modern state.[47] Classic studies of Populism by John D. Hicks and Alex M. Arnett published before *Tom Watson* found significant continuity between agrarian movements of the Populist and Progressive eras, as did Arthur S. Link's pioneering article, "The Progressive Movement in the South, 1870–1914." Standard institutional histories of farm organizations follow that line, focusing on the Farmers' Union as successor to the Farmers' Alliance and on agrarian radicalism within the Democratic Party.[48] In *The Age of Reform* Richard Hofstadter's characterization of "the alliance between agrarians and the urban middle class that consti-

---

47. In a recent review of this literature, historian Morton Keller discovers "a fair prospect for convergence between political science and political history, and in a most unexpected venue," and reports that "[t]he structure of the American state and the fundaments of modern public policy are major themes of modern political science, and the Progressive period is a mother lode for inquiry and insight . . . . " "It is here," Keller points out, "that Stephen Skowronek finds the American administrative state taking form, that Theda Skocpol locates the origin of the modern welfare state, that Robert Putnam finds a rich store of social capital upon which the Progressive polity was able to draw." Morton Keller, "Social and Economic Regulation in the Progressive Era," in Sidney M. Milkis and Jerome M. Mileur, eds., *Progressivism and the New Democracy* (Amherst, Mass., 1999), 127–29 (first and second quotations on p. 127; third quotation on p. 129). See also James T. Kloppenberg, *Uncertain Victory: Social Democracy and Progressivism in European and American Thought, 1870–1920* (New York and Oxford, 1986).

48. Hicks, *Populist Revolt*, chap. 15; Arnett, *Populist Movement in Georgia*, 226–27; Link, "Progressive Movement in the South," 179. For studies of farmer organizations, see in particular Theodore Saloutos, *Farmer Movements in the South, 1865–1933* (Berkeley and Los Angeles, 1960), chaps. 12–13; Carl C. Taylor, *The Farmers' Movement, 1620–1920* (New York and other cities, 1953), chap. 13; and Theodore Saloutos and John D. Hicks, *Agricultural Discontent in the Middle West, 1900–1939* (Madison, Wisc., 1951), chaps. 2–6. One historian of southwestern socialism notes the strong influence of Populism on that vibrant movement, particularly in Oklahoma, but he also cautions against overemphasizing Populist influences, particularly after 1907 when the movement was shaped more by the Socialist Labor Party than by Populism. James R. Green, *Grass-Roots Socialism: Radical Movements in the Southwest, 1895–1943* (Baton Rouge, 1978), 12–13.

tuted the Progressive movement" stands in sharp contrast to Woodward's dichotomy of urban progressives and rural reactionaries.[49]

In a 1963 article based on roll-call analysis of legislation before Congress in 1906–1913, Anne Firor Scott reported that "wherever progressivism took its impulse from agrarian reform the South was in the forefront of progressive legislation." Scott concluded that "from 1906 onward an increasing number of Southern congressmen were responsive to a broader progressive impulse . . . ."[50] The question of why this might have been so was not immediately pursued by other scholars. By 1963 most students of Progressivism were shifting their attention away from legislative matters to the administrative state, which they concluded had been captured by business and professional interests.

This now dominant interpretation, which cast Progressive reform as an element of "corporate liberalism," is being reexamined by scholars who seek forgotten alternatives to the modern bureaucratic state. While some of those pursuing this agenda are still mining the urban, eastern, and European sources of Progressive reform, others are revisiting the politics of sectionalism in the congressional arena and finding new life in the old left-fork agrarian coalition.[51]

Chief among the latter group is political scientist Elizabeth Sanders, whose *Roots of Reform: Farmers, Workers, and the American State, 1877–1917,* provides a valuable counterweight to the now orthodox view of Progressivism associated with Gabriel Kolko, James Weinstein, and others. Like Anne Scott, Sanders pays close attention to congressional legislative histories, and she concludes that "agrarian movements constituted the most important political force driving the development of the American national state in the half century before World War I."[52]

---

49. Hofstadter, *The Age of Reform,* 239. At least when it comes to the twentieth century, the historiographical fault line between Woodward and Hofstadter is more complex than is usually acknowledged.

50. Anne Firor Scott, "A Progressive Wind from the South, 1906–1913," *Journal of Southern History,* 29 (February 1963), 53–70 (quotations on p. 70).

51. As an example of recent work on the urban and European roots of Progressivism, see Daniel T. Rodgers, *Atlantic Crossings: Social Politics in a Progressive Age* (Cambridge, Mass., and London, 1998).

52. Elizabeth Sanders, *Roots of Reform: Farmers, Workers, and the American State, 1877–1917* (Chicago and London, 1999), 1 (quotation), 2, 421 n. 4; Gabriel Kolko, *The Triumph of Conservatism: A Reinterpretation of American History, 1900–1916* (London and New York, 1963); James Weinstein, *The Corporate Ideal in the Liberal State: 1900–1918* (Boston, 1968).

Following a methodology developed by Richard F. Bensel, Sanders analyzes voting patterns along regional lines and reaches an overall conclusion about the shared economic interests of the "periphery" (South and West) that Tom Watson himself could have applauded. Sanders's most original contribution is in her reading of the legislative histories of such Progressive-era measures as the Hepburn Act, Federal Reserve Act, Clayton Antitrust Act, Federal Trade Commission Act, and the Federal Farm Loan and Warehouse Acts. She finds southern congressmen and senators pushing for features in those bills that would have—and in some cases did—write into law Populist demands on regulation of the railroads, trusts, and banking and credit (shades of the subtreasury!). Among the southern champions of this "agrarian statist agenda" were certified agrarian radicals like Joseph H. Eagle and Robert Henry of Texas, Robert Owen of Oklahoma, Otis Wingo of Arkansas, and J. Willard Ragsdale of South Carolina. But their number also included Ben Tillman, Hoke Smith, and James K. Vardaman. All of them were now seated within the "Bryanized" Democracy. "The national Democratic Party," Sanders concludes, "having absorbed the Populist Party and rebuffed its own northeastern conservative wing, became the bearer of agrarian demands in national politics. Thus it was that so much of the old populist program could be enacted years after the Populist Party and the Farmers' Alliance had faded away."[53]

Sanders's passion for a usable democratic past is reminiscent of Woodward, the young historian-with-a-purpose. But if Woodward's enthusiasm was tempered by the widening "dichotomy between dispossessed farmers and possessing farmers," Sanders appears to lump both together, along with the South's emergent commercial interests, under one "agrarian" banner.[54] And if Woodward never successfully explained the racism and xenophobia of Watson and other white Populists, Sanders never seriously engages the same issue in analyzing the legislative careers of her southern agrarian Pro-

---

53. Sanders, *Roots of Reform*, 3 (first quotation); 7 (second quotation); 199–202 (on Hepburn Act); 236–61 (on Federal Reserve Act); 282–89 (on Clayton Antitrust Act); 291–93 (Federal Trade Commission Act); 259–61, 298–303 (Federal Farm Loan Act and Warehouse Act); 412–13 (third quotation). On the methodology see Richard F. Bensel, *Sectionalism and American Political Development, 1880–1980* (Madison, Wisc., 1984), 415–50; and Sanders, *Roots of Reform*, 23–25.

54. Woodward, *Tom Watson*, 404. Furthermore, Sanders's singular focus on the agrarian legislative agenda prevents her from acknowledging the role of professional- and expert-led aspects of municipal and state reform of the type that Woodward, Tindall, and others have addressed.

gressives. In a perceptive review Robert D. Johnston challenged her, and all who still seek a usable past in the populist heritage: "Populists only have a world to gain by a thorough exploration of the relationship between race and agrarianism . . . ."[55]

Add to Johnston's admonition the need to explore the connection between the economic condition of whites and African Americans in the Progressive era and the ability to mobilize some sectors of the rural population for economic and political action. Then we will have described the work to be done before we can make sense of a long agrarian moment that encompasses Populism, Progressivism, and "the nadir" of southern race relations.[56]

The "unity of all producers" was little more than a slogan even by the 1890s, and the one-two punch of disfranchisement and the making of a black rural proletariat through sharecropping ended any hope of biracial agrarian politics. But for southern agriculture as a whole in the years just before World War I, times were much better than they had been during the preceding half century. Cotton prices rose sharply after the turn of the century, dropped in 1907–8, and then reached record levels again in 1909, 1910, and 1913. Furthermore, according to Gavin Wright, "[t]he big jump in the tenancy rate during the 1890s [for the South as a whole] slowed to a crawl after 1900 and stabilized between 1910 and 1920." In 1900 about 25 percent of black farmers in the South owned the land they tilled, and black landownership continued to increase until it peaked in 1910.[57]

With an agricultural economy that was heavily commercialized and with commodity prices that were relatively high but volatile, the South was actually fertile ground for organizations that promised farmers continued economic independence. At least some farmers had enough cash in their pockets to pay the initiation fee, and they recognized the need for cooperative action in a situation where transportation costs and commodity and credit prices seemed rigged against them. The Farmers' Union, founded in Texas in 1902 by a former Farmers' Alliance organizer, spread across the South in a fashion reminiscent of the Farmers' Alliance. Its cooperative program emphasized warehousing and "holding" of the cotton crop for top

---

55. Johnston, "Peasants, Pitchforks, and the (Found) Promise of Progressivism," 396.

56. Rayford W. Logan, *The Negro in American Thought and Life: The Nadir, 1877–1901* (New York, 1954).

57. Gavin Wright, *Old South, New South: Revolutions in the Southern Economy Since the Civil War* (New York, 1986), 117–19 (quotation on p. 117); Edward L. Ayers, *The Promise of the New South: Life After Reconstruction* (New York and Oxford, 1992), 208.

prices, and its political agenda (though pursued through the Democratic Party) reflected the interests of farmers bent on maximizing return and holding onto their land.[58]

In the age of segregation the all-white Farmers' Union was even more ambivalent about cooperation with African Americans than the Alliance had been. But Union members recognized that blacks produced enough of the region's cotton to influence the success of their crop-holding program. Oklahoma Union members "concluded that there were many 'well-to-do, thrifty, industrious, and landowning negro farmers' worthy of admission" into the Union along with whites. But only with misgivings did white Unionists support even the separate organization of African Americans. In some instances white Unionists abjured biracial cooperation altogether in favor of other time-tested methods: night riders appeared at the homes of African American farmers and other holdouts to demand that they join the cotton-holding campaign.[59]

As with the discovery of Populists' intimidation of black Democrats in Georgia, we should not be surprised when the "unity of all producers" mutated into coercion of the dispossessed by the possessing. The support of former Populists for disfranchisement in some instances was only one other manifestation of ways in which the movement, as previously noted, "became isolated and went reactionary."[60] At the extreme, consider the remarks of Rebecca Latimer Felton before the Georgia State Agricultural Society in a speech entitled "Women on the Farm." After pleading for educational opportunities for farm women, this confidante of Tom Watson and the most

---

58. The history of the Farmers' Union in the South is summarized in Saloutos, *Farmer Movements in the South,* chap. 12; Taylor, *Farmers' Movement,* chap. 14; and Dewey W. Grantham, *Southern Progressivism: The Reconciliation of Progress and Tradition* (Knoxville, 1983), 326–32.

59. Saloutos, *Farmer Movements in the South,* 193 (quotation), 198–99. Similar tactics were used by white tobacco farmers in Tennessee and Kentucky. Organized by the National Tobacco Growers' Association to resist the monopoly power of the American Tobacco Company in what became known as the "Black Patch war," white farmers terrorized individuals who failed to cooperate, sometimes whipping or shooting them or burning their crops. Some, but not all of the victims were black. Saloutos, *Farmer Movements in the South,* 171–76. For these tactics in still another industry see Karin A. Shapiro, *A New South Rebellion: The Battle Against Convict Labor in the Tennessee Coalfields, 1871–1896* (Chapel Hill and London, 1998), 235–43.

60. Worth Robert Miller, "Building a Progressive Coalition in Texas: The Populist–Reform Democrat Rapprochement, 1900–1907," *Journal of Southern History,* 52 (May 1986), 163–82; Gregg Cantrell and D. Scott Barton, "Texas Populists and the Failure of Biracial Politics," *Journal of Southern History,* 55 (November 1989), 659–92.

prominent woman in reform politics in Georgia, if not the South, went on to chastise white men for their failure to "put a sheltering arm about innocence and virtue." If "it needs lynching to protect woman's dearest possession from the ravening human beasts," she concluded, "then I say lynch, a thousand times a week, if necessary."[61]

Episodes such as this force us to look again at the issue of agrarian reform and race and to consider the possibility that the racism so clearly evident after 1900 was there all along, that it was as James R. Green says of the Southwest, "an organic part of progressive reformism."[62] It is not a happy assignment, but Robert Johnston is right: We have only a world to gain.

That brings me finally to reconsider an article of faith of Woodward the presentist who recalled that "in writing in the 1930s about the strivings and troubles of the Populists in the 1890s, I could not help being influenced by analogies between their times and my own, by the similarities between the depression in which they struggled and the one in which we were then still floundering. . . . It was no dead past I was trying to bring to life, but one very much alive and full of meaning." The story of a past "very much alive and full of meaning," a story conceived in one depression and calling to mind another, was intended to show southerners, white and black, something of how their agrarian forebears had struggled to create a just society.[63]

Times change. By 1951 the Great Depression was a memory, and fashions in historical studies were shifting toward a consensus school that minimized economic conflict and located the source of social discontent in the "status anxiety" of the discontented. The Cold War was heating up, and with it came opportunistic anticommunists who scared the daylights out of eastern liberals and their academic fellow travelers. In a desperate effort to understand this exotic political specimen from somewhere west of the Hudson River, social scientists discovered populism and determined it to be the source of the unpleasantness. One declared solemnly that "American fas-

---

61. LeeAnn Whites, "Love, Hate, Rape, Lynching: Rebecca Latimer Felton and the Gender Politics of Racial Violence," in David S. Cecelski and Timothy B. Tyson, eds., *Democracy Betrayed: The Wilmington Race Riot of 1898 and Its Legacy* (Chapel Hill and London, 1998), 148–49 (Felton quotation on p. 149).

62. Green, *Grass-Roots Socialism,* 63.

63. Woodward, *Thinking Back,* 37. This was also the Woodward who in 1936 had written to Glenn Rainey, perhaps with tongue-in-cheek but perhaps revealing more about himself than he would later do in print: "As an educator (sic) I have about decided what education should be: besides teaching people what to hate and what [to] cherish it should equip them with proper heroes and proper villains. Rather an old fashioned idea." Woodward to Rainey, July 12, 1936, Folder 1, Box 22, Rainey Papers.

cism has its roots in American populism." Another, somewhat geographically challenged, associated the Populists with "xenophobia [and] Jew-baiting" and proclaimed that "[o]ut of the western Populist movement came such apostles of thought-control and racist bigotry as Tom Watson."[64]

These were not the Populists Woodward knew, but the pronouncements of intellectuals about a tradition they little understood threatened to undercut the "history-with-a-purpose" that he had made his life's work. Woodward responded in 1959 with an essay entitled "The Populist Heritage and the Intellectual." There Woodward acknowledged, as always, that the positive reading of the Populist experience had to be qualified: "it cannot be denied that some of the offshoots of Populism are less than lovely to contemplate and rather painful to recall. Misshapen and sometimes hideous, they are caricatures of the *Populist ideal,* though their kinship with the genuine article is undeniable." Nevertheless, Woodward contended, "The intellectual must resist the impulse to identify all the irrational and evil forces he detests with such movements because some of them, or the aftermath or epigone of some of them, have proved so utterly repulsive. He will learn all he can from the new criticism about the irrational and illiberal side of Populism and other reform movements, but he cannot afford to repudiate the heritage."[65]

Here is Woodward the presentist, with no apology, calling future generations of intellectuals to a life of civic engagement in the populist vein. But in these passages we see Woodward shouldering a burden of southern Populism that has limited scholarly inquiry and hampered our ability to allow the past to speak wisely to our present needs. If, after all the half-concessions have been made, there is still a "Populist ideal" that must be defended as the "genuine article," and if that ideal is to be found more with leaders and their ideas and personal choices than with the rank and file gathered in homes and neighborhoods where they found *their* voices, then how will we ever come closer to understanding the original Pops, warts and all, let alone the likes of Vardaman, Tillman, and Hoke Smith who led congressional Progressives into battle with the same determination they had displayed in securing white supremacy? How will we bring the populist legacy to bear in an age when some working men and women—people who define themselves

---

64. The first quotation is from Victor C. Ferkiss and the second and third from Peter Viereck. Both men are quoted in Woodward, "The Populist Heritage and the Intellectual," 147 (second quotation), 148 (first quotation), and 149 (third quotation).

65. Woodward, "The Populist Heritage and the Intellectual," 163–64 (first quotation; italics added for emphasis), 166 (second quotation).

as consumers and taxpayers more than as producers—connect with David Duke or George Wallace, if they attend to electoral politics at all? And how will the populist tradition speak wisely to a nation where a few of the "little platoons" of civil society look more like the Aryan Nation than the Brothers of Freedom?

The legacy of Populism, in both its short and long forms, is very complex, very human, and also very southern and very American. Neither a reified populism nor one artificially delimited in time serves well the larger purposes that Woodward sought to accomplish in *Origins of the New South* and in his lifelong work of illuminating the burden and opportunity of southern history. Furthermore, these interpretations of populism form an unnecessary impediment for those who still seek in that legacy forgotten alternatives of what America could have become. I would like to believe that by opening up new perspectives we will encourage a new generation of scholars and citizens to pursue Woodward's purposes.

Gender and *Origins of the New South*

We might forgive our graduate students if they reduce the fact-filled paragraphs and biting arguments in C. Vann Woodward's 542-page masterpiece, *Origins of the New South,* to three words: change versus continuity.
Even though we understand that all history is about change, especially the
degree of and reasons for change, countless professors have urged countless
graduate students to take their stands in this dichotomous debate. I remember the day I received this assignment and, ultimately, found myself standing
behind Vann Woodward.[1]

Reprinted from *Journal of Southern History,* 67 (November 2001), 769–88, the Woodward symposium issue.

1. C. Vann Woodward, *The Origins of the New South, 1877–1913* (Baton Rouge, 1951).
Page numbers for subsequent references to *Origins* in this essay are inserted parenthetically in
the text. The first edition's pagination is retained in later reprint editions. Even more than
usual, writing this paper became a collaborative event and, in the process, a lot of fun. I am
grateful to Karen Leathem, Katherine Charron, Adriane Smith, Jane Dailey, Timothy Tyson,

George Brown Tindall had paired *Origins* with Carl N. Degler's *Place Over Time* for my southern history class.[2] We met in Tindall's office, a space filled with moon pies, RCs, baseball caps, and photos of Elvis. There, amid these cultural artifacts, it didn't feel that all that much had changed lately. But Tindall made us choose sides: Would it be Woodward or Degler? As I often did when I was confused in graduate school, I turned to the primary source in my head—my grandmother, Candy Lovin, born in 1887, who brought me up. Which would it be, Candy? Change or continuity?

Candy Lovin was herself reared outside of Hanging Dog, North Carolina, in a family that earned its living by raising fighting cocks. In the 1950s we found ourselves in suburban Greensboro, North Carolina, living in a house-on-a-slab with a "great" room and patio. Out back, where my mother had graded the yard for a tennis court, Candy had insisted on planting rows of corn, "those Kentucky runners," and summer squash. Twice a day, in the dew of the morning and in the cool of the evening, Candy would put on a "house dress," roll down her thick stockings, pull on her men's work boots, don her sunbonnet to keep the Cherokee in her from popping out, hoist her hoe to her shoulder, and go out to tend to the garden. Once she set to hoeing, she would sing at the top of her lungs, off-key, in her mountain twang. Her repertoire ranged from dozens of verses of "Barb'ry Allen," to plaintive Hank Williams songs, to a particularly nasal rendition of "Amazing Grace." Sometimes, if in a mellow mood, she would croon that smash hit of the 1890s, "After the Ball." I could scarcely ask for a more convincing demonstration of continuity.[3]

Next door, though, our neighbors seethed. They had bought a double lot, erected a huge house with sixteen sliding glass doors, and settled in to entertain clients by their pool. He was the regional sales manager for the Dale Carnegie seminars "How to Win Friends and Influence People." They *might* have a lot of money, my mother sniffed, but they aren't *from* here. As they and their business victims sipped Bloody Marys poolside, Candy would treat the group to her spirited renditions and pre–World War I attire. Fi-

---

Stephen Kantrowitz, Bryant Simon, Laura Edwards, Marjorie J. Spruill, and Jacquelyn Hall for their marvelous ideas, their responses to *Origins*, their editing, and their application of restraint where necessary.

2. Carl N. Degler, *Place Over Time: The Continuity of Southern Distinctiveness* (Baton Rouge, 1977).

3. For the score and lyrics of one of hundreds of versions of "Barb'ry Allen" that exist, see "Barb'ry Ellen," in Margaret Bradford Boni, ed., *The Fireside Book of Favorite American Songs* (New York, 1952), 316. See also Charles K. Harris, "After the Ball" (1892), in Boni, ed., *Fireside Book*, 35–40.

nally, the Newer South neighbors built a high fence to screen her out. Even then, they couldn't shut her up. She simply sang louder and switched to medleys of slightly off-color songs from the 1920s. ("You take the legs off some ol' table, you take the arms off some ol' chair, you take a neck off some ol' bottle, and from a horse you take some hair . . . you take some hair.")[4]

As historians, how we determine the extent and nature of change depends on the analytical tools we use to measure it. In my own Newer South, folk culture survived: an anthropologist would have had a field day with Candy. Nevertheless, the politics of World War II, the social transformations that made divorce more common in the 1950s, and the market economy had combined to set us adrift, ultimately, to wash up in our suburb. There, blotting out the farms where Albion W. Tourgée had set *A Fool's Errand*, Newer South developers had imposed two *cul de sacs* in the largest sense of the term.[5] A national franchise market had landed Dale Carnegie's Newer Man of the Newer South next door, even as regional isolation bound my mother to toil all her life as a secretary at a down-at-the-heels cotton brokerage, while dreaming of tennis, which she did not know how to play. But one analytical tool can explain more about our situation than all the others combined: gender. This was a family of three white women who had lived without a man in the house for the better part of twenty years. Gender had painted our possibilities and drawn our boundaries on a canvas of whiteness confined by a class frame.

Within these parameters of class, race, and gender, change rolled through our lives in the 1950s like Sherman rolled through Georgia; by the 1980s, when I came under Tindall's tutelage, there were no longer cotton brokerages, Kentucky runners, or sunbonnets in my South. Despite Candy's example of continuity in my memory, I needed a past that allowed for the possibility of change. In *Thinking Back,* Woodward hits upon this very same explanation to account for the general acclamation and lack of scholarly criticism that followed the publication of *Origins*. His readers needed him: "With all that pandemonium of contemporaneous upheaval and daily

---

4. Candy's song, written anonymously circa 1920, was a takeoff on the Washington and Lee University "swing" song. A version was published as "I Can Get More Lovin' From A Dum-Dum-Dummy (Than I've Been Getting from You)" in 1925 by Shapiro, Bernstein, and Company. At this time, the New York publishers attributed the music to Ray Henderson and the lyrics to Lew Brown and Billy Rose.

5. [Albion W. Tourgée], *A Fool's Errand* (New York, 1880).

change of the 'unchangeable' during the fifties, sixties, and into the seventies, what was there left to say about continuity?"[6]

If one uses gender to analyze southern history, change overwhelms continuity. Within the past twenty years, historians have proven that southern women played important roles in southern history that shaped both public and private life. Moreover, we have discovered that conceptions of manhood and womanhood—of gender—have driven politics, the law, and race relations throughout southern history. Indeed, this body of work suggests that the South was hypergendered: the difference between male and female roles was especially sharp, and these accentuated roles functioned in a variety of ways to define not only gender relations, but class politics and racial controls as well.

Yet, in *Origins,* the Change Manifesto for southern history, women are scarcer than hen's teeth, and nowhere does an explicitly gendered analysis appear. In other words, not only does Woodward exclude women, he does not think about how gendered ideas influenced the white men who created the new political and economic culture that consumes his attention. When, over the past few months, I mentioned that I would be speaking on gender and *Origins,* more than one wag remarked, "Now, that's going to be a short paper." In *Origins of the New South,* Woodward used most of the analytical tools available to him in 1951, wielding political and material analysis with dazzling proficiency. The language that we speak today when we use gender to analyze historical problems, however, was completely unavailable to Woodward. Indeed, twenty years later, both women in history and gendered analyses remained missing from interpretations of the period. Neither Charles B. Dew's marvelous "Critical Essay on Recent Works" in the 1971 reprint of *Origins* that described research on the New South undertaken since 1951 nor Sheldon Hackney's touching 1972 retrospective essay in the *Journal of Southern History* could incorporate gendered insights into the historiography.[7]

---

6. C. Vann Woodward, *Thinking Back: The Perils of Writing History* (Baton Rouge, 1986), 68 (151 in this volume). On change versus continuity see Dan T. Carter, "From the Old South to the New: Another Look at the Theme of Change and Continuity," in Walter J. Fraser Jr. and Winfred B. Moore Jr., eds., *From the Old South to the New: Essays on the Transitional South* (Westport, Conn., and London, 1981), 23–32.

7. Charles B. Dew, "Critical Essay on Recent Works," in C. Vann Woodward, *Origins of the New South, 1877–1913* (1951; reprint, Baton Rouge, 1971), 517–628; Sheldon Hackney, "*Origins of the New South* in Retrospect," *Journal of Southern History,* 38 (May 1972), 191–216 (25–49 in this volume).

Beyond the mere absence of women characters in *Origins,* we must ask ourselves two questions: How valuable is *Origins* for those now writing gendered histories of the period, and how valuable might gender be in unraveling some of *Origins*'s mysteries? My sense is that Woodward's masterpiece still points the way toward changes that Woodward himself did not describe. By putting women into the period 1877–1913 and using gender to analyze the era, we can seize the further possibilities for change that Woodward has left for us.

From *Origins* the reader is hard put to discover that any women lived in the South from 1877 to 1913. In 1951 recuperative work on southern women's history had barely begun. Indeed, before 1950 only a handful of scholars had written on women or topics touching them. Most of these remained unpublished. Among published articles that Woodward could have used in *Origins,* he had surely read Marjorie Stratford Mendenhall's 1934 article "Southern Women of a 'Lost Generation'" in the *South Atlantic Quarterly* and A. Elizabeth Taylor's "The Origin of the Woman Suffrage Movement in Georgia," which appeared in the *Georgia Historical Quarterly* in 1944. Anne Firor Scott's "The 'New Woman' in the New South" was still eleven years away. The equivalent of *Origins* in southern women's history, Scott's *The Southern Lady: From Pedestal to Politics, 1830–1930,* would not be published for two decades.[8]

So perhaps it is not surprising that Woodward does not include women as actors—or as objects—in *Origins.* Of the 540 people listed in its index, 16 are women. Today, the women's absence is most striking when one looks at prominent couples. *Origins* gives us John, but not Lugenia Burns, Hope; William, but not Rebecca Latimer, Felton. We know that when Woodward lived in Atlanta, he knew John Hope. Did he know Lugenia Burns Hope?

---

8. Anne Firor Scott, "A Progressive Wind from the South, 1906–1913," *Journal of Southern History,* 29 (February 1963), 53–70; Jacquelyn Dowd Hall and Anne Firor Scott, "Women in the South," in John B. Boles and Evelyn Thomas Nolen, eds., *Interpreting Southern History: Historiographical Essays in Honor of Sanford W. Higginbotham* (Baton Rouge, 1987), 454–61; Marjorie Stratford Mendenhall, "Southern Women of a 'Lost Generation,'" *South Atlantic Quarterly,* 33 (October 1934), 334–53; A. Elizabeth Taylor, "The Origin of the Woman Suffrage Movement in Georgia," *Georgia Historical Quarterly,* 28 (June 1944), 63–79; Scott, "The 'New Woman' in the New South," *South Atlantic Quarterly,* 61 (Autumn 1962), 473–83; Scott, *The Southern Lady: From Pedestal to Politics, 1830–1930* (Chicago and London, 1970). See also Scott, ed., *Unheard Voices: The First Historians of Southern Women* (Charlottesville and London, 1993). Thanks to Anne Scott for sending her "Women in the South: History as Fiction, Fiction as History," in Lothar Hönnighausen and Valeria Gennaro Lerda, eds., *Rewriting the South: History and Fiction* (Tübingen, Ger., 1993), 22–34.

Woodward arrived at Emory as a junior six years after Rebecca Latimer Felton became the first woman to serve in the U.S. Senate by occupying the fleeting moments of Tom Watson's term after his death in 1922. Felton and Watson were political allies and confidants. The University of Georgia acquired her papers after her death in 1930. Yet Woodward does not mention the Rebecca Latimer Felton Collection in his "Critical Essay on Authorities" in *Origins* (pp. 482–84).[9]

Of the sixteen women who do make it into his pages, most often Woodward simply nods in their direction. For example, on southern writers in the last decades of the nineteenth century, he remarks, "A dozen lesser luminaries, among them Grace King and Kate Chopin, took their first bows within the same years" (p. 165). Three other novelists, Mary Noailles Murfree (pen name Charles Egbert Craddock), Mary Johnston, and Ellen Glasgow, are mentioned by name (pp. 429, 431, 434–36). Five down, eleven to go. Of the remaining eleven, one is Jane Addams (p. 423), another Harriet Beecher Stowe (p. 20), a third "Mrs. Jefferson Davis" (p. 156), a fourth Irene Langhorne, who became the Gibson Girl (p. 149), and a fifth is Mary E. Lease, who came from Kansas "to raise less corn and more *Hell*" in the South (p. 253).[10] Ten down, six to go. Three of these six are professionals: rare women in history, Ethel Armes and C. Mildred Thompson, and in geography, Ellen Churchill Semple (pp. 127, 442, 161).

In the text Woodward places only three women in the public arena: Irene Ashby, Kate Barnard, and Julia Tutwiler. Both Ashby and Barnard were child labor reformers. Woodward praises Ashby for her "extensive investigation" of labor conditions in the South, and he cites approvingly A. J. McKelway's evaluation of Barnard's position in Oklahoma as "'what Jane Addams is to Chicago, its First Citizen'" (pp. 417, 423). Woodward calls Julia Tutwiler of Alabama "a moving spirit in the reform movement" to break the convict lease system (p. 215). Woodward thus reveals that he knew something about women's role in reform—in introducing and managing change—but he stops short of using that knowledge to advance his argument by bringing on women reformers. Why?

---

9. John Herbert Roper, "C. Vann Woodward's Early Career—The Historian as Dissident Youth," *Georgia Historical Quarterly,* 64 (Spring 1980), 9; Roper, *C. Vann Woodward, Southerner* (Athens, Ga., and London, 1987), 31–42; Jacqueline Anne Rouse, *Lugenia Burns Hope: Black Southern Reformer* (Athens, Ga., and London, 1989); John E. Talmadge, *Rebecca Latimer Felton: Nine Stormy Decades* (Athens, Ga., 1960), 137–49 and 178.

10. For Mary E. Lease's role in southern Populist campaigns and her famous quotation, see John D. Hicks, *The Populist Revolt: A History of the Farmers' Alliance and the People's Party* (Minneapolis, 1931), 159–60.

It is possible, of course, to explain the case of the missing women as a typical product of its author's times. Four years later Richard Hofstadter mentioned seven women in the text of *The Age of Reform: From Bryan to F.D.R.* and confined his discussion of arguably the most important reform of the time, the Nineteenth Amendment, to this: "[V]arious reforms intended to promote direct democracy were debated—and to these one should add the proposal for women's suffrage . . . ." Hofstadter writes in the passive voice to avoid any mention of those who debated the amendment—might women have had a word or two to say here?—even as he incorrectly terms it women's, not woman, suffrage. The comprehensive historiographical collection *Writing Southern History,* published fourteen years after *Origins,* contains only three references to the subject of "women" in the index.[11]

Thus, we might see Woodward as simply a product of his time, but that would be a thoroughly unsatisfying explanation, doing an injustice both to Woodward and the time. After all, Sigmund Freud predated Woodward, Lillian Smith's *Killers of the Dream* preceded *Origins,* and the only picture on Woodward's office wall was one of William Faulkner. Ten years before *Origins,* W. J. Cash had written *The Mind of the South,* a dreamy, tragic, whirlpool of a book that exuded sexuality and hopelessness, while it denied southern white class consciousness.[12]

I think it is possible that Vann Woodward deliberately excluded women from *Origins* and that he did so with an ulterior motive. Imagine how different southern historiography might have been if, in the 1930s, Vann Woodward had written a biography of Rebecca Latimer Felton rather than one of Tom Watson.[13] Felton offered Woodward many gifts: extensive papers, sharp wit, one of the best political minds of the nineteenth century, and a long life. Yet Felton goes unmentioned in the text of *Origins.*

Finally, one finds Felton where Woodward has hidden her, in his essay on "authorities." There, he includes the "Georgia Independent Rebecca L. Felton" in a five-member pantheon of white southern radicals, ranging from Readjusters to Populists, that represented "the voice of political dissent" in the period. Not only, then, did Woodward know Felton, but he knew her to

---

11. Richard Hofstadter, *The Age of Reform: From Bryan to F.D.R.* (New York, 1955), 263 (quotation); Arthur S. Link and Rembert W. Patrick, eds., *Writing Southern History: Essays in Historiography in Honor of Fletcher M. Green* (Baton Rouge, 1965), 502. See also Hall and Scott, "Women in the South," 454–55.

12. Lillian Smith, *Killers of the Dream* (New York, 1949); W. J. Cash, *The Mind of the South* (New York, 1941).

13. C. Vann Woodward, *Tom Watson, Agrarian Rebel* (New York, 1938).

be a "political dissent[er]" and an "Independent," whose brand of radicalism was not easily categorized (p. 488). He understood her, moreover, to be a politician before woman suffrage, an insight that was slow dawning on practitioners of women's history. Felton and Woodward needed each other; yet, there was to be no relationship between them, a snub I believe Woodward intended.

While Woodward was writing *Origins,* he was also writing note cards on African Americans that he filed in a different drawer. *The Strange Career of Jim Crow* emerged from these cards three years after *Origins* as the James W. Richards Lectures at the University of Virginia.[14] I've always thought of the two books as a one-two punch. First, Woodward demolishes the myth of white unity and offers up a South in which grasping middle-class white men whipped real democracy in the Populist movement, put women and children to work in factories, and sold out the region's natural resources to avaricious Yankees. In other words, he frees white southern readers from being beholden to their betters by stripping those betters of their pretensions to aristocracy and of their patina of paternalism. Then he tells those same readers that not only did they not have to listen to the old white families in their communities anymore, they could look back to a time when the South had been more open to African American rights, back to a time before these same betters had gotten everyone into this segregation mess. Woodward wrote liberation history that released white southerners to facilitate change in the 1950s.

Yet the two narratives work together only if the women remain missing from the story. No women, no sex. No sex, presto, no race "problem." (Accordingly, only three women appear in the text of the first edition of *Strange Career:* Elizabeth H. Botume, Mahalia Jackson, and Eleanor Roosevelt.) If Woodward had included women reformers, the specter of interracial sex would have instantly appeared. He scrupulously avoided Felton, for example, and thereby circumvented the rape/lynch discussion. In the 1950s South, even white liberals feared interracial sex: They did not think it was right, and they thought it would derail the movement for civil rights. Only once in *Origins* does Woodward mention rape, rapists, or rape scares (p. 352), and he simply does not discuss them in *Strange Career,* despite many treatments of lynching. Woodward had opened the barnyard doors to allow change to stampede in; he could not afford to have any unprotected hens in the coop. Bringing up the woman problem in any way—women in public,

---

14. C. Vann Woodward, *The Strange Career of Jim Crow* (New York, 1955).

women as reformers, women as voters, white women as rape victims, black women as rape victims, women as antilynching activists—would have put Vann Woodward in the middle of the race/sex dilemma. If he touched Rebecca Latimer Felton, he would have been forced to address her famous comment, "if it will save one white woman, I say lynch a thousand black men."[15] Woodward knew that racists would say that where there was smoke there was fire; they would not have been able to separate rape scares from actual rape. Indeed, they were already saying that the civil rights movement was about social equality, and that they did not want their lil' white girls sitting beside some big black Negro in school. Woodward painted a possible future by painting a possible past.

By excluding women in his southern history, Woodward removed a sticking point in the race "problem"—interracial sex—for his 1950s white southern readers. By the time that Jacquelyn Dowd Hall recoupled race and sex almost twenty-five years after the first release of *Strange Career,* her readers accepted interracial consensual sex and fought images of black men as rapists and white women as victims.[16] Had Woodward done anything similar, his book would have lost its usefulness for white southern liberals in the 1950s.[17] White supremacists had preserved a mythical, monolithic, continuous past, at the same time using sexual terror to portray white women as victims and black men as criminals, in order to keep African Americans and women in their places. By refusing to open this Pandora's box, Woodward instead portrayed a changeable past that pointed to a possible future. Did he spurn Rebecca consciously? Or did he simply fail to see her in his zeal to apply a material analysis to a place drowning in mythical historiography? In his own work, did he fail to overcome "the human limitations imposed by the temper of his times"?[18]

---

15. LeeAnn Whites, "Rebecca Latimer Felton and the Wife's Farm: The Class and Racial Politics of Gender Reform," *Georgia Historical Quarterly,* 76 (Summer 1992), 354–72; Whites, "Love, Hate, Rape, Lynching: Rebecca Latimer Felton and the Gender Politics of Racial Violence," in David S. Cecelski and Timothy B. Tyson, eds., *Democracy Betrayed: The Wilmington Race Riot of 1898 and Its Legacy* (Chapel Hill and London, 1998), 143–62 (Felton quotation on p. 149).

16. Jacquelyn Dowd Hall, *Revolt Against Chivalry: Jessie Daniel Ames and the Women's Campaign Against Lynching* (New York, 1979).

17. Thanks to Jane Dailey for suggesting to me the idea that Woodward might have deliberately left women out of the accounts, and for her analysis of the connections between race and sex in the late 1940s and 1950s.

18. George B. Tindall, "Southern Negroes Since Reconstruction: Dissolving the Static Image," in Link and Patrick, eds., *Writing Southern History,* 337.

Historians of every stripe follow Michael O'Brien's dictum to "begin with Woodward."[19] How, then, if *Origins* embraces no women and supplies no gendered analysis, could it be of value to those who write about women and use gender? Beginning with Woodward is necessary for three reasons. First, *Origins* gives us the facts, and lots of them. Second, albeit inadvertently, Woodward restores to importance the period in which southern women changed the most and had the most influence on change. Third, Woodward opens a sense of possibility by bringing to light a hidden southern past. Hidden pasts are just where one goes hunting for gendered stories.

First to the facts. *Origins of the New South* was a synthetic treatment of a period written prior to the monographic literature. Woodward provided a map through the forest. A few months ago, I worked in Vann Woodward's kitchen sifting through mounds of papers, notebooks, and small file boxes that had been left behind after his death, as the family, the movers, and the archivists came and went. I sat as a court of last resort, a reprieve from the yawning dumpster in the driveway. There was correspondence with Merle Curti, an unreturned essay submitted by a graduate student named James McPherson (grade: A), and the note cards for *Origins of the New South.* Long metal card files, crammed with little cards on which Woodward painstakingly had typed up his research. Here in my hands was the stuff that stuffed *Origins* so full of facts: notes on newspaper stories, manuscript sources, and secondary sources, all meticulously recorded and then put to use by a master who worked without laptops or even copy machines. The weight of the research, literally, served as a reminder that *Origins* filled a huge void in southern history when it was written. Scholars had previously neglected an entire period simply because they thought they already knew what had happened—not much. Michael O'Brien credits the rehabilitation of that period to *Origins:* "Seldom can a subject have been raised from such obscurity to such illumination at a single bound. Just as a piece of technique, an effort of research, it was a virtuoso performance."[20]

But Woodward did not write an encyclopedic treatment that purported to be the final word. Asking as many questions as he answered, he littered *Origins* with road signs for future historians. How many of these secret signs have pointed writers on gender and women in the right direction, we may never know. For example, Woodward is discussing "The Divided Mind

---

19. Michael O'Brien, "C. Vann Woodward and the Burden of Southern Liberalism," *American Historical Review*, 78 (June 1973), 589.

20. *Ibid.*, 597.

of the New South"—how torn southerners were between clinging to old ways and embracing northern modernity—when he happens upon Irene Langhorne:

> Irene Langhorne of Virginia established her claim to the title of the all-American "Gibson girl" by marrying Charles Dana Gibson in 1895. About Miss Langhorne there was said to be "no trace of languor." She was "in tune with the times," "capable and energetic." Even Southern belles could be brisk and businesslike. And over the gilded court of New York's exclusive Four Hundred, as arbiter of a thousand fine points . . . , presided the renegade Georgian, Ward McAllister. On his arm Irene Langhorne led the grand march at the New York Patriarch's Ball in 1893 (p. 149).

This is one of the most gendered moments in *Origins*. Woodward uses Langhorne to point out both a continuance of cavalier custom and, with her marriage to Gibson, a reconciliation between North and South after Redemption through the union of northern men and southern women. Moreover, he comes as close as he ever will in *Origins* to introducing his readers to the New Woman of the New South: "Even Southern belles could be brisk and businesslike."

Leaving matters here, Woodward has planted a signpost for Nina Silber to follow in *The Romance of Reunion: Northerners and the South, 1865–1900*. Signpost or no signpost, it is inconceivable that Silber could have written her incisive analysis of that sectional romance before the mid-1980s. She uses a language of gender to connect the private to the public, to discuss images of manhood and womanhood, and to put politics in a cultural and emotional context. And she takes off from *Origins:* "Not unlike the southern proponents of the New South revolution described by C. Vann Woodward, northerners, too, often possessed a 'divided mind' about building up a new South while longing for the old."[21]

Other road signs indicate more circuitous routes. Woodward's chapter, "The Divided Mind of the New South," made it clear to me that there were two sorts of white men in the 1890s—those who looked backward and those who looked forward; those who stayed on the land and those who came to town. My master's thesis sprang from trying to clarify this case for North Carolina, my characters drawn from *Origins,* white men one and all. There I found Josephus Daniels, whom Woodward quoted as believing his

---

21. Nina Silber, *The Romance of Reunion: Northerners and the South, 1865–1900* (Chapel Hill and London, 1993), 5.

North Carolina was " 'a community free from caste or social chasms, as true a democracy as the world has known' " (p. 54), Leonidas L. Polk, the valiant Populist politician, Furnifold M. Simmons "bulldoz[ing]" the Populists (p. 537), and Charles B. Aycock, "simple [and] unassuming" to Woodward (p. 375). I used Woodwardian arguments to tell the story of the clash between the Redeemers, the Populists, and these New South men. Even though I was writing thirty-four years after Woodward, I never mentioned manhood, masculinity, or gender. Indeed, when I transferred to Chapel Hill and began to write the dissertation that became *Gender and Jim Crow,* I didn't think about the men who populated that M.A. thesis. When I remembered them, they seemed to float over the narrative as abstract disfranchisers. Only after I finished the dissertation did I look back at the thesis and back at Woodward to add the chapter "Race and Manhood." There I grapple with what manhood meant to these white supremacists, unblooded sons of Confederate veterans. Although I use gendered discourse and include protection of white women as a central image in political culture, when I look back at Woodward, I see that we are describing the same bunch: upwardly mobile, urban, capitalistic, self-consciously modern white guys who want to run things. It was Woodward who caused me to think of these New White Men as a political fraternity. Then, by incorporating them into my story, I could see that their definition of manhood left no room for the Best Men of the black race, that "uplift" would fail, and that race had trumped class. There could only be one kind of man—a white one—in the world the disfranchisers created. Woodward's treatment of this generation of white men begs for a gendered analysis, and it suggests work that has appeared on masculinity, generational change, and politics.[22]

Woodward restored to importance the period—except perhaps for the 1960s—in which southern women changed the most. *Origins* tells the story of urbanization, industrialization, and middle-class formation in the South

---

22. Glenda E. Gilmore, "Agrarian Unrest and Urban Remedies: The Progressive Solution in North Carolina" (M.A. thesis, University of North Carolina at Charlotte, 1985); Gilmore, "Gender and Jim Crow: Women and the Politics of White Supremacy in North Carolina, 1896–1920" (Ph.D. dissertation, University of North Carolina at Chapel Hill, 1992); Gilmore, *Gender and Jim Crow: Women and the Politics of White Supremacy in North Carolina, 1896–1920* (Chapel Hill and London, 1996), chap. 3, pp. 61–89. I was particularly influenced by Gail Bederman, *Manliness and Civilization: A Cultural History of Gender and Race in the United States, 1880–1917* (Chicago and London, 1995); and Ann L. Stoler, "Making Empire Respectable: The Politics of Race and Sexual Morality in 20th-Century Colonial Cultures," *American Ethnologist,* 16 (November 1989), 634–60.

and rejects the old narrative of unchanging racial repression, paternalistic planters taking care of poor whites and blacks, agrarian-centered politics, and relentlessly reactionary social policy. This new vision of a bourgeois, modernizing South made it possible for southern historians interested in women to lay claim to a narrative history of women in America that until the 1980s was based overwhelmingly on northern women's experiences. Northern women's history taught us that industrialization brought poorer women and their children into textile mills in places like Lowell and Fall River, resulting in changed domestic relationships. We learned that industrial capitalism drove a wedge through the rural household in New York State that separated paid and unpaid work, created "spheres" for middle-class families, encouraged women to organize through religious and voluntary associations, and obliged men to give over to women some of the business of social housekeeping. We found some "disorderly women" on the edges of these stories, maybe in Chicago, and some radical women determined to push the limits of heterosocial culture, probably lurking in Greenwich Village. We came upon some pious women rescuing their less fortunate sisters, and some educated women teaching them how to confront urbanization in settlement houses. In other words, industrialization and urbanization changed women's role in society in a myriad of ways and brought them into public space.[23]

Woodward's exposition of southern middle-class formation turned these northern stories into truly American stories. After Woodward disabuses us of the myth of planter elites turned paternalistic mill owners, we are able to see LeeAnn Whites's Augusta mill girls, as well as the families in *Like a Family*. After Woodward recovers a Progressive movement in the South, we discover, through Anne Scott, that women led it. After Woodward recenters the action in urban areas, we can focus on Elisabeth Lasch-Quinn's black settlement houses. Without Woodward's class analysis, we might fail to see

---

23. See, for example, Mary P. Ryan, *Cradle of the Middle Class: The Family in Oneida County, New York, 1790–1865* (Cambridge, Eng., and New York, 1981); Nancy A. Hewitt, *Women's Activism and Social Change: Rochester, New York, 1822–1872* (Ithaca, N.Y., and London, 1984); Nancy F. Cott, *The Bonds of Womanhood: "Woman's Sphere" in New England, 1780–1835* (New Haven and London, 1977); Carroll Smith-Rosenberg, *Disorderly Conduct: Visions of Gender in Victorian America* (New York, 1985); Gerda Lerner, "The Lady and the Mill Girl: Changes in the Status of Women in the Age of Jackson, 1800–1840," in Nancy F. Cott and Elizabeth H. Pleck, eds., *A Heritage of Her Own: Toward a New Social History of American Women* (New York, 1979), 182–96; and Christine Stansell, *City of Women: Sex and Class in New York, 1789–1860* (New York, 1986).

the differences Marjorie Spruill finds among southern suffragists, or the agrarian connections among antisuffragists for which Elna C. Green argues.[24]

Woodward's material analysis stripped southern gender history of its chivalric cloak and brought us face-to-face with southern capitalist formation. By taking up Charles A. Beard's point that the Civil War marked a conflict between a new industrial system and an old agrarian system, Woodward took the risk of appearing hopelessly old-fashioned in the consensus-driven 1950s when he instead pointed to class struggle in the industrialization of the South.[25] It is this analysis that ultimately made possible a gendered analysis of southern history.

Third, *Origins* opened a sense of possibility in southern history simply by moving the Civil War from center stage in the region's past. Perhaps this shift was most important to the generation of scholars writing women's history in the 1980s simply because they had gone to elementary and secondary school in the 1950s and 1960s. The slow drip of academic revisionism had not seeped into our textbooks—at least for those of us in the South witnessing the civil rights movement. We had been taught a story of more or less happy slaves, voluntary segregation after the Yankee occupation, paternalistic first families, and a Scarlett behind every Rhett. Woodward's New South was nowhere to be found in those textbooks. In their pages, the rest of the nation changed, rushed on and did its business, while the South stagnated.

Reading *Origins*, then, turned on a light of possibility that enabled us to search for women. For Laura F. Edwards, it was "like having someone wipe the intellectual slate clean—the book swept aside a whole lot of assumptions that I had, and even if I didn't accept the ones Woodward put in their place, the fact that the old ones were gone meant a great deal." For Marjorie J. Spruill, it meant that the South was "open to lots of possible developments,

---

24. LeeAnn Whites, *The Civil War as a Crisis in Gender: Augusta, Georgia, 1860–1890* (Athens, Ga., and London, 1995); Jacquelyn Dowd Hall, James Leloudis, Robert Korstad, Mary Murphy, Lu Ann Jones, and Christopher B. Daly, *Like a Family: The Making of a Southern Cotton Mill World* (Chapel Hill and London, 1987); Scott, *The Southern Lady;* Elisabeth Lasch-Quinn, *Black Neighbors: Race and the Limits of Reform in the American Settlement House Movement, 1890–1945* (Chapel Hill and London, 1993); Marjorie Spruill Wheeler, *New Women of the New South: The Leaders of the Woman Suffrage Movement in the Southern States* (New York and Oxford, 1993); Elna C. Green, *Southern Strategies: Southern Women and the Woman Suffrage Question* (Chapel Hill and London, 1997).

25. For the way that Woodward relocated Beard's class conflict from an interregional arena to an intraregional one, see Woodward, *Thinking Back,* 66 (149 in this volume).

with no foregone conclusions." Meeting Woodward after a white school-girl's education of southern ladies and dashing cavaliers suggested that alter-native, usable pasts might exist; in Edwards's recent title, it meant that *Scarlett Doesn't Live Here Anymore.*[26]

If *Origins* had proven valuable to those recovering the history of south-ern women, how might a gendered analysis have proven valuable to Wood-ward? Before I explore three examples of ways one might add gender back into *Origins,* I'll share this true story. Vann Woodward and Peter Gay sat side by side at a late 1990s academic conference through an endless series of papers and comments. Finally, along about late afternoon, Vann turned to Peter and said, in the stage whisper of those who wear hearing aids, "Peter, what *is* gender?"

As for me, I'm delighted that Woodward did not understand gender in 1951, since I wrote a book suggested by a paragraph in *Origins* on the racial violence in North Carolina in 1898. I'll quote from that paragraph at length:

> [Charles B.] Aycock's campaign managers staged "White Supremacy Jubi-lees," in which hundreds of armed men paraded in red shirts. Ben Tillman came up from South Carolina to lend a hand, and sympathizers in Richmond told of 50,000 rounds of ammunition and a carload of firearms shipped to North Carolina a few days before the election of 1898. The Negroes remained quiet. Shortly after the whites of Wilmington won the election over a thor-oughly cowed black majority, a mob of 400 men led by a former Congress-man demolished a Negro newspaper office, set it on fire, shot up the Negro district, killed 11 Negroes, wounded a large number, and chased hundreds into the woods (p. 350).

Going under in the search for a dissertation topic, I clung to two lifelines: evidence I had found of black women turning up at the polls in 1920 and Woodward's rendering of the formal institution of white supremacy in the 1890s in *Strange Career of Jim Crow.* This paragraph from *Origins,* then, with its "thoroughly cowed" "Negroes [who] remained quiet," rang false to me, even as it proved a source of inspiration.

If Woodward had used gender, he would have found that the "hundreds of armed men parad[ing] in red shirts" were followed by white women on

---

26. Laura F. Edwards, e-mail to the author, January 22, 2001; Marjorie J. Spruill, e-mail to the author, January 8, 2001; Laura F. Edwards, *Scarlett Doesn't Live Here Anymore: South-ern Women in the Civil War Era* (Urbana and Chicago, 2000).

floats carrying signs beseeching them to "Protect Us." The "former Congressman" would have become the fading, elderly Alfred Moore Waddell, whose cousin, Rebecca Cameron, whipped him up into a masculine frenzy with these words, "Solomon says, 'There is a Time to Kill.' . . . We are aflame with anger here . . . . I wish you could see Anna. She is fairly impatient and blood thirsty. These blond women are terrible when their fighting blood is up." The "Negro newspaper office" would have become Alexander Manly's press at Love and Charity Hall, burned by the white supremacists because Manly had dared speak the truth that some white women had consensual affairs with black men. The "quiet Negroes" would have become loud black women pushing white women off the sidewalks of Wilmington and threatening to label the black man who would not stand up to the red shirts " 'a white-livered coward who would sell his liberty.' "[27]

If sometimes Woodward suggests gendered topics by the absence of clues, at other times he scatters clues about his text. Mysteries surface frequently in *Origins;* when Woodward comes across an intriguing point he could not or had not the time to solve, he turns to address the reader *entre nous.* For example, here is Woodward musing on the domino theory of demagoguery: "By some obscure rule of succession, Bleases tended to follow Tillmans . . . . The new type of leader could hardly be said to have had a program or a party. Instead, he had prejudices and a following." And here we veer toward gender: "The leader often flouted sober conventions, sometimes consorted with lewd company, and in numerous ways proclaimed himself one of the boys" (pp. 392–93).

Stephen Kantrowitz and Bryant Simon have recently given us contextualized, biographical, and above all, gendered studies of the ol' boys themselves, Ben Tillman and Cole Blease, that illuminate Woodward's "obscure rule of succession."[28] At the risk, in Kantrowitz's words, of Woodward's "ironic throwaway, . . . lead[ing] us down the path of reductive social science," I asked Simon and Kantrowitz how gender helped them understand their subjects and how they related their work to *Origins.* Simon reflects,

---

27. Gilmore, *Gender and Jim Crow,* chap. 4, pp. 91–118 (Cameron quotation on p. 110, black women's threat on p. 107).

28. Stephen Kantrowitz, *Ben Tillman and the Reconstruction of White Supremacy* (Chapel Hill and London, 2000); Bryant Simon, *A Fabric of Defeat: The Politics of South Carolina Textile Millhands, 1910–1948* (Chapel Hill and London, 1998). For a discussion of the problem of manhood and white politics, see Kantrowitz, "Ben Tillman and Hendrix McLane, Agrarian Rebels: White Manhood, 'The Farmers,' and the Limits of Southern Populism," *Journal of Southern History,* 66 (August 2000), 497–524.

"On the surface this [Woodward's comment] is obviously true[,] . . . but [Tillman and Blease] are different politicians with different messages. . . . [W]hile there is perhaps a succession between the two demagogues, the context changes dramatically. Industrialization is a break in the history of the upcountry and this break raises new questions about white masculinity and patriarchal power." Kantrowitz argues, "Tillman and his ilk represent an appeal to a partly dying, partly mythic white yeoman South—one that can appeal to white men's traditional conceptions of themselves against a familiar constellation of enemies . . . . Blease, . . . on the other hand, represents an almost entirely symbolic protest rooted in resentments and confusions of race and gender identity created in large measure by the adjustment to factory work . . . ." Moreover, Simon and Kantrowitz agree that "white men" changed dramatically from Tillman's time to Blease's with this economic transformation. This change in their constituencies' concepts of their own manliness meant that for Tillman "demagoguery had been a useful tactic" to appeal to white yeomen's fears of future loss, while "for Blease it was intrinsic and essential" to appeal to white mill worker's realizations of actual loss.[29]

Finally, Jane Dailey's *Before Jim Crow*, a new gendered history of the Virginia Readjusters, might have sprung from both the ungendered *Origins* explanation that rang false and the Woodwardian ironic throwaway. Woodward tells us that Readjuster William Mahone thought of himself as Julius Caesar or Napoleon Bonaparte, and that Mahone's third party, the Readjusters, represented " 'a very real and a very debasing tyranny' " (pp. 97, 98). Caesar? Napoleon? Tyranny? Such hot imagery leaves the modern reader cold as to why people could be so stirred about readjusting the post–Civil War debt. But add this Woodwardian throwaway: "School superintendents and local boards were replaced with men in 'touch with the people' . . ." (p. 97). Dailey tells us that some of those new men on local school boards were African American Readjusters, whom Democrats immediately portrayed as being dangerously close to being "in touch with the people"—their white female pupils. In a dress rehearsal for the 1890s, Virginia Democrats played on concepts of manhood, womanhood, sex, and power to emphasize African American participation in the Readjusters and to force white men back into the Democratic Party.[30]

---

29. Bryant Simon, e-mail to author, January 18, 2001; Stephen Kantrowitz, e-mail to author, January 18, 2001.

30. Jane Dailey, *Before Jim Crow: The Politics of Race in Postemancipation Virginia* (Chapel Hill and London, 2000), 96–98.

Woodward might not have understood the vocabulary of the social construction of sex roles until the late 1990s, but once he did, he quickly embraced the value of gendered analysis for southern history and recognized its significance for the Woodward thesis. Not long after I arrived at Yale, I met C. Vann Woodward for the first time at a cocktail party. After someone unfortunately introduced me to him as "John Blum's replacement," he rightly scowled at the suggestion that anyone could replace John Blum and asked, "What else do you do?" In a tiny little voice, I answered, "Southern history?" Before his eyes, I had transformed myself from John Blum's replacement into C. Vann Woodward's replacement. The scowl deepened, and he responded, "Well, I guess someone has to do it." When *Gender and Jim Crow* appeared, I screwed up my courage and sent it to him with a note. Three days later, I picked up the telephone to hear, "Professor Gilmore, this is Vann Woodward, I have read your book, and I suggest we meet."

As we talked over lunch, I found my perfect reader. Woodward and I had visited and loved the same place, but we had arrived separately. I carried different baggage, but we saw the same people and came to similar opinions about what had happened there. As we talked over old friends and enemies—Furnifold Simmons, Josephus Daniels, Alexander Manly—it was like gossiping about relatives. He approached my book as if it told him what they had been doing since he had left home.

Woodward became enthusiastic about using gender to rewrite southern history. And it liberated him to speak the unspeakable. This is Woodward in 1998: "Getting at the truth of such subjects as fornication, rape, bastardy, adultery, divorce, and domestic violence is difficult enough in any case. But when they are mixed with constantly changing attitudes about race, class, freedom, slavery, servitude, and male authority and honor, especially in times of civil war, invasion, defeat, and slave emancipation, and accompany the politics and violence of white supremacy, the search for 'truth' often seems hopeless." Here is a brand-new Woodward, postmodern and feminist, praising Martha Hodes's *White Women, Black Men: Illicit Sex in the Nineteenth-Century South*. Noting that "historians have tended to avoid such subjects and the frustration they involve," Woodward calls Hodes "courageous, but not reckless." Finally, he applauds Hodes's Woodwardianness: "Hodes's searching study of sexual politics confirms and extends the findings of earlier scholars that white supremacy, in all its legal and institutional manifestations, became more rigid and punitive at the end of the century than at any other time since the Civil War."[31]

---

31. C. Vann Woodward, "Dangerous Liaisons," *The New York Review of Books*, 45 (February 19, 1998), 14 (first three quotations), 16 (final quotation); Martha Hodes, *White*

The last piece that Vann Woodward wrote for publication was a preface for an anthology that Jane Dailey, Bryant Simon, and I edited on southern politics from 1865 to 1955. The articles reinterpret traditional southern historiographical arguments or tell well-known stories in new ways. Each one deals with white supremacist politics, race, and gender simultaneously. In asking Woodward to write the preface, we explained our debt to him for wrenching a changing South—a contested South—out of a period when "nothing happened." Our book collects moments when African Americans fought back against white supremacy so hard that white supremacy had to reinvent itself at every turn, with both sides wielding gendered tools. In other words, in the "nadir" of African American history, in a period of continuous oppression, the authors in our book argue for continuous challenges and, hence, continuous change.[32]

C. Vann Woodward realized how much our collection owed to *Origins*. He commented that these articles represented historians who began to write at the end of the twentieth century, while he had begun to write back at the beginning. His words look back on *Origins,* even as they establish an ironic continuity in breaking with the past. In his last paragraph he reveals that he too had mastered new tools of analysis. Woodward concludes, "None of the last several generations of southern historians could ignore such subjects as race, slavery, Civil War, Reconstruction, violence, segregation, and politics. What distinguishes the new history is not only its inclusion of subjects that the old history neglected, but the new questions it raises and the way it treats the traditional subjects. That includes attention to the roles played and leadership provided by a race, a gender, or a class, that had heretofore been treated by historians not as participants, but as helpless spectators or victims." Woodward had the flexibility of mind and the generosity of spirit to welcome and appreciate new ways, including gender, of making old stories new again.[33]

In the preface to the 1971 edition of *Origins of the New South,* Woodward reveals his philosophy of change—this time, historiographical change—as alive and elastic:

Women, Black Men: Illicit Sex in the Nineteenth-Century South (New Haven and London, 1997).

32. Jane Dailey, Glenda Elizabeth Gilmore, and Bryant Simon, eds., *Jumpin' Jim Crow: Southern Politics from Civil War to Civil Rights* (Princeton and Oxford, 2000); Rayford W. Logan, *The Negro in American Life and Thought: The Nadir, 1877–1901* (New York, 1954).

33. C. Vann Woodward, "Preface," in Dailey, Gilmore, and Simon, eds., *Jumpin' Jim Crow,* ix–xi (quotation on p. xi).

Had I written the book in the early 1970's instead of the early 1950's, I should have taken advantage of this recent scholarship and produced a different and, I hope, a better book. I should also have had the advantage of the added perspective and the stimulus of new questions raised by the swift changes and historical developments of recent years. It is even possible that I should have been able to make use of some of the new historical techniques . . . . But that would have been a different book, the product of another period, written under other circumstances and influences . . . . I have decided to risk letting this book "stand on its own." Revision where it is needed must be the task of others. More important, a new synthesis awaits the pen of a historian with another world view, fresher insights, and perhaps a different philosophy of history. It would already appear to be time for *him* to be about *his* work.[34]

In 1999, a half century after *Origins* and almost thirty years after this comment, he praised "[o]ur new historians, men and women, . . . of a quite different order" than "older generations of historians." Change versus continuity? At ninety-one, C. Vann Woodward continued to embrace change.[35]

---

34. C. Vann Woodward, "Preface to the Present Edition," *Origins* [1971 edition], viii (emphasis added).

35. Woodward, "Preface," in Dailey, Gilmore, and Simon, eds., *Jumpin' Jim Crow*, x (first quotation) and ix (second quotation).

The Political Economy of the New South: Retrospects and Prospects

A conference to evaluate and assess the influence of C. Vann Woodward's *Origins of the New South* a half century after its publication is certainly remarkable.[1] Few historical studies have the staying power that would justify such a conference, especially in these days of almost instant revisionism. Ordinarily, fifty-year-old books, if not completely forgotten and ignored in new scholarship, are mentioned as documents that illustrate the views of the time they were written but are now obsolete. Rarely are they considered to be important interpretive contributions to the problems being studied.

The career of *Origins* has been quite different. Over the years, many

Reprinted from *Journal of Southern History,* 67 (November 2001), 789–810, the Woodward symposium issue.

1. C. Vann Woodward, *Origins of the New South, 1877–1913* (Baton Rouge, 1951). Page numbers for references to *Origins* in this essay are inserted parenthetically in the text. The first edition's pagination is retained in later reprint editions.

scholars have argued that the book's basic interpretive thrust remained viable even in the face of revisionist efforts. After surveying the scholarship on issues raised by *Origins* in the twenty years since its publication, Sheldon Hackney declared that the book had "survived relatively untarnished"; a decade later J. Morgan Kousser and James M. McPherson announced that Hackney's assessment still remained valid. Woodward also offered his own assessment. His 1986 memoir, *Thinking Back,* is a sensitive and insightful discussion of his career and scholarship in which he gives recognition to his critics—at least some of them—in the form of both modifying (somewhat) and clarifying his positions, but in a usually convincing, if sometimes slippery, manner that leaves the basic structure of his work intact.[2]

The staying power of *Origins* is revealed in another way in the bibliographies and historiographical essays dealing with all aspects of the period 1877 to 1913.[3] These surveys do not show that all of Woodward's interpretations stand undisputed or unscathed, but they do demonstrate how much of the literature deals with the same questions he asked a half century ago—even when the answers sometimes, but certainly not always, differ. Moreover, even when more recent work poses new problems or suggests new approaches, Woodward, as Edward L. Ayers put it in his splendid study, "was never far from my mind." Indeed, one rarely comes across a book or essay concerning the post-Reconstruction South where the author fails to indicate how his or her interpretation fits into the literature and arguments that stem from Woodward's work.[4] In sum, Woodward's 1951 study turned

---

2. Sheldon Hackney, "*Origins of the New South* in Retrospect," *Journal of Southern History,* 38 (May 1972), 191–216 (quotation on p. 213, p. 46 in this volume); J. Morgan Kousser and James M. McPherson, "C. Vann Woodward: An Assessment of His Work and Influence," in Kousser and McPherson, eds., *Region, Race, and Reconstruction: Essays in Honor of C. Vann Woodward* (New York and Oxford, 1982), xxxii; C. Vann Woodward, *Thinking Back: The Perils of Writing History* (Baton Rouge, 1986), esp. 59–79 (144–60 in this volume).

3. Woodward's "Critical Essay on Authorities" in *Origins* was 33 pages in length (pp. 482–515). When the book was republished in 1971, Charles B. Dew added a 111-page "Critical Essay on Recent Works," a sign of how the field had developed. Dew's essay contains a section dealing specifically with historiography. Dew, "Critical Essay on Recent Works," in C. Vann Woodward, *Origins of the New South, 1877–1913* (1951; reprint, Baton Rouge, 1971), 517–628, esp. 517–21. More recent historiographical surveys may be found in John B. Boles and Evelyn Thomas Nolen, eds., *Interpreting Southern History: Historiographical Essays in Honor of Sanford W. Higginbotham* (Baton Rouge, 1987); and Howard N. Rabinowitz, "Bibliographical Essay," *The First New South, 1865–1920* (Arlington Heights, Ill., 1992), 187–219.

4. Edward L. Ayers, *The Promise of the New South: Life After Reconstruction* (New York and Oxford, 1992), vi. Although Ayers seldom gets directly involved in historiography in the

our view of the post-Reconstruction South in a different direction, and now, fifty years later, that direction remains dominant.

Because *Origins* has had this remarkable staying power and because it has already been the subject of so many evaluations and assessments, a new and original appraisal becomes difficult, a difficulty compounded by my specific assignment here. My task in this discussion is to consider Woodward's treatment of economic, agricultural, and legal matters. This is obviously a major assignment that includes almost everything in *Origins*, because these matters, given Woodward's clearly articulated Beardian approach, are at the core of his analysis here and in much of his other work as well.[5] (I cannot resist noting that there is a certain irony—very appropriate at a Woodward conference—in the fact that Charles Beard is one of those historians who, unfortunately, in my view, seems to have been revised out of existence and is seldom read these days. But his seemingly faded interpretation is very alive at the heart of Woodward's analysis. Beard's economic interpretation is not without problems, but it is far less crudely reductive than some of his critics have contended and, in any case, far less crudely reductive than the work of some of the still widely read "cliometricians." But that's *obiter dicta,* as a lawyer might say.)

Like Beard, Woodward saw class conflict and the clash of economic interests as central to American history. He was particularly drawn to Charles and Mary Beard, who in their textbook emphasized the industrial-agricultural antagonism that had divided North and South and led to the Civil War, resulting in what they called the "Second American Revolution": the victory of the industrialists and the destruction of southern agrarianism based upon slavery.[6] Woodward thought this revolution also applied to the South as a region, and he discovered much the same conflict within the postbellum South that the Beards had found between North and South before the war. He also found the same results. In *Origins* Woodward argues that

---

text of his work, he does so in his extensive notes, which clearly reveal the importance of Woodward's analysis to his study.

5. Woodward acknowledged his debt to Beard specifically and emphatically in *Reunion and Reaction: The Compromise of 1877 and the End of Reconstruction* (Boston, 1951), ix. He moderated his enthusiasm somewhat in *Thinking Back* but did not "lament or disavow" it. "To concede that economic interpretations have sometimes been overstressed, however, is not to concede that economic motive is unimportant, much less absent." Woodward, *Thinking Back*, 56.

6. Charles A. Beard and Mary R. Beard, "The Second American Revolution," chap. 18 in *The Rise of American Civilization.* Vol. II: *The Industrial Era* (New York, 1927), 52–121.

the defeat of the Confederacy established the domination of business interests at the expense of the agrarians in the South. The victorious northern
Radicals installed business-oriented Reconstruction governments; if the political affiliation of these postbellum state governments proved temporary,
the class they represented did not. Although the fall of the Radical Reconstruction governments in the South drove Republicans from power, Woodward maintains that this change did not alter the business domination of the
southern governments. There was no "sharp distinction between Reconstruction and Redemption"; both were Whiggish and Hamiltonian in outlook (p. 16). Despite the participation of some of the leaders of the old
regime, "Redemption was not a return of an old system nor the restoration
of an old ruling class. It was rather a new phase of the revolutionary process
begun in 1865" (pp. 21–22).[7]

The victory of the business interests, however, did not end conflict in the
postbellum South. The old ruling class who had opposed the demands of
northern business interests had been removed, leaving the section without
its traditional representatives. The new southern rulers made their peace
with northern business by eschewing conflict and accepting a subordinate
and cooperative position. For Woodward, class differences—specifically, the
resistance of the lower classes of small farmers and workers to the domination of the business-oriented Redeemers—were at the center of the political
and economic conflicts that regularly erupted in the South in the late nineteenth and early twentieth centuries.

It is this core economic argument that informs *Origins* as well as Woodward's analysis of Populism that I want to make the focus of my comments
here. As I have noted, and as everyone in the field knows, there are already
extensive bibliographies and historiographies that deal with the literature of
all aspects of the period covered by *Origins;* one more is hardly necessary.
What I want to do in the time allotted me is to consider the extensively discussed matter of continuity and change that stems from Woodward's
Beardian economic approach and the effects of Woodward's interpretation
on the question of southern distinctiveness. I hope my discussion will suggest some different perspectives and fresh avenues for further research. Even
though I shall include some historiography, a full consideration of the state
of scholarship is not my intent. I am certainly not here to bury Woodward's

---

7. Of course, in finding both the Radical and Reconstruction governments to be business-
oriented, Woodward does not find their policies to be identical concerning such matters as race
relations, public education, and other social programs.

ideas but to praise them. I shall, however, raise a few questions and offer suggestions, some that probably would have outraged Woodward and may outrage some who read this essay.

The idea that the Civil War marked a sharp discontinuity in southern history—a discontinuity that profoundly altered the region's economic, social, and political structure—is the most important argument that resulted from Woodward's Beardian approach. This was a strong revisionist argument to make in 1951, because it denied that the Redeemers were part of the antebellum elite and that they brought unity and stability to the region by restoring the traditions of the Old South. When Woodward entered the profession in the 1930s, he remembered later, a general consensus prevailed among southern historians that "proclaimed the enduring and fundamentally unbroken unity, solidarity, and continuity of Southern history" and "papered over the breaks and fissures and conflicts in Southern history with myths of solidarity and continuity."[8] *Origins* challenged both the notions of continuity and of unity by finding that the Civil War brought a fundamental change in class relations and new forms of class conflict to the postbellum South.

From a later perspective and with even a modest familiarity with the outpouring of scholarship on the issues raised by Woodward in *Origins,* we might lose sight of what he had accomplished. In a 1973 article Michael O'Brien summarized it well: Before the publication of *Origins,* there had been very little scholarship on the period. "Seldom can a subject have been raised from such obscurity to such illumination at a single bound. Just as a piece of technique, an effort of research, it was a virtuoso performance." But the book did far more than provide information on a largely neglected facet of southern history. It also presented a "moral" and ironic vision, O'Brien noted. Woodward used irony to express his disapproval of the Redeemers, becoming more staid and serious when dealing with the Populists and others who met with his approval. He put emphasis on the masses, including African Americans, and he "raised the broad issue of social responsibility in Southern politics." Moreover, when he published *Origins* in 1951, his interpretation not only sharply countered the prevailing view of southern history, but it also challenged the growing dominance of consensus interpretations of American history in general.[9]

---

8. Woodward, *Thinking Back,* 23 (first quotation), 27 (second quotation).

9. Michael O'Brien, "C. Vann Woodward and the Burden of Southern Liberalism," *American Historical Review,* 78 (June 1973), 589–604 (first quotation on p. 597, second quotation on p. 599). Woodward's friend (and sometimes critic) David M. Potter made much the same argument in reference to Woodward's first three books (*Tom Watson, Agrarian Rebel* [New

If first Hackney and then Kousser and McPherson found Woodward's interpretation pretty much intact, O'Brien, despite his enthusiasm for what Woodward had accomplished, nevertheless had serious doubts and reservations. Woodward's liberalism, O'Brien argued, led him to cling to the "progressive school of Beard and Turner" with the result "that as Southern history [*Origins*] is probably a dead end."[10] Woodward's biographer, John Herbert Roper, voiced a similar evaluation a decade and a half later, when he argued that "major revisionist scholarship has . . . dislodged some of the very foundation stones of *Origins*." The revisionist "scholars have so thoroughly damaged Woodward's interpretation from so many different angles of approach that one could as well label Woodward the continuitarian, the one clinging to a virtually unchanging faith in Beard."[11]

The damage to Woodward's interpretation would seem to be borne out by some later general studies of the "new" South. The notion of a "New South" dates from the time of Henry W. Grady, and publicists, promoters, boosters, critics, and all sorts of other folks, including historians and other academics, have variously used the term, debated its reality, dismissed it, and accepted it. But there seems to be no agreement and a great deal of ambivalence about when, or indeed if, the South became "new." A bit of this uncertainty may be seen in the last three volumes of the History of the South series. Woodward's 1951 contribution traced the *Origins of the New South, 1877–1913*. Then in 1967 George Brown Tindall devoted more than 500 pages to *The Emergence of the New South, 1913–1945*. What originated in 1877 and began to emerge in 1913 was apparently still emerging by 1945. Then, it seems, it finally arrived several decades after World War II, for Numan V. Bartley entitled his 1995 work, *The New South, 1945–1980*.

York, 1938], *Reunion and Reaction*, and *Origins*) in an essay first published in 1969. Potter, "C. Vann Woodward and the Uses of History," in Don E. Fehrenbacher, ed., *History and American Society: Essays of David M. Potter* (New York, Oxford, and London, 1973), 143–48 (originally published in Marcus Cunliffe and Robin W. Winks, eds., *Pastmasters: Some Essays on American Historians* [New York, 1969]).

10. O'Brien went on to suggest that Woodward's argument for southern distinctiveness rested upon a consensus view of the American experience from which the South departed. When that view of the North faded, so too did Woodward's basis for southern distinctiveness. O'Brien, "C. Vann Woodward and the Burden of Southern Liberalism," 600–602 (quotation on p. 600).

11. John Herbert Roper, *C. Vann Woodward, Southerner* (Athens, Ga., and London, 1987), 159 (first quotation), 305 (second quotation). In using the word *continuitarian*, Roper, of course, was appropriating a term Woodward used to describe some of his critics who disagreed with his notion of discontinuity. Woodward, *Thinking Back*, 70 (152 in this volume).

Bartley argued that once "metropolitan moderates" replaced the "county-seat establishment" the South became more like the North:

> Prior to the ascension of the moderates, the South was distinctively different from the rest of the nation in significant part because of two factors. The southern social system rested on de jure white supremacy in the form of enforced segregation along with disfranchisement and other related practices while that of the rest of the nation did not. The southern governing class was a rural-oriented colonial ruling elite that differed fundamentally from the corporate business and financial establishment and allied upper-middle-class suburbanites who ruled much of the rest of the nation. The moderate victory brought to power in the South metropolitan corporate leaders who had much in common with their northern peers and who accepted the demise of strict Jim Crow segregation. Thereafter, the South became considerably more like the non-South.[12]

Howard N. Rabinowitz solved the problem of the apparently slow arrival of a new South at least to his satisfaction by finding multiple new Souths. He called his study *The First New South, 1865–1920,* and he noted "that at least three separate New Souths have been declared since 1920." Rabinowitz contended, however, that the first new South was not really new, and he even questioned whether "the South had become truly new by the 1960s and 1970s." Finally, he concluded, by the 1990s it "can be at long last correctly called 'the New South.'"[13]

Of course, what is involved in these varying views is not "ambivalence" or "uncertainty," the terms I used earlier, but rather, at least in the case of Bartley and Rabinowitz, a sharp disagreement with Woodward's analysis. Bartley specifically listed the two factors that had to end before the South became truly new: legal segregation and domination by a "rural-oriented colonial ruling elite," a view that Rabinowitz had also suggested three years earlier. The postemancipation South, Rabinowitz concluded, "was characterized to a greater degree by continuity than by change," while those changes that did take place merely "reinforced traditional aspects of southern society." Moreover, both Bartley and Rabinowitz argued that the new

---

12. George Brown Tindall, *The Emergence of the New South, 1913–1945* (Baton Rouge, 1967); Numan V. Bartley, *The New South, 1945–1980* (Baton Rouge, 1995), 460–61 (quotation).

13. Rabinowitz, *The First New South,* 2 (first and second quotations), 185 (third quotation).

South would not really arrive until the South closely resembled the North. In short, these two scholars rejected Woodward's argument that the Civil War and emancipation marked a fundamental discontinuity in southern history by allowing a new ruling elite to gain power, making them, in Woodward's eyes, "continuitarians"—a term he coined to describe historians who held this view.[14] It is to this matter of the nature of the postbellum elite that I next turn.

Two decades ago, Gavin Wright warned that the continuity/change question was unanswerable, that it elicited endless debate leading inevitably to a dead end. "When we encounter studies with such titles as 'How Different Were North and South?' or 'The Postbellum South: Continuity or Discontinuity?' we know in advance that we are not going to get satisfying answers," he wrote.[15] His point is well taken, not, as he suggested, because the questions are not good, but rather because the methods or approaches historians have used to answer them have been inadequate. In times when a president can suggest that there could be some ambiguity concerning the meaning of "is," or more academic types could suggest that all meaning is doubtful because all meaning is socially constructed, we should not be surprised that a great deal of the debate over these questions—as well as more than a few others—revolves around the definitions the debaters give to words.

Nor does it resolve the debate and make the answers better when they are carefully quantified, as the many planter persistence studies amply illustrate. These works differ in their exact methods and results, but they all follow the same general procedure. They take sample counties in one or more states and use the manuscript census, sometimes supplemented by tax records, to find the top wealth holders (of land, slaves, and other property) usually in 1850 and/or 1860 (when both antebellum dates are used, it provides a picture of antebellum persistence rates). They then follow the same procedure, typically for 1870 or 1880: they locate the top wealth holders in the same sample counties and compare the names in the later year with those in the earlier year. When done in this way the research invariably results in "persisting" planters, the percentage varying slightly from study to study. Many—in most instances about half—of the same landowners (or their de-

14. Bartley, *New South*, 460–61 (first quotation); Rabinowitz, "Epilogue: A Real New South?" *First New South*, 181–86 (second and third quotations on p. 186). For Woodward's notion of "continuitarianism," see *Thinking Back*, 70 (152 in this volume).

15. Gavin Wright, "The Strange Career of the New Southern Economic History," *Reviews in American History*, 10 (December 1982), 164–80 (quotation on p. 165).

scendants) are found in the same places and still at the top of the heap in wealth, albeit the extent of that wealth was sharply diminished by the loss of slaves and the decline in land values. But, these studies insist, *relative* to the others in the neighborhood, a large proportion of the antebellum elite remained as part of the postbellum wealthy elite. Hence, many conclude, the Civil War did not bring a significant change or discontinuity to the region, as Woodward claimed. In agriculture, the key sector of the southern economy, the old ruling elite remained, not unscathed to be sure, but still in charge.[16]

If the planters persisted—that is, if they maintained their economic control and with it their political hegemony, their adherence to traditional values, and their ability to impose these values on the postemancipation South despite their defeat in the Civil War and despite the brief hiatus of Radical Reconstruction (which, in any event, they succeeded in overthrowing)— then Woodward's central economic and social thesis would appear to collapse. This, of course, is the view of O'Brien and Roper, as well as many, but not all, of the authors of the persistence studies.[17]

I do not seek to denigrate or dismiss the contribution these studies have made to our understanding of the early postemancipation years. They have provided valuable, previously unavailable information and have stimulated research and debate and, consequently, new thinking about postemancipation economic and social developments. Nevertheless, I would suggest that they are potentially misleading and that if they raise challenges to some of the details in Woodward's thesis, they fail to undermine it significantly. The problems with the persistence studies arise from their emphasis on genealogy and from their limited time frame. These methodological characteristics lead to an aggregation of data and a short-term perspective that make it impossible to see variations and changes over time, thereby clouding our understanding of the significance of emancipation. Curiously—or, given the subject of this symposium, ironically—Woodward's analysis of changes in landownership shares some of these same weaknesses.

---

16. I have discussed many of these studies in "Economic Reconstruction and the Rise of the New South, 1865–1900," in Boles and Nolen, eds., *Interpreting Southern History*, 270–71. See also Ayers, *Promise of the New South*, 457–58 n. 51.

17. Planter persistence into the postbellum years did not necessarily signal the persistence of their agrarian, anti-business values. Michael Wayne argues in *The Reshaping of Plantation Society: The Natchez District, 1860–1880* (Baton Rouge, 1983) that the antebellum elite survived but was transformed by new conditions brought by emancipation. Joseph P. Reidy comes to similar conclusions in *From Slavery to Agrarian Capitalism in the Cotton Plantation South: Central Georgia, 1800–1880* (Chapel Hill and London, 1992).

Woodward's discussion in *Origins* of planter persistence and change comes in "The Unredeemed Farmer," a chapter mainly concerned with tenancy, the crop lien, and the poverty of small farmers, but only peripherally with the nature of the landowning elite. He argues that large-scale landholdings continued to exist after emancipation and correctly notes that the appearance in the census of fewer plantations and an increased number of farms was the result of the landowners' parceling out their lands in small portions to tenants and the census bureau's subsequent counting of each subdivision as a separate farm. Then in a single short paragraph Woodward presents the argument that the persistence studies seek to test. "To say that plantations of a sort were preserved and enlarged is not to say that the antebellum planter was preserved also," he begins (p. 179). On the contrary, he continues, there was a significant change in ownership. But he actually offers scant evidence for this change. First he quotes Roger W. Shugg's conclusion that in the Louisiana sugar areas there was a "revolution in land titles," the old planters being replaced by "a new, capitalistic sugar aristocracy, organized in corporations and financed by banks" (p. 179).[18] He then quotes an 1881 estimate by F. C. Morehead, president of the Mississippi Valley Cotton Planters' Association, "that not one third of the cotton plantations of the Mississippi Valley were 'owned by the men who held them at the [close] of the war'" (p. 179).[19]

Woodward's evidence for the change in landownership is clearly inadequate. Moreover, in its emphasis on genealogy and its short-term perspective, it shares the same problems I have raised concerning the persistence studies. But neither Woodward's thin evidence in *Origins* nor the evidence in the later persistence studies undermines the validity of Woodward's main argument—or, at least, his main argument as I shall amend it somewhat.

Inasmuch as confiscation and redistribution of planters' land was almost nonexistent after the war, it should occasion no surprise that manuscript census and tax records in the early postbellum years reveal that many antebellum landowners or their sons, daughters, or other surviving relatives still owned the family land and remained large landowners—always keeping in mind that the persistence studies themselves often show that as many as half

---

18. The reference is to Roger W. Shugg, *Origins of Class Struggle in Louisiana: A Social History of White Farmers and Laborers During Slavery and After, 1840–1875* (Baton Rouge, 1939), 248–49.

19. The source for Woodward's quotation is [Henry W. Grady], "Cotton and Its Kingdom," *Harper's New Monthly Magazine,* 63 (October 1881), 722. Woodward erroneously identified Morehead as the president of the National Cotton Planters' Association.

did not persist, even in the short run. But if certain *people* persisted as land-owners, much had nonetheless changed. The emancipation of slaves meant a massive loss of the planters' wealth, a loss that destroyed their major capital resource, which lowered their investment possibilities and undermined their ability to command credit and to organize their labor force, to say nothing of the deprivation of the prestige, social status, and personal services that slaves had provided.[20] If the persisters were to survive and prosper, they had to adjust to their very new and different situation.[21]

A more dynamic approach that follows individual experiences over time and, incidentally, beyond 1880 avoids the problems associated with producing snapshots from two census years, even if it does not have the quantitative precision of the persistence studies. Investigations of individuals reveal significant variations among both older planters and newcomers as they adjusted (or failed to adjust) in a number of different ways to the newly imposed free labor system. This approach also permits us to unpack further the transformations among small landowners as they moved into commercial production and adapted to the new conditions.

It is those accommodations in all their variations over time that most of the persistence studies miss. These studies, for example, would pick up the Compsons who continued to own their square mile of land following the Civil War—if I may make my point by using a fictional example from Woodward's favorite novelist as an illustration. As significant landowners

---

20. To refute the conclusions of some scholars that the Civil War left the South economically devastated, Roger L. Ransom and Richard Sutch argue that the end of slavery "did not destroy the 'capital' embodied in the black population. The apparent disappearance of nearly one-half of the southern capital stock represented, not a loss to the South, but a transfer of the ownership of 'capitalized labor' from the slaveholders to the ex-slaves themselves. As free agents, the former slaves 'owned' themselves and the right to profit from their own labor as they saw fit. Apparently, it is because so much of southern history has been written from the perspective of the slaveowner that this transfer of ownership has been incorrectly viewed as a loss to the southern economy." Ransom and Sutch, *One Kind of Freedom: The Economic Consequences of Emancipation* (Cambridge, Eng., and New York, 1977), 52. This is peculiar reasoning. A slave owner had no trouble getting credit by using slaves as collateral or raising cash by selling his slaves. A former slave now owning himself would be in a very different situation.

21. Woodward may be faulted, at least to a degree, for encouraging a more static approach, for while he finds the Redeemers to be new men who created a bourgeois society and allowed it to be subordinated to northern industrial interests, he finds also that they fashioned a backward, labor-intensive, static, agricultural regime dominated by a few staple crops and worked by a dependent, depressed mass of impoverished tenants and small farmers enthralled by the crop lien system and never-ending debt.

the Compsons would appear as "persisting" in 1880, although they were already gradually selling off their land, until the last significant parcel went to a golf course developer in 1910. Like their lands, the family itself petered out, except for Jason IV, a crude, modern business-type who "competed and held his own with the Snopeses, who took over" Jefferson.[22] Although some of the large-scale business plantations or, at least, their precursors, might be detected by persistence studies, most would be missed or seen incorrectly. These business plantations, which used closely supervised black cropper laborers treated as wage laborers, evolved slowly in the cotton areas of the old plantation black belt over several decades following the end of the Civil War and were first recognized by the census in a special report in 1910.[23]

Sometimes these plantations were owned and managed by members of old antebellum planter families—Trail Lake, owned by the Percy family, for example. In other instances newcomers, like the Mississippi Delta Planting Company (which later became the Delta & Pine Land Company) developed them by buying out existing farms.[24] Persistence studies do not extend to the 1890s and beyond when these plantations emerged and therefore do not notice them. If, however, scholars expanded persistence studies to include later decades, they would find some persisters such as the Percy family. But

---

22. The reference is to William Faulkner's early novel, *The Sound and the Fury* (New York, 1929), and to the novelist's history of the Compson family that he wrote to include in *The Portable Faulkner*. See "Appendix: 1699–1945: The Compsons," in Malcolm Cowley, ed., *The Portable Faulkner* (New York, 1946), 737–56 (quotation on p. 750). The Snopes clan were the storekeeper-merchant-landowning descendants of a barn-burning poor white.

23. In its special study for the 1910 census, the Census Bureau termed these large-scale operations "tenant plantations." The workers on such plantations, however, were usually croppers, not tenants, or, at least, were treated as such whatever their legal position. U.S. Bureau of the Census, "Plantations in the South," *Thirteenth Census of the United States, 1910. Vol. V: Agriculture: General Report and Analysis* (Washington, D.C., 1913), 877–89, esp. 878–79. The bureau later published an expanded version of this chapter separately: U.S. Bureau of Census, *Plantation Farming in the United States* (Washington, D.C., 1916). I have discussed the evolution and significance of the law relating to tenants and croppers in *New South—New Law: The Legal Foundations of Credit and Labor Relations in the Postbellum Agricultural South* (Baton Rouge, 1995).

24. On Trail Lake, see William Alexander Percy, *Lanterns on the Levee: Recollections of a Planter's Son* (Baton Rouge, 1941), 279–81. For a brief sketch of the origin and growth of Delta & Pine Land Company, see "Biggest Cotton Plantation," *Fortune*, 15 (March 1937), 125–32, 156, 158, 160; and Samuel Crowther, "Big Business in Cotton," *The Country Gentleman*, 92 (March 1927), 65–66. See also Lawrence J. Nelson, "Welfare Capitalism on a Mississippi Plantation in the Great Depression," *Journal of Southern History*, 50 (May 1984), 225–50.

persistence also declined over time as many landowners (like the fictional Compsons) could not adapt to new conditions and failed, while others sold out, often to newcomers such as the organizers of Delta & Pine Land.

Still another picture emerges in some of the antebellum plantation areas such as the Natchez District, where persisting planters are readily found. These planters, however, did not transform their lands into business plantations but opted instead to become absentee landlords who collected rents while abdicating the day-to-day responsibility of managing the operations, retaining the security for their rents through their automatic prior lien on the crop. In the Louisiana sugar areas some antebellum planters persisted while others did not, but most planters who did transformed former slaves into wage workers rather than tenants or croppers. Finally, the persistence studies miss the newly developing areas of the South where either large business plantations appeared almost from the start or investors purchased huge tracts and then divided them into small rental farms.[25]

While Woodward notes "the survival and expansion of the plantation" in the postbellum South, even citing the 1910 special report on "tenant plantations," he does not consider fully the variety of plantation organizational forms that evolved after the Civil War and that I have sketched here. If he had, he would have found additional support for his discontinuity argument. He fails to see how these "tenant plantations" were characterized by a new aggressive business orientation and instead argues that the new form was

> the plantation minus such scant efficiency, planning, responsible supervision, and soil conservation as the old system provided. It was minus the ordinary minimum of economic virtues associated with proprietorship, for the plantation was usually minus even an owner who lived on its soil and spent the profits of another's labor on his own family. The evils of land monopoly, ab-

---

25. On Natchez see Ronald L. F. Davis, *Good and Faithful Labor: From Slavery to Sharecropping in the Natchez District, 1860–1890* (Westport, Conn., and London, 1982); and Wayne, *Reshaping of Plantation Society*. On Louisiana see Rebecca J. Scott, "Fault Lines, Color Lines, and Party Lines: Race, Labor, and Collective Action in Louisiana and Cuba, 1862–1912," in Frederick Cooper, Thomas C. Holt, and Rebecca J. Scott, *Beyond Slavery: Explorations of Race, Labor, and Citizenship in Postemancipation Societies* (Chapel Hill and London, 2000), 61–83. On newly developing areas in the South, see Neil Foley, *The White Scourge: Mexicans, Blacks, and Poor Whites in Texas Cotton Culture* (Berkeley, Los Angeles, and London, 1997); Jeannie M. Whayne, *A New Plantation South: Land, Labor, and Federal Favor in Twentieth-Century Arkansas* (Charlottesville and London, 1996); and Mark V. Wetherington, *The New South Comes to Wiregrass Georgia, 1860–1910* (Knoxville, 1994).

sentee ownership, soil mining, and the one-crop system, once associated with and blamed upon slavery, did not disappear with that institution but were, instead, aggravated, intensified, and multiplied (pp. 179–80).

In fact, Woodward was wrong about the characteristics of the tenant plantations found in the special 1910 report. They were the most modern, well-organized, closely supervised agricultural operations in the cotton South.[26] Testifying before a Senate committee in 1895, the owner of one of these plantations described the problems he faced because of low cotton prices. His statement revealed much about the organization and operation of these plantations and the thoroughly "business" attitudes of their owners:

> Take a large plantation kept up in good condition working a large number of mules and people, with manager, blacksmith, engineer, carpenters and machinery, and all the expenses incident to and waste inseparable from a large business, and I have no hesitation in saying that there is no profit in the business with middling cotton under 10 cents. At that price a moderate interest upon the capital employed might be assured.[27]

Unfortunately, Woodward does not realize how the emergence of this group of planter-businessmen serves to buttress his basic argument about postbellum economic change. They were those "new men" who replaced the old planter class, and they were part of the enterprising, business-oriented, new postbellum ruling elite.

Woodward also mistakenly links his discussion of the survival of the plantation to the transformation of the yeomen into commercial farmers—a rather different development that took place in different areas than did the

---

26. The organization and structure of the plantations are described in the 1910 census report, "Plantations in the South," 877–89. Later investigations provide more supporting details. See, for example, C. O. Brannen, *Relation of Land Tenure to Plantation Organization,* U.S. Department of Agriculture Bulletin, No. 1269 (Washington, D.C., 1924). For a different view of the tenant plantations, see Jay R. Mandle, *Not Slave, Not Free: The African American Economic Experience since the Civil War* (Durham and London, 1992), esp. 33–43. Ironically, Mandle's view of the tenant plantations is closer to the one Woodward advanced in *Origins,* but Mandle's analysis disputes Woodward's general discontinuity interpretation, finding instead the continuity of a plantation economy.

27. *Senate Reports,* 53 Cong., 3 Sess., No. 986: *Report of the Committee on Agriculture and Forestry on Condition of Cotton Growers in the United States, the Present Prices of Cotton, and the Remedy* (2 vols., Washington, D.C., 1895), I, 331–35.

rise of the business plantations. The commercialization of the yeoman farms involved mainly, but not exclusively, whites rather than blacks, and it had different results. In the years following the war, increasing numbers of small white farmers who had been largely self-sufficient before the war began producing crops, predominantly cotton, for the market. Indeed, by the end of the nineteenth century, white farmers grew more cotton than did black farmers—a reversal of the antebellum situation. As they moved into commercial production, many former yeomen found it increasingly necessary to seek credit to finance their operations, and they received the needed credit by offering liens on their future crops.

Woodward depicts these changes and describes their results from the point of view—even using similar language—of the Alliance and Populist critics with whom he clearly sympathized. He places heavy blame for the farmers' hard times on the crop lien system, which affected whites as well as blacks and "by its economic results alone . . . may have worked more permanent injury to the South" than slavery. The lien system was new to the South, and "it represented one of the strangest contractual relationships in the history of finance" (p. 180).[28] The lien locked the farmer into cotton production and forced him to pay outrageously high interest on the funds borrowed, thereby keeping him in perpetual debt to the merchant or the landowner, who were often the same person.[29]

Woodward's clear contempt for the postbellum "New South" leaders, who he argues had replaced the old planter elite, sharply contrasts with his more favorable view of the Populists. Indeed, at times it appears that Woodward's view of the Populists is similar to the Southern Agrarian critique of modern bourgeois economy and society, suggesting, perhaps, that the Popu-

---

28. In fact, this is only partially true. The antebellum factorage system was much the same as the postbellum lien system in law and in practice, although the parties involved were usually large producers and merchants, and much of the relationship was based upon informal agreements rather than legal obligations. Furthermore, borrowing against a future output (or income) is not as strange as Woodward's statement suggests. What makes the lien system peculiar is the small scale of each individual arrangement and the lack of wealth of many of the borrowers and most of the lenders as well. It should be noted, however, that when a borrower did have wealth of any kind (land, wagons, mules, plows—even chickens, hogs, or household items), these were usually added to the lien in the form of a mortgage to increase loan security. I have discussed these and other matters relating to credit arrangement in *New South—New Law*.

29. Unlike most of the Alliance and Populist critics, however, Woodward did not make the merchant "the villain in the piece." The merchant also paid high interest, and he took high risks. "The merchant was only a bucket on an endless chain by which the agricultural well of a tributary region was drained of its flow" (pp. 184–85).

lists had been forced or mistakenly enticed into the market and were seeking a return to the traditional noncommercial society.[30] At other times, his sympathy for the Populists and his moral outrage at the conditions in which many farmers found themselves make Woodward seem to be the liberal reformer bent on exposing the devastation arising from "unrestrained capitalism."[31] Perhaps this ambiguity in Woodward's view arises from what he later called the various "approaches and ideologies" that shaped his interpretation—"the Agrarians, the Marxists, the Liberals, and ideas associated with the name of Charles Beard."[32]

Whatever its source, Woodward's compassion for the Populists does not lead him to a full analysis and appreciation of the extent of the changes, the results, and the considerable variations involved in the transformation of the yeomen into commercial farmers. As farming in the upcountry became increasingly commercialized, farmers with new needs and problems increasingly found themselves in conflict with a new bourgeois elite that had arisen to meet those needs. Quickly growing towns became business and trade centers and focal points for the conflict. Yet an analysis of conflict in the postbellum South must not be limited to the investigation of rural-urban tensions. Conflict often also extended into the countryside, pitting some

30. Sheldon Hackney, following Morton Rothstein ("The Antebellum South as a Dual Economy: A Tentative Hypothesis," *Agricultural History,* 41 [October 1967], 373–82), suggests that if the antebellum planters were "modern" capitalists, but the yeomen and African Americans comprised a traditional sector of society, "then one of the most far-reaching effects of the Civil War was to force both white and black farmers from the traditional sector into commercial agriculture where they were unable to survive. . . . Populism may have been the cry of the rural masses for the re-creation of a noncommercial community." In another place and context Hackney makes the same point in a slightly different way: "Populists derived not only from inferior economic strata but from a rural segment of society that was being left behind by advancing technology and an increasingly urban society. They were defending a rural way of life, a culture, as well as a way of earning a living." Hackney, "*Origins of the New South* in Retrospect," 212–13 (first quotation, 46 in this volume), 206 (second quotation, 40 in this volume). Similarly, Steven Hahn argues that the white farmers who provided the strongest support for the Alliance and the Populists were resisting their transformation from near self-sufficiency in the antebellum era to commercial production in the decades following the Civil War. Hahn, *The Roots of Southern Populism: Yeoman Farmers and the Transformation of the Georgia Upcountry, 1850–1890* (New York and Oxford, 1983).

31. Woodward's biographer has claimed that the experiences of Woodward's family in Arkansas facing problems of credit and transportation during the historian's youth left Woodward with "a lingering distrust of 'unrestrained capitalism'" that clearly "pervades" *Origins.* Roper, *C. Vann Woodward, Southerner,* 12 (first quotation), 316 n. 11 (second quotation).

32. Woodward, *Thinking Back,* 38.

farmers against others. Because Woodward concentrated on the grievances raised by the Populists, he failed to see the full extent of the changes in the non-plantation areas or upcountry and how these changes created new forms of business and new forms of class conflict, marking a sharp discontinuity from antebellum conditions and providing additional support for his general economic interpretation of the New South.

Postbellum improvements in transportation and other marketing and financing facilities extended the market for commercial production into new areas.[33] As the income possibilities of commercial production became apparent, many of the small farmers found they had surplus land—that is, land beyond what they and their family members could work themselves. They quickly realized that this land, if put into cultivation, could augment their income. This led them to increase their labor force beyond their household by hiring day labor, by using croppers, or by renting land to tenants—or, as was sometimes the case, using a variety of these arrangements.

Whatever process they followed, such farmers faced escalating needs for credit: to pay for necessary supplies on land they worked themselves; to feed and pay day-laborers and croppers before the crop was gathered; to provide for the needs of tenants or, if they did not directly make such provisions themselves, to guarantee that those who did supply the tenants would be paid. A growing number of merchants stood ready to provide the credit, and the towns in which they congregated (and which they sought to expand and develop) soon housed brokers, buyers, storekeepers, ginners, bankers, and others who supplied the needs of nearby farmers and the swelling population of the towns.

When cotton prices were up, these arrangements could prove profitable, raising the incomes of landowners, tenants, and the middlemen with whom they dealt and increasing the wealth of landowners as land values rose. Good times would lead some to sell their land and pocket the capital gains and others to increase their landholdings, and some landless farmers used profits to begin the purchase of land. But when cotton prices fell, as they did periodically in the 1870s and 1880s and then disastrously in the mid-1890s, many landowners found themselves deeply in debt, often losing their land to merchant-lenders or selling portions at depressed prices to pay debts. Those who had bought lands in good times at high prices often lost their land when, as cotton prices fell, they were unable to continue pay-

---

33. The process had begun haltingly before the Civil War but developed apace in the postbellum years.

ments on mortgages or other borrowings. These developments, along with a rapidly growing rural population with few other employment opportunities, forced an increasing number and proportion of white farmers into tenancy, as the census data clearly revealed.[34]

The result of the entry of the yeoman into the market, in Lacy K. Ford's words, was the "rise of a dynamic merchant class that turned Upcountry towns into pulsating nodules of economic activity," and this "Upcountry mercantile community, and some of the large landholders as well," became a "cohesive bourgeoisie anxious to place its own imprimatur on the state of South Carolina." These developments, occurring in states across the South, created conflict between the new business class and the commercial farmers and tenants with whom they dealt. Similar divisions and conflict in various forms took place in the small interior mill towns as described by David L. Carlton, in the larger cities as described by Don H. Doyle, and in Appalachia as described by Ronald D. Eller.[35]

In sum, all of these changes associated with the destruction of the traditional society of the yeomen as they became commercial farmers, mill hands, miners, and even rural and town businessmen, provide additional support for Woodward's theme of discontinuity, the rise of a new southern business-oriented elite, and the development of new forms of conflict within the South. Some of this friction arose from clear class divisions—that is, conflict between employers and employees. But in the case of the differences between landowners and tenants on the one hand and the merchants and other middlemen who marketed and financed their crops on the other, I think the conflict may be more accurately seen as a struggle *within* the business class. I shall return to this in a moment.

---

34. Investigators for a Department of Agriculture study in the early 1920s interviewed more than three hundred farmers and examined tax and census data to provide a rich report tracing these changes over the post–Civil War era. Howard A. Turner and L. D. Howell, *Condition of Farmers in a White-Farmer Area of the Cotton Piedmont, 1924–1926*, U.S. Department of Agriculture Circular, No. 78 (Washington, D.C., 1929).

35. Lacy K. Ford, "Rednecks and Merchants: Economic Development and Social Tensions in the South Carolina Upcountry, 1865–1900," *Journal of American History*, 71 (September 1984), 294–318 (quotations on p. 317). See also Michael R. Hyman's perceptive and important discussion in *The Anti-Redeemers: Hill-Country Political Dissenters in the Lower South from Redemption to Populism* (Baton Rouge, 1990). David L. Carlton, *Mill and Town in South Carolina, 1880–1920* (Baton Rouge, 1982); Don H. Doyle, *New Men, New Cities, New South: Atlanta, Nashville, Charleston, Mobile, 1860–1910* (Chapel Hill and London, 1990); and Ronald D. Eller, *Miners, Millhands, and Mountaineers: Industrialization of the Appalachian South, 1880–1930* (Knoxville, 1982).

The theme of new forms of conflict is clearly evident in the transformation of slaves into free workers. This change, I would add, was more complex than Woodward's analysis in *Origins* suggests, but it does not contradict his basic argument. Indeed, recognition of the complexity not only lends additional support to Woodward's discontinuity thesis, but it also helps to provide a richer explanation of the problems the Populists and other reformers faced in uniting farmers across racial lines. Woodward provides a sensitive discussion of postemancipation African American life, considering such matters as discrimination, disfranchisement, lynching, attempts at racial cooperation, and the development of class differences within the segregated black community. But his analysis of the transition from slavery to freedom as it affected the majority of freedpeople—those who remained in agriculture—is incomplete and fails to distinguish adequately the differences between the experiences of the emancipated blacks and the whites moving into commercial production.

Woodward begins his discussion of the African American experience by arguing that little had changed:

> Much discussion about the Negro's civil rights, his political significance, his social status, and his aspirations can be shortened and simplified by a clear understanding of the economic status assigned him in the New Order. Emancipation and Reconstruction had done little to change that picture. The lives of the overwhelming majority of Negroes were still circumscribed by the farm and plantation (p. 205).

Although some black agricultural workers succeeded in their pursuit of acquiring land, almost all African Americans, nevertheless, remained landless and owned little other property, a fact that clearly differentiated the white and black experience. "It is pretty clear," Woodward continues, "that as a rule the Negro farmer not only worked the white man's land but worked it with a white man's plow drawn by a white man's mule" (p. 206). What Woodward does *not* note, and it is a serious omission, is that many blacks, unlike most whites, also worked under a white man's close supervision and were gradually transformed in law and in practice into a proletariat.

Beginning even as Woodward wrote in 1951 but continuing apace in the half century that followed, there has been an outpouring of scholarship dealing with the efforts of African Americans to give meaning to their freedom by escaping from the domination and control of whites by acquiring their own land or by achieving independence from direct control through tenancy. The details of this scholarship are familiar and need not detain us here except to note significant differences in the black and white experiences, differences that have direct bearing on Woodward's thesis in *Origins*.

When blacks succeeded in acquiring some land or becoming true tenants, they occupied economic positions similar to that of white small landowners and tenants but with important differences beyond simple economic status that would affect attitudes, outlooks, and expectations. For African Americans, becoming a true tenant farmer was a move up, giving them a degree of independence and freedom from that day-to-day supervision of their work that they found reminiscent of slavery. I suspect also that for some blacks, the achievement of the next step, buying land of their own, would have represented increased opportunity for independence through self-sufficiency and freedom from commercial production—in other words, not a step up the agricultural ladder but the choice of a different option.[36] For whites, becoming a tenant farmer often meant a move down, signaling either the loss of land or the inability to acquire land—that is, a frustrating fall from the ladder or the failure to climb.[37]

But not all African Americans became true tenants. Many became croppers on the business plantations and occupied a socioeconomic position very different from that of tenants. This group had none of the independence of tenants; they were closely supervised workers on yearlong contracts, paid not in a portion of the crop produced but according to the value of what they produced. These black laborers had moved from slavery to that peculiar form of wage worker in the South, the cropper.[38] And they worked for that new class of businessmen-planters, those "new men" that Woodward argues replaced the antebellum planter elite. These businessmen consolidated their holdings, experimented with the breeding of seed, planting and weeding methods, and other production procedures, used the best equipment available, and hired experienced professional managers to handle labor relations, finance, and other aspects of their operations. In a word, the business plantations may be best described as emerging agribusinesses, using low-cost black labor.

---

36. Obviously this tentative proposition needs further research to support it and to determine how widespread it was.

37. I realize that this simplifies matters a bit. Some white tenants were renting land from relatives and could count on inheriting the land at a future date, and some white tenants were climbing the agricultural ladder and would get land of their own in the future.

38. Some workers were legally croppers, but they were treated as tenants by absentee landlords or by landowners who did not want to exercise close supervision of their work. I have considered the variations in treatment and status in *New South—New Law,* chap. 3.

Class and class conflicts might therefore be reconsidered—or, more precisely, might be considered somewhat differently in the light of changes I have described. If class and class conflicts are central to Woodward's analysis, race is an important dimension as well. Woodward argues in *Origins* and in his other work, especially in *Tom Watson,* that class could and sometimes did overwhelm racial differences, at least temporarily. To the reasons he offers for the failure of biracial cooperation, I would suggest another arising from significant class differences between blacks and whites living in what only seem to be similar class situations—toiling as tenants or small landowners, dependent upon the income from a commercial crop, and heavily indebted. But for many, though certainly not all, this class similarity was more apparent than real, because a growing number of blacks were croppers on business plantations. They were workers, not tenants, and they did not share the same goals as tenants. Or, to put this in another way, if large-scale planters became the agrarian New South's big businessmen, the former yeomen by becoming commercial farmers—either as owners or renters of the land they worked—became the agrarian New South's small businessmen. And if some former slaves also became commercial farmers, most became part of a new working class.

This puts the class structure of the postemancipation agrarian South in a different perspective. It helps to explain why croppers on business plantations would have different goals and needs from small farmers and tenants even though both suffered from low incomes and poor living standards. And because this class difference roughly, if not precisely, corresponded to race, it offers an additional perspective on race relations during this formative and volatile period. Nor does depicting the former white yeomen, now landowning or landrenting commercial farmers, as businessmen erase significant differences between them and the big planters or diminish the reality of the hardships they faced and their conflicts with the middlemen with whom they dealt. Indeed, in part, the problems of the small farmers arose from their competition with the more efficient big plantations that were located on the most fertile land, used the best available equipment and seed, organized the work more efficiently, and had better access to credit and services. The small farmers worked with inferior equipment on less fertile land and faced higher costs for credit and other necessary services. The problems of small farmers were those of small businessmen—costs of production and competition from more efficient producers—while the problems of the croppers were those of workers—income and working conditions. If tenants and croppers were often poverty stricken, they were nonetheless situated differently enough economically to make joint action on common solutions difficult.

Thus far in this brief survey I have been more Woodwardian than Wood-ward—or, if I may be permitted a bit of arrogance, I have attempted to show how Woodward himself could have been more Woodwardian. Let me con-clude by very briefly considering two other matters of importance in Wood-ward's argument that arise from his economic perspective: comparative history and southern distinctiveness.

Woodward applauded attempts at comparative history, devoting a chap-ter to it in *Thinking Back*. The growing body of comparative studies of post-emancipation societies has provided important insights into the American experience—for the most part by revealing how different changes in the United States were from those elsewhere.[39] Although most of this kind of comparative study came after the publication of *Origins*, Woodward argued that the "comparative perspective" had long been a common feature in studies of southern history, and the results, he insisted, were unfortunate:

> It was not that the South was embarrassed for lack of comparative perspec-tive, or its history for lack of a comparative dimension. In fact the South has, if anything, been plagued by comparisons and its history distorted by them. The trouble lay in the comparative partner with which the South was long stuck, namely the North.[40]

Woodward's point is well taken but, I would suggest, not for the reason he gave. Indeed, if postbellum southern history has been distorted by compari-sons with the North, a significant part of the distortion arises not from a comparison that is not apt, but rather too often the South has been com-pared to a distorted picture of the North.

The litany is familiar enough but may be summarized in a sentence: While the North was growing, industrializing, and prosperous, the South remained stagnant, agrarian, and poor. Although accurate perhaps in an ag-

---

39. Woodward, "Comparing Comparisons," chap. 7 in *Thinking Back,* 121–33. In this chapter Woodward mentions that Frank Tannenbaum's *Slave and Citizen: The Negro in the Americas* (New York, 1946), a study of comparative slavery, predated *Origins,* but the work on comparative emancipations came later. For some of this later work see, for example, Steven Hahn, "Emancipation and the Development of Capitalist Agriculture: The South in Compara-tive Perspective," in Kees Gispen, ed., *What Made the South Different?* (Jackson, Miss., and London, 1990), 71–88 (along with a perceptive "Commentary" on Hahn's essay by Peter Kol-chin, 88–96); Hahn, "Class and State in Postemancipation Societies: Southern Planters in Comparative Perspective," *American Historical Review,* 95 (February 1990), 75–98; and Coo-per, Holt, and Scott, *Beyond Slavery.*

40. Woodward, *Thinking Back,* 121.

gregate sense, the generalization ignores many variations that point to far less difference between the sections. Tenancy was growing in both sections, and, of course, agrarian unrest was not a purely southern phenomenon. The growth of big business in the North had its counterpart in the development of the business plantations in the South. It is not immediately apparent that a laborer working for George Pullman and living in his company town was significantly better off than a cotton mill worker in the South. If disfranchisement was widespread and successful in the South, northern "reformers" at the same time sought to limit the franchise of immigrants. And other examples of North-South similarities might be added.[41]

I do not want to overstate the point and suggest that all North-South differences disappeared. I merely want to suggest that the Civil War and emancipation erased key elements of southern distinctiveness. In some ways, Woodward would seem to have agreed. If the end of slavery can be described, as he wrote in *Thinking Back,* "as the death of a society rather than the liquidation of an investment," producing a massive discontinuity in southern history marked by the displacement of the antebellum elite, then the question arises as to what was the nature of the new society that re-placed the old.[42] If the new southern elite was business-oriented, even if willing to accept a role subordinate to the northern business elite, was not the postbellum South really new in that it was much like the bourgeois North? If so, emancipation should mark the end of southern distinctiveness—or, at least, it put the South on the road to the end of distinctiveness.

The Civil War and emancipation marked a sharp discontinuity in southern history: the transformation of a slave society into a bourgeois society. The change was not immediate but rather gradual, and many traditional features remained in the bourgeois South. Nevertheless, at least by the turn of the twentieth century, it was clear that a "new" South as Woodward described it in *Origins* had emerged. One result of this change was the weakening and gradual disappearance of *significant* southern economic distinctiveness. This, I believe, is the monumental and lasting contribution of this half-century-old volume—even though, I suspect, Woodward himself would have objected to my taking his argument to this conclusion.

---

41. I have discussed the growth of the large-scale business plantations as a phenomenon that parallels the growth of big business in "Class, Race, Politics, and the Modernization of the Postbellum South," *Journal of Southern History,* 63 (February 1997), 3–22. On northern disfranchisement efforts see J. Morgan Kousser, *The Shaping of Southern Politics: Suffrage Restriction and the Establishment of the One-Party South, 1880–1910* (New Haven and London, 1974), 52–53, 250–57.

42. Woodward, *Thinking Back,* 130.

Origins of the New South and the Negro Question

Not the least remarkable fact about C. Vann Woodward's *Origins of the New South* is that, fifty years ago, Woodward knew better than to attempt what I have been asked to do: to discuss Afro-Americans as a subject apart from the subjects of land, agriculture, and rural unrest; industrial development and political economy; class warfare, class alliances, and politics; and literature, the sciences, and the arts, that have occupied the symposium thus far. Then (as now), the more usual procedure was to relegate Afro-Americans to a space of their own, defined as "race relations" and set apart from the study of history properly so called. Woodward never fell into that trap. He understood that the importance of Jim Crow as a subject in no way established its validity as a method.

Never at any point in *Origins* is Woodward unaware of Afro-Americans'

Reprinted from *Journal of Southern History,* 67 (November 2001), 811–26, the Woodward symposium issue.

entire implication within the vital questions of the New South. Meaningless definitions of their predicament that may pass muster today, such as *marginalization* and *exclusion,* did not fool him for a minute. (Marginalized? Excluded? When the planters wanted nothing better than for them to stay conspicuously in their place, working as before?) The opening sentence of chapter 1 sets the tone at once (and with as fine an example as I know of Woodward's flair for mischief). Right there, where no one can miss it, he writes, "Any honest genealogy of the ruling family of Southern Democrats would reveal a strain of mixed blood."[1] The mixture in question was of Whig and Democrat, rather than of black and white. But, beyond doubt, the metaphor was calculated. Trifling with the hallowed conventions of racism by thus juxtaposing the sacred and the profane—ruling-class genealogy and mixed blood—Woodward serves early notice that, in method as in content, *Origins of the New South* will neither fear nor respect the color line. Though he may flirt occasionally with the language of race relations, he only rarely makes concessions to its conceptual apparatus.[2]

Race relations as an analysis of society takes for granted that *race* is a valid empirical datum and thereby shifts attention from the actions that constitute racism—enslavement, disfranchisement, segregation, lynching, massacres, and pogroms—to the traits that constitute race. For racists in the New South, those traits might have included the Negroes' ignorance, laziness, brutality, criminality, subjection to uncontrolled passions, or incapacity for the moral and intellectual duties of civilization. For scholars in our own time who accept race, once ritually purified by the incantation *socially*

---

1. C. Vann Woodward, *Origins of the New South, 1877–1913* (Baton Rouge, 1951), 1. Page numbers for subsequent references to *Origins* in this essay are inserted parenthetically in the text. The first edition's pagination is retained in later reprint editions. I would like to thank Michael R. West and Lauren F. Winner for comments on the manuscript.

2. One of the rare exceptions appears in the chapter on the Atlanta Compromise (chap. 13), where Woodward credits Booker T. Washington with having "framed the *modus vivendi* of race relations in the New South" (p. 356). The framing as race relations was Washington's work, but Woodward's argument in the preceding chapters makes clear that the *modus vivendi* itself had been determined, as it would continue to be, by means of crop lien and sharecropping, law and constitution, rope and faggot. Michael R. West, "The Education of Booker T. Washington: The Negro Problem, Democracy, and the Idea of Race Relations" (Ph.D. dissertation, Columbia University, 2000), 61–62. Even in *The Strange Career of Jim Crow,* which is much more race relations–oriented than *Origins,* Woodward betrays his dissatisfaction with the language of race relations: "The peculiarity most often used to distinguish one order from another, however, has been the relation between races, or more particularly the status of the Negro." C. Vann Woodward, *The Strange Career of Jim Crow* (3d rev. ed., New York, 1974), 5. Note the shift from "relation between races" to "the status of the Negro."

constructed, as a valid category of analysis, the relevant traits are more likely to be "difference," "Other-ness," "culture," or "identity." Either way, however, objective acts, the real substance of racism, take second place to subjective traits, the fictive substance of race; traits that would be irrelevant to explaining racist acts even if their empirical validity could be established.

Quincy Ewing, a white southerner writing in the *Atlantic Monthly* while Woodward was an infant, refuted on empirical grounds the various racial explanations of the problem: the Negroes' purported ignorance, laziness, criminality, and the like. But such rationales, he maintained, were beside the point in any case. The problem would persist even were there "no shadow of excuse for the conviction that the Negro is more lazy, or more ignorant, or more criminal, or more brutal, or more anything else he ought not to be, or less anything else he ought to be, than other men." Nor, according to Ewing, could the problem be laid to "difference" (an old favorite that has returned to favor in recent scholarship, often graced with a capital *D*): "There is nothing in the unlikeness of the unlike that is necessarily problematical," he pointed out; "it may be simply accepted and dealt with as a fact, like any other fact."[3] Like or unlike, Ewing declared, no race problem arises unless "the people of one race are minded to adopt and act upon some policy more or less oppressive or repressive in dealing with the people of another race." He concluded:

> The problem, How to maintain the institution of chattel slavery, ceased to be at Appomattox; the problem, How to maintain the social, industrial, and civic inferiority of the descendants of chattel slaves, succeeded it, and is the race problem of the South at the present time. There is no other.[4]

Woodward is more attentive than Ewing to how white people differed among themselves in social and economic standing, objectives and aspirations, and ability to mobilize political power. But, like Ewing, he recognizes

---

3. Quincy Ewing, "The Heart of the Race Problem," *Atlantic Monthly,* 103 (March 1909), 390–92 (first quotation on p. 390), 396 (second quotation). An example of the current vogue for "difference" as a category of analysis is Patrick Wolfe, "Land, Labor, and Difference: Elementary Structures of Race," *American Historical Review,* 106 (June 2001), 866–905. Wolfe regards race as "one among various regimes of difference." After asserting that land and labor are the key to understanding colonial regimes, he chooses to concentrate instead on "discourses of miscegenation" (p. 867).

4. Ewing, "The Heart of the Race Problem," 396.

that the essence of the situation was power and the contest over it: not just the contest (grotesquely unequal as it was) between white and Afro-American people but also that among white people themselves. If allowed the rights of citizenship, Afro-Americans potentially held in their own hands the balance of power between contending groups of white people. If stripped of the rights of citizenship, they still potentially held the balance of power, only not in their own hands. Settling the future of Afro-Americans in the New South inevitably also meant settling the future of white people there, for better or worse (that is, better for some white people and worse for others).

That is why my title refers to the "Negro Question," rather than to any of the common variations on the theme of race or race relations. *Negro Question* (or *Negro Problem*) has the virtue, as Michael R. West has argued, of setting the predicament of Afro-Americans firmly within, rather than at a tangent from, the major questions of political, economic, and social power that were up for settlement in the New South. It also reveals without euphemism the illegitimacy of the problem in the context of a democratic polity. Proposing to decide the fate of people occupying the nominal status of citizens otherwise than with their participation and assent is a profoundly undemocratic, indeed anti-democratic, undertaking. West argues that *race relations* as an ideological formation of the problem, popularized with genius by Booker T. Washington, arose precisely as a way to disguise the anti-democratic essence of the problem by providing for it both a definition and a solution apparently capable of bypassing the issue of naked power that lay at its core.[5]

From the moment Woodward introduces the Redeemers, discusses their social provenance, and characterizes their political program, he makes clear that the central issue for their regimes was how to forestall democracy. The "most common characteristic" of Redeemer state constitutions, he asserts, was "an overweening distrust of legislatures" (p. 65). Quincy Ewing leaps from chattel slavery before Appomattox to social, industrial, and civic inferiority after. Woodward, however, does not forget that Reconstruction fell between, although he neither exaggerates its extent nor takes at face value the Redeemers' charges against their predecessors. ("[T]he Radical regime in the average state . . . lasted less than three and a half years. The amount of good or evil the Radicals could accomplish was limited by this fact if by no other" [p. 22].) Woodward attributes the intensity of the reaction against

---

5. West, "The Education of Booker T. Washington," 13–17, 61–62. West uses the more brutally honest formulation, "Negro Problem."

democracy to the radicalism of its brief tenure, observing that the investment of freed slaves with citizenship and the franchise was unprecedented (p. 53).[6] He weighs the varied significance that the legacy of Reconstruction held for different groups of white people, as well as for Afro-Americans. White planters of the Black Belt, for example, gained a greater measure of control over white people in the uplands than they had enjoyed under slavery, when their prerogative of casting ballots on behalf of voteless Afro-Americans was three-fifths, instead of five-fifths (p. 79). For Afro-Americans, Reconstruction kindled a hope whose loss Woodward evokes movingly, if briefly, by drawing attention to the somber coincidence that took Frederick Douglass off the stage in the same year that Booker T. Washington emerged onto it (pp. 356–57).

The intricacies of fusion, that odd policy of forming tactical political unions with the lesser enemy against the greater, are a sufficient reminder that nothing to do with politics among white southerners was separate from Afro-southerners and vice versa. That is especially true of disfranchisement which, as Woodward makes clear, rested on an old struggle between predominantly white counties and predominantly black counties. The Reconstruction constitutions, sponsored by Republican regimes confident about controlling the votes of the newly enfranchised former slaves, heightened the struggle by upsetting antebellum arrangements that had limited the power of planters in the Black Belt over the white-majority counties. Some scholars may be tempted to attribute all the fuss and feathers to the working out of something they call "white racial identities." But white residents in white-majority counties were not naive enough to make the same mistake. A Populist newspaper in Louisiana roundly charged the Democrats with " 'maintaining white supremacy (?) with the Negro votes,' " (p. 276).[7] A white-county delegate at Virginia's disfranchising convention scornfully rejected complaints by Black Belt delegates of Negro domination in their

---

6. Considering the volume of private property expropriated without compensation, the investment of former slaves with citizenship, the franchise, and the right to hold governmental office, and the former slaveholders' loss—albeit temporary—of power within the national state, emancipation in the United States was radical compared to the emancipation of serfs in Europe and slaves elsewhere in the Americas during the nineteenth century. See Barbara Jeanne Fields, "The Advent of Capitalist Agriculture: The New South in a Bourgeois World," in Thavolia Glymph and John J. Kushma, eds., *Essays on the Postbellum Southern Economy* (College Station, Tex., 1985), 73–94; and Steven Hahn, "Class and State in Postemancipation Societies: Southern Planters in Comparative Perspective," *American Historical Review*, 95 (February 1990), 75–98.

7. The question mark appears in Woodward's source.

home counties—and not from solicitude for the rights of Afro-American voters: " 'I ask you gentlemen of the black belt, . . . How do you happen to be here if the Negroes control down there?' " (p. 328). As Woodward makes clear, the question was not white supremacy but "*which whites* should be supreme" (p. 328, Woodward's italics).

White residents in the white-majority counties of Mississippi sought disfranchisement in 1890, according to Woodward, to overthrow their domination by white people in the black counties (p. 329).[8] In the end, they suffered the same fate as the Afro-Americans at whose disfranchisement they had connived. The Mississippi Plan stripped the franchise from the Afro-American majority and lodged with a minority of white people control over the rest. In the face of the resulting hostility, the convention decided against submitting the new state constitution for ratification by the electorate (pp. 340–41). Disfranchisement not only directly robbed Afro-American as well as white voters of the franchise, but, according to Woodward, it also prepared the way for the apathy that steadily reduced electoral participation, a trend that has continued up to the present (pp. 343–46).

It is not done, however, to interpret these matters as issues of democracy and its abrogation, particularly not where Afro-Americans are concerned. The rubric of the hour is race. Though discredited by reputable biologists and geneticists, race has enjoyed a renaissance among historians, sociologists, and literary scholars. They find the concept attractive, or in any case hard to dispense with, and have therefore striven mightily, though in vain, to find a basis for it in something other than racism. The most recent pedigree papers trace it to culture or identity, at the same time implicating its victims as agents of its imposition. " '[R]ace,' as an embodied category of difference and a constructed aspect of identity, is not imposed by one group upon another," the author of a recent book insists. "[I]t is a product of an ongoing dialogue . . . ."[9]

The effort to redefine race as culture or identity is bound to come a cropper just as did the effort to define race as biology. Indeed, it already has come a cropper, though the fashionable preference for "complicating" anal-

---

8. Citing the work of his student J. Morgan Kousser, Woodward later conceded that he had overstated the initial enthusiasm for disfranchisement among white residents of white counties. See C. Vann Woodward, *Thinking Back: The Perils of Writing History* (Baton Rouge, 1986), 69, 97; and J. Morgan Kousser, *The Shaping of Southern Politics: Suffrage Restriction and the Establishment of the One-Party South, 1880–1910* (New Haven and London, 1974).

9. Joanne Pope Melish, *Disowning Slavery: Gradual Emancipation and "Race" in New England, 1789–1860* (Ithaca, N.Y., and London, 1998), 3–4.

ysis may conceal from the unwary the difference between complexity and muddle. Race as culture is only biological race in polite language: No one can seriously postulate cultural homogeneity among those whose racial homogeneity scholars nonetheless take for granted. The only veil hiding the conjuror's apparatus from full view of the spectators is the quicksilver propensity of *culture* to change meaning from one clause to the next—now denoting something essential, now something acquired; now something bounded, now something without boundaries; now something experienced, now something ascribed.[10]

Scholars are quick to assimilate the commonplace that race is "socially constructed"—which a German shepherd dog or even an intelligent golden retriever knows without instruction—to the popular but mistaken view that race is equivalent to identity.[11] For example, Jane Dailey offers as proof "that racial identity in Virginia was neither static nor superficial" a Virginian ex-Readjuster's demand to know " 'how many white men in Lynchburg will go back on their race and make negroes of themselves' " by voting for the Mahoneite Readjusters.[12] But of course the remark proves nothing about "racial identity," not even that there is such a thing. No white politician could have suggested, even metaphorically, that Negroes who allied with the opposing faction or, for that matter, who allied with his own faction thereby turned themselves into white men. Whereas white men might "make negroes of themselves" by improper or undignified conduct, a black man could make a white man of himself only by an act of misrepresentation or concealment that, if discovered, could under the right circumstances land him in jail or at the end of a rope dangling over a bonfire.

Race as identity breaks down on the irreducible fact that any sense of self intrinsic to persons of African descent is subject to peremptory nullification by forcible extrinsic identification. Such nullification occurs when police of-

---

10. A rich discussion of the history of *culture* as a concept, and of the changing relationships among its varied meanings, may be found in Terry Eagleton, *The Idea of Culture* (Oxford, 2000).

11. My own attempt to account historically for the emergence of racial ideology in the United States, attributing it to the juxtaposition of slavery and freedom during the Revolutionary era, is regularly cited as an argument for the "social construction" of race—which is its starting point, not its conclusion. See Barbara Jeanne Fields, "Slavery, Race and Ideology in the United States of America," *New Left Review,* 181 (May/June 1990), 95–118. Melish cites this article and sketches a similar historical argument but neglects to attribute the argument to the article. Melish, *Disowning Slavery,* 5.

12. Jane Dailey, *Before Jim Crow: The Politics of Race in Postemancipation Virginia* (Chapel Hill and London, 2000), 149 (first quotation), 148 (second quotation).

ficers shoot an unarmed black civilian or, even more flagrantly, when they shoot a black fellow officer, their identification of him as a black man—and, ipso facto, a candidate for summary execution—lethally overriding his self-definition as a policeman. Whatever Afro-American people's identity may be (and a well-argued recent article proposes doing away with the concept altogether), it cannot be equated with their race.[13] After years of probing them for something of value or use, W. E. B. Du Bois repudiated all efforts to define race as a characteristic or attribute of its victims, whether the definition hinged on biology, culture, or identity (supposing "identity" to mean an individual's or a group's sense of self). The black man is not someone of a specified ancestry or culture, he decided, and certainly not someone who so identifies himself. A black man "is a person who must ride 'Jim Crow' in Georgia."[14]

Forced to ride Jim Crow is the key. Not identity as sense of self, but identification by others, peremptory and binding, figuring even in well-meant efforts to undo the crimes of racism. Not the perpetrator's tangible racism, but the victim's intangible race, is the center of attention. Thus, racist profiling goes by the misnomer "racial profiling," and the usual remedy proposed for it is to collect information about—what else?—the victims' "race."[15] Like a criminal suspect required to confess guilt before receiving probation, or a drunk required to intone "I am an alcoholic" as a prerequisite to obtaining help, persons of African descent must accept race, the badge that racism assigns them, to earn remission of the attendant penalties. Not justice or equality but *racial* justice or *racial* equality must be their portion. "[I]n [Ben] Tillman's world," writes Stephen Kantrowitz, " 'racial

---

13. Rogers Brubaker and Frederick Cooper, "Beyond 'Identity,' " *Theory and Society,* 29 (February 2000), 1–47.

14. W. E. B. Du Bois, *Dusk of Dawn: An Essay Toward an Autobiography of a Race Concept* (New York, 1940; reprint, New Brunswick, N.J., 1992), 153. Jane Dailey mistakes Du Bois's blunt definition of race as something imposed by political power for a statement about the "linkages between social interactions and the construction of individual identity." Dailey, *Before Jim Crow,* 133.

15. The columnist Richard Cohen insists that white police officers' automatic identification of a black man as a criminal stems from "race—but not racism," thus implying that mistaken identity is an inborn trait of the mistaken, rather than an act committed by the mistaker. Richard Cohen, "Profile of A Killing," Washington *Post,* March 16, 2000, p. A27. No doubt Cohen would spot the fallacy at once if police randomly harassed and frisked middle-class white adolescent boys on grounds of their color, arguing (correctly) that school mass murderers tend to be white.

equality' was an oxymoron."[16] In mine, too, I must confess, except that I would replace *oxymoron* with *contradiction in terms*. An oxymoron is a figure of speech. *Racial equality* and *racial justice* are not figures of speech; they are public frauds, political acts with political consequences. Just as a half-truth is not a type of truth but a type of lie, so *equality* and *justice*, once modified by *racial*, become euphemisms for their opposites.

Du Bois's thumbnail summary—forced to ride Jim Crow—represents the end of the odyssey that Woodward chronicles in *Origins*. Woodward offers an equally laconic summary of the beginning of that odyssey:

> Much discussion about the Negro's civil rights, his political significance, his social status, and his aspirations can be shortened and simplified by a clear understanding of the economic status assigned him in the New Order. . . . The lives of the overwhelming majority of Negroes were still circumscribed by the farm and plantation. The same was true of the white people, but the Negroes, with few exceptions, were farmers without land (p. 205).

"Farmers without land" makes as good a summary of the starting point of Afro-Americans in the New South as "forced to ride Jim Crow" does of their destination. The same passage reminds us why Jim Crow will not do as a method of analysis:

> It remained for the New South to find . . . a definition of free labor, both black and white; for the white worker's place in the New Order would be vitally conditioned by the place assigned to the free black worker (p. 205).

(Note: Woodward's use of "assigned," emphasizing that an undemocratic settlement where Afro-Americans were concerned necessarily meant undemocratic limits on white people.)

It is perhaps in order, at this point, to say a few words about Woodward's observation that "[i]t took a lot of ritual and Jim Crow to bolster the creed of white supremacy in the bosom of a white man working for a black man's wages" (p. 211). The phrase may seem to echo W. E. B. Du Bois's "psychological wage" (the beloved pet of so-called whiteness studies at the moment) and tempt someone to connect Woodward's argument to arguments about white identity. In fact, however, Woodward's remark dif-

---

16. Stephen Kantrowitz, *Ben Tillman and the Reconstruction of White Supremacy* (Chapel Hill and London, 2000), 2.

fers from Du Bois's both in substance and in register. While Du Bois's remark is declaratory, Woodward's is sardonic. "It must be remembered," Du Bois explains, "that the white group of laborers, while they received a low wage, were compensated in part by a sort of public and psychological wage."[17] To Woodward, "ritual and Jim Crow" is more a symptom of white people's exploitation than a remedy or compensation for it. His point is not that Jim Crow compensated white people for exploitation but, rather, that white people suffered plenty of exploitation that needed compensating for. A few pages on in the same chapter, Woodward makes the point explicit:

> The rituals and laws that exempted the white worker from the penalties of caste did not exempt him from competition with black labor, nor did they carry assurance that the penalties of black labor might not be extended to white. The propagandists of the New-South order, in advertising the famed cheap labor of their region, were not meticulous in distinguishing between the color of their wares (p. 221).

Like everything race relations touches, segregation is liable to suffer trivialization on contact, typically in the form of the equation of segregation with separation. That equation is what possessed Joel Williamson to refer to the "peculiar kind of racial integration that slavery required" and John Anthony Scott, in a mirror-image fallacy, to consider slavery " 'the ultimate segregator.' "[18] Both are wrong, and for the same reason: Slavery was a system for the extortion of labor, not for the management of "race relations," whether by segregation or by integration. Woodward usually resists the confusion. (Not always: It was in the successive revisions of *Strange Career,* under the influence of various sociological nostrums, that he was most liable to the error.)[19]

---

17. W. E. Burghardt Du Bois, *Black Reconstruction in America: An Essay Toward a History of the Part Which Black Folk Played in the Attempt to Reconstruct Democracy in America, 1860–1880* (New York, 1935), 700.

18. Joel Williamson, "Wounds Not Scars: Lynching, the National Conscience, and the American Historian," *Journal of American History,* 83 (March 1997), 1233 (first quotation), 1239; John Anthony Scott, "Segregation: A Fundamental Aspect of Southern Race Relations, 1800–1860," *Journal of the Early Republic,* 4 (Winter 1984), 425 (second quotation). The same impulse leads Scott to classify the withdrawal of monastics from the secular world as another, albeit voluntary, manifestation of the same generic phenomenon of "isolation." Scott, "Segregation," 427.

19. In the preface to the third revised edition, Woodward refers to the "strange career of segregation," rather than of Jim Crow—a much narrower concept; and he speculates about Afro-Americans' "ambivalence" toward integration and "yearning for separate racial identity." In "The Career Becomes Stranger," the concluding chapter that he wrote for the third

In *Origins*, at least, Woodward understands segregation to be an act of political power, as well as a constitutional and moral wrong—an act of power that, whatever the popular sentiment behind it, gained its force from the authority of the state. Neglecting the act-of-power aspect accounts for scholars' treating the establishment of independent Afro-American churches and the passage of Jim Crow laws as the same phenomenon or as related or similar phenomena. The near-totemic significance often attached to the notion of powerless people's *agency* can lead to the conclusion that initiative in forming independent churches proves agency in bringing about segregation as a legal and political fact. It may also lead to a facile dismissal of segregation laws and the timing of their passage as matters of no importance in themselves, a view from which Afro-Americans who actually lived through the era when segregation laws took effect have dissented.[20] To equate segregation with separation, however (and why ever) accomplished, is to vacate questions of power and citizenship, making a mystery of the New South and, equally, of the civil rights movement. "Freedom now!" was a slogan to inspire the sacrifice of livelihood and even of life. "Integration now!" could scarcely inspire the expenditure of the breath required to shout it.

Woodward presents in *Origins* a relentlessly social-structural argument. He devotes much of his attention to getting a line on the social provenance, political connections, and economic projects and intentions of the ruling class. Letting hitherto unheard "voices" from the past speak, not in order to pose or answer questions deemed to be of moment, but for the pure antiquarian hell of it, is a doubtful enterprise. It did not interest Woodward and, I must say on my own account, is strictly an acquired taste. In our own time, when the overwhelming power of capitalist markets and their protagonists over nation-states and their hapless citizens passes virtually without comment or criticism, Woodward's insistence on getting to grips with capitalism

---

edition, he does not pursue his own insight that the civil rights movement completed a nineteenth-century agenda, rather than tackling a twentieth-century one. He therefore ends on a note of false paradox, emphasizing Afro-Americans' simultaneous demands for integration and separation but losing sight of the social predicament to which both were irrelevant. Woodward, *Strange Career of Jim Crow*, v (first quotation), vi (second quotation), vii (third quotation), 193. See also Howard N. Rabinowitz, "More Than the Woodward Thesis: Assessing *The Strange Career of Jim Crow,*" *Journal of American History*, 75 (December 1988), 842–56; and Woodward's response to his critics, "*Strange Career* Critics: Long May They Persevere," *ibid.*, 857–68.

20. For example, see Mamie Garvin Fields with Karen Fields, *Lemon Swamp and Other Places: A Carolina Memoir* (New York, 1983), 45–46.

may strike a quaint and rather archaic note. In discussing the proselytizing zeal of the industrialist Daniel Augustus Tompkins, Woodward is at some pains to make clear that it is not just industrialism for which Tompkins and his fellows sounded the trumpets, but "laissez-faire capitalism, freed of all traditional restraints, together with a new philosophy and way of life and a new scale of values" (p. 148).

The moonlight-and-magnolias nostalgia for slavery and the Old South, along with the cult of the Lost Cause, was part of the new order, according to Woodward, not an echo of the old. The " 'bonny blue flag,' " symbol of the Confederacy long before Lee's battle flag usurped that role, " 'is the symbol of nothing to the present generation of Southern men,' " Henry Watterson said in 1880 (p. 155). (He meant "white Southern men"; that was long before otherwise sane people began to believe the legend of a black Confederate phalanx.) Only in the 1890s did the Confederacy become an emotional symbol.[21] Woodward associates the "cult of racism" with that of archaism, all part of a new order seeking to burnish its claim to antiquity (pp. 154–57, quotation on p. 249).

Lynching and racist violence in many forms turn out to be one of the novel elements of the New South. That Woodward's discussion of lynching is brief is now a commonplace observation. Even in its brevity, it is valuable for its insistence that an overall tendency toward violence in the South provides the essential terms of reference for analyzing lynching and pogroms; and for its recognition that racist violence occurred in the context of the political settlement for which Booker T. Washington's Atlanta Exposition address provided the public ratification (pp. 350–54). Appropriately, much has been written about lynching since *Origins*. Some of this literature has been worthwhile, answering the questions why, where, who, when, under what circumstances, with whose permission, facilitation, or connivance, and with what result.[22] Some of it has added little beyond moral posturing.[23] Some of it has positively darkened counsel. For example, the authors of one study about lynching bend a perceptive observation by John Dollard—"Every Negro in the South knows that he is under a kind of sentence of death; he does not know when his turn will come, it may never come, but it

---

21. During the civil rights era the battle flag became a symbol of segregationists. Only in recent years has it been claimed as a symbol of "white heritage"—whatever that is.

22. See, for example, Jacquelyn Dowd Hall, *Revolt Against Chivalry: Jessie Daniel Ames and the Women's Campaign Against Lynching* (New York, 1979); and W. Fitzhugh Brundage, *Lynching in the New South: Georgia and Virginia, 1880–1930* (Urbana and Chicago, 1993).

23. Williamson, "Wounds Not Scars," 1221–53, is a particularly egregious example.

may also be at any time"—into a statement about contingency and agency, rather than a statement about living in fear for one's life. "The kind of contingency Dollard identified was tightly circumscribed, to be sure; it was without doubt criminal and terrible in its living and for a time nurturing of white supremacy," they argue. "But, still, it represented an indeterminateness predicated on and fostering agency."[24]

At every stage of a lynching-in-the-making, the authors inform us, something could happen to make events unfold differently. Their concluding non sequitur is that we had much better attend to the steps along the way rather than the finished process or (still less) the collective and aggregate phenomenon of lynching.[25] The essence of Damocles's predicament, it seems, is the tensile strength of the hair from which the sword hangs, rather than the circumstance that a sword is hanging over him by a hair in the first place. For all his brevity in dealing with lynching, Woodward never forgets the sword or how it came to be hanging by a hair over a man's head.

Origins is steeped in the South, full of its flavors and textures. Woodward remains alert, nonetheless, to the international context. More important than the direct international comparisons he occasionally makes (for example, in analyzing the credit system [pp. 180–81], homicide rates [p. 159], and regional disparities in wealth [p. 111]) is his exploration of foreign investment in the South, during a period when the bourgeoisie of England were scouring the earth for places to invest their surplus capital (pp. 118–20). In one of his wonderfully dry, satirical passages, he compares the New South "natives" with those of the European imperialist powers:

Such wretchedness [as that of white migrants to Arkansas and Texas] belonged to those "backward peoples" whom the leading imperial powers of Western Europe were in those days seeking to "develop," and to whom was applied by common international usage the curious term "natives." The teeming millions of kerchiefed Negroes in the Black Belt, with their "happy-go-lucky disposition," and the quaint "highlanders" of the mountains, with their "Elizabethan flavor" (invariably noted), fitted conveniently into the imperialistic pattern of "backward natives." But the observant traveler from the Northeast found some difficulty in accounting for other millions of Southern-

---

24. John Dollard, *Caste and Class in a Southern Town* (New Haven, 1937), 359 (first quotation); Larry J. Griffin, Paula Clark, and Joanne C. Sandberg, "Narrative and Event: Lynching and Historical Sociology," in W. Fitzhugh Brundage, ed., *Under Sentence of Death: Lynching in the South* (Chapel Hill and London, 1997), 40–41 (second quotation on p. 41).

25. Griffin, Clark, and Sandberg, "Narrative and Event," 41–42.

ers of approximately the same economic status who were not black, who bore English, Scotch, and Irish names, and about whom there was no appreciable Elizabethan flavor (p. 109).

Despite Woodward's deliberate concentration on power and those who wielded it, he does not treat Afro-Americans as passive objects rather than active subjects of history. His comments about Afro-American Protestant denominations (p. 453), about the Colored Farmers' Alliance (pp. 192, 220–21, 255–56), and about Afro-Americans' distaste for fusion in 1894 (p. 277) refute any such accusation. And even the most zealous apostles of "agency" would have to concede that Woodward credits Booker T. Washington with an ample share (pp. 356–67). But *Origins* does not, where Afro-Americans or anyone else is concerned, emphasize the inwardness of people's lives for its own sake. Woodward is much less interested in how Afro-southerners (or, for that matter, Euro-southerners) made lives for themselves within the cramped space available to them than in how and by whom that space was delimited and what rules governed life within it. Even his treatment of literature, the arts, and the sciences is not a rumination on these matters in, of, or for themselves, but on their relationship to the novel set of social relationships that constituted the New South.

The valid observation that much less secondary literature concerning Afro-Americans was available at the time Woodward wrote *Origins* (and that *Origins* stimulated much of the literature since produced) is not, therefore, an adequate explanation of why *Origins* focuses on some questions to the exclusion of others. Even if the large body of scholarship about Afro-Americans in the South that now exists had been available in 1951, *Origins* would still have emerged as a book about power and its ramifications rather than a book about the self-activity of the powerless. After all, Woodward made broader use than most of his contemporaries of the secondary literature about Afro-Americans, including much that others avoided because it fell on the wrong side of the color line or the line of political acceptability (or both, as in the case of W. E. B. Du Bois). Furthermore, Woodward has attributed great importance to his acquaintance with J. Saunders Redding during his stint at Georgia Tech and with Langston Hughes and other figures of the Harlem Renaissance during study at Columbia University in 1931–32, as well as to his later close intellectual relationship with John Hope Franklin.[26] His footnotes illustrate the debt he owed to such associa-

---

26. Woodward, *Thinking Back,* 85–86, 89.

tions. No doubt, had it been available to him, he would have drawn upon literature such as Peter J. Rachleff's study of Afro-American working-class political activism in Richmond, Eric Arnesen's study of Afro-American dockworkers in New Orleans, and James D. Anderson's study about educational philanthropy and Tuskegee.[27] Literature of that kind is more relevant to Woodward's questions than the kind in which the self-activity of the exploited and downtrodden is important just because it is self-activity, regardless of its efficacy.

Woodward was capable, of course, as are we all, of errors of judgment and fact. I have never been convinced, for example, by his analysis of class structure among Afro-Americans. "Soon after the war," he writes, "Negroes began to break up into differentiated social and economic classes that eventually reproduced on a rough scale the stratified white society" (p. 218). And later: "One of the most important developments in Negro history . . . was the rise of a whole separate system of society and economy on the other side of the color line. . . . Beginning as a largely undifferentiated class of former slaves, the race was soon sorted out into all the social and economic classes of the white capitalistic society upon which it was modeled" (pp. 365–66). Lacking a bourgeoisie, Afro-American society was, at best, a truncated facsimile of the white class structure. It cannot have been a true replica given that those at the bottom of Afro-American society did not answer to those at the top, while those at the top answered to white superiors.

I cannot resist closing with a reflection on an issue—language—that I wish Woodward had dealt with: not because it necessarily belongs in *Origins,* but because he could have dealt with it as no one else will ever do. Woodward did not write about language in *Origins,* though his quotations offer a rich sampling of the varied flavors of southern speech. I wish he had, because his comparativist instinct and his brisk way with foolishness would have made short work of the reified entity known to true believers as black English and attributed by them to the powerful surviving influence of an African meta-language. (I say "African meta-language" because even the true believers concede that Africans enslaved in North America spoke many different languages.) Ever the comparativist, Woodward would have wondered why there is no parallel concept of black Spanish, black Portuguese,

---

27. Peter J. Rachleff, *Black Labor in the South: Richmond, Virginia, 1865–1890* (Philadelphia, 1984); Eric Arnesen, *Waterfront Workers of New Orleans: Race, Class, and Politics, 1863–1923* (New York and Oxford, 1991); James D. Anderson, *The Education of Blacks in the South, 1860–1935* (Chapel Hill and London, 1988).

or black French, even though classical Yoruba (not just bits and pieces of grammar and vocabulary) survived in religious rituals in Cuba and Brazil well into the twentieth century, while Haiti and the Franco-Caribbean developed African-descended creole languages that are still spoken today. He would have noted the entire absence of a creole language in the Hispanic Caribbean and its presence in some and absence in other parts of the Anglo-Caribbean.[28]

It would not have taken Woodward long to notice that, despite a large influx of migrants whose mother tongue is some form of Jamaican Creole, there is no "black English" in Britain. Though typically bilingual in English and Creole, second-generation Caribbean Britons speak English in the accent of their class and region, just as white Britons do. For the most part, their children are not even bilingual. They may understand Creole if spoken slowly and may even be able to say a few heavily accented words in it; but most are monoglot speakers of a language indistinguishable from that of comparable white Britons. Having reached that point, Woodward would have found himself on familiar ground: the history of segregation in America. The speech patterns of Afro-Americans do not reflect a stronger survival of African linguistic patterns among Afro-Americans, as compared to Anglo-Caribbeans. Instead, they testify to the greater prevalence, strength, and rigidity in the United States, as compared to the United Kingdom, of segregated schooling, residence, and sociability, especially among the working class.

That, of course, is where Woodward came in. All the elaborations and internal linguistic analysis that make so-called black English seem a product of itself or a reflection of its speakers' identities or a fruitful arena for the exploration of subaltern cultural expression and creativity are secondary, at best, to the central point that it is one of the many outcomes of segregation. Which is to say that it is a result of the power of some people over others; an illustration, not of race (let alone racial identity) but of racism. It is black only in the sense that sharecropping or lynching is black. Precisely because it is an outcome of Jim Crow, a Jim Crow approach cannot account for it.

Woodward's refusal to jim-crow Jim Crow is the great gift that *Origins* has bestowed on the study of Afro-southerners. Recognizing the centrality

---

28. For a valuable discussion of the origin and current (as of 1985) status of creole languages in the Caribbean, see Mervyn C. Alleyne, "A Linguistic Perspective on the Caribbean," in Sidney W. Mintz and Sally Price, eds., *Caribbean Contours* (Baltimore and London, 1985), 155–79.

of the Negro Question, not just for the aspirations of Afro-southerners but for those of all southerners, Woodward placed the issue in the same zone where the big questions were to be engaged. But time does not invariably bring wisdom, and momentum is not necessarily progress. Whether we will put Woodward's gift to appropriate use and build on it—in our politics, our scholarship, our morals, our manners—remains to be seen.

Reflections on Woodward's *Origins*

I grew up in Yazoo City, Mississippi. When I left there in 1955 to attend college, I took with me beliefs and values common to white Mississippians of the time. Throughout four years of undergraduate education in the Midwest, I remained an unreconstructed southerner. In 1957, when President Dwight D. Eisenhower sent troops into Little Rock, I was outraged. If James C. Cobb thought E. Merton Coulter was bad on race relations, I am glad that he did not know me in those days.

In the spring of 1960 I took Morton Rothstein's seminar on late-nineteenth-century United States history at the University of Delaware, where I had enrolled in the M.A. program. The list of research topics included the New South. I had no idea what that term meant, but I was intrigued and decided to pursue it. At that point Rothstein and Walter J. Heacock, a Howard K. Beale student from the University of Wisconsin, conspired. They suggested that I start by reading W. J. Cash's *Mind of the South*.[1] For me, reading that book was like undergoing a religious conversion. My views of the South began to change, as did many long-held beliefs. After completing Cash, I read C. Vann Woodward's *Origins of the New South* and *Tom Watson, Agrarian Rebel* and went on to write a seminar paper comparing Watson and Ben Tillman.[2]

By the end of the semester, I knew that I wanted to study southern history, and in the fall of 1961 I entered Rice University, which had a tiny graduate program where I got a lot of individual attention, sometimes more than I wanted. Frank E. Vandiver was kind enough to let me escape the Civil War and do a dissertation on a New South topic. Although I worked at Rice, Woodward was a major intellectual guide. Shortly after arriving in Houston, I bought my own copy of *Origins,* which I reread and constantly consulted.

When I first taught a New South course in 1965, I taught Woodward because my lectures came largely from his works. By the time I offered that course for the final time in 2000, I had incorporated a lot of additional material, including the works of James C. Cobb, Barbara J. Fields, Glenda E. Gilmore, Robert C. McMath Jr., and Harold D. Woodman. But I still taught Woodward. So it is an honor to comment on the able articles written to commemorate the fiftieth anniversary of *Origins*'s publication.

Cobb's article stands apart from the others in that it rests largely on primary research. Reading extensively in the correspondence of Coulter, Glenn W. Rainey, Charles W. Ramsdell, and Wendell Holmes Stephenson enabled Cobb to develop a fresh account of the challenges Woodward confronted in writing *Origins*. When Woodward entered the profession in the 1930s, a reigning orthodoxy prevailed in southern history that closely resembled the New South Creed. Reconstruction had been a terrible mistake from which the Redeemers rescued the South. The Redeemers represented the restoration of the antebellum order, and they ushered in an era of honest government, economic growth, and racial and class harmony. Woodward had few historiographical models to follow in challenging the prevailing orthodoxy, but he drew inspiration from early writers of the Southern Literary Renaissance. He launched his own assault on the existing historiography by writing

---

1. W. J. Cash, *The Mind of the South* (New York, 1941).
2. C. Vann Woodward, *Origins of the New South, 1877–1913* (Baton Rouge, 1951), and *Tom Watson, Agrarian Rebel* (New York, 1938).

Tom Watson, a book so fine that it earned for him the opportunity to do the New South volume in the History of the South series.

In writing *Origins,* Cobb tells us, Woodward exploded New South myths. Nowhere did Woodward better illustrate this than in his treatment of the Redeemers. Instead of representing continuity with the policies of the antebellum leaders, Woodward argued, the Redeemers marked a sharp break. They encouraged the wasteful exploitation of the South's national resources, repressed African Americans, and ignored the plight of the agricultural masses. *Origins* also foreshadowed the Woodward thesis on the beginning of segregation, which received its full development in *The Strange Career of Jim Crow.*[3] As Glenda Gilmore noted, this was Woodward's one-two punch: first, he demolished the myth of the noble Redeemers, and then he explained that southern race relations were more complex after Reconstruction than Americans of later generations realized.

Cobb's article presents a stimulating account of the intellectual climate that Woodward confronted in writing *Origins.* The article also demonstrates that Cobb possesses a rare gift—the ability to make us laugh while also thinking critically about our history.

If the Redeemers were the bad guys in Woodward's story, the Populists were the good guys, and Robert McMath focuses most of his attention on these agrarian rebels. McMath finds that Woodward's interpretation of Populism remains largely intact. The movement represented an uprising of small, landowning farmers against the merchant supply system and the excesses of capitalism, which by the 1890s had fallen increasingly under the domination of large corporations. In view of the sizable body of Populist scholarship over the past half century, the survival of Woodward's interpretation is impressive.

One of the few weak points that McMath discovered in *Origins* involves the sharp distinction that Woodward drew between Populism and Progressivism. McMath argues that the two movements were closely related. To understand this relationship, as well as to acquire a more unified view of southern history for the period covered in *Origins,* McMath proposes expanding the perimeters of agrarian protest back into the Reconstruction era and forward into the administration of Woodrow Wilson. Tracing the beginnings of the agrarian uprising back into the 1860s demonstrates the continuity of rural protest over the course of the late nineteenth century, and

---

3. C. Vann Woodward, *The Strange Career of Jim Crow* (New York, 1955).

there is a lot of support for this view.[4] But the attempt to demonstrate a close link between Populism and Progressivism enters onto more controversial grounds. John D. Hicks suggested this approach long ago, and in 1999 Elizabeth Sanders made the strongest case to date for the decisive role that agrarian congressmen from the South and West played in enacting a broad array of Progressive-era reforms.[5] Given the recent appearance of Sanders's book, it remains to be seen how pervasive her influence will be in shaping the way historians view the relation between Populism and Progressivism.

There is, moreover, a substantial body of historical work that demonstrates fundamental differences between the two movements.[6] The Populists had strong faith in grassroots democracy, believing that the electorate, if given the opportunity, would make wise decisions. The Progressives tended to rely more on experts and bureaucratic agencies. Education reform illustrates this difference. The Southern Farmers' Alliance called for local control of schools that would give parents a greater voice in their children's education; the Progressives supported school consolidation and centralization of authority that weakened local control.[7] On the economic front, the Populists spoke harshly of large businesses that they perceived as threatening small producers. Their rhetoric and programs had leveling tendencies that people who subscribed to the New South Creed found disturbing. The Progressives, in contrast, supported programs that seemed less threatening. Identifying more closely with industrial and urban development, the Progressives found the economic and social systems that emerged in the late nineteenth century more compatible than did the Populists. It is possible that the Progressives shared more in common with the Redeemers than they did with the Populists. The Redeemers championed a form of economic development that the Populists took issue with, but the Progressives accepted

4. Theodore Saloutos, *Farmer Movements in the South, 1865–1933* (Berkeley, 1960), 31–87; Robert C. McMath Jr., *American Populism: A Social History, 1877–1898* (New York, 1993), 19–82.

5. John D. Hicks, "The Legacy of Populism in the Western Middle West," *Agricultural History*, 23 (October 1949), 225–36; Elizabeth Sanders, *Roots of Reform: Farmers, Workers, and the American State, 1877–1917* (Chicago, 1999).

6. Sheldon Hackney, *Populism to Progressivism in Alabama* (Princeton, 1969), 108–46; Robert W. Cherny, *Populism, Progressivism, and the Transformation of Nebraska Politics, 1885–1915* (Lincoln, 1981), 149–66; O. Gene Clanton, "Populism, Progressivism, and Equality: The Kansas Paradigm," *Agricultural History*, 51 (July 1977), 559–81.

7. Theodore R. Mitchell, *Political Education in the Southern Farmers' Alliance, 1887–1900* (Madison, Wisc., 1987), 124–49, 176–96; William A. Link, *The Paradox of Southern Progressivism, 1880–1930* (Chapel Hill, 1992), xi–xii, 10–16, 125–42.

the Redeemers' goal of an industrial and modernized society. To help achieve that goal, the Progressives added programs for improved public roads, schools, and health programs.

When McMath discusses relations between white Populists and African Americans, he is on more solid ground. In *Origins* and *The Strange Career of Jim Crow* Woodward argued that Populism offered a constructive alternative to the harsh expressions of racism associated with the Democratic Party. McMath finds that the Woodward thesis still stands, but like many others who have pondered it, he insists that the thesis requires substantial qualification. A fine line always divided the Populists and the Democrats on race. Early in the 1890s, for example, Tom Watson called for black and white farmers to join forces in addressing common problems, but a decade later Watson supported disfranchisement of blacks. Woodward explained this change in Watson in terms of a Jekyll and Hyde interpretation that presented two Watsons, the first a young crusader who rallied the Populists, the second an older man embittered by the losses he had sustained in his congressional campaigns.

McMath does not accept Woodward's explanation. Instead, he sees one Watson who consistently and simultaneously embodied positive and negative characteristics. In the heyday of the People's Party Watson saw the benefits of interracial cooperation, but by the Progressive era his racist instincts predominated. Watson was not alone in embodying racism and reform. This was true for many white southerners who became active in the agrarian organizations of the late nineteenth century and who supported Progressive programs early in the twentieth century. Between the Civil War and World War I southern reform movements had their dark sides along with their more positive manifestations, and McMath correctly reminds us to view the movements in their entirety.

Barbara Fields discusses Woodward's treatment of African Americans without giving attention to his thesis on the origins of Jim Crow legislation. She commended him for not treating African American experiences as an appendage of southern history. Instead, Woodward recognized the centrality of blacks in shaping southern history, and he discussed them within the broad developments affecting land, agriculture, industry, and politics. Since Woodward emphasized the relation between economics and politics, he recognized that the ruling class of whites mobilized power to relegate blacks to an inferior caste. Reconstruction had enabled blacks to participate in democratic processes, and the Redeemers worked to curtail that trend. At first, they relied on practices like replacing elective offices with appointive offices and on state laws like one in South Carolina that required voters to deposit ballots correctly in eight separate ballot boxes. Beginning in 1890 white leaders rewrote and amended state constitutions to disfranchise blacks along with poor whites.

As she has argued previously, Fields does not accept race as a valid category that has an empirical base in biology or culture.[8] Woodward also did not take that approach in discussing African Americans, and that is a major reason Fields finds *Origins* so attractive. Nor did Woodward make the mistake committed by later historians who equated voluntary forms of racial separation, like black churches and fraternal organizations, with segregation statutes that mobilized government power to require blacks to ride Jim Crow railroad cars.

It is possible that Woodward's discussion of African Americans, more than any other feature, accounts for *Origins*'s long life. In contrast to other scholars who had completed volumes for the History of the South series by the time *Origins* appeared in 1951, Woodward was far ahead of his time in the treatment of black southerners.

Of the five speakers at the symposium, Glenda Gilmore had the most challenging assignment: to discuss the role of women and gender in *Origins*, issues that Woodward did not even address. I wondered how she would do it. Then I read her paper and discovered that she fulfilled her assignment very effectively. Throughout his career Woodward propounded the importance of change as a force in shaping southern history. He demonstrated that himself in writing *Origins* as he wiped the slate clean of older interpretations and presented a fresh way of looking at the South. Historians who came into the profession late in the twentieth century and who included gender in their work have found *Origins* a good starting point because Woodward broadened the possibilities of southern history. In her book *Gender and Jim Crow*, Gilmore examined some of the people and events that Woodward had discussed earlier.[9] By including the role of gender, Gilmore deepened our understanding of what happened in North Carolina race relations late in the nineteenth century and early in the twentieth century. Her work, of course, has implications for the entire South, and on reading her book Woodward immediately understood its importance.

---

8. Barbara J. Fields, "Ideology and Race in American History," in J. Morgan Kousser and James M. McPherson, eds., *Region, Race, and Reconstruction: Essays in Honor of C. Vann Woodward* (New York, 1982), 143–77.

9. Glenda Elizabeth Gilmore, *Gender and Jim Crow: Women and the Politics of White Supremacy in North Carolina, 1896–1920* (Chapel Hill, 1996).

Harold Woodman reminds us of the importance of the Beardian approach that Woodward used to demonstrate that the Civil War marked a sharp dividing line in southern history. First with the Radicals of Reconstruction and then with the Redeemers, the South came under the influence of middle-class leaders. Of the two groups, the Redeemers had far more influence because they laid the foundations for the modern South's approach to race, politics, economics, and law.

Woodman focuses on aspects of *Origins* that have come under fire. But instead of conceding that the criticisms undermined Woodward, Woodman suggests ways in which the criticisms actually strengthen Woodward's arguments for the importance of change and class conflict in shaping southern history. The most intriguing issue that Woodman dealt with involved the role of the planters. Woodward argued that the antebellum planter class did not survive the war and that a new business-oriented middle class became the dominant force in the region. Since the 1970s a stream of studies have argued against Woodward by marshaling evidence for a high degree of persistence within the planter class from 1850 to 1880. Instead of a new order taking control after Reconstruction, these studies argue, the old planter elite continued to rule. While not denying the value of the studies that argue for persistence, Woodman suggests that they focused on too narrow a time span. By the early twentieth century there arose a new class of large business plantations like the Delta & Pine Land Company in Mississippi and the big units that Neil Foley described in the coastal bend region of Texas.[10] These business planters represented the very kind of new men whom Woodward believed replaced the antebellum planter class.

In explaining how the business planters became a strong force by the early twentieth century, Woodman helps us understand the importance of time in the development of the New South. The bourgeois economic order that the Redeemers worked for did not suddenly triumph immediately after Reconstruction. As Woodman noted, the descendants of the antebellum planters actually enjoyed a high level of persistence as late as 1880, but twenty years after that a new class of planters had arisen. By 1900, moreover, Populism, the last major protest against the new business-industrial order, had fallen, and onto the scene came the Progressives, who would

---

10. Neil Foley, *The White Scourge: Mexicans, Blacks, and Poor Whites in Texas Cotton Culture* (Berkeley and Los Angeles, 1997); Foley, "Mexicans, Mechanization, and the Growth of Corporate Cotton Culture in South Texas: The Taft Ranch, 1900–1930," *Journal of Southern History*, 62 (May 1996), 275–302.

carry on the work of the Redeemers by making sure that the South did not abandon its newly acquired bourgeois status. Jump ahead a half century to 1949. Then V. O. Key could point to a one-party political system, racial segregation, and the rule of black belt elites to argue that the South remained markedly different from the rest of the country.[11] After another twenty years even those institutions fell, and the South had come ever closer on its journey to full integration with prevailing national norms. Has the South now lost its last vestiges of regional distinctiveness? I won't open that can of worms, but I agree with Woodman's point that the South reached the key turning point in losing its distinctiveness at the end of the nineteenth century, by which time it had made the transition to a bourgeois society.

The articles originally presented at the Rice University symposium on February 23–24, 2001, deepen our appreciation for *Origins* and help us to understand why we still read the book a half century after its publication. As I reflected on the articles, I asked myself what southern history would be today if C. Vann Woodward had never lived. More than any other single person, Woodward shaped the field. We have discussed *Origins,* but one can argue that *Tom Watson* is a stronger book, one that has the potential to last even longer than *Origins.* Has any American historian ever written a more successful dissertation? Published by a major commercial house soon after its completion, *Tom Watson* speaks to readers today in ways that are as meaningful as the ways it spoke to readers in the 1930s. And there are the essays that Woodward wrote in the 1950s that appeared in *The Burden of Southern History.*[12]

One January day in 2001 I had lunch with a Mississippian visiting the University of Georgia. I asked her how she planned to vote in the upcoming referendum on changing the Mississippi state flag. She said something about wanting to preserve southern heritage. I almost tried to persuade her to vote for changing the flag, but I kept quiet. Later that day I copied Woodward's "Search for Southern History" and mailed it to her.[13] If that essay did not start her on the road to reconsidering southern heritage, nothing I could say would help.

---

11. V. O. Key Jr., *Southern Politics in State and Nation* (New York, 1949), 3–12, 664–75.

12. C. Vann Woodward, *The Burden of Southern History* (Baton Rouge, 1960).

13. C. Vann Woodward, "The Search for Southern Identity," *Virginia Quarterly Review,* 34 (Summer 1958), 321–38, reprinted in *The Burden of Southern History,* chap. 1.

Gender and Vann Woodward

I didn't dare tell John Boles that I almost backed out of commenting on these papers last week after I came across a review of the John H. Roper biography of C. Vann Woodward in which our favorite curmudgeon, Ben Wall, wrote that "lesser historians as well as those of some stature have buzzed around his books and essays like gnats around a sweaty mule."[1] None of my colleagues today qualify as gnats, but I have grave fears for myself. Then I found Woodward himself writing that it is better to be criticized than forgotten, so I took heart.[2]

The papers we have heard at this symposium have been so carefully done that even a dedicated critic would have a hard time coming up with useful

---

1. Bennett H. Wall, "C. Vann Woodward, Southerner: An Essay Review," Louisiana History, 30 (Winter 1989), 85–90 (quotation on p. 88).

2. C. Vann Woodward, Thinking Back: The Perils of Writing History (Baton Rouge, 1986), 5.

questions. I propose instead to pick up on Glenda Gilmore's remarkable paper—a paper Vann would certainly have admired for its imaginative construction and literary excellence. What I propose is a variation on a theme by Gilmore.

While Gilmore's thoughts about clues historians of women might find in Woodward's work are intriguing, I want rather to talk about the clues he might have found for himself but did not. Beginning with *Tom Watson,* Woodward noted that Mrs. Watson—though appearing as a fragile southern lady—had in fact run several farms and taken care of all the family's business affairs; thus, Woodward wrote about her "relieving her husband," presumably for more important work. It did not occur to him to follow this thread, to ask how typical she might have been, to ask why the image was so different from the reality. In fact, that's all we hear about Mrs. Watson until several hundred pages later where she is described as "aging rapidly" and Tom is said to have been seeking "compensation" (Woodward's word) with one Mrs. Lytle—"a large, vigorous young woman of Irish extraction." The relationship, the apparently Puritan Mr. Woodward assured us, was not scandalous, no matter what the rumors said.[3]

One paragraph in *Origins of the New South* includes statistics about women and children "driven into the mills" and quotes with apparent approval the comments of the U.S. Commissioner of Labor about the deplorable "moral condition" of the "working girls." Woodward made no connection between this observation and the extremely low pay of those factory girls. In *Origins* he also observed that the Farmers' Alliance as well as the Populists admitted women to their deliberations, but he evinced no interest in what brought the women there or what part they played in the development of the party. He mistakenly gave the Farmers' Alliance credit for providing the first opportunity for women to take a public role. (The Woman's Christian Temperance Union [WCTU] had been doing that for years.)[4]

If we turn to the chapter "Progressivism—For Whites Only," more questions arise. Had Woodward been a little acquainted with the local and state associations of black women, of which there were hundreds in the South, and with the work they were doing, he could have found black Progressives in considerable numbers. Of course he paid no attention to the even more

---

3. C. Vann Woodward, *Tom Watson, Agrarian Rebel* (New York, 1938), 46 (first quotation), 417 (second and third quotations).

4. C. Vann Woodward, *Origins of the New South, 1877–1913* (Baton Rouge, 1951), 226 (first quotation), 227 (second and third quotations), 195.

numerous white women's voluntary associations that played such an important part in creating what came to be labeled Progressivism in the South. He
wrote about the lottery problem in Louisiana but did not recognize the
major anti-lottery campaign that was carried out by Louisiana women. It is
no excuse to say that there were no monographs—all these organizations
were clearly visible in the primary sources he used.[5]

The pattern of failing to understand women as significant historical
actors continued. Woodward referred to a couple of comparatively minor
figures among southern women activists but seems to have been unaware of
the significant leaders who changed the South: Nellie Nugent Somerville in
Mississippi, Jean and Kate Gordon in Louisiana, Laura Clay in Kentucky,
Mary Munford and Lila Meade Valentine in Virginia, Mary Latimer
McLendon in Georgia, and many, many others. Ida B. Wells-Barnett is nowhere to be seen, nor is Lugenia Burns Hope or any other black women
leaders.

When Woodward wrote that the work of Charles D. McIver for improved education in North Carolina had "small results," he seemed to be
unaware of McIver's major achievement, the creation of the North Carolina
Normal and Industrial College, which opened the possibility of higher education (and by extension certain careers) to numbers of North Carolina
women. Nor is there any reference to Lulu McIver, who both during her
husband's lifetime and after made major contributions to North Carolina
women's education.[6]

The pattern changed a little in his seventies when Woodward discovered
Mary Chesnut and, it seemed to me, quite fell in love with her. Perhaps her
literary gifts drew him, or her feisty personality. But in any case she was a
late acquisition and was not an activist in *his* period.[7]

Gilmore offers an intriguing hypothesis: that Woodward *did* understand
the significance of women in southern social and political history but chose
to leave them out of his analysis because he did not wish to stir up the old
arguments about white women/black men and the emotions connected with
lynching. I said earlier that he would have liked her paper, but on this point
I think he would have said, "My dear, you give me too much credit. In fact,
I just didn't notice."

---

5. *Ibid.*, chap. 14, and pp. 11–14.

6. *Ibid.*, 398.

7. C. Vann Woodward, ed., *Mary Chesnut's Civil War* (New Haven, 1981); Woodward
and Elisabeth Muhlenfeld, eds., *The Private Mary Chesnut: The Unpublished Civil War Diaries* (New York, 1984).

Indeed, that the history of southern women activists could have contributed so significantly to his purpose of subverting the received wisdom suggests to me that he would not have missed the chance to thus strengthen his case had he recognized the possibility that was there.

All the clues suggest that Woodward did not take women of any persuasion seriously. He wrote of WCTU members as "White Ribboners" in a slightly derisive tone, leaving the impression that they were somewhat ridiculous. These women were major reformers. He said nothing whatever about their serious contribution to doing away with the convict lease system and to prison reform. Similarly, the section in which he wrote about Kate Barnard is pure southern gentleman: "A pretty and apparently irresistible champion of the underdog, Miss Barnard at the age of twenty-seven was made state commissioner of charities and corrections of Oklahoma by the Farmers' Union and labor-union men, who . . . cheered her every utterance." The implication is clear that she got the job because she was pretty (and sexy?).[8]

This treatment of the few women he did notice is instructive. I am reminded of a footnote to a long-ago critique of Richard Hofstadter's *Age of Reform* that might serve equally well for his dear friend Woodward:

> A novelist achieves his effects not merely through the substance of what he says but by the effectiveness of his technique. A critic needs, therefore, to be as aware of the one as of the other. . . . [For] a scholar having the special literary skills of Richard Hofstadter it becomes important. . . . [R]esults are sometimes achieved by the author's talent in the art of suggestion rather than by explicit argument and supporting fact. Individuals are hung, drawn and quartered but in such an innocent and disarming way that no unfriendliness seems intended. The skillful imputation of faintly discreditable motives; the artful selection of illustrative materials; damning with the faintest of praise these and other techniques are used to belittle, patronize and ridicule without striking a direct blow. When this kind of technical virtuosity is combined with the imagination and genuine brilliance of a writer . . . , it is difficult for the reader not to relax the standards of verification to which less talented writers are held.[9]

In short, although Woodward is known to all of us as an intellectual subversive, his ambition to redraw the nature of southern history did not in-

---

8. Woodward, *Origins of the New South*, 391 (first quotation), 423 (second quotation).

9. Andrew M. Scott, "The Progressive Era in Perspective," *Journal of Politics*, 21 (November 1959), 687–88 n. 7.

clude rethinking the way women were perceived. Because his work was so important, we hold him to a higher standard than his contemporaries, almost none of whom paid any attention to women in their scholarship. We think that someone as insightful as he was should have noticed—but in this area he shared the cultural blindness of his time.

I believe there is a close connection between his failure to recognize women as historical actors and his view of women as historians. My evidence comes from personal experience. Vann and I met—when he was forty-one and I was twenty-nine—at that memorable Southern Historical Association meeting when he and a couple of others had arranged to tweak the old-timers and strike a blow for justice—integration—by arranging for John Hope Franklin to give a paper.

I was there because my Harvard mentor, with typical Harvard certainty, had assured me that there was only one person doing decent work in southern history, and of course I must meet him at once. So I was introduced as a just-passed-her-orals graduate student preparing to write on southern Progressives. Vann was polite but skeptical, and not exactly forthcoming. I was stung enough to note in my journal that he was "not as impressive in person as he is in writing." Only years later did I understand how it might strike a rising leader in the field when an untried young person appeared to say she was writing on a subject about which he was about to publish a pathbreaking chapter, and a young person who happened to be female.

He was far from alone in his day and generation. I remember quite well arriving in Chapel Hill after teaching in an all-male college in Pennsylvania only to be told that the University of North Carolina history department had "never had a woman and never planned to." A few years earlier Guion Griffis Johnson had been assured, by one of the old fogies who had so offended the young Woodward in other ways, that women simply couldn't "do history." This to one of the most gifted historians of her generation! There was quite a stir when Fletcher M. Green, faced with unexpectedly high enrollments, hired me as a part-time visitor—to teach three sections of the introductory course five days a week—because I was already there and inexpensive. When I showed up at the department, nobody had thought to arrange an office, and the secretaries were not sure they should type my articles.

A couple of years later Richard Watson, who would become a beloved friend, wrote politely to ask if I would be willing to teach at Duke "until they could find somebody." The clear assumption was that "somebody" meant a man.

Years after the fact I learned that my early essay "The 'New Woman' in the New South" caused a furor at an editorial meeting of the *South Atlantic Quarterly:* was it, the members demanded, really history or just politics? The staff was overruled by the editor, who announced that he knew that women had played significant roles in the past. After all, he studied English history.[10]

Fast-forward a few years: In 1970 it was my job to present recommendations from the Organization of American Historians (OAH) committee on women to the board of that organization. Among other things we laid before the nearly all-male board was a careful analysis of four or five of the most widely used American history textbooks—including one of which Vann was a coauthor—documenting their almost total inattention to women. He sat frowning and as soon as I finished said, "Surely, Anne, you aren't suggesting *censorship!*" If only my scholar's instinct had told me to record my answer—it is lost, unless the board minutes took note, which I doubt they did. But the remark was, as a psychologist I once knew was fond of saying, "highly diagnostic."

Though he clearly thought Willie Lee Rose and Barbara Fields could do excellent history, neither of them were historians of women. Nothing in his writing showed that he had read any of the flood of southern women's history that began to flow in 1970. Year after year I waited in vain for him to say something, anything, about *The Southern Lady.*[11] He never did. As late as 1985 he still routinely spoke of historians as "he." In the index to *Thinking Back* three women's names appear: Margaret Bourke-White, Gertrude Stein, and Barbara Fields, only one of the three a card-carrying historian.

On a slightly different tack: Vann was, as we hear over and over, a man who loved irony. Did he ever, I wonder, notice the irony that a man so reserved that he often puzzled even his closest friends was becoming, possibly, the most exhaustively documented of any twentieth-century historian? Or one whose scholarly work was so often discussed in connection with his life experience?

I even wonder whether in spite of his well-known reticence, at some level he wished to be understood. Otherwise how explain the hours and hours of interviews he gave to John Herbert Roper, all carefully reconstructed by his auditor and made available to readers in the Southern Historical Collec-

---

10. Anne Firor Scott, "The 'New Woman' in the South," *South Atlantic Quarterly,* 61 (Autumn 1962), 473–83.

11. Anne Firor Scott, *The Southern Lady: From Pedestal to Politics, 1830–1930* (Chicago and London, 1970).

tion?[12] How explain his cooperation in allowing Roper to interview a long list of people whom he had encountered at some stage of his life? Among those interviewed there were three or four women, three who had taught him early in his life, and there was some reference to U. B. Phillips's daughter. But none of the adult women of his own generation or those who had been his students is on the list of interviewees. Perhaps therefore bits and pieces of my own experience may add a little to Roper's impressive, if somewhat suspect, archive.

Despite the rocky start and an occasional bad patch, Vann and I were friends for fifty years and corresponded regularly. He typed his own letters; they were usually brief and, one might say, laconic. Not what you could call outgoing. Yet when the Woodwards came to our house for dinner, he showed a different side—by paying such close attention to the children that they thought he was simply great and remembered him ever after.

Every now and then he abandoned his normal reserve, and there were surprising little bursts of confidentiality. The White House Conference on Civil Rights in 1966 was one such occasion. The setting spurred him to response; we sat together through two days and carried on a whispered commentary on what we were witnessing—if only I could reconstruct that commentary now, this would be a real contribution to his biography!

One of the difficult moments in our friendship came in 1979. I had been flattered and challenged by being asked to comment on his OAH paper on Mrs. Chesnut. I had spent an inordinate amount of time preparing for this, trying to live up to his own standards for English prose, and was pleased with what I had come up with. It was not a profound critique but a suggestion of things about the diary that he had overlooked, things that seemed to me significant. Yet when we went for coffee afterward, I waited in vain for some comment about my carefully crafted comments. He talked about all kinds of things but said not a word about my paper—what a letdown! I think being ignored is even worse than being criticized. Then, preparing for this meeting, I finally read the introduction to *Mary Chesnut's Civil War,* published two years after that panel, and there, to my amazement, I found my argument incorporated. Had he heard me after all? Or (it happens to all of us!) had it come back to him as his own idea? I will never know.

---

12. It should be noted, however, that these reports often tell more about Roper than they do about Woodward. Roper did not use a tape recorder but "wrote up" the interviews after the fact. Presumably he sent them to Woodward to be corrected, but a good deal of what is there cannot be independently corroborated. See John Herbert Roper, *C. Vann Woodward, Southerner* (Athens, Ga., and London, 1987).

He did become somewhat conservative as he grew older. There was the inexplicable Herbert Aptheker affair, his criticism of the students who took over Harvard buildings, his objection when the OAH decided to engage in some outreach activities. Scholars should do their work, he said testily, not proselytize—this despite his own history of skillful persuasion under the guise of history.

But I begin to sound like one of Ben Wall's gnats.

When all is said, he was a great man. In his memoir he quoted H. Stuart Hughes with approval: "Unless there is some . . . elective affinity linking the student to his subject, the results will be pedantic and perfunctory. . . . The man who does not feel issues deeply cannot write great history about them."[13] From very early he aspired to write great history. And, more than most of us, he succeeded.

I believe that at the end he was still ambivalent about being a historian, wondering if he should have chosen literature. At Emory University his closest friends were two poets. At Yale University he was much attached to Robert Penn Warren. The large picture of Faulkner over his Yale desk is legendary, and he said to Roper that Faulkner had influenced him perhaps more than he knew. But he also knew he did not have the gift for fiction, at least not purposeful fiction. Yet he did not want to be the kind of historian who had so offended his own young sensibilities at Chapel Hill in the 1930s.

As early as 1979 my journal notes that he was fretting a bit about aging. About that time, Roper's notes indicated that *he* worried that Woodward was too frail for some of the things he insisted on doing. Neither of them could foresee a saga that happened twenty years later when the Southern Historical Association planned a ninetieth birthday party for Woodward. He set out to get to the meeting. First his plane was canceled in New Haven, so he drove, alone, to Hartford in a pelting rainstorm, which made him miss the turn to the airport. Eventually he found his way back, only to face another canceled flight. Still, he showed up in Birmingham not, apparently, much the worse for wear and suggesting that we go at once to find a drink.

William S. McFeely probably offered the best summary in a comment to me: "He was a very complex man who showed different sides of himself to different people. Nobody fully knows him." Certainly I did not but could say, as he said of Faulkner, of course he influenced me, probably even more than I realized.

We should all be so lucky as to be the subject of such serious inquiry two generations or more after we began.

---

13. Quoted in Woodward, *Thinking Back*, 30.

C. Vann Woodward and the Confessions of a "Continuitarian"

The age of C. Vann Woodward in southern studies has now come to a close. As these trenchant and valuable articles disclose, his work, however, continues to inform us. Since he is no longer alive, we can reminiscence with less constraint and criticize without embarrassing him or ourselves. But while challenging some of Woodward's most tenaciously held ideas, these articles retain the deep respect that his long tenure in the profession and his brilliance of thought fairly demand. In using some personal recollections, I will avail myself of the precedent set by one of the speakers at the symposium where these articles were first presented.

Glenda Gilmore's article marvelously combines a personal reminiscence, an informative survey of gender in southern history, and an elegant appreciation of Woodward's unanticipated openness to change. She justly points out how *Origins of the New South* does not meet current feminist requirements. But Gilmore notes that Woodward himself, the champion of change over continuity, did change to a remarkable degree. Thanks to her splendid *Gender and Jim Crow*, which, to her surprise, he much admired, he became a convert to feminist history.[1] Moreover, she recalls his telling her how much he regretted that *Origins of the New South* had not been composed at a later stage in life. Such a delay, he confessed, would have offered him the advantage of reading works like hers and expanding the intellectual breadth of his study. Surely Vann Woodward's own continuity—reaching almost a century—provided him with the time to reconsider old assumptions.

On this point I differ a little from the approach of Woodward's worthy successor at Yale. Continuity seems to me no less significant than change. Glenda Gilmore's southern experience has apparently taught her the relevance of unexpected transformations. As a transplanted Yankee at an early age, I was more struck by what seemed the timelessness of southern life than she. Like her, I, too, was steeped in the lore of a now departed South. My highly intellectual and Victorian grandmother, Eliza M. Little of Montgomery, presiding over my early years, had something to do with a lifelong devotion to history. She was as dedicated to books as Gilmore's grandmother Candy was to truck farming in a Greensboro suburb. She used to have me read to her a paragraph from a dry eighth-grade history textbook, shut it, and then recite the chief ideas in the passages selected before moving on to the next. Why this did not turn me off from history forever remains mysterious. But my father, raised in Eufaula, Barbour County, Alabama, was the authority to introduce me to the lore and history of the South. At bedtime he often read aloud from the Reverend Abram Ryan's collection of melancholy post-Confederate poems. The Catholic priest's lugubrious "The Conquered Banner" was so much a favorite that I memorized it. It closes with the immortal lines:

> Furl that Banner, softly, slowly!
> Treat it gently—it is holy—
> For it droops above the dead.
> Touch it not—unfold it never,
> Let it droop there, furled forever. . . .

My father's efforts took place in the quite alien environment of Harrisburg, the state capital of Pennsylvania—and my birthplace—in the 1930s. At age

---

1. Glenda Elizabeth Gilmore, *Gender and Jim Crow: Women and the Politics of White Supremacy in North Carolina, 1896–1920* (Chapel Hill, 1996).

eight, however, I was sent by my parents to live in Sewanee, Tennessee, with Mrs. Little, who had recently moved there from the fourth floor of the family residence in Harrisburg. For me it was indeed a sharp break from the continuity of Yankeedom that I had up to then experienced. My writing *Southern Honor: Ethics and Behavior in the Old South* many years later had something to do with early and not altogether positive reactions to the new locale. Sewanee was steeped in Episcopalian ritual, Confederate nostalgia, and the seemingly everlasting conventions of Jim Crow and white supremacy throughout the forties and mid-fifties. At the latter point in time, I had left the South forever. (After all, Florida, or at least Gainesville with its liberal politics, is not really southern anymore.) Continuity or discontinuity in a life experience—which was more important? Without a doubt, we all have a little of each in our makeup. But Woodward's own move from the South to the cold North suggests his own preference for discontinuity.

Glenda Gilmore notes how Vann Woodward, as he aged, proved surprisingly more flexible on entertaining new ideas and reexamining his old ones, even those that challenged his ideas about abrupt change. I thoroughly agree. His combining historical interpretation and literary craftsmanship in his own work helps to explain his open-mindedness. If a book or article were soundly researched and well written, he had the acuity to appreciate it whether he agreed with the conclusions or not. Not all critics, alas, are so fair-minded. On a visit with him, just a few weeks after his lamentable and ultimately fatal heart-valve operation in late July 1999, he proudly handed me a review he had just published of Eugene D. Genovese's *A Consuming Fire*. While taking exception to much of the argument, Woodward concluded that the "small volume" had been "written with intellectual rigor and impressive scholarship." He recommended that it be placed "on the required reading list of all seriously interested in Southern history."[2]

More important, as Gilmore illustrates, his insistence on the breaks in southern history, which *Origins* did so much to illustrate, did not remain as single-minded and doctrinaire in his own opinions as he grew in years. Aging sometimes freezes the old in the stasis of the past. As a life lengthens, continuity may be deemed preferable to abrupt change, which might seem to augur mortality's relentless advance. Not so in Vann Woodward's case. In any event, as we who worked under his direction well know, he had always adhered to a cardinal principle. He was firmly convinced that students

---

2. C. Vann Woodward, "Confederate Theology and Yankee Economics," *Civil War Book Review*, 1 (Summer 1999), 5.

must find their own way, reach their own conclusions, scrutinize reigning ideas, including even his own. On occasion, his subalterns might have compelled him to adjust or even retract long-treasured interpretations that seemed no longer supportable. That is certainly why Woodward's students from Johns Hopkins and Yale have been so clannishly loyal. Not that he was any pushover, mind. You certainly had to substantiate your arguments and offer them in prose as lucid as talent and experience permitted.

But to return to the issue of continuity and discontinuity in his thinking. On the occasion of Woodward's retirement, James M. McPherson, J. Morgan Kousser, and publisher Sheldon Meyer put together a festschrift for him, entitled *Region, Race, and Reconstruction*.³ At a meeting of the Organization of American Historians in Philadelphia in 1982, we presented it to Vann at a memorable banquet at Bookbinder's. At Meyer's request, Vann had just finished reading *Southern Honor* and recommended it for publication. When we chanced to meet in the hotel lobby on the way to the dinner, his words of enthusiasm meant more to me than a score of favorable reviews.

I had had good reason to worry, though, about how my former supervisor would react to the work. In the opening pages I had proposed the long continuity of a regional ethical system pretty much along the lines that W. J. Cash in *The Mind of the South* had sketched. Woodward had always had little use for Cash. He accused the North Carolina journalist of denigrating southern letters, dismissing the contribution of the Jeffersonian enlightenment, and underrating the significance of the Populist insurgency. In addition, Woodward charged Cash with neglecting any signs of southern disunity, dissent, discontinuity, and diversity and of portraying a seamless past from the building of Jamestown's fortress to the rise of Atlanta's skyscrapers. With regard to the jackhammers and swinging cranes to erect them in the year that the First World War began, Cash had remarked, "Softly; do you not hear behind that the gallop of Jeb Stuart's cavalrymen?" Woodward retorted, "The answer is 'No!' Not one ghostly echo of a gallop. And neither did Jack Cash. He only thought he did when he was bemused."⁴

I had long thought that Woodward had missed the point. Cash had continued, "Do you not recognize it for the native gesture of an incurably ro-

---

3. J. Morgan Kousser and James M. McPherson, eds., *Region, Race, and Reconstruction: Essays in Honor of C. Vann Woodward* (New York, 1982).

4. C. Vann Woodward, "The Elusive Mind of the South," in *American Counterpoint: Slavery and Racism in the North-South Dialogue* (Boston, 1971), 261–83 (quotation on p. 282).

mantic people, enamoured before all else of the magnificent and the spectacular?" After a few more lines of text, Cash retreated a pace or two and admitted to a fanciful indulgence. But he refused to relinquish his primary point: white southern pride—Texas-size bravado, one might say—prompted such extravagance. Goaded by critics of slavery and frightened by vastly superior northern development, a defensive rejection of regional inferiority had surely appeared before and during the Civil War, as Cash had stressed. The post–Civil War South's adoption of Yankee ways—skyscrapers, banks, and Rotary Club notions of Progress—did not mean genuine ethical and moral change, that is, a substantial change of heart. To achieve the kind of moral advance that Woodward earnestly sought would take a half century, another world war, and what Woodward in a Cash-like metaphor called "the Bulldozer Revolution."[5] In fact, Cash and Woodward shared a certain literary bent, even a common talent for the memorable phrase or apt metaphor.

Yet there were differences, too. Cash was himself a victim of New South propaganda about the alleged horrors and failure of Republican Reconstruction. As Jim Cobb mentioned during the question and answer session after his symposium presentation, Woodward blamed the North Carolinian for perpetuating the tired myths about Reconstruction and Redeemer glory, and on that point he had every reason to complain. The return of the old planter elite and the rise of New South boosters were not something that Cash ought to have celebrated. He had felt as strongly as Woodward had about the Redeemers' sins of hypocrisy and worker coercion. But Cash was still drawn to some of the myths that he was fiercely determined to unmask.

Whatever his visceral reactions to Cash, Woodward could not ignore the persistent intrusiveness of the past upon the present, nor did he really wish to. After all, William Faulkner's picture hung on his office wall. And even on that wonderful evening at Bookbinder's, Woodward quoted Quentin Compson's famously unconvincing bellow at Shreve about not hating the South. In his classic collection of essays, *The Burden of Southern History,* Woodward quoted approvingly Faulkner's comment that "there is no such thing as *was*—only *is*."[6] In later years, he enjoyed calling me a tried and true "continuitarian."

Change, Woodward well knew, had to be set against a distinct and pal-

---

5. W. J. Cash, *The Mind of the South* (New York, 1941), 219–20 (quotation on p. 219); C. Vann Woodward, *The Burden of Southern History* (3d ed., Baton Rouge, 1993), 6, 10.

6. Woodward, *Burden of Southern History,* 279.

pable continuity, or the result would be a constant, unbearable flux. In an article in the *Journal of American History*, he openly wrestled with the rival claims of change and continuity with regard to the writing and revising of *The Strange Career of Jim Crow*, a short study that won a popular as well as academic audience. Woodward conceded that he had not sufficiently distinguished between urban and rural styles of race oppression, as critics, notably the late Howard Rabinowitz, had revealed. But he justified his interpretation on the grounds of the contemporary context. "My first concern was to overcome the prevailing impression" in the 1950s "that race relations in the South remained basically unchanged, that changes in law, whether associated with slavery, emancipation, Reconstruction, or segregation, had been superficial and resulted in no real change in relations between races. No changes, no history." Some critics, he continued, preferred to stress changelessness in hopes of perpetuating the segregationist style. Others wrung their hands in liberal despair that the South would forever remain intractable. Despite all the fuss, unnecessary diversions, and misapprehensions over the character of the book and its several revisions, Woodward proudly and rightly claimed that he had made a significant point: "race relations *had* a history"—even though, he added, that very fact opened a "Pandora's box" of historical "troubles." One of them was the peril of moralizing about the past: "the integrity of the art over which Clio presides can be threatened by the just as well as the unjust, the righteous as well as the unrighteous, the moral as well as the immoral." He admitted his own tendency to teach uplifting lessons through the good offices of the historical muse just referred to. In fact, "some corruption of history by morals was unavoidable" in the fight against white racism.[7]

Slyly Woodward implied that his original mischaracterization of the period before Jim Crow cracked the racial whip in the 1890s had served high moral purposes for which he need not apologize. In fact, he wrote a note to me on the offprint: "Bert, a rare opportunity to retaliate—Vann." In the article, he did not need to remind his readers that Martin Luther King Jr. had referred to *The Strange Career of Jim Crow* as "the historical Bible of the civil rights movement." In *Thinking Back*, however, he recalled the circumstances of the head-swelling encomium. On the march to Selma, in which Woodward participated, King had made that statement. As the procession moved along, Woodward noticed the silent throngs of whites who

---

7. C. Vann Woodward, "*Strange Career* Critics: Long May They Persevere," *Journal of American History*, 75 (December 1988), 857–68 (quotations on pp. 860, 861, 867, and 868).

watched the spectacle of white Yankee liberals and even some southern academic leaders, nuns and clergy, young people and old, and black activists singing songs of brotherhood. In reaction to King's words, Woodward confessed to "mixed feelings." For such "sedentary types" as he, "a certain Yale professor of Southern origins," the praise seemed not altogether warranted. Woodward recalled that the Reconstruction schoolmarms had not stayed the full course, nor were the righteous, high-minded young men and women from privileged northern backgrounds ready to do much more than march in a romantic gesture toward Selma. Change in race relations once again faced the nation—the riots in the Yankee ghettoes and the reaction to them in both white and African American minds, Woodward explained.[8]

For all his emphasis on the volatility and rapid drifts in human affairs, Woodward was always more inconsistent on the relative degrees of continuity and change than he admitted in the *Strange Career* article and elsewhere. He stressed change in the 1940s and 1950s because of his conviction that the South had too long honored its continuities. The region required a moral, political, and historical jolt to forward his goal of equal and color-blind rights for all. Woodward's aim was morally beyond dispute. Yet the depth of racism and white southern suspicion of liberalism was much more ingrained than his strategy of reform could remedy. Glenda Gilmore points out that, in light of the new studies by Jane Dailey, Stephen Kantrowitz, and Bryant Simon, he also underestimated the power of demagogic appeals to poor whites on the basis of manhood. Actually Cash, Woodward's nemesis, made the point with vivid imagery and memorable phrases—the "slashing hell of a fellow," an "honor complex," the "lily-pure maid of Astolat," and the demagogue's "hell-for-leather bluster that the South demanded in its heroes and champions."[9] The work of these recent scholars has indeed given us a more Cash-like than Woodward-like rendition of the Populist and Jim Crow eras.

Helpful as the new investigations are, for the late nineteenth and early twentieth centuries, the term *honor* might be more serviceable than manhood to grasp southern motivation. With no apology, I prefer it, anyhow. The ethic of honor includes adherence to the hierarchies of white over black,

---

8. C. Vann Woodward, *Thinking Back: The Perils of Writing History* (Baton Rouge, 1986), 92.

9. Cash, *Mind of the South*, 46, 73, 86, 284; Bryant Simon, *A Fabric of Defeat: The Politics of South Carolina Millhands, 1910–1948* (Chapel Hill, 1998); Stephen Kantrowitz, *Ben Tillman and the Reconstruction of White Supremacy* (Chapel Hill, 2000); Jane Dailey, *Before Jim Crow: The Politics of Race in Postemancipation Virginia* (Chapel Hill, 2000).

male over female, and localism over state centralism in politics, affecting gun control, environmental laws, abortion, taxation, and welfare. All these are bound together. Manhood or whiteness of skin are essential constituents but not the sole elements in an ethical system that has survived—though in many ways greatly diminished—the many changes wrought in the former slave states. Whether that point is valid, there is no doubt that Gilmore's fine appraisal and Woodward's willingness to keep up with current concerns and preferences have brought a new apprehension of just how important issues of gender and race have been in southern history.

As Harold Woodman, and indeed all the speakers at the symposium, observed, Woodward's texts live on in a way denied most historians. How did he do it? First of all, the brashness of youth or, to be more generous, the boldness to say something new was a part of his success. The invitation to contribute to the highly prestigious History of the South series was itself an inspiration to the youthful author, just thirty years old at the time. He had already shown considerable contempt for the elder scholars in his field. As Jim Cobb notes, Woodward had found the work in modern southern history sadly wanting as he started graduate study at the University of North Carolina. "That first plunge was chilling," he recalled. Robert McMath has already quoted those memorable lines, but I dare repeat them here. "Plodding through volume after volume," Woodward remembered years later, "I began to wonder if I had ever encountered prose so pedestrian, pages so dull, chapters so devoid of ideas, whole volumes so wrongheaded or so lacking in point."[10] For many a midnight hour he paced up and down Chapel Hill's Franklin Street pondering if he had entered the wrong profession. Earlier, at Emory University, as Cobb points out, he had thought about writing a novel, so strong were his literary interests. Luckily, Gibbon's volumes on Rome, read for a seminar, a discovery of other historians with literary gifts, and the revelation that archival research "could be fun" swung him back to history.[11]

When the offer to contribute to the History of the South series reached him, Woodward saw a chance, he said, to play the "mole to subvert the establishment." The young rebel sought to expose the manipulations of the moneyed class and the racial intolerance that New South boosterism engendered. It was time to set the historical sails in a new direction. As he recalled in *Thinking Back*, however, he was nearly dumped from the series. He later

---

10. Woodward, *Thinking Back*, 21.
11. *Ibid.*, 22.

discovered that the editors had had second thoughts. In his autobiographical volume, Woodward explained their doubts: "This prospective author was so young and so impressionable, and rather erratic to boot." But, Woodward continued in his recollections, they failed to act in spite of clear evidence, as one put it with categorical certitude: "Woodward can't write." Obviously the critic meant he could not convey history in fittingly lifeless, academic prose.[12]

By the time the volume appeared, however, twelve years had passed. Apparently, his literary proficiency had quite remarkably improved. But more important, he had had time to grow intellectually as well. Four different teaching appointments in various parts of the nation, three summers of instructing undergraduates at Florida, Harvard, and Chicago, and a lengthy war of some importance stood between him and completion of the text. Although he was already the author of a classic work, *Tom Watson, Agrarian Rebel*, the young naval lieutenant took the journeyman's role by writing three books, two of them classified, for his military superiors in Washington. Only *The Battle for Leyte Gulf* appeared in print.[13]

The naval assignment taught him many lessons—how to conduct research of events more complex than a biography like *Tom Watson* could involve and how to deal with the idiosyncracies of commanders, the odd contingencies of events, the signals of unwarranted personal ambition, and the outrageously stupid errors that leaders could unwittingly contrive. Once the war was over, he appreciated more than ever a positive development in the South—the outpouring of artistic creativity that his native region was undergoing. To be sure, no "renaissance" had arisen in history, he wrote, "no rebirth of energy, no compelling new vision" had emerged, but the same unresponsiveness no longer seemed to inhibit playwrights, novelists, and poets of the South.[14]

Another reason for Woodwardian durability was the theoretical foundation of *Origins*. Perhaps Charles Beard and company no longer stir young imaginations. In Woodward's time, however, such an approach became the artillery to blast away the encrustation of smug New South self-congratulations. Robert McMath notes how "Woodward told stories of long-forgotten southerners, black and white, who struggled to create better futures for themselves and their people." Of course, as McMath further elaborates,

12. *Ibid.*, 44.
13. C. Vann Woodward, *The Battle for Leyte Gulf* (New York, 1947).
14. Woodward, *Thinking Back*, 23.

Woodward's association with leftist and progressive thinkers encouraged such an endeavor. Given the current historical interest in the economically deprived in the nation, *Origins* still serves to enlighten readers.[15]

Yet the stimulation that the Beardian perspective gave him does not fully account for the enduring strength of *Origins of the New South*. Instead, we must not forget the aesthetic element that he exemplified in that and all his other work. Over the years, Woodward shared the artistic temperament with his artist friends—Robert Penn Warren, William Styron, Cleanth Brooks, and other notables in the literary field. He was as much if not more at home in their profession than he was in the field of history.

Another factor that has helped keep Woodward's work alive may be easier to document than his indefinable literary gifts. It was his insight into a theme upon which Harold Woodman has so well elaborated—the sense of a deep chasm or unhealing scar in the southern psyche. By that Woodward meant, if we need reminding, the reality of Confederate defeat, the transfer of political and economic power from a planter elite to a new commercial breed, and the eventual overturn of black Republican Reconstruction race relations to oppressive forms of apartheid and racial proscriptions. Woodman points out just how liberating and innovative this proposition proved to be. At the time Woodward wrote *Origins,* a seamless past in southern history was the prevailing assumption.

The Woodward thesis of discontinuity was very appropriate for the political climate of the early 1950s. Few southern historians have ever been more aware of the tragic implications of regional history than he was. Thanks to Woodward, as Woodman observes, post–Civil War ruin, poverty, and undercapitalization became the focal point of historical interest in the period before the First World War. In addition, we have Bob McMath's thoughtful and original reexamination of the failed political uprising at the close of the nineteenth century. His appreciation of Woodward's idealistic but substantive account of Populism underscores how *Origins of the New South* drove home the point of southern political failure.

Yet in Woodward's determination to distance himself and his themes from the dead weight of the historiographical past—E. Merton Coulter and company—he went too far in privileging change. Jim Cobb notes Woodward's own recognition of a tendency to overstate. That predisposition is almost unavoidable when dealing with sweeping interpretations. Another

---

15. Robert C. McMath Jr., "C. Vann Woodward and the Burden of Southern Populism," *Journal of Southern History,* 67 (November 2001), 742 (190 in this volume).

factor is the difference in perspective that separates the history of politics and the history of social and cultural topics. In institutional and political forms, change may arise without eradicating venerable, underlying customs, forms of prejudice, and demands for consensus—all of which inhabit the substrata of class and political structures. Take, for example, Woodward's interpretation of the Lost Cause. What he saw was the exploitation of community nostalgia by the Snopesian elite. New South boosters appropriated the rituals and rhetoric of the past while undermining that past at every turn. True enough. But Woodward's analysis leaves open a major question: why did constant, mournful blowing of taps for Rebel Dixie work so efficiently and so deeply in the popular mind? Why was race so easily invoked to abort the Readjuster movement in Virginia, a biracial effort, and later Populism, as Barbara J. Fields and Bob McMath have ably explained?

Woodward, I think, was so justifiably eager to point a way out of the deathly swamp of the historical past that he did not fully recognize how deep-seated these matters were. It is just as well. Hope must arise, even in the face of daunting odds. But as Fields shrewdly notes, Woodward showed his "flair for mischief" in *Origins*. With his usual genius for irony, he juxtaposed the "mixed blood" of Whig and Democrat in the post–Civil War era and the actuality of racial intermingling in the ruling class. Woodward shattered the old icons with well-aimed blows. But to return to the Lost Cause, a conquered people had to mourn in tones that perhaps sounded inauthentic later. Yet to admit that the Confederate dead had lost their lives in vain—who was ready to make so bold, so unholy a claim? The Lost Cause and its blistering backlash against African Americans that allegedly caused the Rebel downfall had its own tragic rationale. Even though, as Fields proposes, Woodward's passages on lynching were all too sketchy and brief, he knew this very well. Yet he could not countenance an unbroken line from the slaveholding past to the racist present. It might forestall change in race relations.[16]

These issues, however, are basically a secondary problem. More important was Woodward's facility in breaking the chains of racial assumptions and proscriptions and exploring issues of colonial, capitalistic domination over southern resources—material and human—small farmers, laborers, and especially black freedpeople. Fields captures the Woodwardian message with her usual vigor of language. She notes that even if the secondary literature about African Americans had been available, Woodward's "*Origins*

---

16. Barbara J. Fields, "*Origins of the New South* and the Negro Question," *Journal of Southern History,* 67 (November 2001), 811–26 (quotations on p. 811, p. 262 in this volume).

would still have emerged as a book about power and its ramifications rather than a book about the self-activity of the powerless." Appropriately, she also recognizes his misidentification of black class structure and regrets that he did not do more with black speech and its African origins. Her article closes, though, with a testament to a major aspect of the work: Woodward's bold readiness to integrate the African American experience and trials into the text. In other hands, the period from 1877 to 1913 would have been treated with as segregated an approach as the Jim Crow laws were intended to achieve in most other spheres of southern life.[17]

As Harold D. Woodman, and indeed all our speakers, asserted, Vann Woodward's published works live on in a way denied all of our feeble attempts at remembrance, popular or even academic. He possessed the self-confidence and the maturity to accept criticism graciously and learn from it. That modestly expressed yet proud sense of himself helped him bear—with considerable delight—the barbs leveled at his major work. Although so accused, he never claimed for the South in general "a special wisdom—only with a potential if largely untapped source of wisdom."[18] Woodward might have said the same for himself, but he was too temperate to be so presumptuous.

We historians may strive for the preeminence that Woodward achieved. Yet hard as it is to admit, we know that the results of our labor will soon be as wind-scattered and dry to future generations of scholars as Isaiah's withering grass. Will there be any anthologies devoted to criticism of our work, any festschrifts, panels at conventions, workshops, special symposiums, or other forms of academic paraphernalia to memorialize our contributions? It's not likely.

In sum, we have been blessed with as sophisticated and beautifully styled a set of articles as one could ever expect from any sort of academic conference. I think that the subject himself has been the source of that inspiration. If some of the remarks challenge Woodward's position, he would scarcely mind. Woodward once commented, "In America, historians, like politicians, are out as soon as they are down. There is no comfortable back bench, no House of Lords for them."[19] Our speakers and the organizers of this symposium have helped to ensure that consignment to oblivion will not be Woodward's fate. He is gone from our midst, but we miss his intellect, challenging ideas, and understated wit as much as ever.

---

17. *Ibid.,* 823 (274 in this volume).
18. Woodward, *Thinking Back,* 136–37.
19. Woodward, "Elusive Mind of the South," 261–83 (quotation on p. 282).

Contributors

JOHN B. BOLES is the William P. Hobby Professor of History at Rice University and Managing Editor of the *Journal of Southern History*.

JAMES C. COBB is the B. Phinizy Spalding Distinguished Professor in the History of the American South at the University of Georgia.

BARBARA J. FIELDS is professor of history at Columbia University.

GLENDA E. GILMORE is the Peter V. and C. Vann Woodward Professor of History at Yale University.

SHELDON HACKNEY is professor of history at the University of Pennsylvania.

CARL V. HARRIS is associate professor of history at the University of California, Santa Barbara.

WILLIAM F. HOLMES is professor of history emeritus at the University of Georgia.

BETHANY L. JOHNSON, formerly Associate Editor of the *Journal of Southern History*, now lives in Durham, North Carolina.

ROBERT C. McMATH is professor of history and vice provost at the Georgia Institute of Technology.

ALLEN W. MOGER was professor of history at Washington and Lee University.

JAMES TICE MOORE is professor of history emeritus at Virginia Commonwealth University.

ANNE FIROR SCOTT is the William K. Boyd Professor of History emeritus at Duke University.

HAROLD D. WOODMAN is professor of history emeritus at Purdue University.

C. VANN WOODWARD was Sterling Professor of History emeritus at Yale University.

BERTRAM WYATT-BROWN is the Richard J. Milbauer Professor of History at the University of Florida.